Reuben Chappell

Pierhead Painter

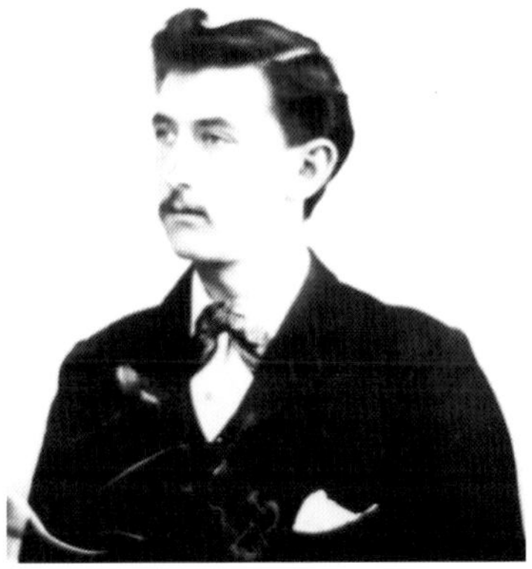

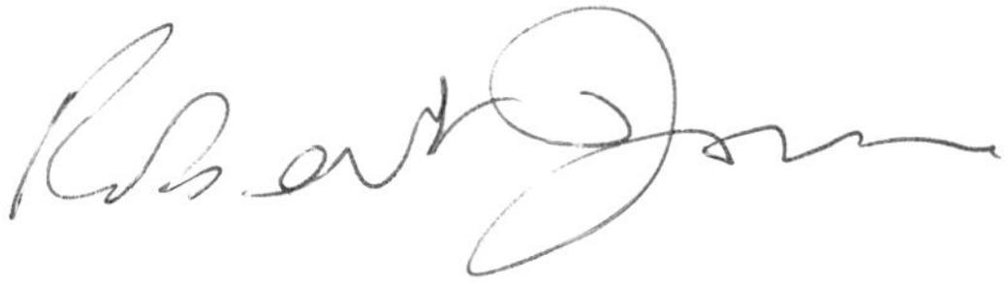

Robert Jones

First Light

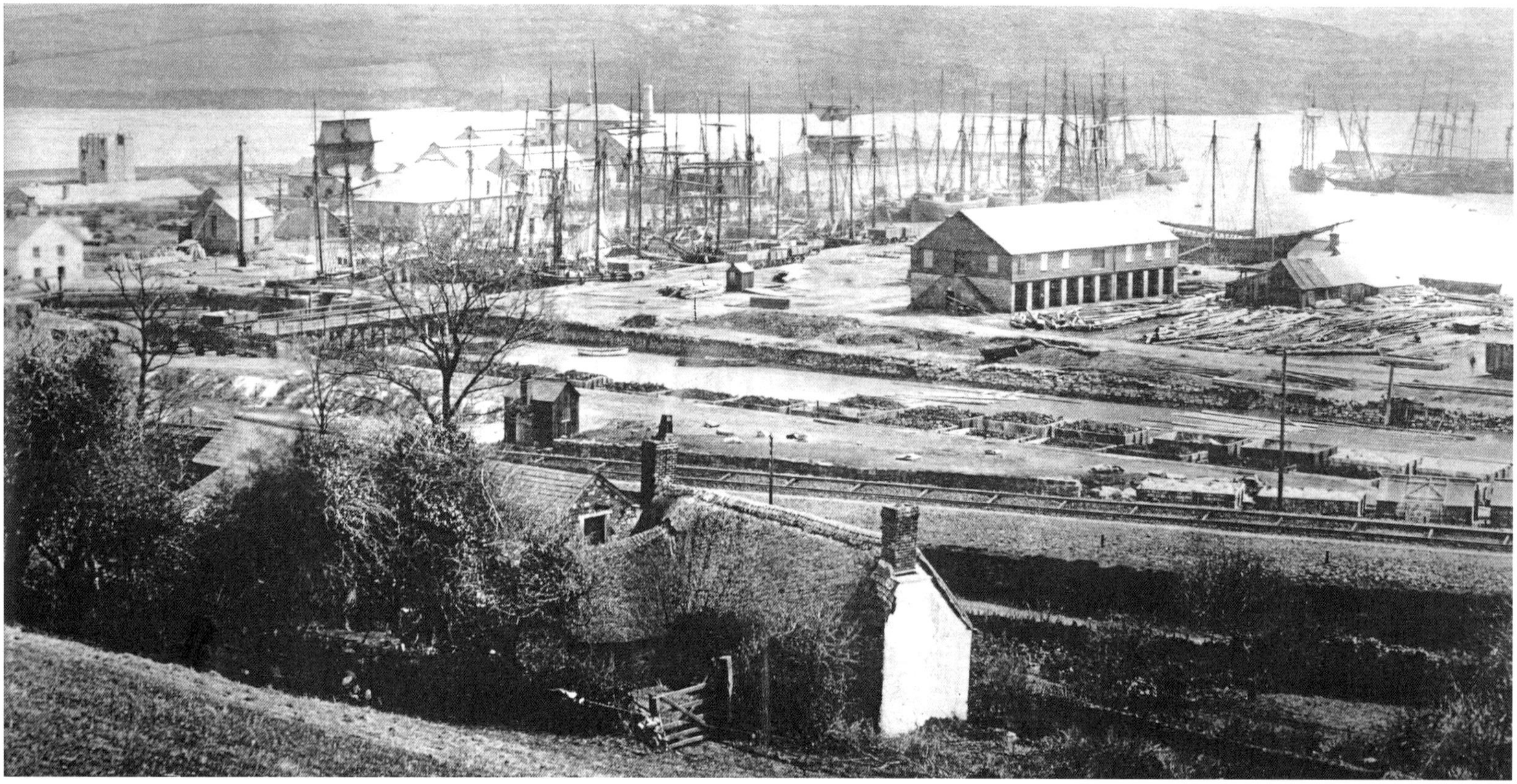

Par Docks *Photo China Clay Museum*

I am grateful for the help I have received from all those people who offered invaluable advice and support while I was preparing this book including:

Janet Tierney and Peter Appleyard, Goole Museum and Art Gallery, Goole, Yorkshire

Brian Masterman, Goole, Yorkshire

Arthur Credland, Hull Maritime Museum, Yorkshire

Henne Jensen, Svendborg County Museum, Denmark

Kjeld Soberg, Holm Petersen Maritime Collection, Denmark

Erik Kromann and Henning Terkelsen, Marstal Maritime Museum, Denmark

Ulla Graham, Ærøskøbing Museum, Denmark

Captain George Hogg, National Maritime Museum, Falmouth

Ron Openshaw, Bartlett Library, National Maritime Museum, Falmouth

Liz Chard, China Clay Museum

John Buckingham, Padstow Museum

David Taylor and Doug McCarthy, National Maritime Museum, Greenwich, London

Heather Ball, National Trust, Overbecks, Salcombe, Devon

Jonathan Holmes and all at Penlee House, Penzance

Lucinda Middleton and Robert Cook, Royal Cornwall Museum

Michael Charles, The British Mercantile Marine Memorial Collection

Eric Cawthorne

Clive Carter, Cornish maritime author and artist

Jenny Pery, art historian and author

David J. Dixon, Great Grandson of Reuben Chappell

Sue Corfield, restorer, Sancreed, Cornwall

Simon Cook, photographer, Penzance, Cornwall

Janet Cave, Design and Print, Hayle, Cornwall, for her skill and patience

In particular, I would like to thank Reuben Chappell's Grand daughter Jean Dixon for all her help and encouragement

Contents

In shipping tonnage does not refer to the weight of the vessel, but the volume, i.e, the internal capacity available for carrying cargo, a registered ton being 100 cubic feet of internal measurement. The word tonnage is an international means of measuring ships, and is handed down from early days when dues were collected on vessels carrying wine in 'tuns', meaning a large wine cask. Net tonnage is the enclosed space of a vessel available for cargo and does not include engine room, accommodation etc. ie gross tons.

Official numbers were issued to all British sea going vessels in 1855. They gave each ship a unique identity. The same number remained with the ship throughout its life, and avoided confusion between ships of the same name. While ships changed their name or port of registery, the official number remained unaltered.

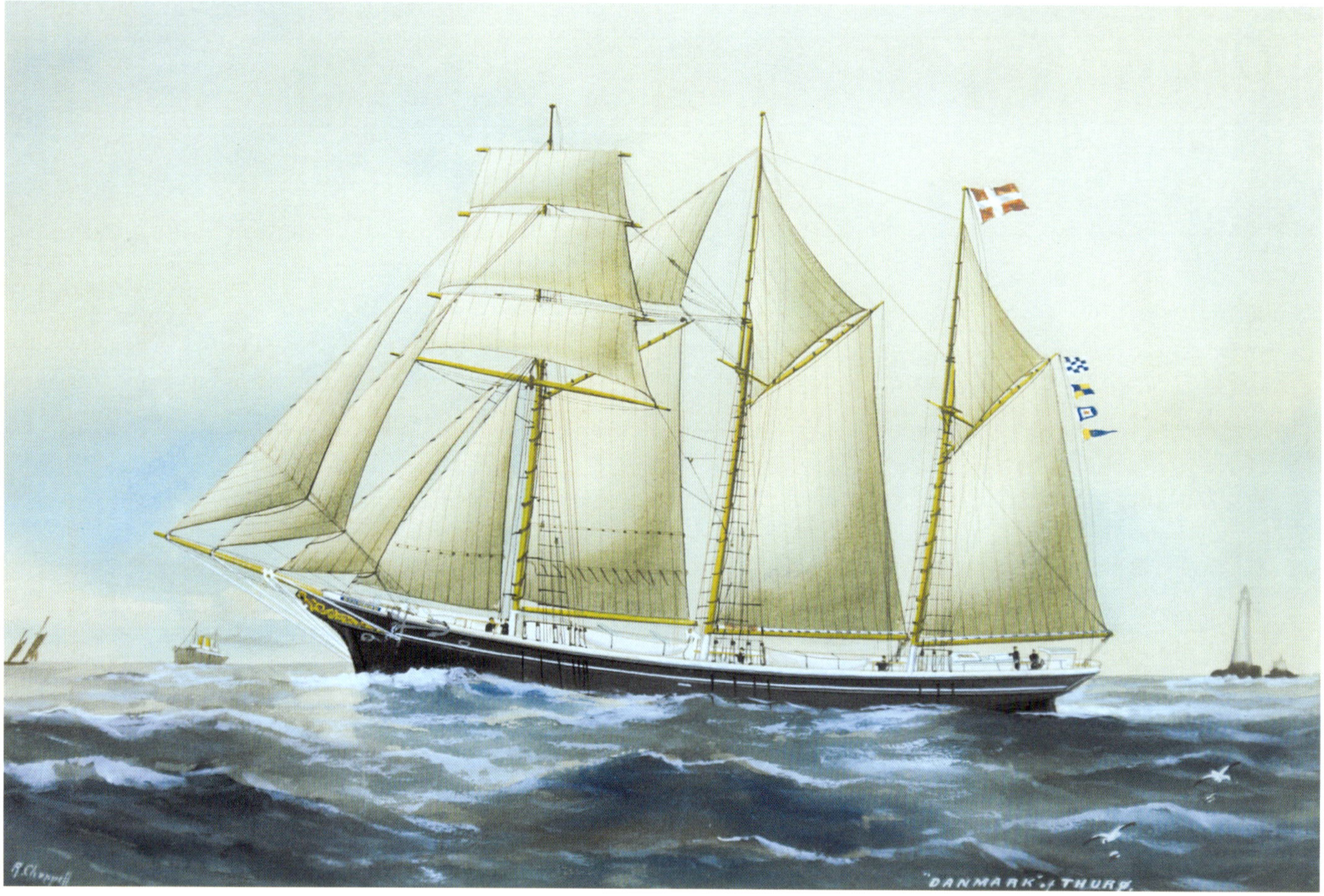

Private Collection

Danmark of Thurø

Three-masted wooden schooner; built Thurø by C. Bom; 103.5' x 22.10' x 11.6'; owned by R.S. Hansen.

On 31st January 1911 the Danish three-masted schooner Danmark entered the Dover Straits bound for Fecamp in Normandy, having sailed from Køge in Denmark with a cargo of wheat. In Esjberg, the official enquiry into her loss heard that the sea was rough that night and the captain was in his cabin when the seaman on watch mistook the flashes from the South Foreland Lighthouse for those of the Sandettie Lightship. The ship was on the wrong course when she went aground on the Goodwin Sands. By the time the Ramsgate lifeboat reached them, all the ship's crew were in the rigging, the ship and cargo awash. This would have dated the picture within the five years after 1904 when Reuben Chappell had moved to Par.

Foreword

Reuben Chappell was one of the last, and arguably one of the finest, of the so-called 'Pierhead Painters', the men who earned their living painting portraits of the merchant shipping sailing in and out of Britain's ports. He was also one of the most prolific, with an estimated output in excess of 12,000 paintings, but although he must have produced his work in haste – many of his customers were sailing on the next tide – his work shows little sign of it, being as meticulous in the detailing of each individual ship as in visual appeal.

Victorian photographers tended to be interested in the romantic and the picturesque; steam ships being neither, at any rate as far as the late 19th century was concerned, they were usually photographed either as part of an overall dockyard scene, or in extreme close-up as a backdrop for a group portrait of the crew. However, while photography was popularly established by the end of the 19th century for personal portraits, seamen and ship owners preferred to have a painting of their vessel, subject to two basic criteria – it must be attractive, and it must be accurate. Unlike George Race of Grimsby, his near-contemporary at the other end of the Humber, who never painted a sailing vessel, Reuben Chappell recorded both sail and steam, both in his home port of Goole and later in Cornwall. For a historian, this is the great importance of Chappell's work; his ship portraits are not just works of art, but also important documents, recording, as he does so meticulously, not only the gradual transition from steam to sail, but also those workaday, taken for granted steam ships of the late 19th and early 20th century. Indeed, Reuben Chappell's paintings are often the only pictorial record of a vessel to survive.

Until Basil Greenhill (later Director of the National Maritime Museum) wrote a brief appreciation of Reuben Chappell in a 1948 Sea Breezes article, Chappell's work was largely unknown except to the families of the seamen and ship-owners who bought his paintings. Short articles have followed periodically since then, but, somewhat surprisingly, Chappell's work has not so far been deemed to merit a deeper and more scholarly appraisal. Robert Jones's study is long overdue, and much to be welcomed by all who appreciate the work of this most modest, industrious and distinctive artist.

Janet Tierney - Curator of Goole Museum and Art Gallery

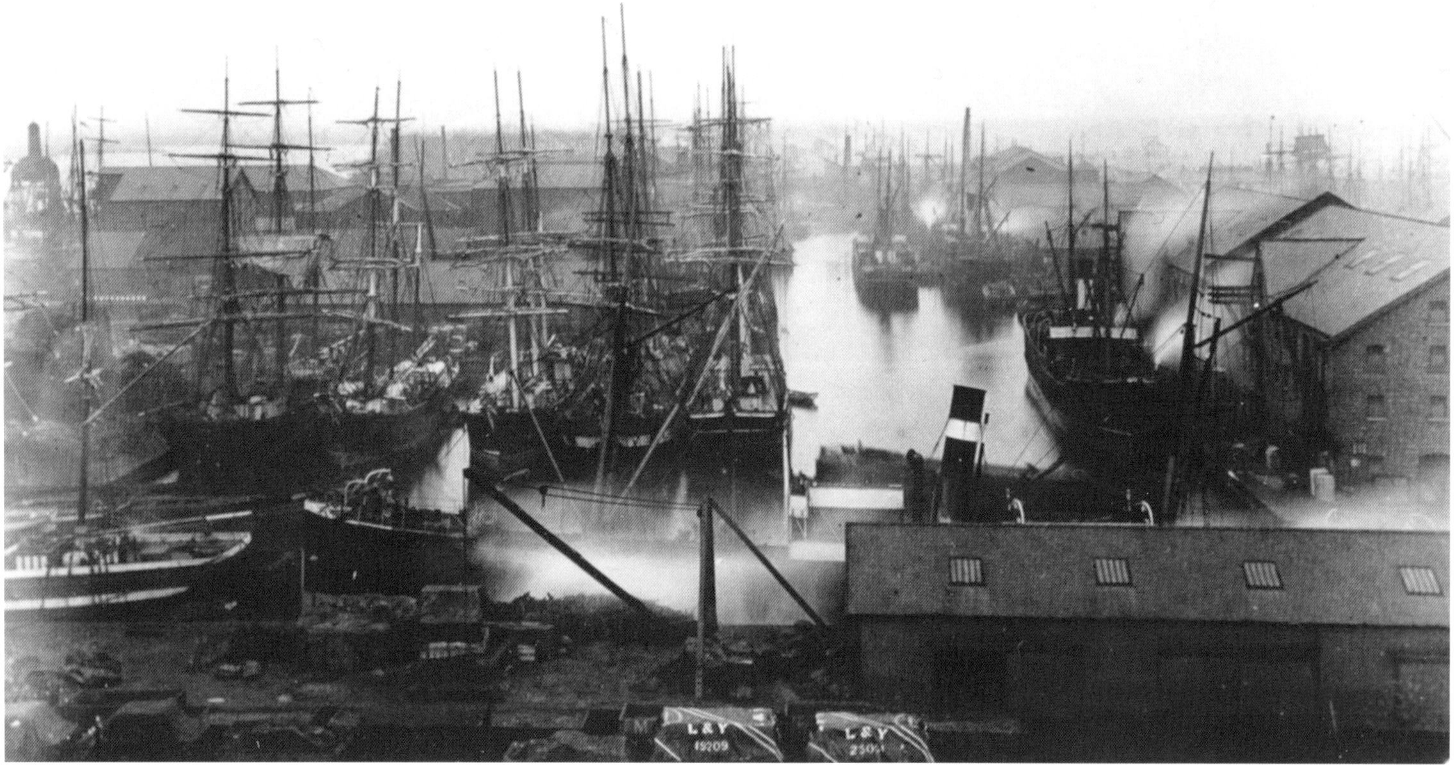

Aldam Dock, Goole 1896 *Masterman Collection*

Introduction

The sea is integral to the art of Robert Jones. Most of his paintings are concerned with the sea, its weather states, shipping and its coastal landscape. As a figurative painter Jones's principal enthusiasm is the look of sea and coast, but his perceptive eye is supported by an extensive knowledge of all things marine, the history of shipping and the lives of the seamen in one of the world's most dangerous occupations. For many years he worked as the skipper of various inshore fishing vessels, and came to know the coastal waters of his native Cornwall intimately. Despite his name, he is a Cornishman, and has lived for most of his life in Cornwall. His services to his native county have been recently been recognised in his election as a Bard of the Cornish Gorsedd. Jones combines his deep interest in maritime history with an equal interest in painters of the sea and ships. It was his dual fascination with both marine art and the history of seafaring that impelled him to write Alfred Wallis - Artist and Mariner (published in 2001), a percipient book in which he demonstrates that Wallis's unique 'memory paintings' were based on first-hand experience. It was the same rare conjunction of interests that compelled Robert Jones to research and write this first book on the pierhead painter Reuben Chappell. In it he shows that Chappell possessed not only a complete understanding of the ships he was commissioned to paint, but that he was also an artist of considerable stature; and that a pierhead portrait of a ship, often denigrated by art historians, could be both an historical record and a celebratory work of art. In similar fashion Robert Jones, with art and seafaring in his blood, has produced a compelling factual record that is also a valuable work of art history.

Jenny Pery - Author and art historian

Pierhead Painting

This book is about the life and work of Reuben Chappell, an artist who painted portraits of ships for seamen. It is also about the ships and shipbuilders, the men who crewed the vessels, and the trades that took them over the seas to the ports of Europe, Scandinavia, the Mediterranean and across the Atlantic to North and South America.

Reuben Chappell's customers were the captains and crew of the ships that visited the ports where Chappell worked. It was their ships that he painted. These were the small merchant ships, sail and steam powered vessels, which visited the port of Goole where he lived until 1904. After his move to Cornwall, he made portraits of the ships that came to the clay ports of Charlestown, Fowey and Par, where he practised until the latter part of his life. It was not only British vessels that featured in his work as his paintings were also very popular with seamen from foreign ports. Ships from Denmark regularly visited both Goole and the Cornish clay ports and he made paintings of many of these vessels.

Reuben Chappell witnessed and recorded the zenith and decline of the great days of commercial sail. His paintings also record the ascent of steam power, and show a part of our maritime history that has now gone for ever. Built to move bulk cargoes across the seas for commercial ends with their design determined by their function, these ships were remarkable examples of man's ingenuity and industry, and in themselves things of beauty. There is an understandable romance attached to the age of sail.

The graceful lines of the ships contrasts strongly with the life aboard them. There were times when the conditions under which their crew worked were harsh and dangerous. The seamen were poorly paid, yet they still felt great affection for and pride in the vessels and this feeling could be expressed in no better way than in the possession of a painting, a portrait that would be a lasting momento of their vessel on perhaps a particular voyage. In ports around the world artists were practising ship portraiture for the crews of visiting vessels, and because of the circumstances in which the paintings were commissioned these artists became known as pierhead painters. Their work was created, not for galleries and the art market, but for men whose lives and livelihoods were intimately entwined with the subject of the painting. Such seamen may have known or cared little about art, but they would have recognised a good ship painting. They were not wealthy men, yet they bought these paintings, and in so doing created a market for this unique art form.

The seamen who commissioned the paintings would have been demanding customers, knowing every detail of their ship and expecting the painting to be right. Although they were not paying a great deal of money for each painting, for them it still represented a significant sum. These paintings had to be cheaply and quickly produced, yet they tell us far more than any photograph could.

In the 19th century the market for these works developed along with increasing commerce. There was a steady increase in the number of ships launched and as the size of the merchant fleets grew, so the number of ship portrait painters increased. Schools of painting sprang up in the seaports of Northern Europe, around the Mediterranean, and in China and America. In many ports several artists would have been practising and in many cases it was not only individual artists, but families of artists who were employed in the production of ship paintings.

Though sometimes painted in oil, because of their quick drying qualities watercolour and gouache were the most frequently used medium. Most of the paintings were bought and taken home to be framed, and they now appear in a curious variety of frames. Obviously they were valued and cherished by the seaman and his family. These paintings record vessels which are now long gone and it must be the case that for many ships, apart from perhaps a reference in a ships list such as Lloyds, the painting is the only evidence of a vessel's existence.

The importance of these merchant vessels' role in the history of trade must not be underestimated. Their voyages regularly took them around the British Isles, across the Channel and North Sea to Continental, Scandinavian and Baltic ports. They carried cargoes to and from the Mediterranean, and crossed the Atlantic to Canada and North and South America. The cargoes these vessels carried, though small by modern standards, were fundamental to trade at that time. The trades they plied and the goods they carried formed the foundations of the economy. Comparatively little has been written about the history of the small merchant sailing and steam ships which Chappell painted. Although their stories were often more dramatic they did not have the glamour of the clipper ships or the ocean liners. They were so ubiquitous around the coasts, harbours and ports at the time that their continuing presence was taken for granted, and their gradual disappearance seemed to go almost unnoticed.

Reuben Chappell was, and still is, considered to be one of the best, and certainly most prolific, of the pierhead painters. It is obvious that he was highly regarded by those who bought his paintings, but as there was a limit to what they could afford to pay Chappell's prices had to be low and his output large. The paintings often had to be produced quickly, in just the time that the ship was in port, unloading and loading cargo. In spite of all this his work has a quiet dignity and a presence which is remarkable.

The format Chappell used, nearly always portraying the ships side on, was in keeping with the established tradition of pierhead painting. Side-on views were part of the conventions of ship portraiture as a whole. That is what his customers wanted, and was the most informative way of portraying the ship.

In Chappell's paintings one senses a respect for the seamen and their lives at sea. His customers became his friends. Reuben Chappell was not simply an observer in their world, his work was also a part of the maritime culture. His paintings recorded their ships, and in doing so also gave meaning and importance to the seamen's way of life. Yet pierhead paintings, Reuben Chappell's work included, were for many years regarded as a secondary art form, and were excluded from auctions of fine art. Instead, they would appear in furniture sales.

Today these paintings contain an abundance of nautical and historical information presented in an unpretentious and direct manner and speak to us of a bygone age. However, Reuben Chappell was not necessarily concerned with recording history. Although he usually signed or initialled his work, named the ship and the port of registery, and sometimes included the name of the captain, he did not date his work.

Chappell's paintings demonstrate a great awareness of the scale and proportion of each part of the vessel, and his architectural sense gives a sense of elegance to his subjects. His paintings were admired by his customers for the accuracy of detail, and were clearly informed by a real understanding of the working of a ship.

In common with other pierhead painters, Reuben Chappell repeated certain motifs in the backgrounds of his paintings, a particular piece of cliff, a lighthouse, lightships etc. One might dismiss these topographical features as merely repeated decorative backgrounds, and to some extent it was a formula he used, but the vessels he painted had for the most part recently sailed to the port where Chappell practised. Their journey could have taken them, for example, along the south coast of England, probably some miles from, and at times, out of sight of land. They would have passed several lightships off Kent, warning of the Goodwin Sands and other sandbanks. Off Plymouth, the Eddystone Reef was marked by a lighthouse and the stump of one earlier destroyed. But of course the lightships and lighthouses were not there for decorative purposes, they were were significant features of the voyage and were there to warn seamen to keep clear of very real dangers. Before the Second World War there were no radar or electronic navigation systems. The men aboard ship would have been anxious to see these lights to know that they had passed danger safely and to establish their position. One can imagine how difficult it would have been for them in stormy weather, squalls, reduced visibility, fog. The landmarks may also have denoted a change of course.

Start Point Light on the South Devon Coast would have been an important landmark when ships were approaching from the east. This would have been a welcome sight, signifying final stages of their journey, and so Reuben Chappell tells us a story of 'journey's end.' In other paintings he places details to show departing ships, and they signify the beginning of a new voyage. For the seaman who bought the paintings these topographical features were not just decorative, but would also have represented important landmarks that they saw on their voyage.

As well as the lights and landmarks in the paintings there are generally other vessels seen in the background. Again, these may seem an attractive decorative device, perhaps giving a sense of scale to the main ship in the painting, but those who have spent time at sea will know that a constant lookout is required for other vessels. Despite the 'rules of the road' the risk of collision at sea was a very real one. Ships did collide and larger vessels regularly ran down smaller ones with fatal results. Danger aside, passing shipping would have been a constant feature of a voyage, and a source of interest to the seamen. The variety of vessels which Chappell depicts in the background or on the horizon reflects the variety of shipping to be seen at the time, both sail and steam, from ocean liners to fishing boats.

We now take for granted weather forecasts on radio and television. The shipping forecast gives detailed reports on all the sea areas around the British Isles, and vessels now have ship to ship and ship to shore radios. None of these facilities existed before the earlier part of the twentieth century. Mariners would have relied on a barometer, the rising and falling of which would give some indication of approaching weather, and they would also have drawn on their experience of watching the sea and sky conditions for signs of change.

Reuben Chappell made his paintings for experienced seamen, and in his work they saw something more than just an acceptable depiction of their ship. Perhaps the quality which really distinguished his work is what has been described as his liquid seas and skies. His paintings satisfied the seaman's eye for weather.

Life

REUBEN CHAPPELL 1870 - 1940

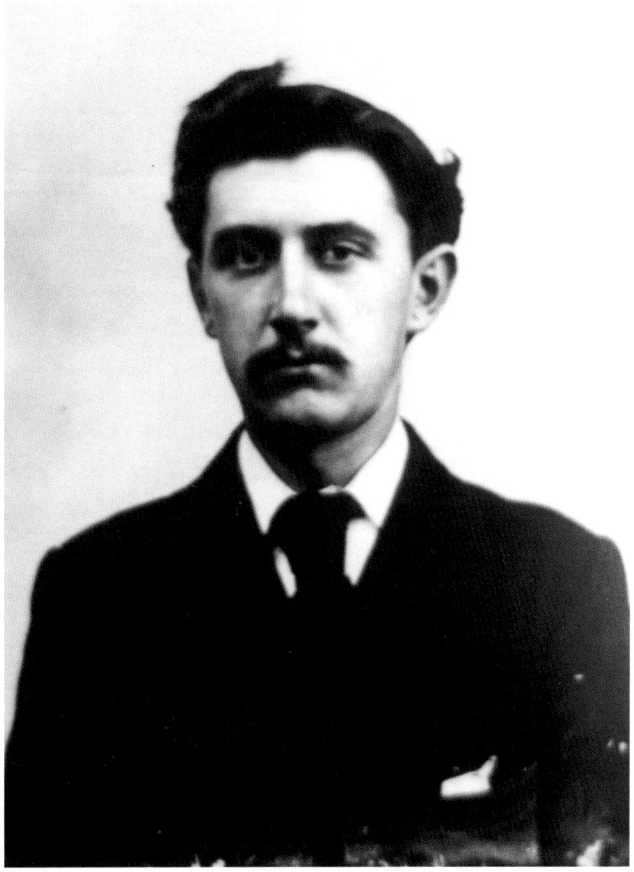

GOOLE

The port of Goole lies on the River Ouse at the head of the Humber Estuary, 50 miles from the North Sea. It is a creation of the nineteenth century - a canal town founded on the coal trade, coal that was brought down the canal and river systems of East Yorkshire to Goole. Ships, large and small, came up the Humber to the docks from all over Europe to load coal from Yorkshire pits.

Goole was a busy port, most families in the town were connected in some way with the docks, the ships there and the sea, and many local people owned shares in vessels. The masters and crew of the local sailing ships and the Humber steam ships also came from the area. Over 400 sailing vessels were registered in Goole, and fifty ship owners lived at the inland port.

Large sailing ships came up the Humber carrying all manner of cargoes, for example, Baltic timber, wheat, fustic from the West Indies for dyeing, and vegetable oil from the Mediterranean. As well as coal, general cargoes were shipped to continental ports in the holds of Goole-owned steamers. The masts and rigging of the visiting schooners could be seen in the docks alongside the local vessels.

It was here, in a street near the docks that Reuben Chappell was born and grew up. Reuben Chappell can be seen as a product of his environment, his work growing directly from his experience of life in the port of Goole.

Reuben Chappell was born on the 21st July 1870, in Doyle Street, Hook, which is now a part of Goole, Yorkshire. He was the youngest of six children. His father was a skilled

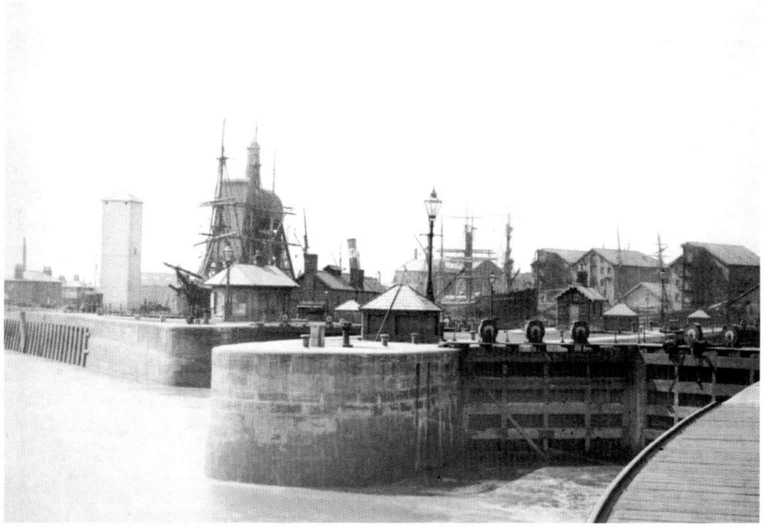

Entrance to Victoria Lock, Goole. *Masterman Collection*

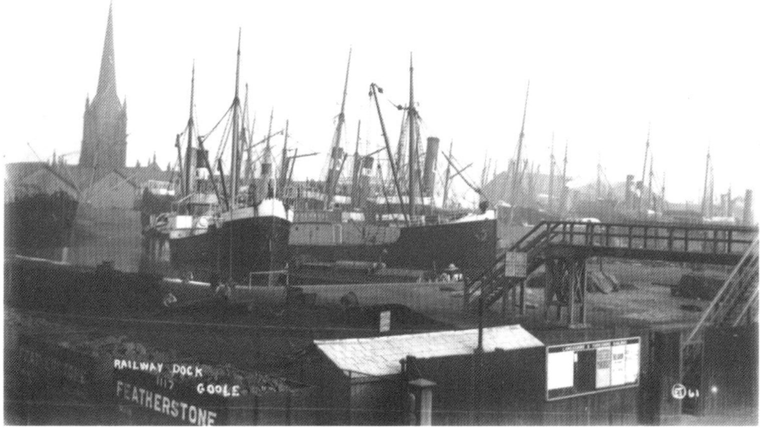

Forrest of masts in Railway Dock, Goole 1906/07. *Masterman Collection*

cabinet maker. Other members of the family were self employed tradesmen whose work was connected with the maritime life of the town. Doyle Street was near the docks, so as Reuben Chappell grew up he would have been familiar with the colourful environment of ships and seamen.

As a boy he made drawings of the ships that were close by his home. His father encouraged his interest in drawing and painting, and he won a scholarship to the privately-run Goole grammar school. From childhood he had suffered from bronchitis which may have influenced his decision to become an apprentice in a local photographic firm when he left school, rather than go sea or perhaps work in the docks as many of his contemporaries would have done. Part of the work he did at Harrisons involved hand-tinting photographs. Throughout this time he was developing his interests in art and paintings of ships. Before he was twenty he had drawings published in local newspapers. His paintings were becoming well known and around this time he advertised himself in the Goole Times as 'photographer and artist.' As demand for his paintings grew, his interest in photographic work declined. Apart from a few painting lessons, Reuben Chappell was largely self taught, and by the age of 20 he was earning his living from his paintings. His father built a studio for him at 7 Jackson Street, Goole, where he painted the ships that he saw in the busy inland seaport. His studio was destroyed by bombing in the Second World War.

Most of Chappell's early work was oil on canvas, but as his paintings became more sought after, he started to paint in watercolour and gouache. These water-based mediums were quicker to dry, so they were the traditional alternative to oils used by many pierhead painters.

There was interest in Chappell's work from local owners, masters and shipbuilders. He painted the colourful keels and sloops which were then a common sight on the Humber. They were the traditional sailing vessels associated with the river and its network of canals and waterways. He also made paintings of the steamships and packets that sailed to the Continent. SS Wharfe is one such vessel. He displayed a painting of her in the window of a local furniture shop to attract the interest of seamen going to and from the docks in Goole. Known as 'the greyhound of the Humber,' Chappell made several oil paintings of this ship.

Chappell's paintings of ships were particularly admired by Scandinavian seamen, in particular those from Denmark, who came to Goole in their schooners bringing Baltic timber. Many Reuben Chappell paintings of Danish schooners went back to Denmark with these sailors and their cargoes of coal. They returned to ports such as Svendborg, Marstal, and

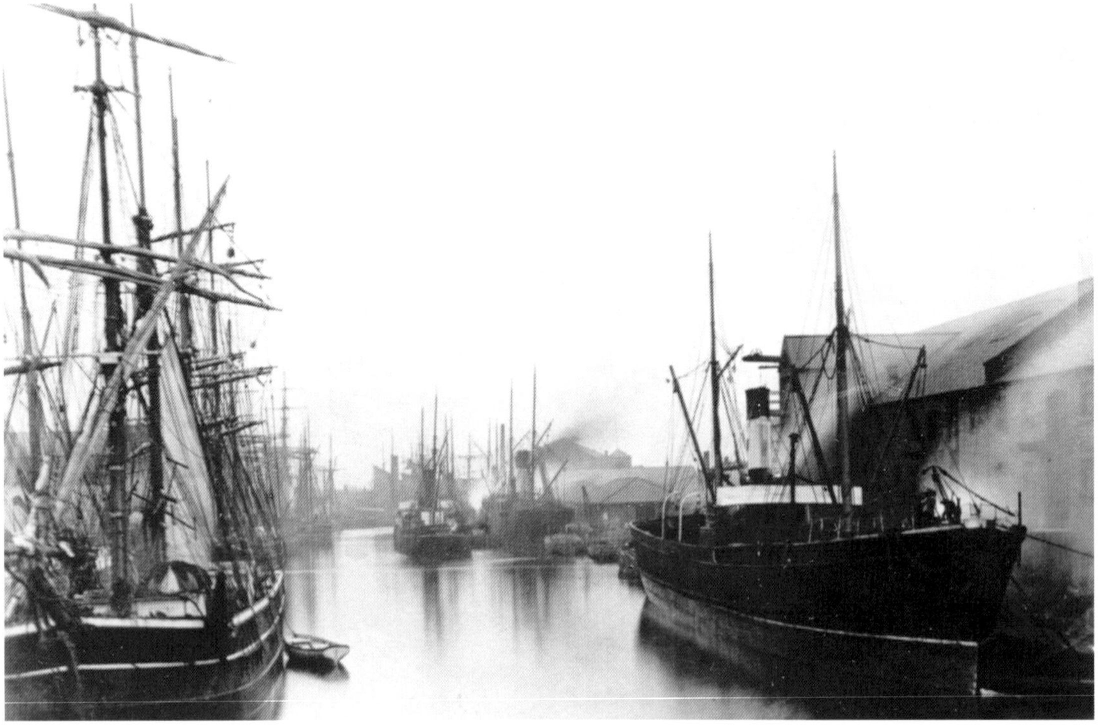

Ship Dock, Goole 1896. *Masterman Collection*

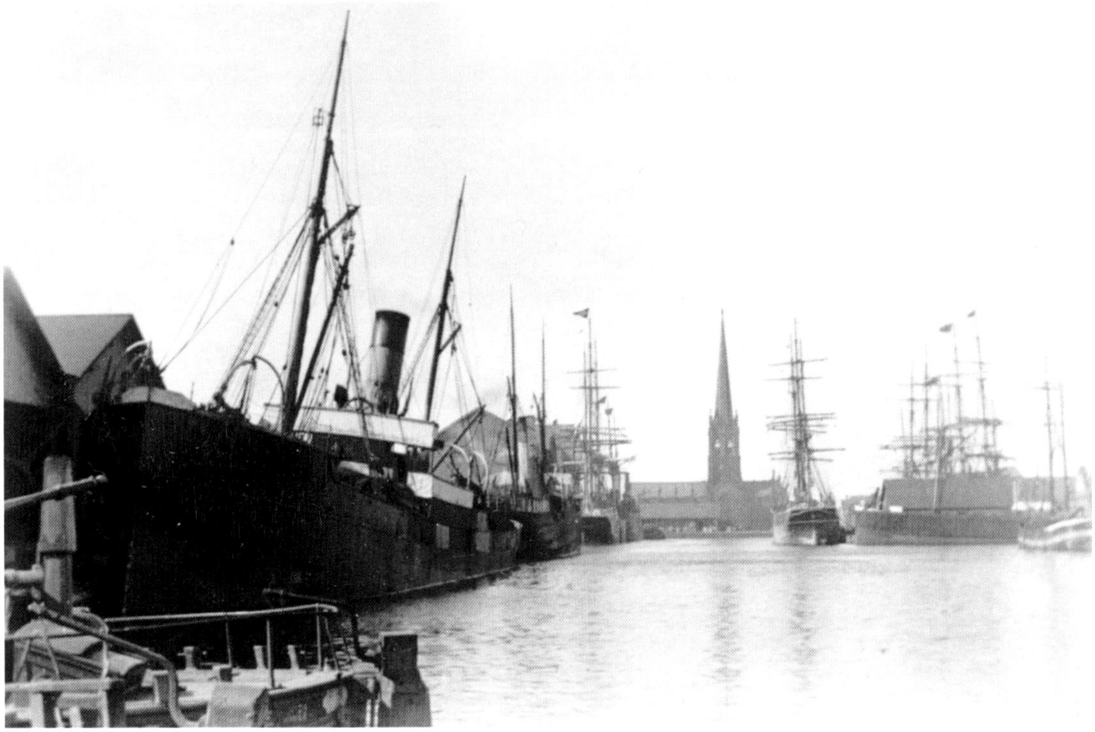

Ship Dock, Goole 1896. *Masterman Collection*

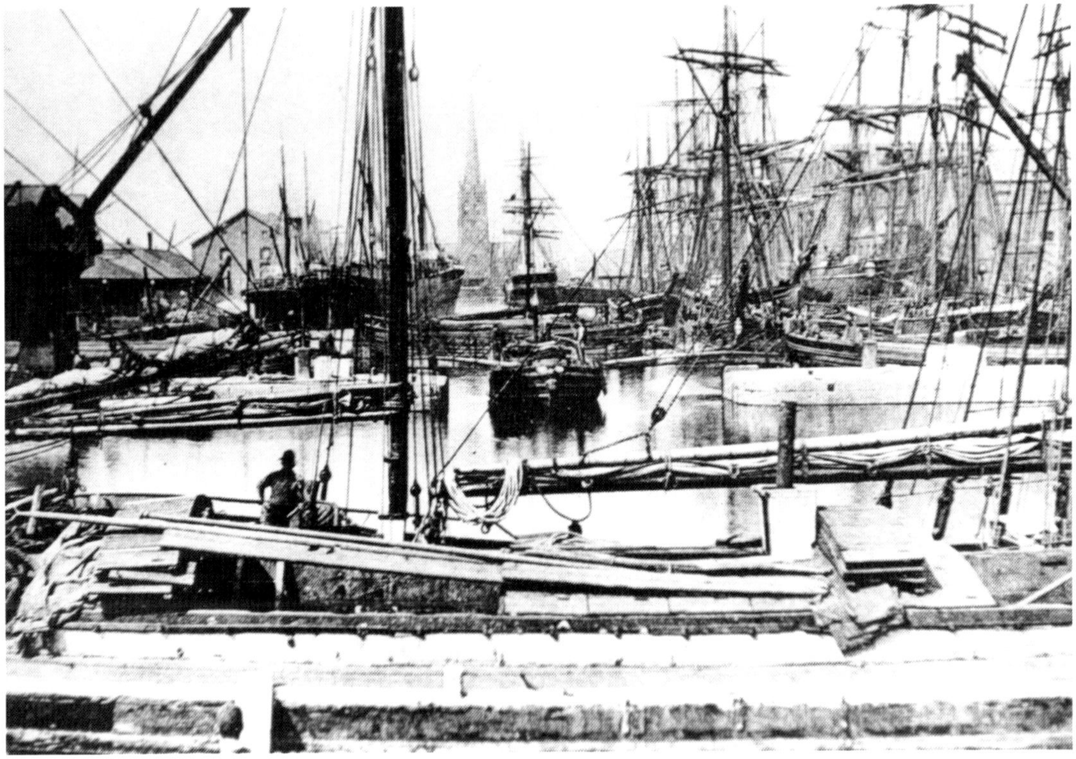

A packed Barge Dock and Ship Dock, Goole c1898. *Masterman Collection*

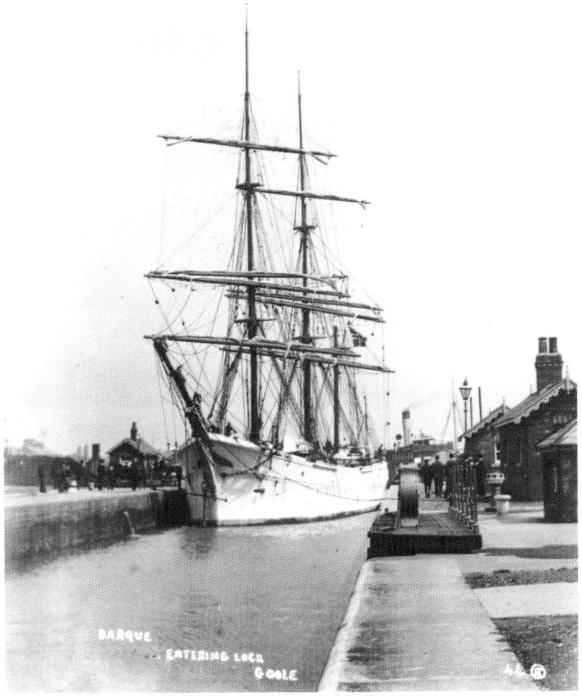

Norwegian Barque entering lock, Goole.
Masterman Collection

Ærø, where the paintings are to this day, still highly valued by the families and descendants of the seamen, and where several Danish maritime museums have large collections of his work.

Reuben Chappell is only known to have made two sea trips, one to Hamburg and one to Par in Cornwall. The voyage to Cornwall was in a 75 tonne Yorkshire Billy Boy called Daisy. The captain's name was Capt. Cawthorne. It seems there was an incident when the Daisy broke her moorings in a gale and was washed ashore on the coast at Par. As later events were to show, what Reuben Chappell saw of Cornwall must have made a good impression on him. It is likely that he found that the Danish schooners he knew in Goole also traded into the Cornish clay ports of Fowey, Par and Charlestown.

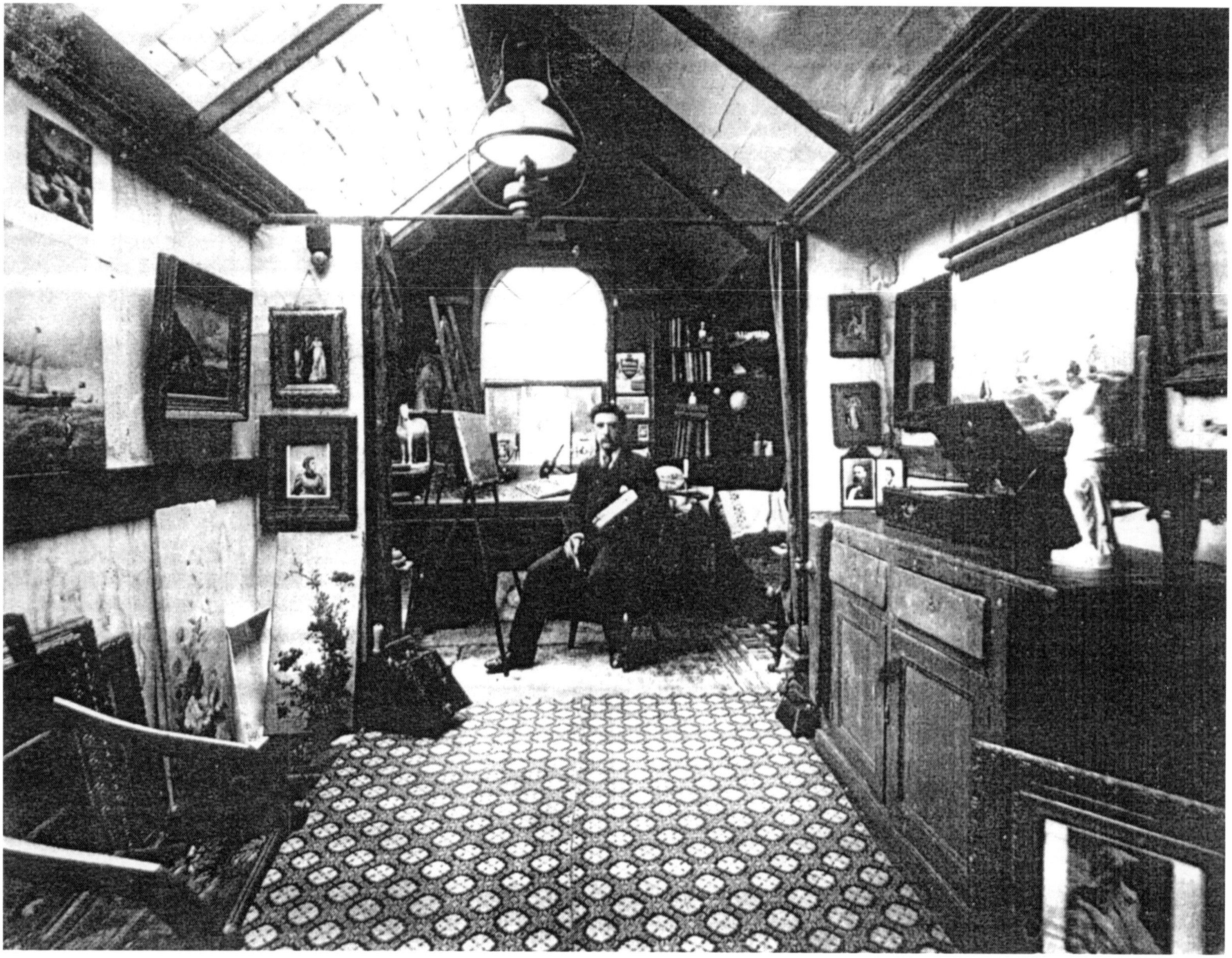

Reuben Chappell in his studio, Goole — Goole Museum and Art Gallery

We do not know how long the visit lasted but in all events Reuben Chappell returned to Goole and continued with his work. His business was doing well, and at the age of twenty five he married Caroline Amelia Bayford of Thorne, known as "Carrie." She wrote poetry and short stories and her poems were regularly published in local newspapers. They were to have three sons, Cecil, Edward and Leo.

His business was thriving, and with the commissions Chappell obtained from visiting seamen, he also continued to make paintings of the great variety of locally-owned vessels, both sail and steam. Keels, sloops, ketches and schooners, many registered in Goole or Hull, all appear in his paintings of this period. These were commercial sailing vessels carrying cargo to destinations all around the coast of Britain and across the North Sea to Baltic and European ports. There were also steam ships, the smaller vessels involved in the coastal and home trade as well as the larger passenger steam ships which ran regular services to the continent, and were increasingly seen on the Humber.

However, Chappell continued to suffer from bronchitis, and in 1904 when he was in his mid thirties, his doctor advised him to move away from the harsh east winds of Yorkshire. The decision was taken to move to Par and the milder climate of the south west. One can imagine what a tremendous wrench it was for Reuben and Caroline to leave Goole. They were leaving behind their family, friends, his studio, and his business with all the contacts he had built up over the years, but his doctor had advised him to move. In the circumstances it seems understandable that he decided to go to Par, remembered from his trip on the Daisy, and Cornwall certainly offered a much milder climate than Yorkshire, without the biting winds of the east coast.

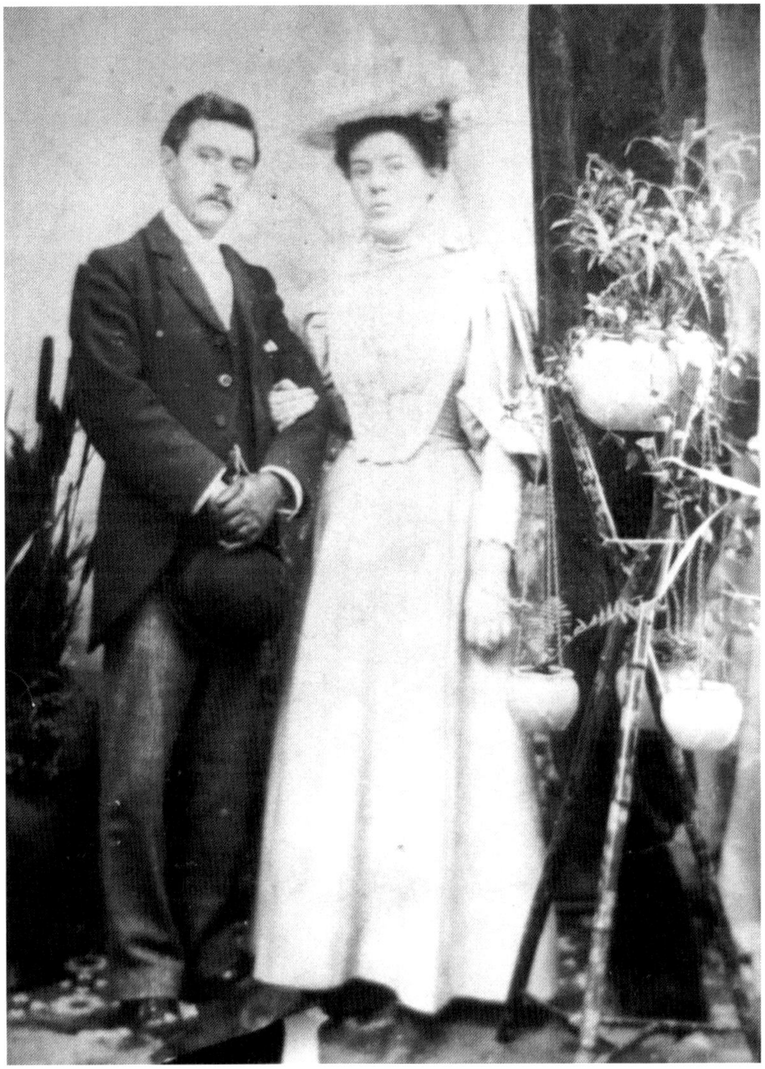

Reuben and Caroline

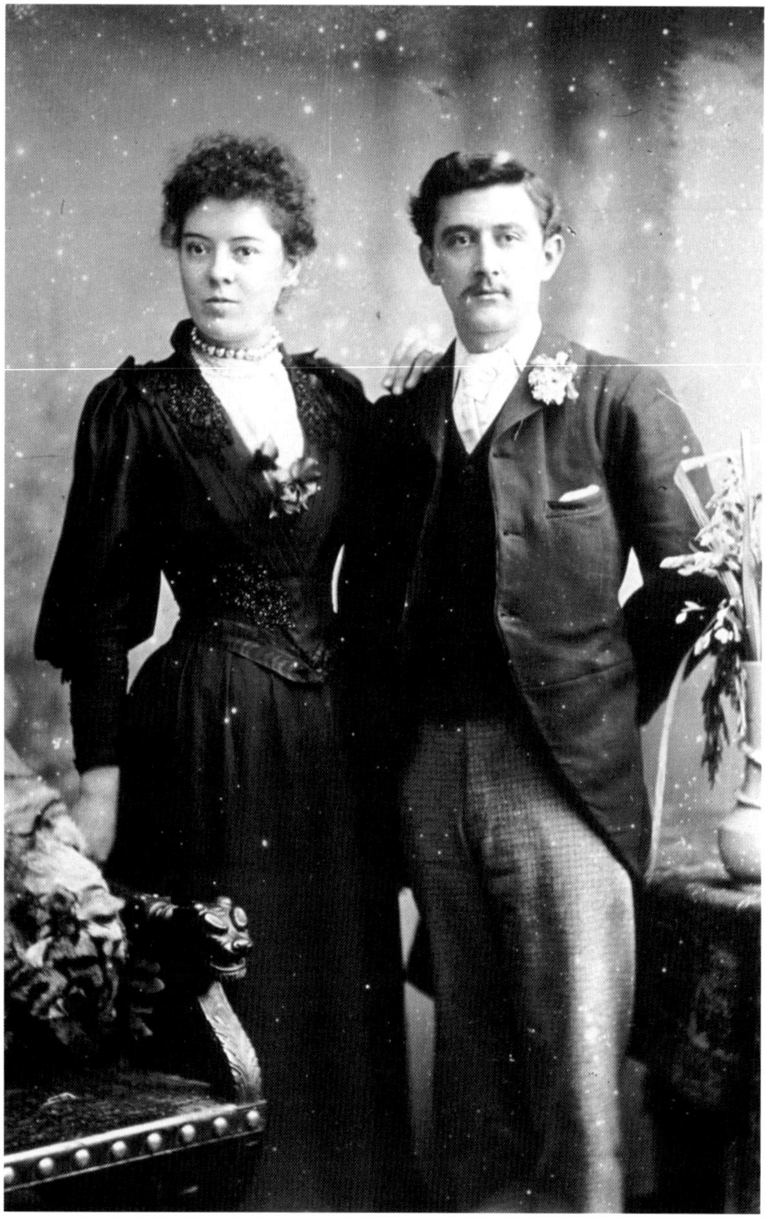

Reuben and Caroline - 1896

A crucial factor in his decision must have been that he knew his friends from Denmark, who had been his first customers in Goole, also visited Par, Fowey and Charlestown in their schooners. The principal cargo they brought to Cornwall was Baltic timber, and they returned to Denmark from Cornwall with china clay. Reuben Chappell would also have been aware that a large amount of shipping, both sail, steam and oil-powered was associated with the china clay ports at this time.

Par

In 1904 Reuben Chappell left Goole for Par. At first he moved there alone, living in lodgings while he tested the market for his paintings. He then sent for Carrie and the children, and they rented a house, formerly number 67, (now number 44,) Par Green, where he used an upstairs room with north light as a studio. From the back of the house he had a view of the beach and the docks. He and Carrie were to live there for the rest of their lives.

Par and nearby Fowey and Charlestown were frequented by ketches, schooners and small coastal steam ships, the sort of merchant sailing vessels familiar to Reuben Chappell. As in Goole, besides British vessels there were foreign ships, in particular ships from Denmark. The harbours were known collectively as the clay ports, and ships had come there for the most part for one particular product: china clay. This white clay enabled potteries to make white porcelain, and up until the discovery of china clay in south east Cornwall, in the mid 18th century, the process was a closely guarded secret of the Chinese. China clay, which was also

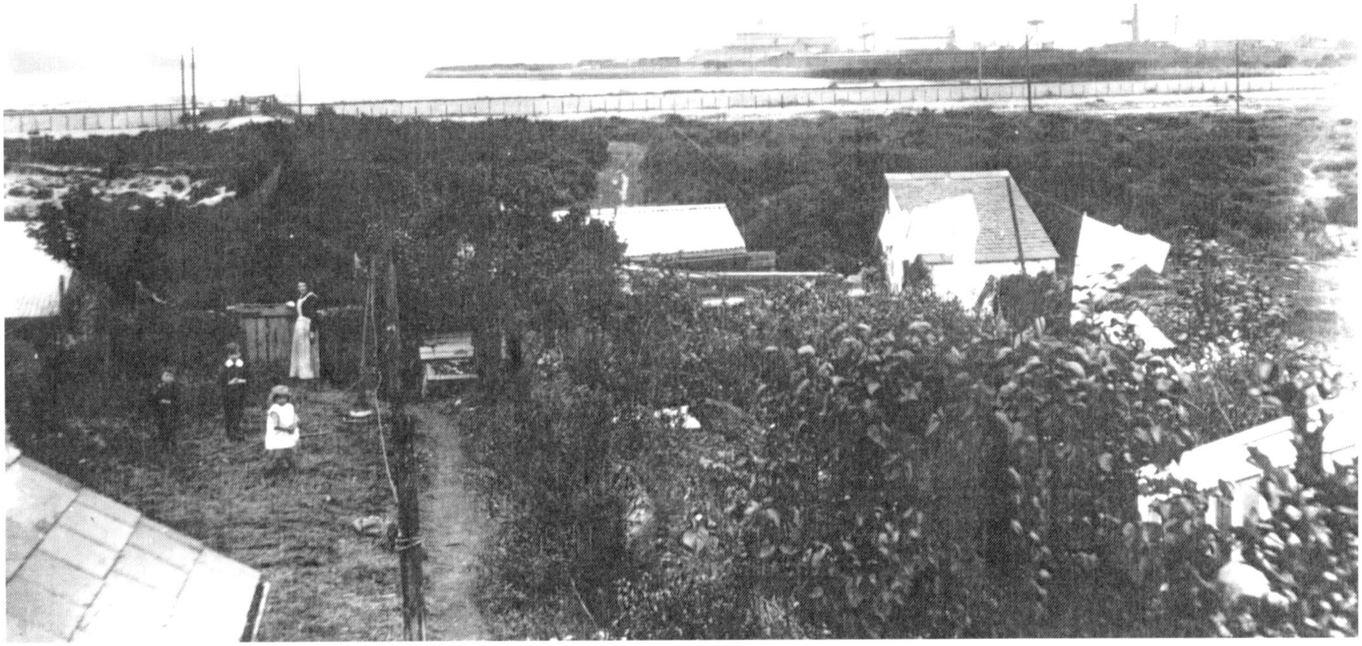

View from the back of the house in Par with the Docks in the distance and Caroline and three boys in the garden.

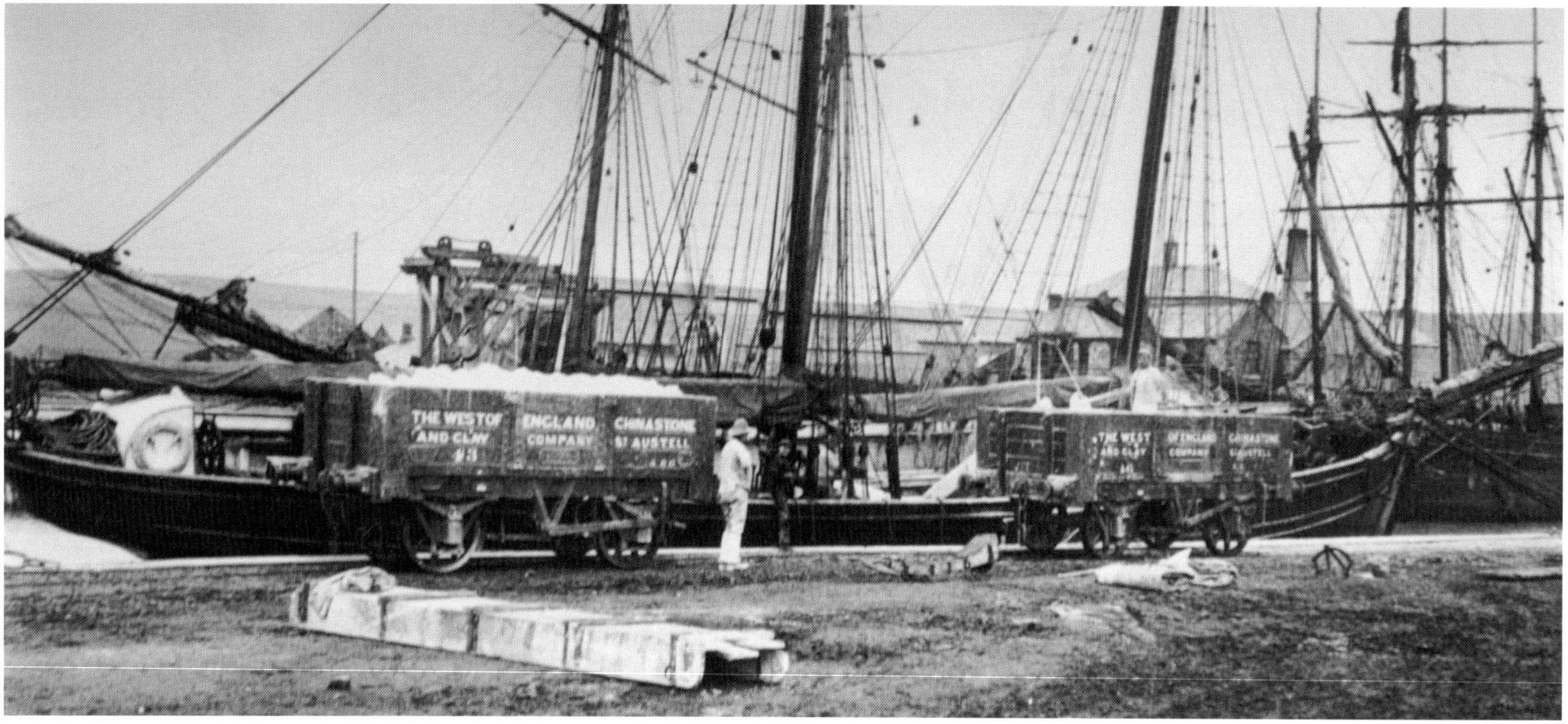

Schooner loading china clay in Par Docks. *China Clay Museum.*

used in paper making, was in demand and the clay ports were full of ships. So here in Par, almost at the bottom of Reuben Chappell's garden, ships lay alongside the quays, their rigging white from the china clay they were loading.

Reuben Chappell would solicit commissions from the captains and crew of the visiting vessels. He became a familiar figure on the quayside, summer and winter, dressed in his Norfolk suit with examples of his work rolled under his arm. He would discuss the settings and details to be included in the picture with the customer - fair or foul weather, and perhaps places or events seen on the voyage.

Despite his photographic training he did not employ the camera to assist him in his work. Having gained a commission Chappell made preparatory notes and drawings in a series of linen-covered sketchbooks. They showed carefully drawn details of parts of the particular vessel, the bow with any decoration it might carry, details and layout of deck buildings, ship's boats and stern. The proportions and layout of the masts and rigging, yards, gaffes and booms were all indicated. Occasionally there are notes on the setting up of the rigging or that the vessel's rail was painted white, or that the bulwarks were dark green. It was accuracy in such points that endeared Chappell to his patrons who wanted above all else correctness of detail. They were experts in their field, knowing the significance and importance of every detail of their vessel. That knowledge was essential not only for their livelihoods, but their lives also depended on it. There was a great deal of mariner's pride in their association with the particular vessel and the painting would commemorate their feeling for their ship. In the tradition of pierhead painting Chappell's ships were portrayed broadside on and often included other vessels in the distance and some topographical interest, for example a particular

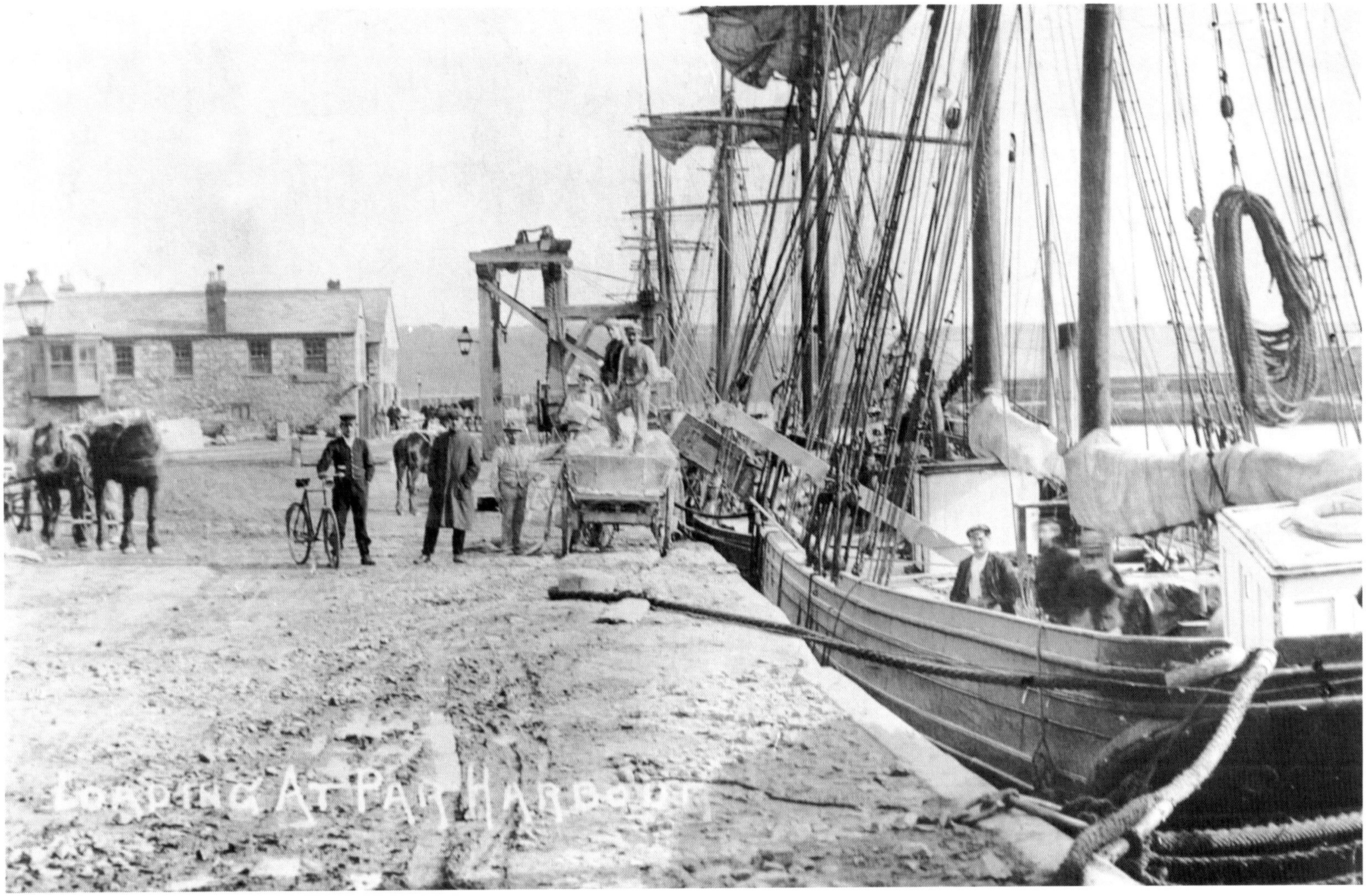

Par Docks. *China Clay Museum.*

piece of coast or a lighthouse that the vessel might have passed. Frequently Start Point and the Eddystone light would have been significant landmarks on a voyage to and from the clay ports. There exist examples where clearly the seaman ordering the painting has asked Reuben Chappell to depict a particular event, for example the painting of the Mary Jones depicted, dismasted off Godrevy on 19th February 1919.

The flags flying on the ships in the paintings all have meanings. Firstly there is the Red Ensign carried by all British merchant vessels, or the national flag in the case of Danish or other foreign vessels. Often there is a group of four small flags which refer to the unique code signal of the vessel. The ship owner's and insurance company's flag are sometimes depicted, and often a decorative pennant bearing the ship's name is included.

Reuben Chappell's paintings were never shown in galleries. He sold his work directly to the seamen and those associated with the ships he painted. He needed to make his paintings affordable and this perhaps

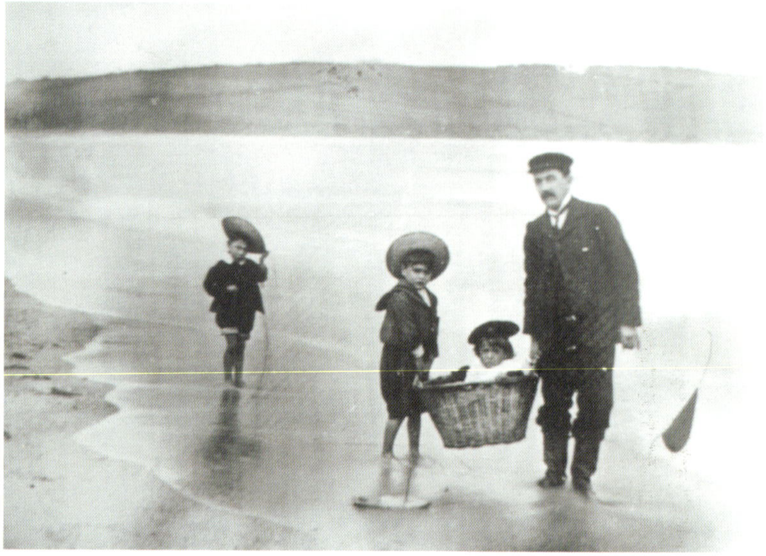

Reuben and sons on Par Beach.

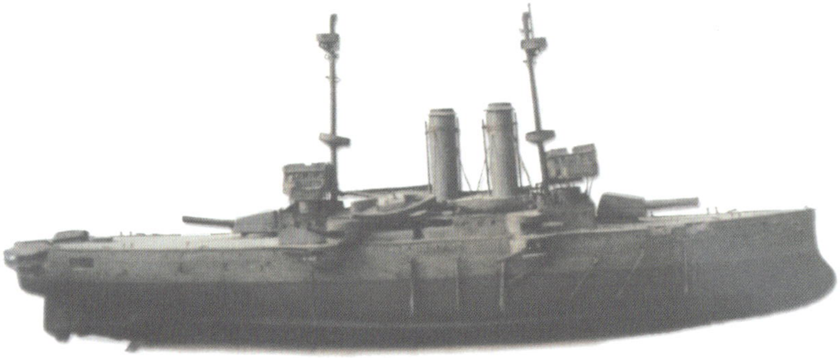

Model of World War One battleship made by Reuben.

explains why he produced such a large number of paintings. In his early years at Par the prices that Reuben Chappell charged started at between 2/6d and 5/-, and rose to 12/6d in 1925. Although his pictures were sold unframed, even then this was not a lot of money; a ship portrait would have been a luxury. In the early 1900s the master of the sort of vessel Reuben Chappell painted would have earned about £5 per month, the mate about £4, and the crew far less. Each painting would have had to be completed and delivered before the ship sailed. There were times when the ships were leaving port the next day, and Chappell worked into the night to complete and deliver the painting before the vessel departed on the morning tide.

In Par Reuben and Caroline were part of the community. Caroline was a respected member of the Mother's Union there. Reuben did not paint on Sundays, but attended church at Par Green with his family, and in the afternoons the family would go for long walks, sometimes to the Luxulyan Valley, Pridmouth, Gribben Head or Polkerris. Sometimes they would go to Par Beach with model boats Reuben had made for his sons, and they sailed them on the pool, a place popular with people who also brought their boats to race and sail.

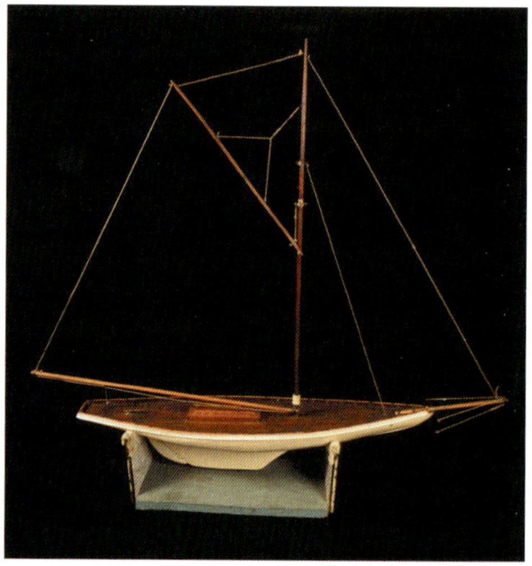

Reuben might go to the local pub for a beer once a week, and the family went to listen to the brass bands and male voice choirs which were a strong tradition of the St Austell area. When at home, Caroline sang and played the piano. There is no evidence that they owned a car, so it is likely that Reuben caught the bus or walked the 5 miles from Par to Fowey in the east, or the 6 miles from Par to Charlestown in the west. During weekday mornings he would go to the china clay ports, carrying a roll of his paintings as samples to show the seamen as he sought commissions. At times the order might be for more than one painting, perhaps a pair of paintings depicting the ship in fair and foul weather. He painted the merchant ships, either sail or power, which plied the small ports, but never painted naval shipping.

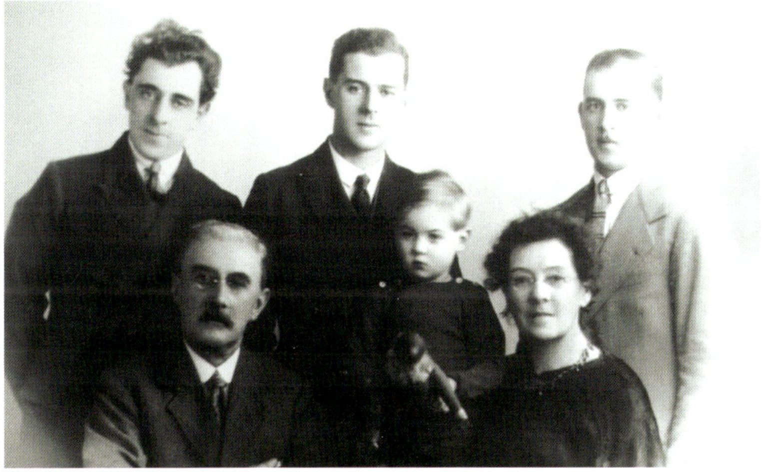

From left; Edward, Reuben, Cecil, his son Trevor, Caroline and Leo

It is important to note that although Chappell saw the ships he painted mainly when they were in port with their sails furled, he depicted them as if they were at sea under full sail. This fitted the convention of the ship's portrait, but nevertheless required considerable imagination and a knowledge of sails and rigging, enabling him to show which sails would be set in different weather conditions.

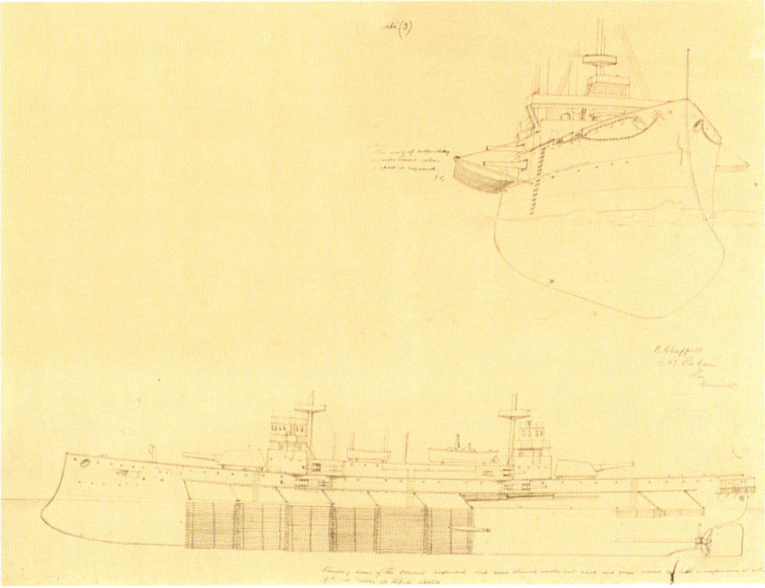

Designs for ships' defenses

During the First World War security laws prohibited the sketching of sensitive information including ships. By that time Chappell was so familiar with the form and layout of his subjects that he managed to remember the details needed to complete the painting. Shipping, of course, continued throughout the war and, even during this period, he managed to obtain sufficient commissions to support his family. He also sent a considerable number of designs to the Ministry of Imperial Defence to help the war effort: portable nets fixed to the bows of ships to protect against mines, and screens suspended over the sides of ships to protect against torpedoes. He had ideas for smokescreens and dummy warships and devised methods for attacking zeppelins.

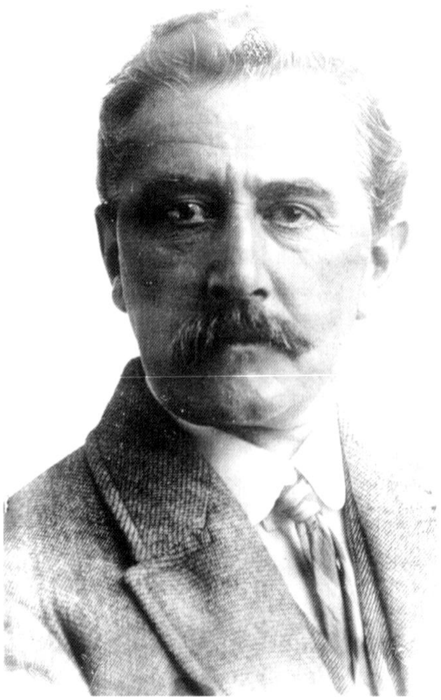

Reuben Chappell

Imaginative methods for disguising trenches and soldiers as well as ways of deploying barbed wire were some examples of Chappell's extraordinary ingenuity. In wartime their eldest son Cecil joined the Royal Engineers. While he was in Mesopotamia in 1918, Caroline woke up in the middle of the night in tears having dreamt that Cecil was desperately ill. Indeed he was, with dysentery. Eventually he was brought home. Later Cecil worked for Marconi, and then the textile industry. Chappell's second son Edward had joined the merchant navy in the Great War. He later travelled the world making a number of voyages to Africa, Australia and North and South America. He then went to Canada to work for the Hudson Bay Company. He eventually settled in Scarborough, Canada, and there, for the rest of his life, made a living as an artist. Leo was still at school during the war. He became a draughtsman, working on the Bristol Brabazon, which at the time was the world's biggest plane, and he subsequently went to Australia.

Reuben Chappell's paintings are honest and unpretentious. He never romanticises or exaggerates. Even in the foul weather paintings, one senses he is underplaying the sea states and dark skies. Storms could in reality be far worse than those he depicted. His intention was to portray the vessel accurately, in convincing sea and weather conditions. Any romance we sense in these paintings is connected with nostalgia for the age of sail and steam.

C Ward Jackson has studied Reuben Chappell's diaries, and although the years are not complete he has calculated that Reuben Chappell may have produced as many as 12,000 paintings. This figure has been disputed by some, and it does seem an extraordinary amount, but as evidence C Ward Jackson shows us that in 1916, for example, Chappell painted 395 ships, in 1917 he painted 345 ships, and in 1919, 483. In 1920 an amazing 509 ship portraits were produced. After this the numbers decline, but it is quite clear that during his most productive years Reuben Chappell was producing an average of more than one painting a day. His paintings show an accomplished technique which he was clearly able to apply to each new subject. It is also likely that he sometimes produced more than one version of the same ship commissioned by different seamen. What Reuben Chappell had witnessed and recorded was the end of an era. The age of sail, or at least the age of commercial sail, was coming to an end. As Chappell's paintings record the decline of sail, they also record the rise of steam powered vessels. Sometimes his practice was to produce a pair of paintings, one depicting the vessel in full sail, sailing in fine weather, the other in foul weather with reduced sail. Progress of Bideford is an example. The paintings were not dated, but most included the name of the vessel, her home port, and sometimes the name of the master. He continued to sign his paintings R Chappell of Goole for a number of years after he moved to Par, presumably to let people know he was the same painter well known in Goole. There are other paintings which are signed "R Chappell" "R.C." and "R.C.G." During the latter part of his career Chappell had a series of postcards made of some of his paintings.

In 1922 The Cutty Sark, then under Portuguese ownership, came into Falmouth, sheltering from a storm. She was bought by Captain Wilfred Dowman who was at the time running a training ship for young seamen in Falmouth. The Cutty Sark stayed in the port for some years, and during this time Chappell was asked to make a model of her.

In 1925 Reuben Chappell suffered a minor stroke which affected his eyesight, and after this his health started to decline. His wife Caroline died in 1930 and was buried in Fowey. Chappell remarried Mrs Ada Jane Turner, a widow, three years later. He died 20th July 1940 of bronchial pneumonia and was buried next to Carrie in Fowey cemetery.

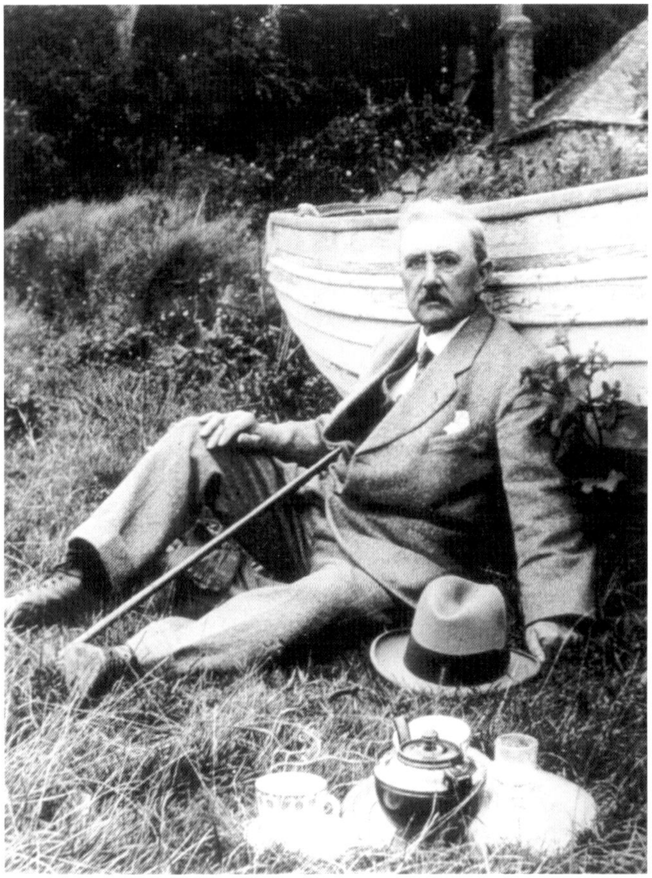

Ships of the Humber

By his early twenties Reuben Chappell was an established ship portrait painter in his home town of Goole. His customers were the owners and masters of vessels connected with the area. A great variety of vessels were registered in Goole or Hull. There were the keels and sloops whose work took them up and down the Ouse and Humber, and by way of the canal systems, to towns and cities far inland. Sailing ships of all sizes were to be seen, as were the large steamships, some of which were owned by the railway companies running regular services to northern European ports. Many visiting ships came up the Humber and Ouse to Goole. British and foreign vessels, and Danish sailing ships in particular were regularly seen in the port.

Clearly Goole was a very busy port for the period that Reuben Chappell lived in Goole. All sorts of vessels, large and small, sail and steam powered, were there. Chappell's paintings are now a poignant record of the ships that were to be seen on the Humber and Ouse in the two decades prior to his move to Cornwall in 1904.

On the East Coast of England the Humber stretches over 50 miles from the North Sea to the river Ouse and Goole, where it is connected with the Aire and Calder rivers and canal systems of East Yorkshire. The system of rivers that radiate from the upper reaches of the Humber have had a history of continuous commercial traffic since the middle ages. In the 18th century they were improved with locks and artificial cuts, some rivers like the Aire and Calder being almost completely canalised by the mid 19th century.

Keels & Sloops

The traditional small sail trading vessels of the area, the keels and sloops which Chappell painted were shallow draught vessels made for carrying freight. Their flat bottoms enabled them to sit on the beds of rivers and creeks when the tide was out, and they were built narrow and shallow enough to fit the canal systems. On the canal the keels would be hauled by horse, man power, or steam tugs. If there was a was a favourable wind the sails were set. In open water the square rig could be handled to allow the vessel to work well to windward, the lee boards gripping the water. A keel with an 80 ton capacity could be handled by two men.

While Yorkshiremen remained faithful to the keel, the sloop was the favourite of the Lincolnshire side of the Humber. The sloop had the same hull form but the rig was fore and aft; indeed the terms 'keel' and 'sloop', refer to the rig rather than the hull form, and keels were altered to sloop rig. Sloops made coastal passages, and some were big, with capacities of up to 200 tons. Their size depended on the limitations of which waterway or canal they used. Vessels could carry a surprising amount of cargo, a capacity of 100 tons

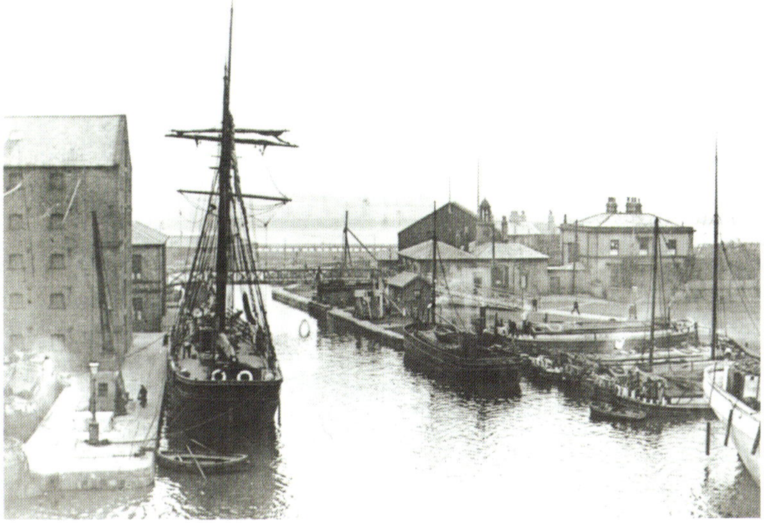

Entrance to the harbour basin, Goole c1900 *Masterman Collection*

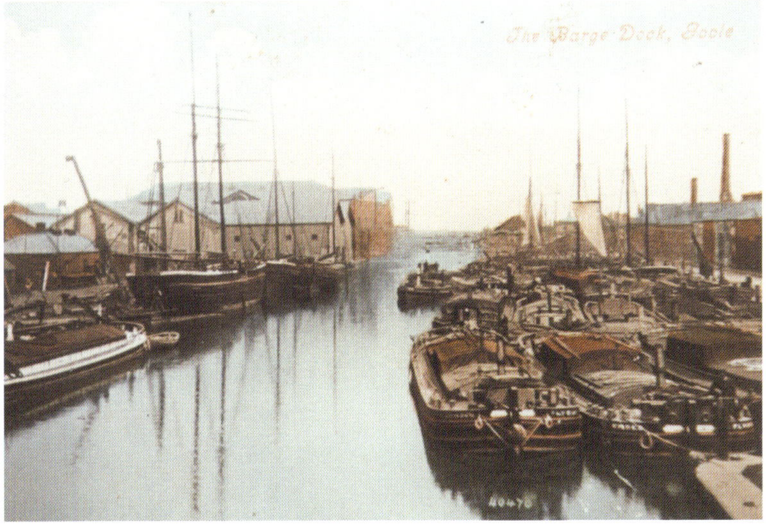

The Barge Dock, Goole postcard *Masterman Collection*

not being unusual. As would be expected most of the vessels' space would be devoted to the cargo hold, which when loaded was covered with boards and canvas.

On entering the canal system the mast could either be lowered or unstepped and left ashore, to enable the ship to pass under bridges. On some sections of river or canal steam tugs were available when winds were not favourable, and they would often tow several vessels at once. In other sections of the canal there were men with horses who could be hired to tow the vessel. But tugs and horses, if they were available, had to be paid for. The alternative, if there was no wind to sail, was man power.

These little cargo ships would travel many miles inland to deliver and collect cargo from the many towns, mines and farms and factories served by the canals. The canal and river systems stretched to towns and cities far inland, to such places as Sheffield, Doncaster, Rotherham, Mexborough and York.

Yorkshire coal was an important export, but was also used locally to bunker trawlers in Hull, fuel gasworks, mills and factories as well as being used as house coal. Keels and sloops brought raw materials to factories far inland along the canal system, and carried their products back on the return trip. Cocoa in its various forms went to Rowntrees of York. China clay which had been brought by topsail schooners and ketches from Cornwall was delivered to the potteries. Farm products, barley, maize, rye, oats, fishmeal and fertilisers, metals such as copper and iron, manufactured goods including tractors and canned foods, wheat and flour, potatoes and olive oil, phosphates, gravel, hides, are just a small selection of the cargoes carried by these vessels.

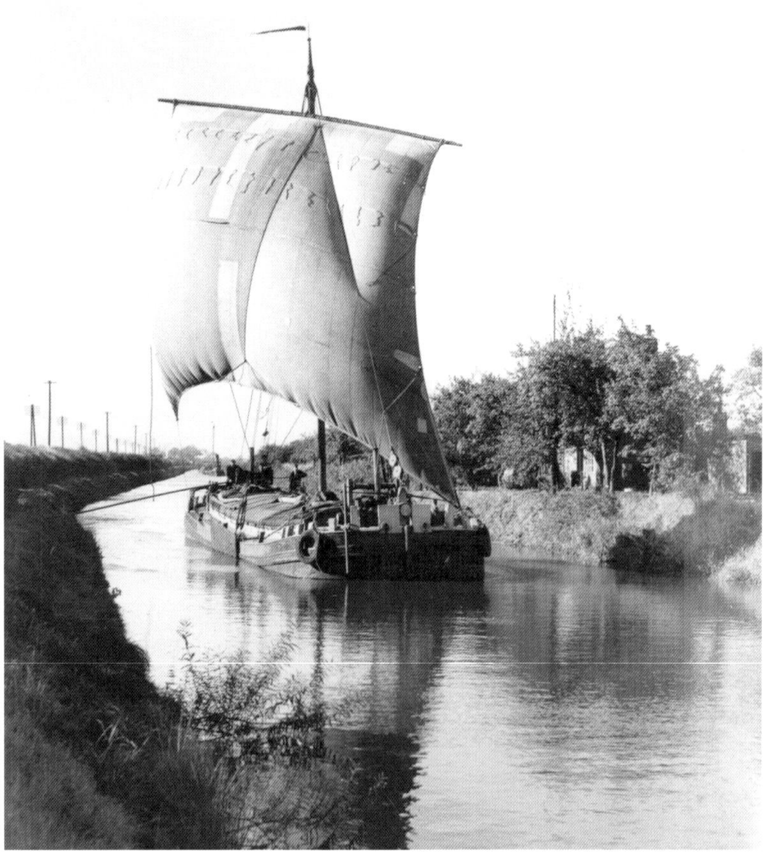

Hull Maritime Museum

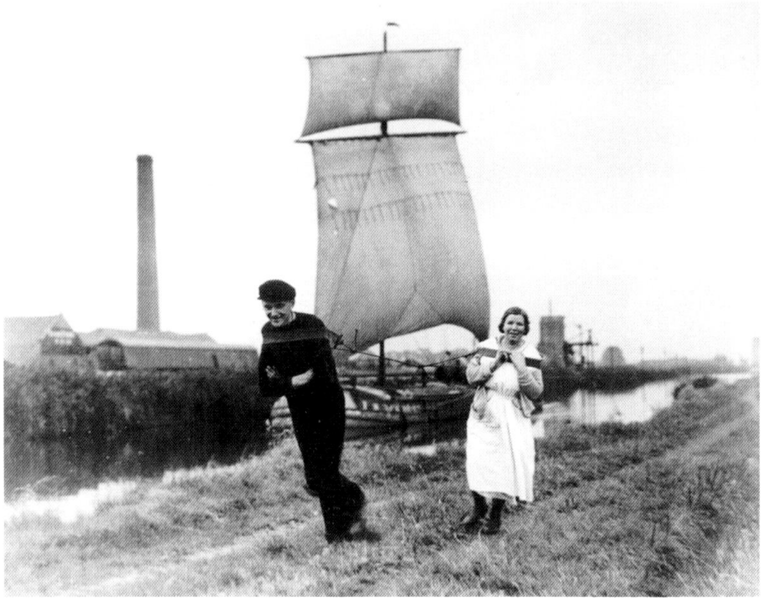

Hull Maritime Museum

The accommodation was in the stern of the vessel below the after deck, reached by way of a nearly vertical ladder. With stove bunks, panelled cupboards, table etc., it made a compact home. These vessels could be worked by two men, the skipper and a mate, whose accommodation was below the foredeck. But often they were crewed by a family, the skipper, his wife and children, and the ship was their home.

It is still possible to see two of these ships sailing on the Humber and its tributary rivers the Trent and Ouse. The keel Comrade and the sloop Amy Howson have been restored by the Humber Keel and Sloop Preservation Society and are sailed during the summer months.

There are three public collections which contain Reuben Chappell paintings in this area: Hull Maritime Museum, the Ferens Art Gallery, Hull and the Garside Collection at Goole Museum.

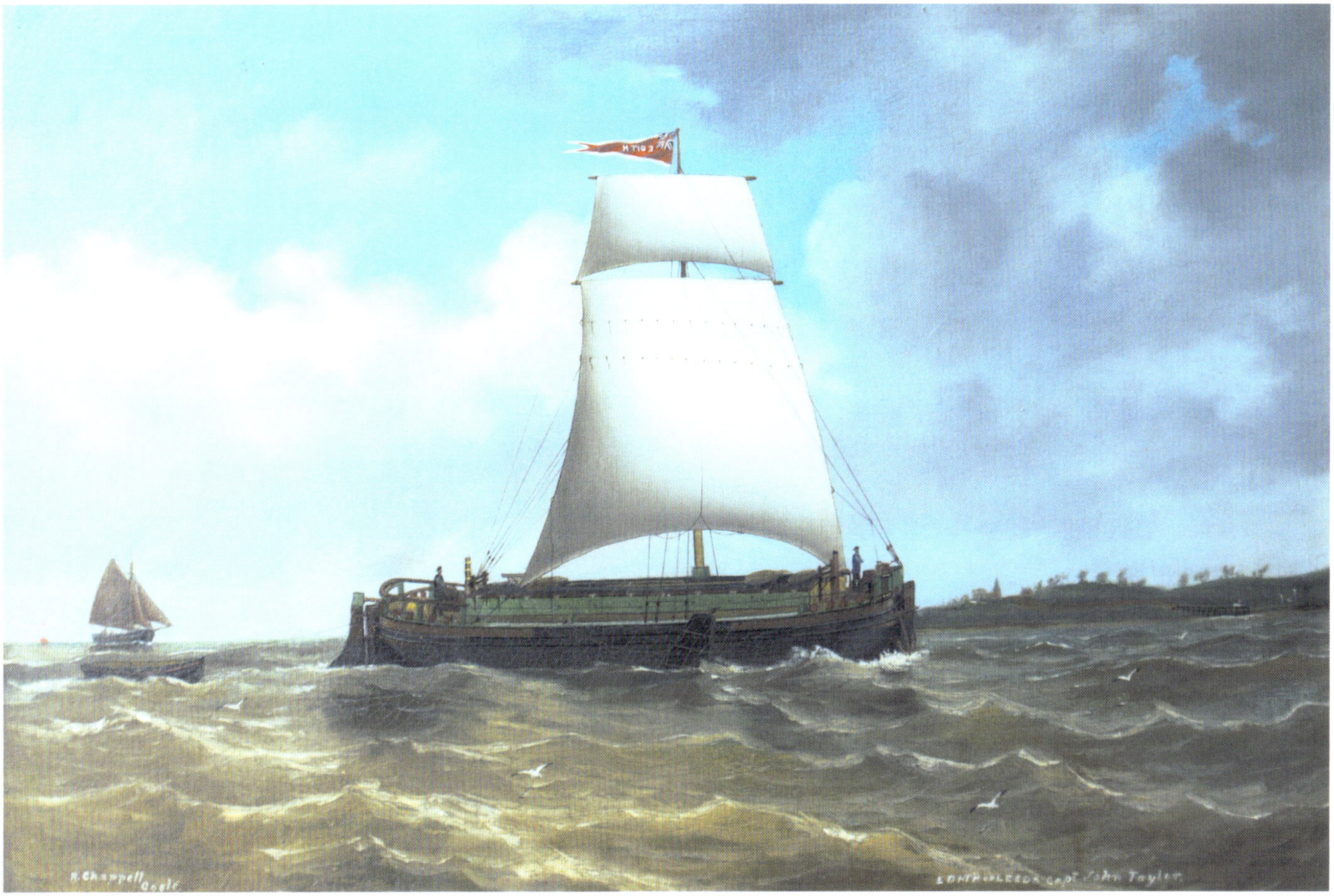

Goole Museum and Art Gallery

Edith of Hull

The keels were very distinctive vessels and their square sails were obviously of ancient origin. They were built to trade on the Humber and connecting rivers and canal systems of Yorkshire. On the canals the vessels were usually handled by men and horses, the sail hoisted in favourable winds. On the rivers and sea, their square sails set, they sailed well, using lee boards instead of a keel.

These little ships were often owned and run by a family who worked and lived aboard. Quite understandably their owners had considerable pride in and affection for these vessels. Reuben Chappell's paintings of them would have been treasured by their owners. This oil on canvas painting was commissioned by her master Capt. John Taylor and shows the Humber Keel Edith sailing in the mouth of the Humber.

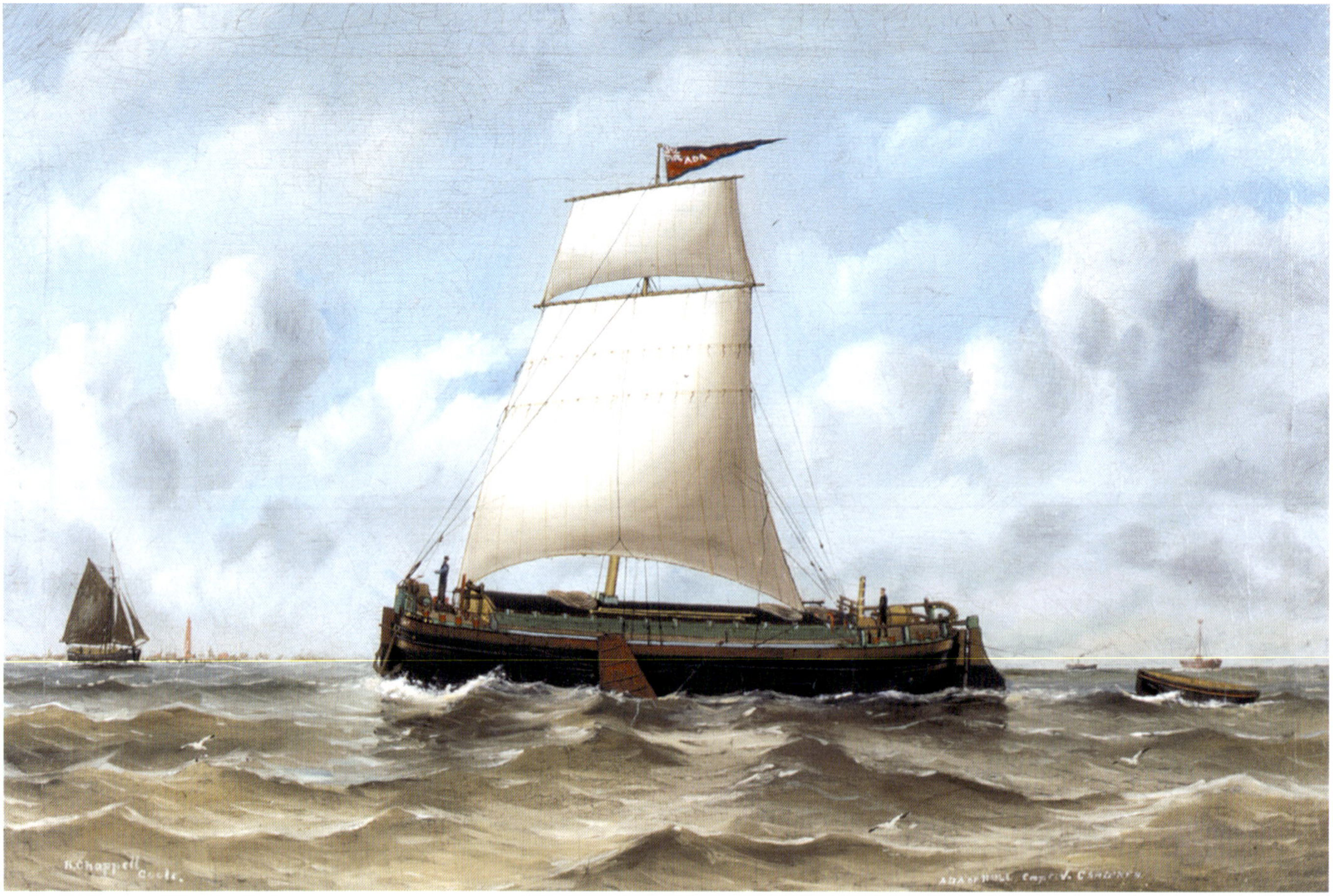

Hull Maritime Museum

ADA OF HULL

The Humber keel Ada was built in 1889 and owned by James Gardiner of Hull, captained by his brother William Gardiner. This painting shows Ada entering the Humber. The Middle Lightship is shown in the distance.

A reported tragic incident took place on the Humber which involved a Captain Cawthorne. As there were a number of captains of that name, this may not necessarily be the same Captain Cawthorne who took Reuben Chappell on his first visit to Par. He had taken delivery of a new keel, and to mark the event had taken his wife and two children out for a trip. The vessel was anchored in the Humber for the night and the family asleep when she was hit by one of the Humber steamships. The keel was cut in half and sunk by the force of the collision. Captain Cawthorne escaped but his wife and children were drowned. In those days collision at sea was a constant danger. It was common for fishing vessels and sailing ships to be lost in this way.

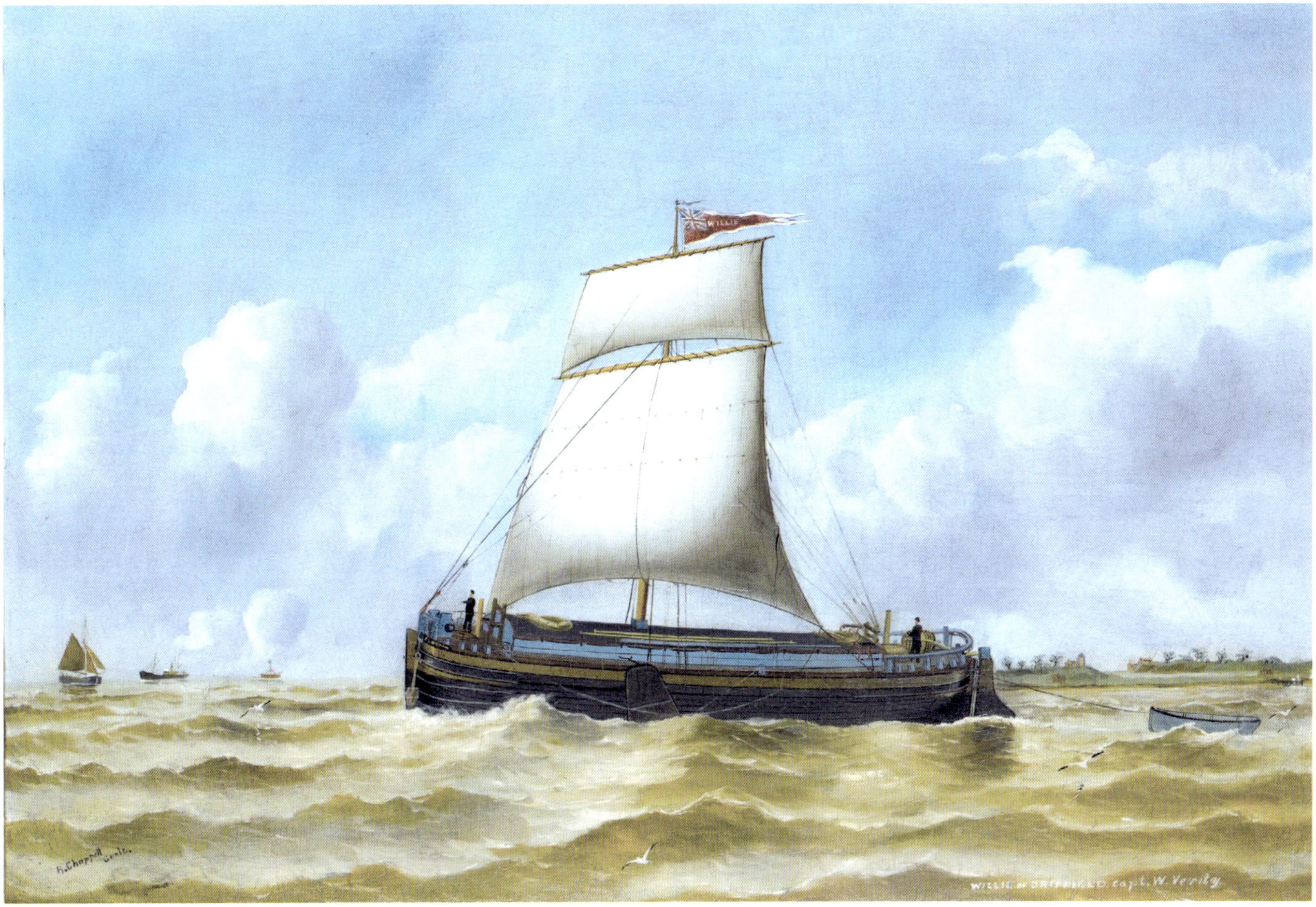

National Maritime Museum

Willie of Driffield

In this oil painting Chappell shows the Humber keel Willie at the mouth of the river. The incredible muddy colour of the water of the Humber is apparent here. On the horizon are several vessels including the lightship at the mouth of the river.

Cog Boats

These tenders had many uses and were essential to the efficient working of a keel or sloop. Chappell rightly shows their importance by including the ship's cog boat either being towed behind the vessel or being carried on deck.

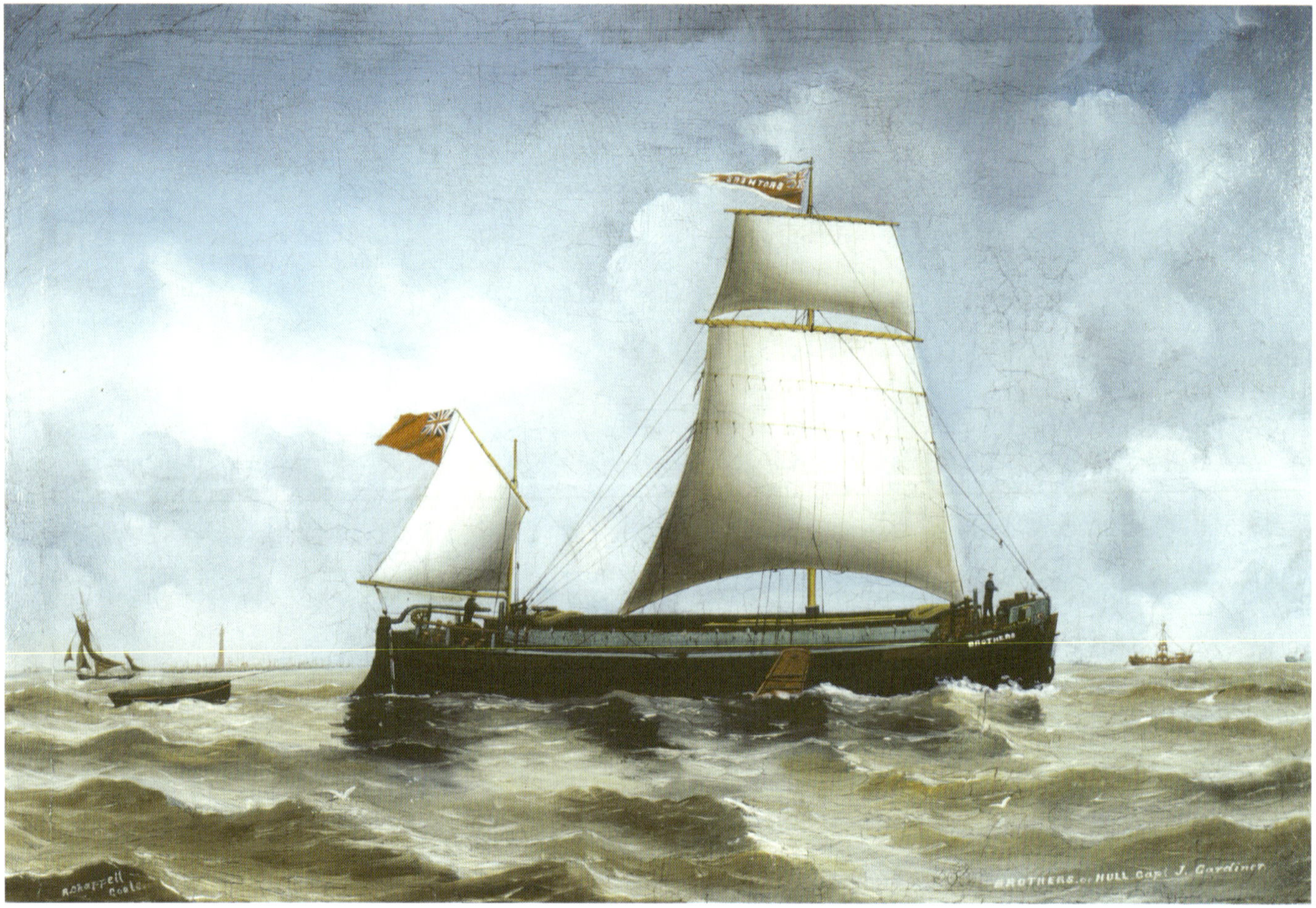

Hull Maritime Museum

Brothers of Hull

Ketch; built in 1887; 53 reg. tons; 74'9" x 14'; owned by James Gardiner of Hull.

The Trent catch or ketch Brothers is known to have made regular coastal passages. In this oil on canvas painting Reuben Chappell shows the ketch in the Humber off the Middle Lightship.

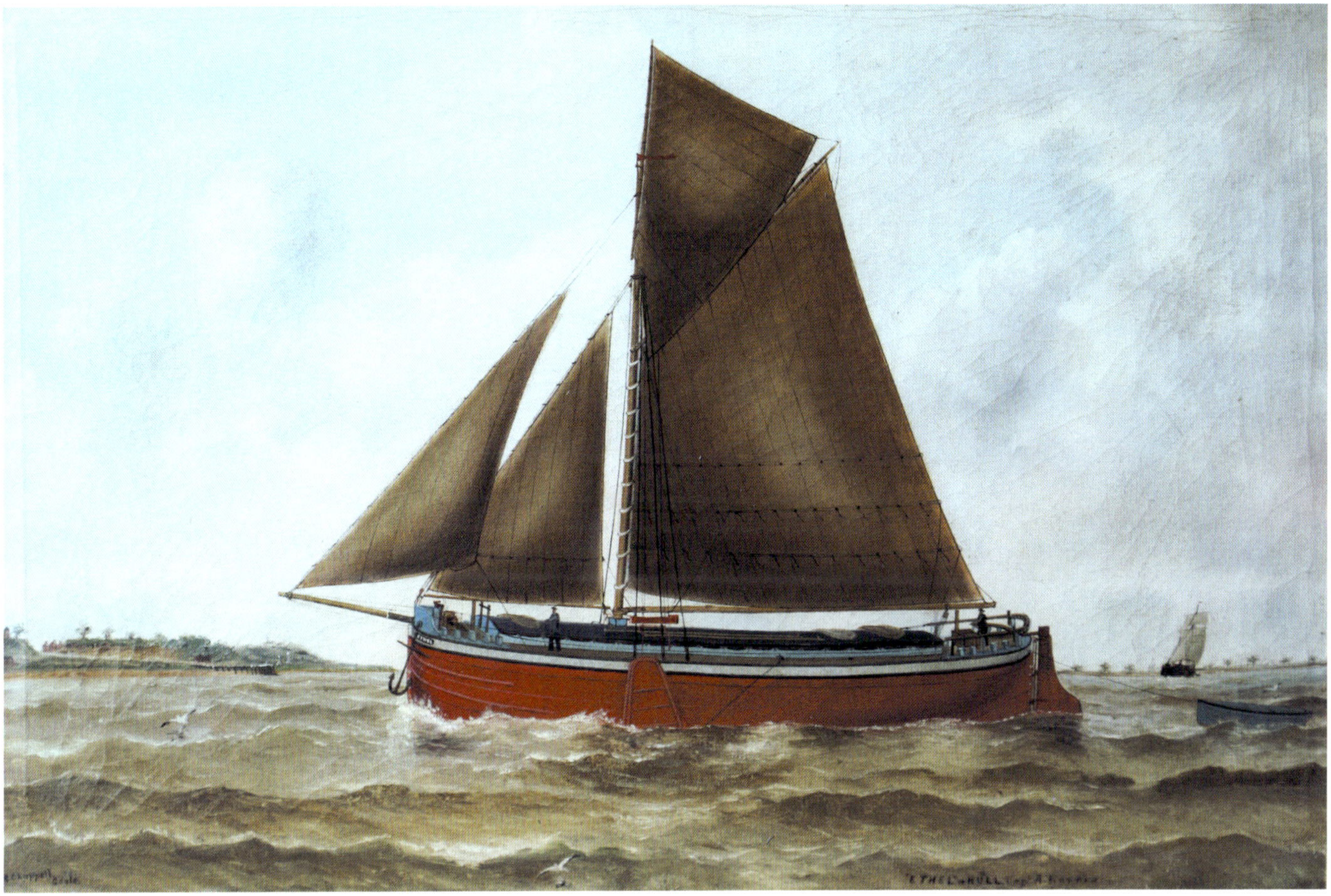

Goole Museum and Art Gallery

Ethel of Hull

The land seen to the left of this picture is possibly Trent Falls with the church and former jetty at Whitton. The sloops were peculiar to the Lincolnshire side of the Humber. In this painting Reuben Chappell shows a Humber keel in the distance.

In 1912 Ethel was carrying a cargo of timber from Hull to Sheffield when she became stranded near St Andrews Dock. Although the crew were saved, the vessel was lost.

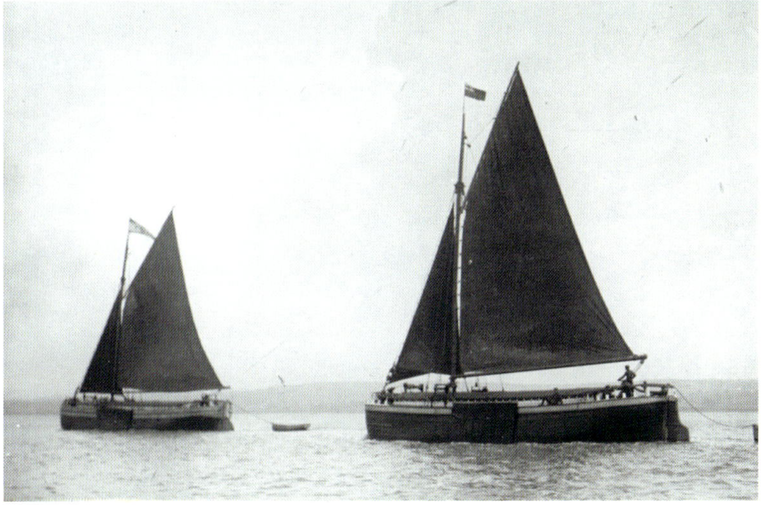

Sloops Phylus and Eva Lucy *Hull Maritime Museum*

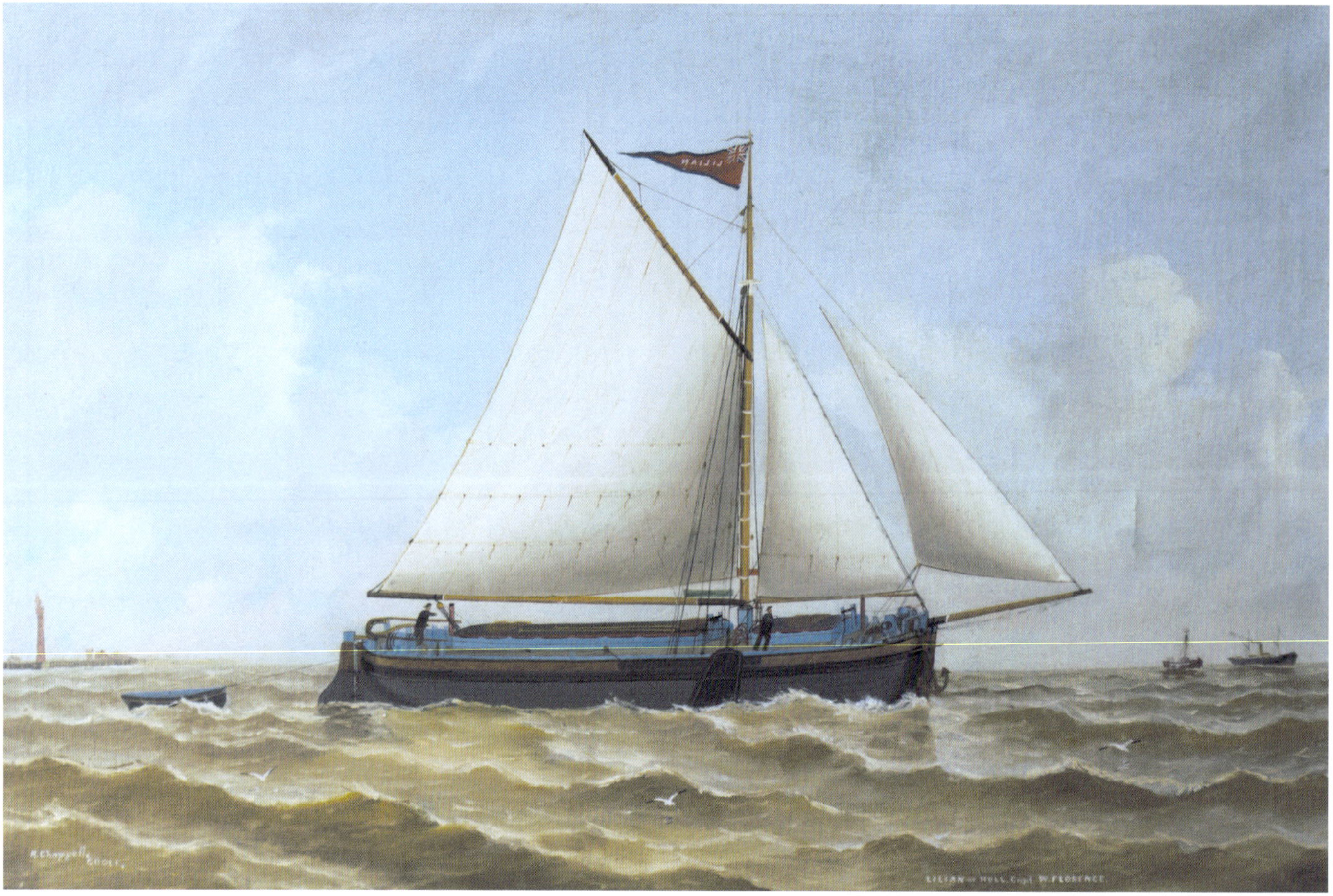

Goole Museum and Art Gallery

Lilian of Hull

The Sloop Lilian was built in 1896 at Barton, on the Lincolnshire side of the Humber. She was still afloat in 1947, only disappearing from the Mercantile Navy list in 1951.

The painting, commissioned by her Master, shows Lilian off the coast. The port of Grimbsy with its hydraulic tower is seen in the distance.

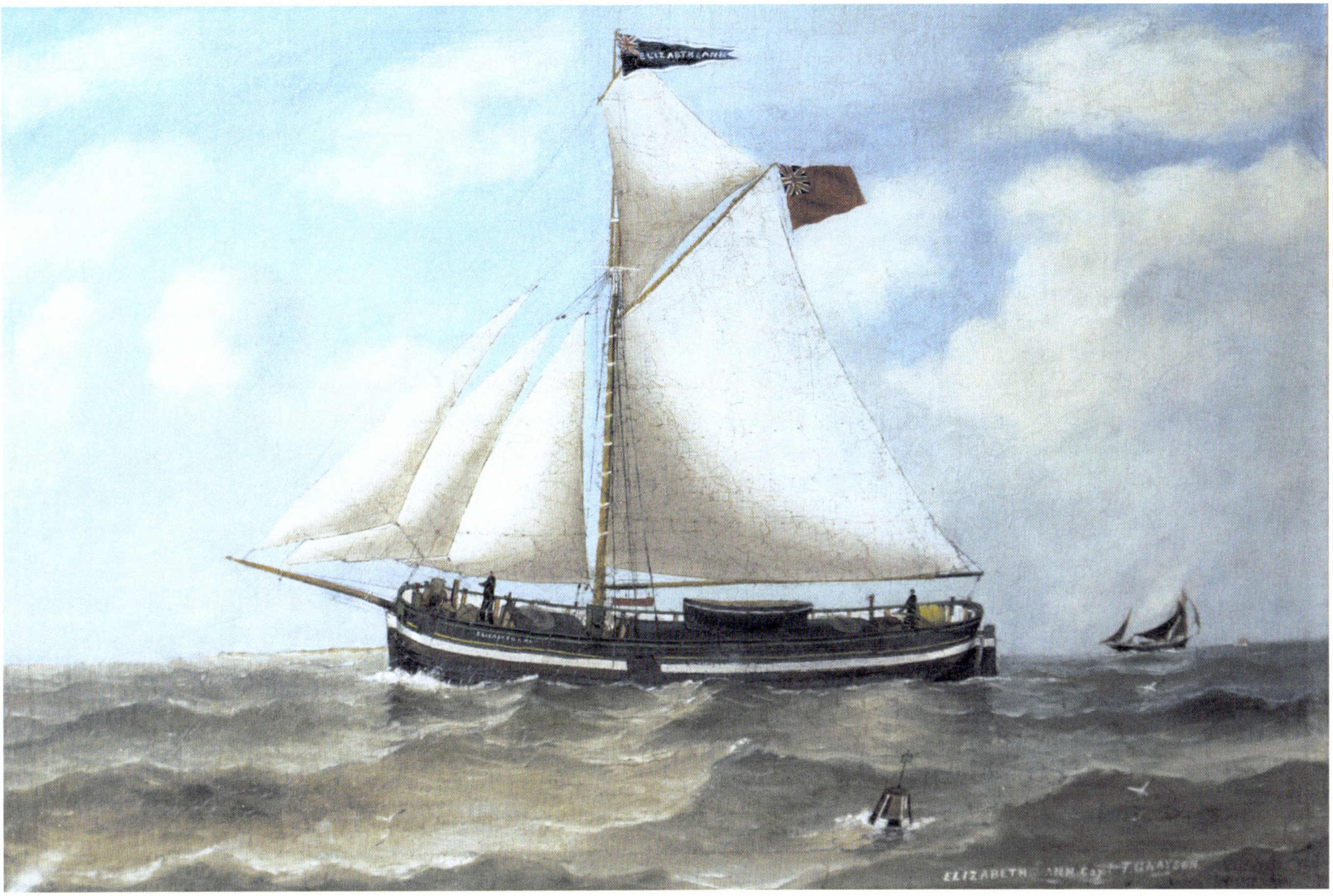

Goole Museum and Art Gallery

ELIZABETH AND ANN

Reuben Chappell painted this portrait of the Humber sloop Elizabeth and Ann for the master of the vessel Capt. T Grayson. The painting shows her near the confluence of the Trent and Humber on the Lincolnshire side of the river near Whitton.

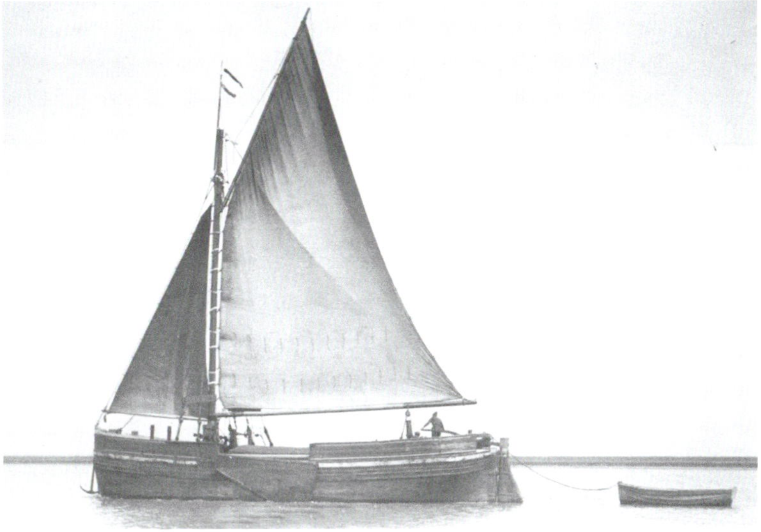

The sloop Bee *Hull Maritime Museum*

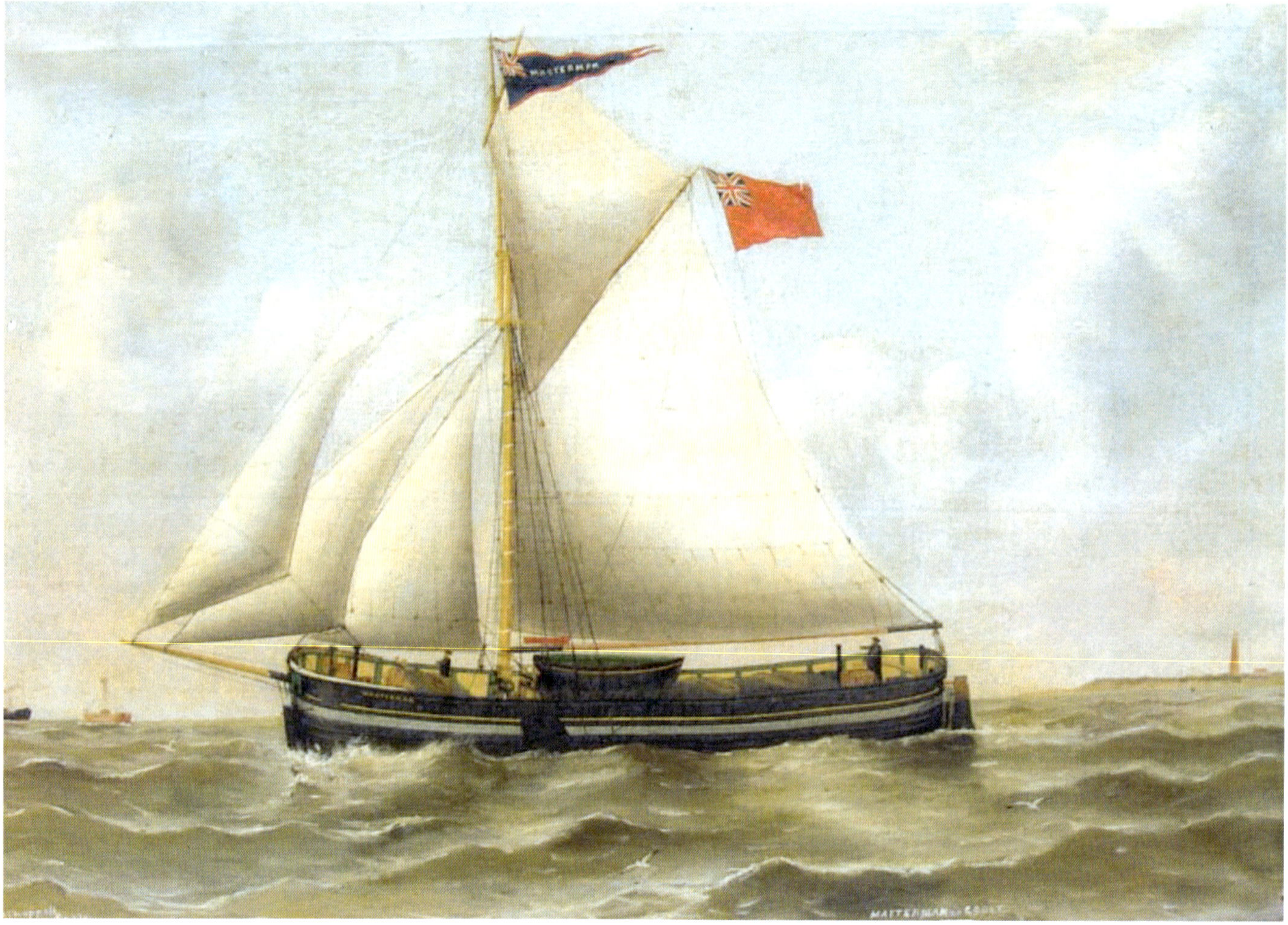

Goole Museum and Art Gallery

MASTERMAN

Reuben Chappell painted this striking portrait of the Humber sloop Masterman at the end of the 19th century. The vessel was registered in Goole and was lost in a tragic incident that illustrates the dangers associated with navigating the Humber.

An article in the Goole Times of 29th June 1906 headed 'A Goole Sloop Capsizes - Fearful Disaster off Whitton. Five Lives Lost' describes how the vessel, which left South Ferriby with a cargo of chalk, had to wait for the tide and anchored for the night. On board were skipper Alfred Eastwood, his wife Emily, her three sisters aged 15, 9 and 7, and their mother as well as the first and second mates. In the early hours the sloop started to drag her anchor until she became grounded on Whitton Ness. The tide took the sand away from beneath the vessel and she listed over. With the women and children still in the cabin, water poured into the vessel. The cabin filled in less than a minute and the five occupants were drowned. The three men managed to escape and eventually walked nearly twenty miles to Hull to report the incident. Nothing of the vessel or its occupants was ever recovered.

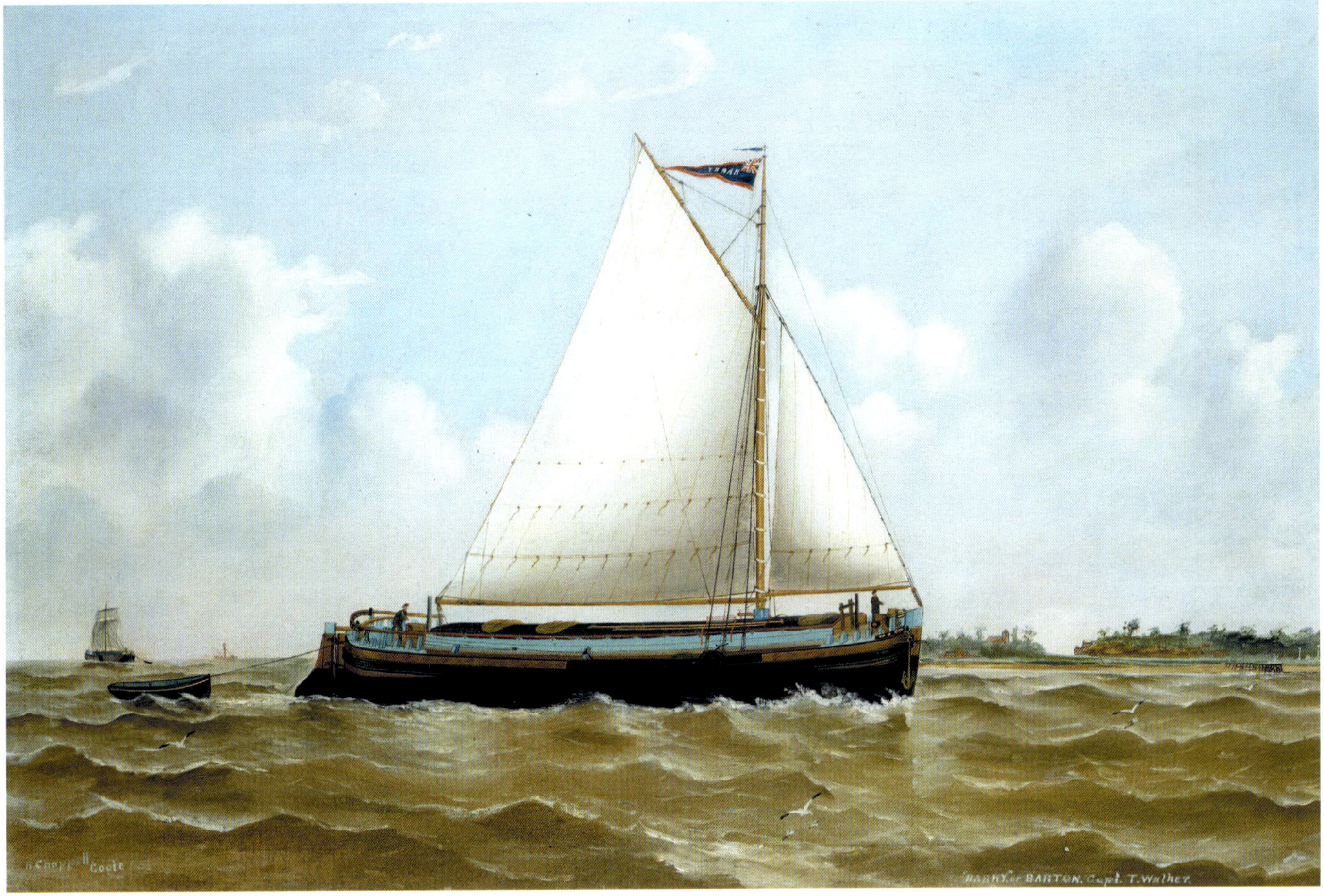

National Maritime Museum

HARRY OF BARTON

Harry, built in 1892 by Brown and Clapson of Barton. A typical sloop of the day, rigged fore and aft with a single head sail. Originally crewed by skipper Tom Walker and mate George Sweeting. Reuben Chappell has depicted Harry and her two-man crew in the mouth of the Humber off Whitton Nes.

The terms keel and sloop refer to the way the vessels were rigged and not to the form of the hull. The sloop had the same shallow draught barge-like hull form as the keel, but the sails were rigged fore and aft. The sloop was preferred on the Lincolnshire side of the Humber while the Yorkshiremen favoured the keel. Some keels were altered to sloop rig. Early sloops and keels were built of timber but there were also many built of steel. Some sloops were quite long, with capacities of up to 200 tons and made sea passages from the Humber. The Harry was still sailing in 1927.

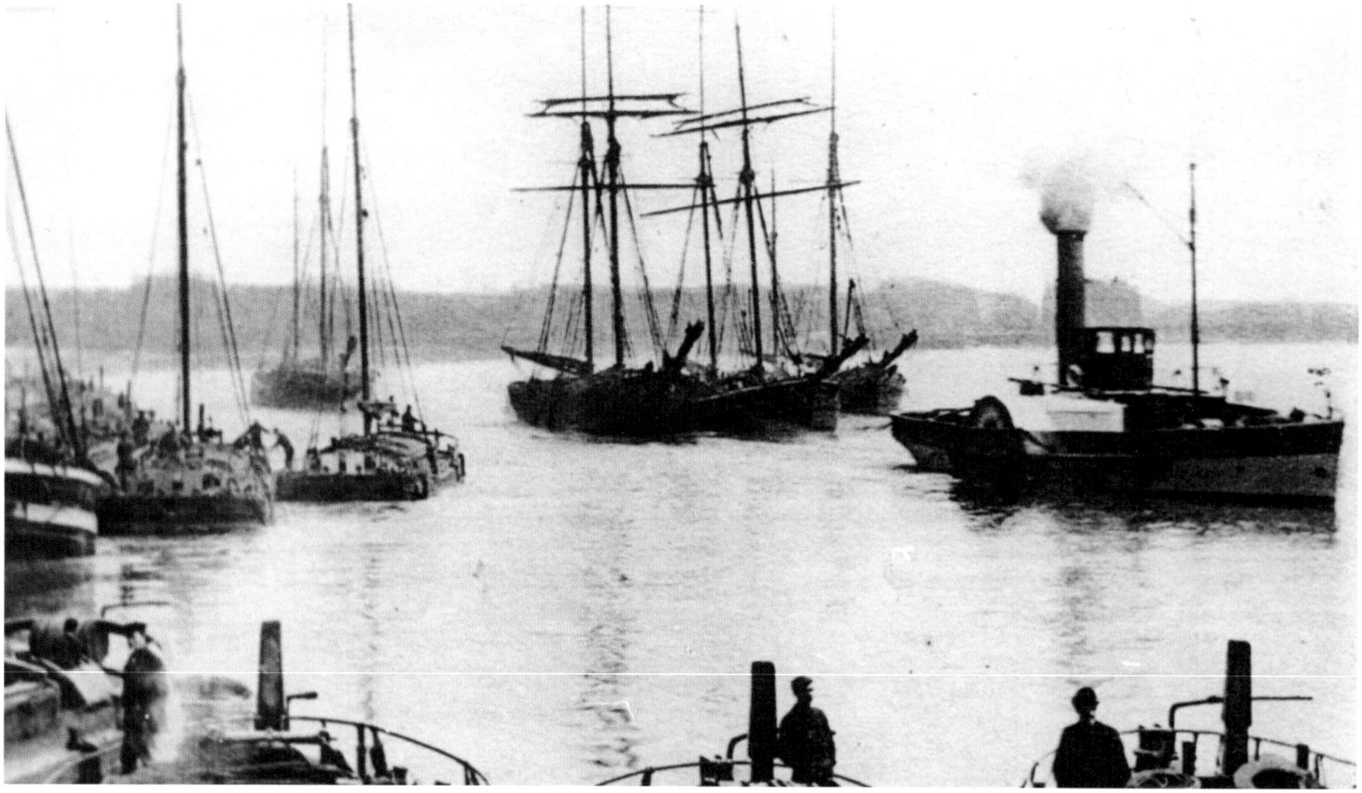

Schooners, ketches and sloops waiting to enter the locks, Goole 1901 *Masterman Collection*

Humber Schooners and Ketches

In the latter part of the 19th century Goole was a colourful and busy port with ships of all sorts coming and going. Besides the keels and sloops, and the steamships carrying passengers and cargo across the North Sea, there were schooners and ketches registered in Goole or Hull as well as many visiting ships.

In the 19th century and up until the First World War sailing vessels proved an efficient method of transporting goods around the coast. They were relatively cheap to build and run, the wages of the crew were low and the wind was free. They carried all manner of goods, building materials, bricks and stones, flint, timber, cement, all the materials and machines that built the new towns and factories, and the goods that were produced: farm and market garden produce to feed the town, and malt and barley for the breweries. But their principal cargo was coal. It was the coal trade that created the demand for these vessels, and at least a third of all voyages made by them were carrying coal around the coast of Britain and across the Channel or North Sea to Continental ports. The industrial revolution in Britain was driven by the power of steam engines. The boilers of the steam engines were fired with coal from the collieries of the North east of England, and from South Wales and most of this coal was carried around the coast by small merchant sailing ships.

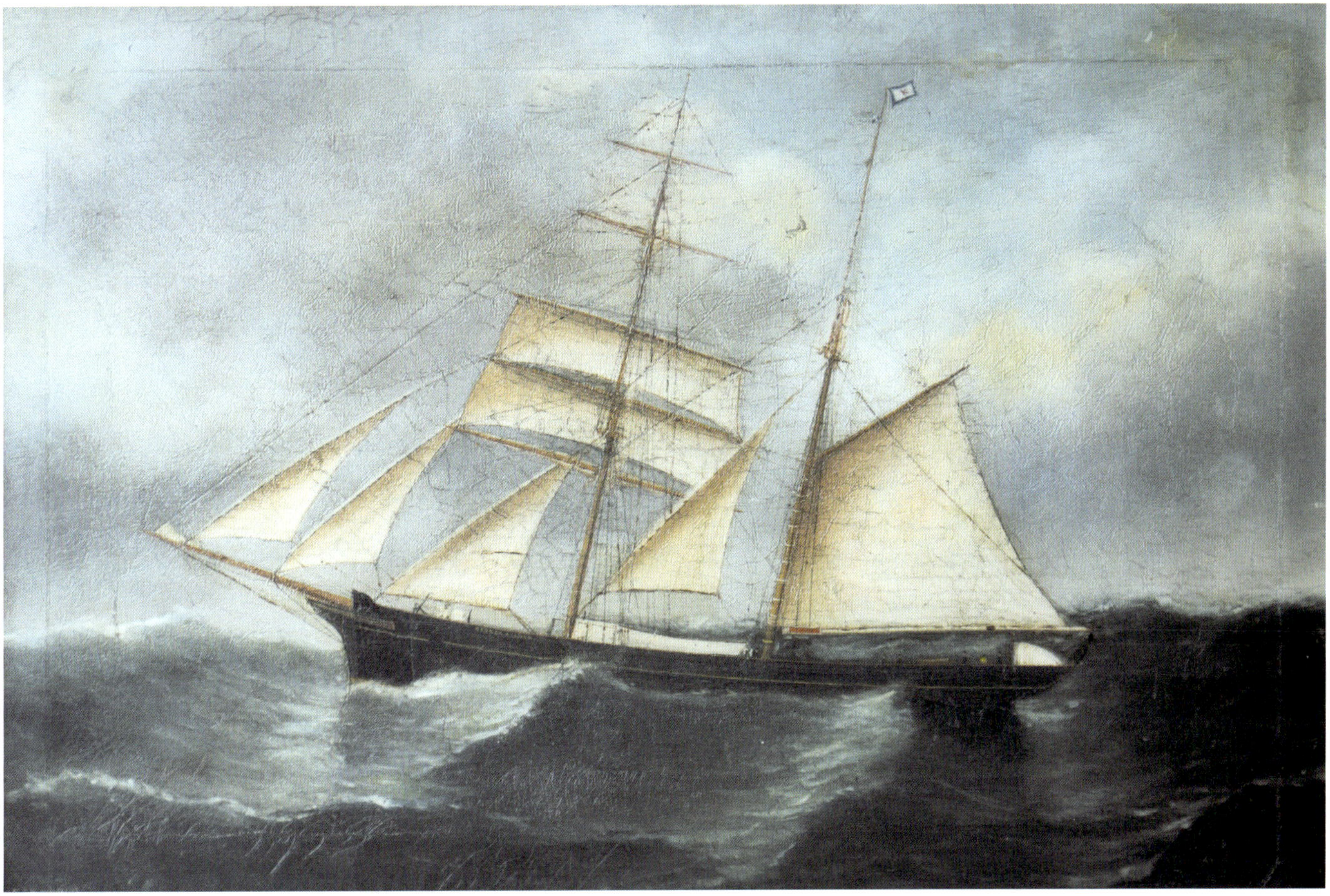

Goole Museum and Art Gallery

George Kilner

ON 91324; brigantine; built 1891 at Howden Dyke; built by Mr. Caisley; 124 reg. tons; managing owner George Kilner. Her first master was a Captain Rees.

John Kilner 1792 -1857 founded a firm in Yorkshire that produced airtight preserving jars. The Kilner Jar was made of glass with a rubber seal and a metal screw-cap, and was used for bottling fruit, jams, pickles, chutneys and no doubt many other preserves. In the days before refrigeration Kilner Jars became essential items in the kitchen. The business, later run by his four sons, was highly successful. Kilner's award-winning jars were sold in Europe, America and Australia.

The ship George Kilner, named after one of the owners of the company, was used to transport their products. Chappell painted a number of Kilner's vessels, and this early oil painting shows the George Kilner with reduced sail in heavy seas.

Jane Knox

ON 44216; schooner; built 1862 Perth; 94 gross tons; managing owner Richard Legott; Reg. Goole.

A fair-and-foul-weather pair of paintings commissioned by her owner and master Captain William Farmery.

Jane Knox is typical of the small topsail schooners which traded from Goole during the latter part of the 19th century She carried cargoes to Northern European ports, Scandinavia and the Baltic.

In October 1917, while sailing from Briton Ferry to Saint Brieux with coal the ship was wrecked at Portcawl and the crew were drowned.

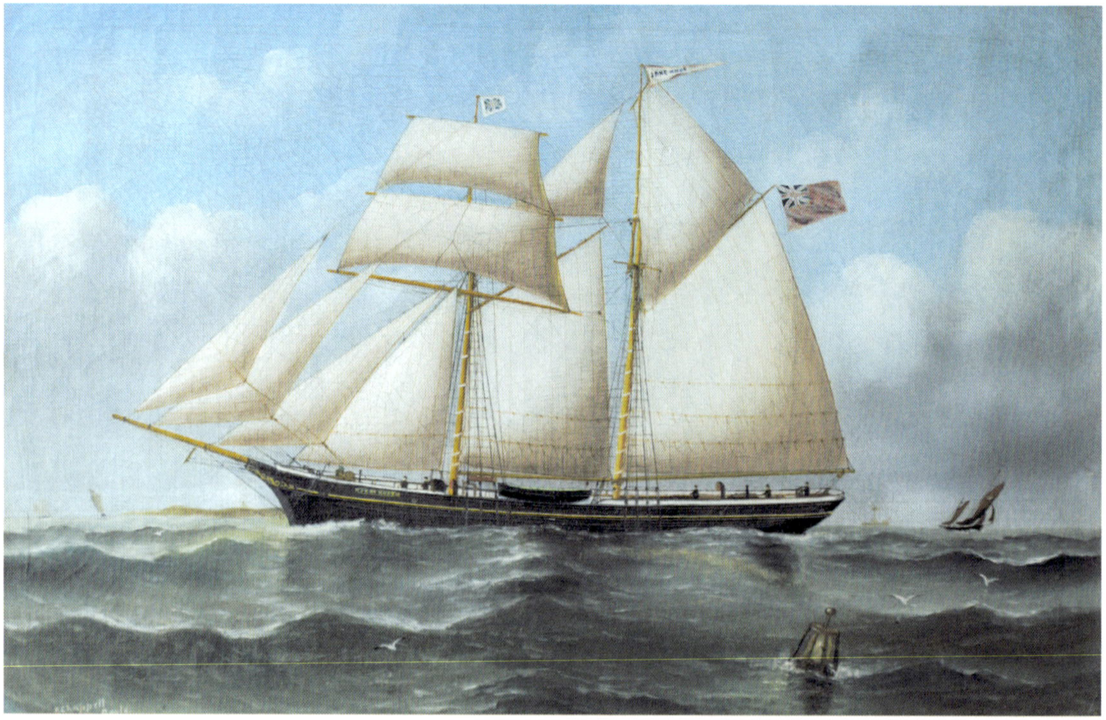

Goole Museum and Art Gallery

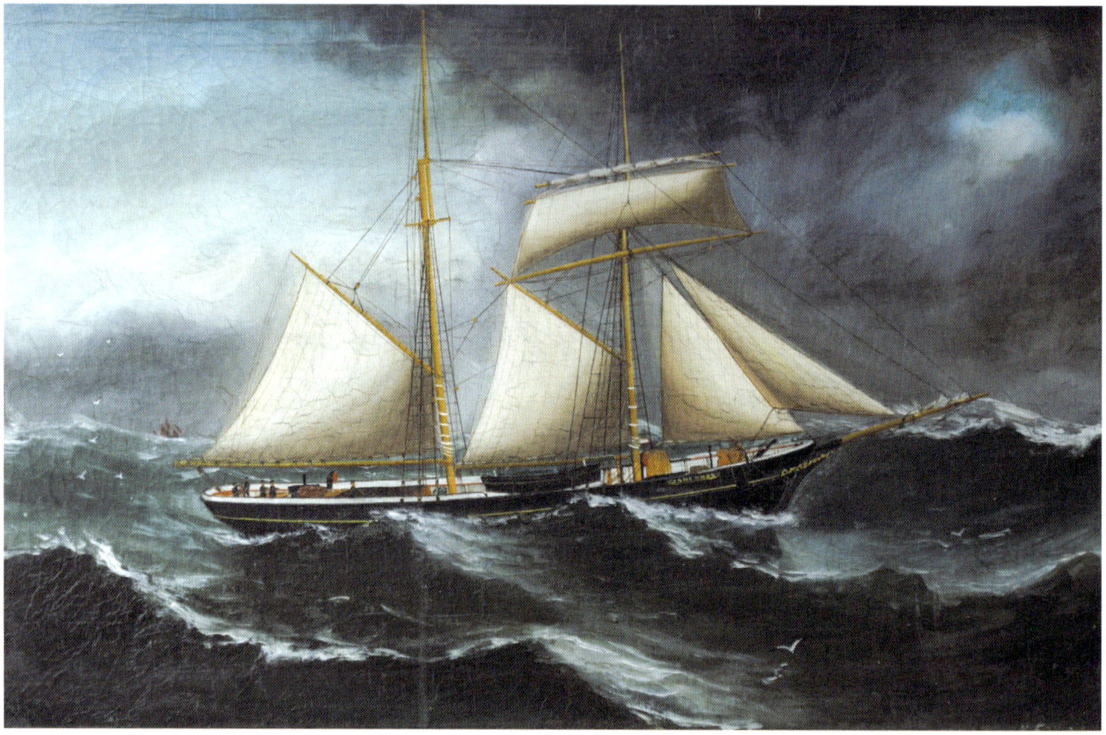

Goole Museum and Art Gallery

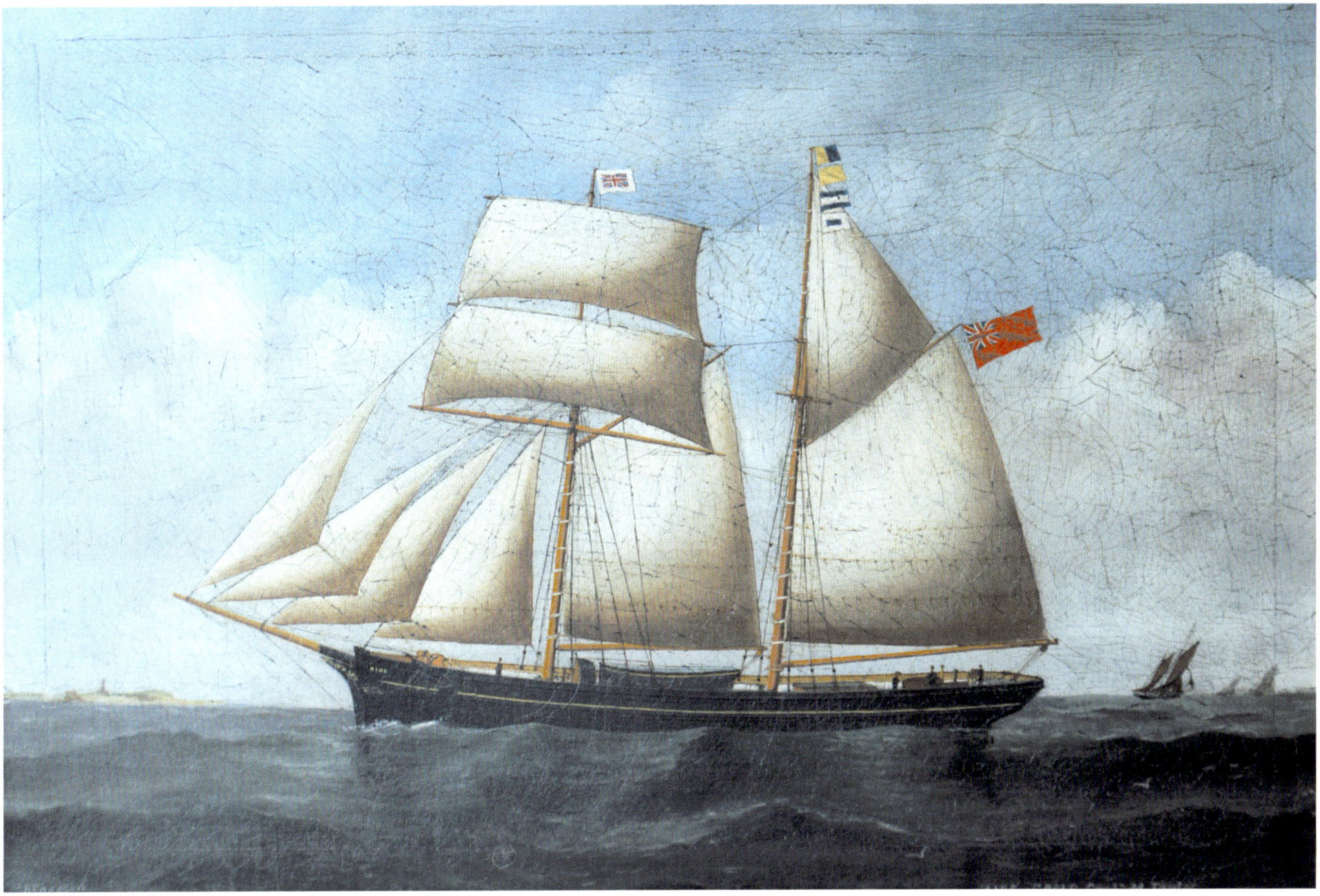

Goole Museum and Art Gallery

AIRE

ON 58748; schooner; built 1871 by A. Palmer, Yarmouth; 92 gross tons; 77.6' x 19.5' x 10.2' reg. Goole.

In this early oil painting Reuben Chappell shows Aire in the Humber Estuary off Spurn Point. The ship was built in Yarmouth and registered in Goole where she was owned by the Turgoose family who were prominent in the shipping business in Goole. While sailing from Newcastle to Invergoden with coal the ship foundered in a gale off St. Abbs Head. Her owner/master Alexander Smith and all three crew were saved.

Paintings that Chappell made of Goole shipping, most of which date from before 1904, are to be seen in a comprehensive body of his work held in the Garside Collection in the Goole Museum. The original collection of Chappell paintings was donated by Harold Garside, a local photographer and amateur historian. To this collection other paintings have been added over the years, many donated by families of the seamen who had commissioned the paintings.

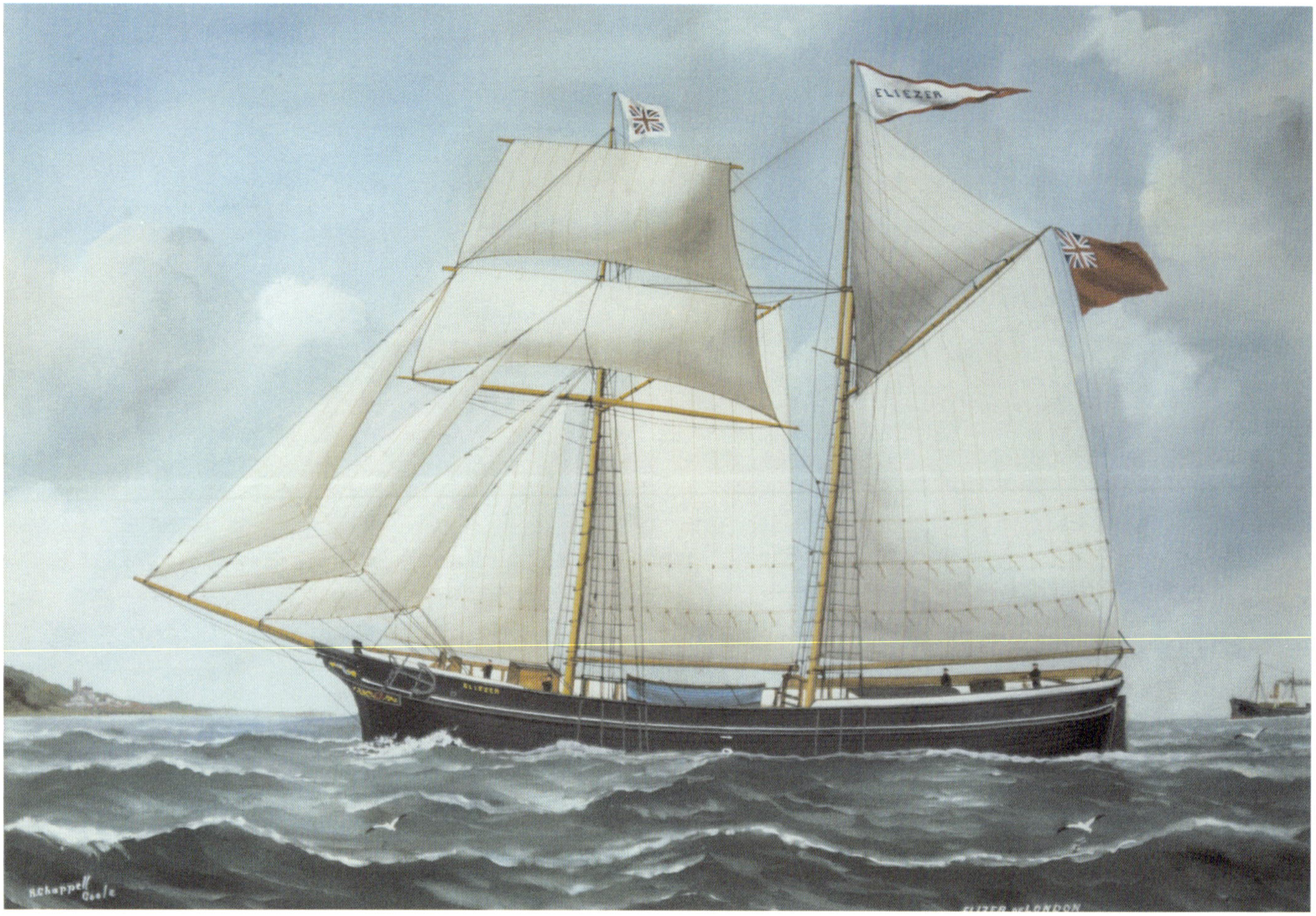

Goole Museum and Art Gallery

ELIEZER OF LONDON

ON 44028; 76 gross tons; 77.1' x 18.1' x 9.4'.

Built 1862 by Thomas Cliffe and Sons of Knottingley. The ship, like many of the vessels in Goole at that time, was owned by a consortium - Joseph Hargrave of Knottingley, Caleb Kilner of Goole, and two London based owners, William and John Kilner. Joseph Hargrave was the sole owner when she disappeared from the records in 1887, and it was probably he who commissioned the painting from Chappell.

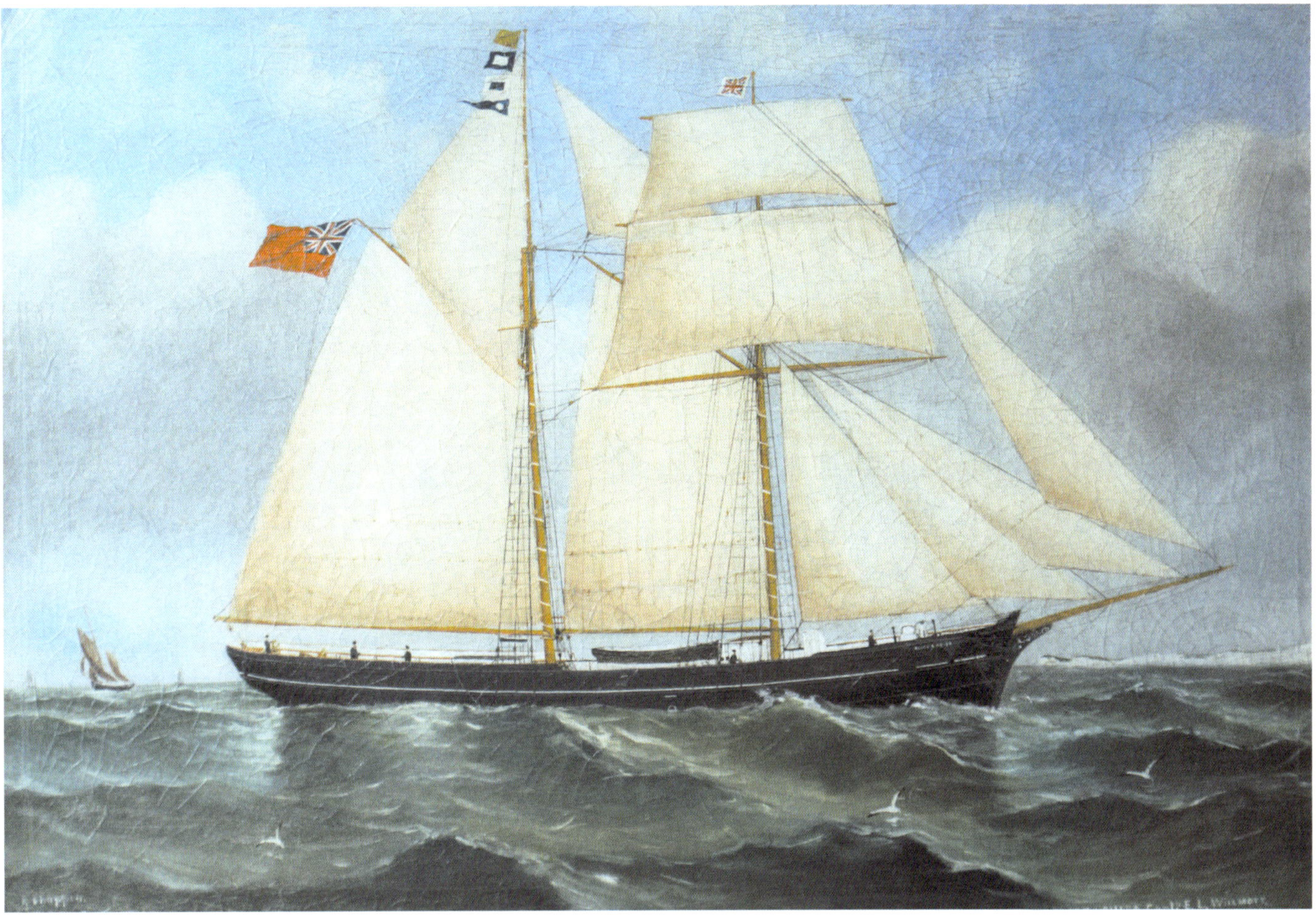

Goole Museum and Art Gallery

Alice Louisa

ON 58728; wooden schooner; built 1868 at Selby, Yorkshire; 101 gross tons; 83.6' x 20.5' x 9.9' owner Edward Wilmmott, Goole; reg. Goole.

Built for J. Rhodes at Selby on the Yorkshire Ouse, the Alice Louisa was registered at Goole. Her first master was Edward Wilmmott who became owner master in 1883. The vessel was employed in the coastal trade, and before they had a family Captain Wilmmott's wife accompanied him aboard. In 1901 on a voyage from Poole in Dorset to Goole carrying a cargo of pipe clay the Alice Louisa was lost on Donna Nook, River Humber whilst owned by William Caisley of Howden Dyke.

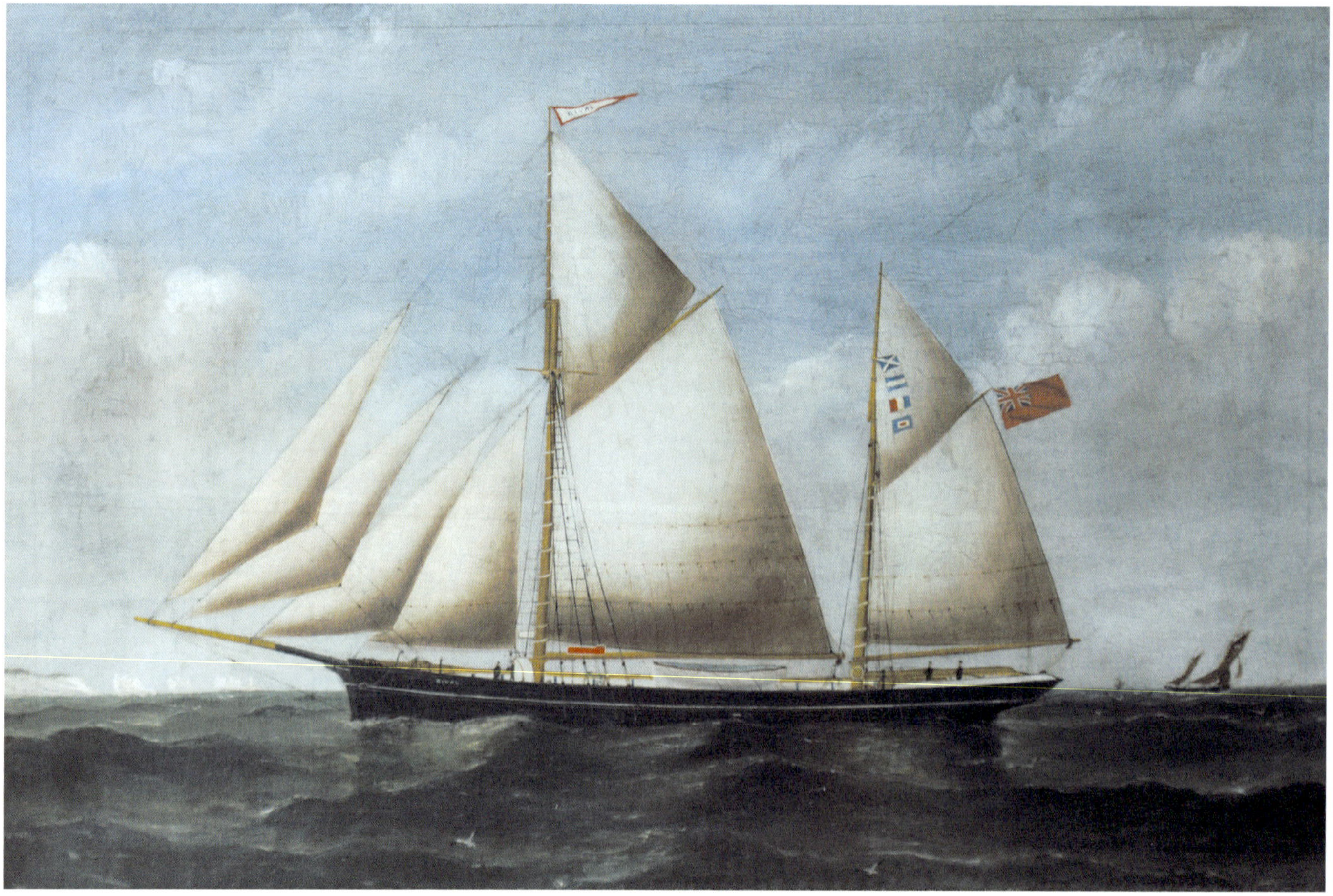

Goole Museum and Art Gallery

RIVAL OF RYE

ON 62251; built "Sandwich, within the port (area) of Rye" 1869.

Reuben Chappell made this painting of the ketch Rival for her owners and it remained in the family until it was given to the East Riding Museum. The ship which was owned by the Carman family was built in the port of Rye in east Sussex. She sailed from there for many years until in 1911 she was lost off Glamorgan while sailing in ballast from Appledore to Newport. The painting shows Rival passing the white cliffs, a notable feature of her voyages around the south coast of England.

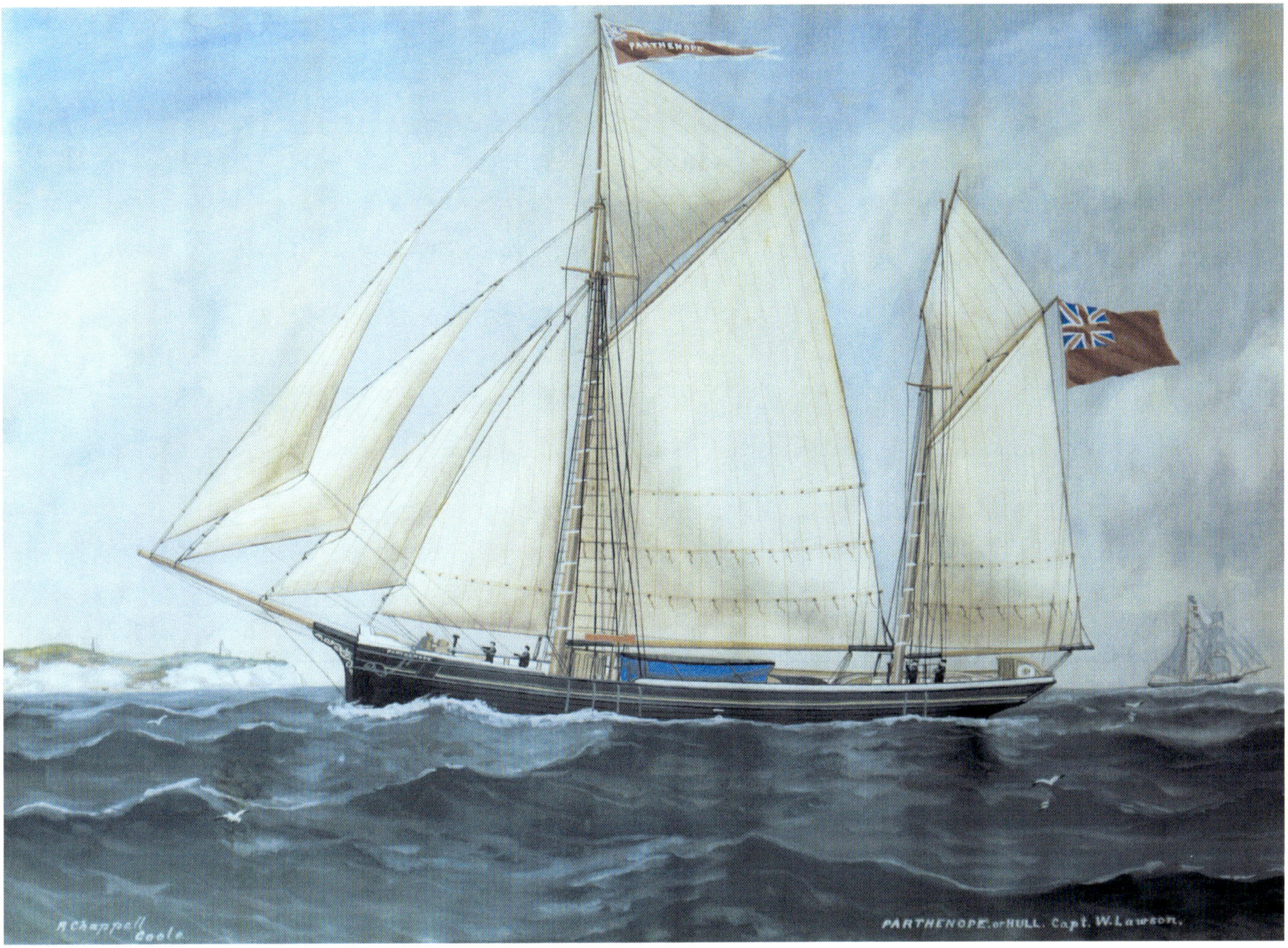

Goole Museum and Art Gallery

PARTHENOPE OF HULL

ON 91428; ketch; built 1885 at Howden Dyke; 90 reg. tons; 81.6' x 21.3' x 10.5' owners John Holmes, Neptune Street, Hull; reg. Hull.

This wooden ketch was named after one of the dangerous Sirens encountered by Odysseus in Homer's Odyssey. She was built by William Caisley of Howden Dyke near Goole, for himself. The brigantine in the distance is thought to be the Kinnaird of Liverpool.

Humber Steamships

Steam engines were first used to pump water from mines, and later as their design developed they were used to power railway locomotives and ships. In the first part of the 19th century steam engines driving paddle wheels were used, first in steamboats on rivers and lakes, and later in seagoing vessels. The risks involved in putting steam engines into wooden vessels were clearly very real, so for obvious reasons, iron, and later steel, became favoured for steam-powered ships. The development of screw propulsion made steamships more efficient. Realising this, I. K. Brunel changed the design for his ship, the Great Britain. She first sailed to New York in 1845.

However, steam ships were more expensive to build and operate than sailing vessels. By 1850 only three per cent of the ships in the Continental and coasting trades were steam-powered. In spite of its reliance on the weather the sail trading vessel was still the most economic method of moving cargo.

By the latter part of the 19th century steam-driven ships were becoming more common and many were built to carry coal along the east coast of England to London. Several steamship companies were formed, some owned by railway companies, their ships offering passenger and cargo carrying services to northern European and Baltic ports. Several of these companies were based on the Humber, and Reuben Chappell depicted their ships embarking on, or returning from, their voyages across North Sea.

A feature of the early years in the development of the design of steam-powered ships was that the vessels also carried sails. They were of obvious use in the case of mechanical breakdown, and also may have provided some economy in fuel use. This interesting period in ship design, known as transitional, continued for quite some time. Ships in the home and coasting trades continued to be seen with both power and sail well into the 20th century.

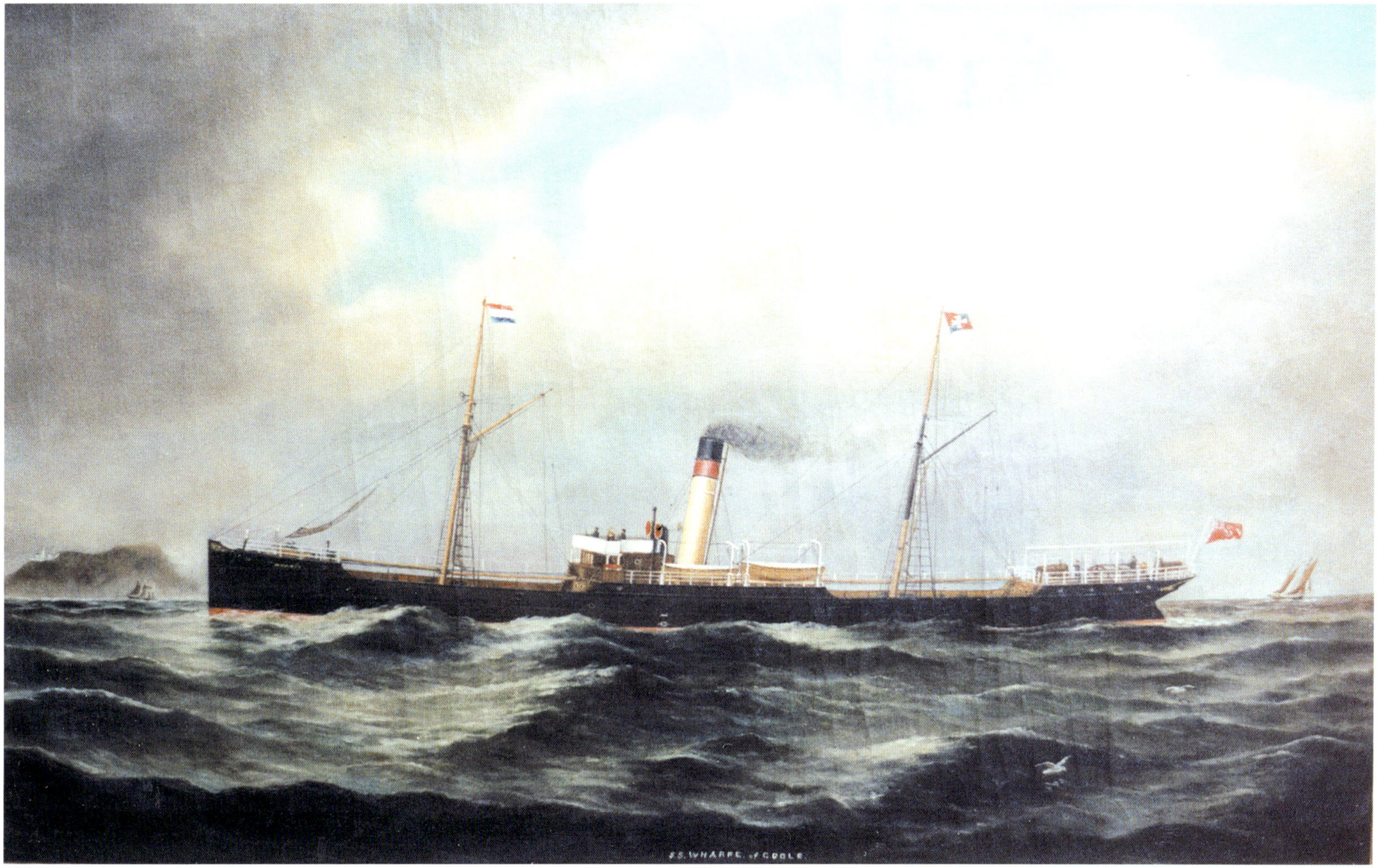

Private Collection

SS Wharfe

ON 369; 914 tons gross; 245' x 32.7' x 15.7'; built 1890 by W. Dobson & Co. for the Goole Steam Shipping Company, sold later to the Lancs & Yorks Railway Co; reg. Goole.

This ship was named after the river Wharfe, a tributary of the Humber. Obviously considered a fast vessel of her time, she was known in the 1890s as the 'greyhound of the Humber.'

She entered service in June 1890 and ran a twice-weekly service, from Goole to Rotterdam. These ships had buff funnels with a red band and a black top. They were owned by the Goole Steamship Company, known locally as the Soot, Blood and Suet line.

Chappell produced a number of paintings of this vessel, one of which was placed in the window of a local furniture shop to attract the interest of seamen going to and from the docks in Goole.

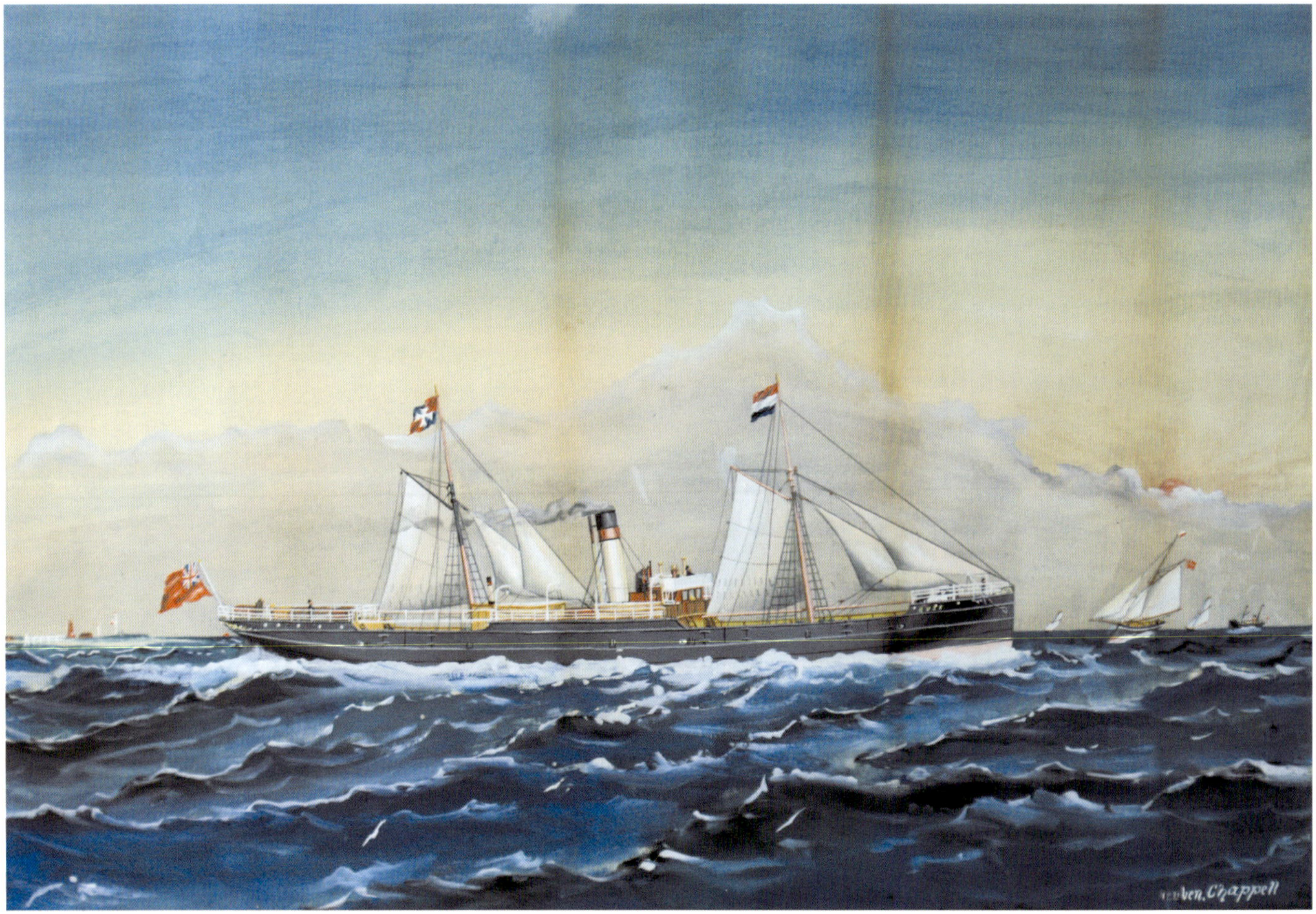

Goole Museum and Art Gallery

SS Ouse of Goole

ON 565; steel, screw schooner-rigged steamship; built 1884 by William Dobson & Co. Low Walker; 763 tons gross; 220' x 28.7' x 13.7'.

Built for the Goole Steam Shipping Company and later sold to the Lancs & Yorks Railway Co. SS started service in September in 1884, Goole/ Rotterdam service. She had space for horses and cattle besides passengers and cargo, and was the first ship in the company to be given a Yorkshire river name.

Reuben Chappell shows her passing Spurn Point flying the Dutch national flag indicating her destination. She is also flying the Goole Steamship Company flag and the Red Ensign. There are other steam and sailing ships in the distance.

In 1890 the captain was W Gravel, and in that year she collided with a barque in the North Sea which sank with all hands. Following this incident the mate of SS Ouse had his licence suspended for six months. When she was sold in 1909 she was renamed Goole Trader.

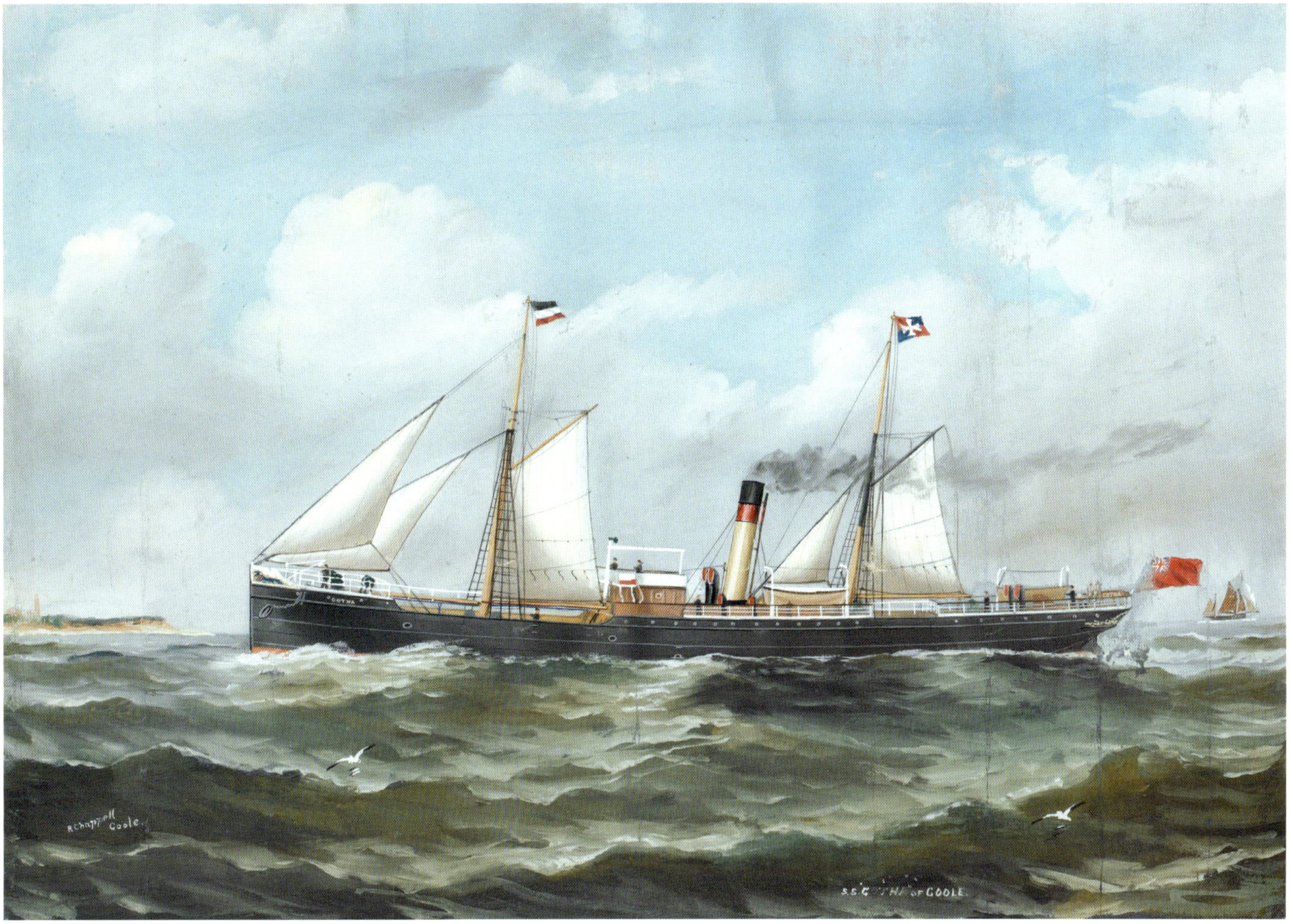

National Maritime Museum

SS Gotha of Goole

ON 91315; steel screw steamer; built 1888 by the Earls Company, Hull. 257 tons net; 220.5' x 29.1' x 13.7'; reg. Goole.

A general cargo carrier for the owners, the Yorkshire Coal & Steamship Company. In this painting SS Gotha is flying the flag of the Goole Steamship Company and her funnel is in their distinctive 'soot, blood and suet' colours.

This map shows the shipping routes operated by the Great Central Railway from Grimsby to Northern Europe. Of course, steamships owned by other railway companies operated similar routes from Hull and Goole. These ships carried passengers, goods and livestock to and from the major European ports. It was possible for European passengers bound for the USA and Canada to book their tickets from the same company for their voyage across the North Sea to connect with trains that took them to Manchester and on to Liverpool where they would join their ship for the voyage across the Atlantic.

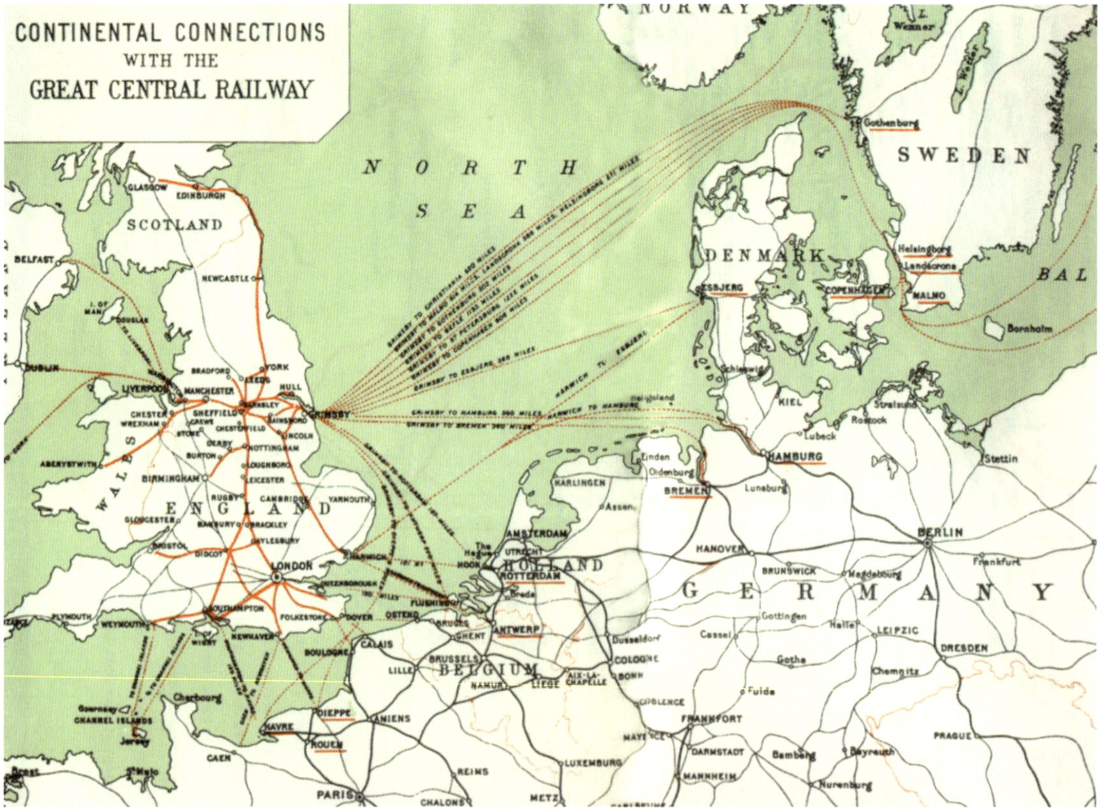

Shipping services operated by the Great Central Railway 1903

The River Humber

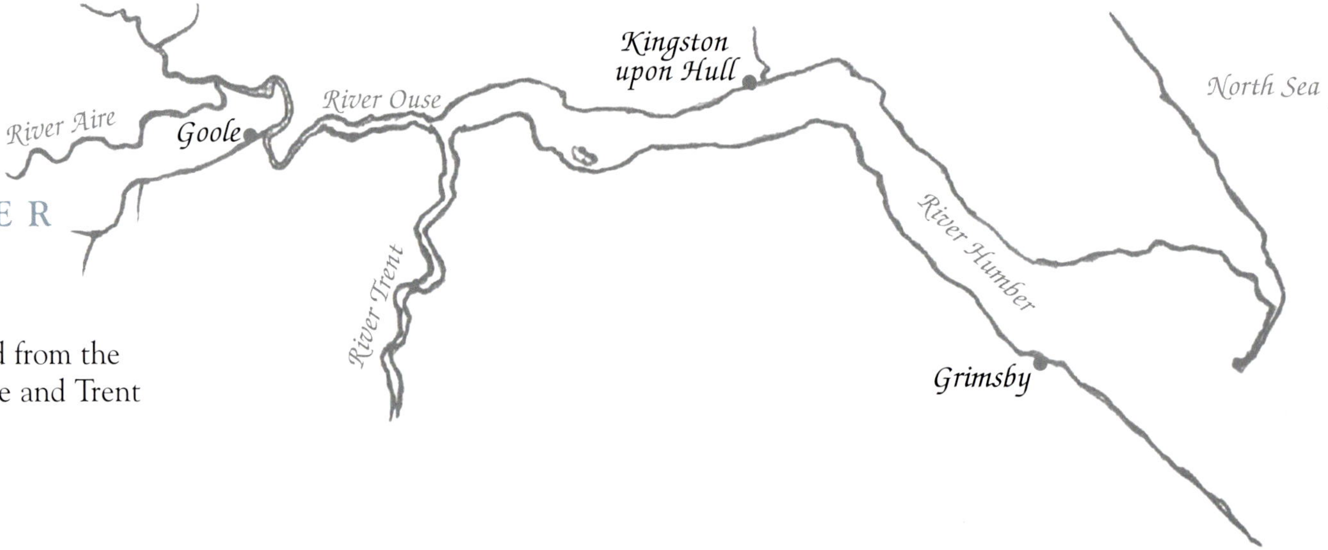

The Humber is formed from the confluence of the Ouse and Trent rivers.

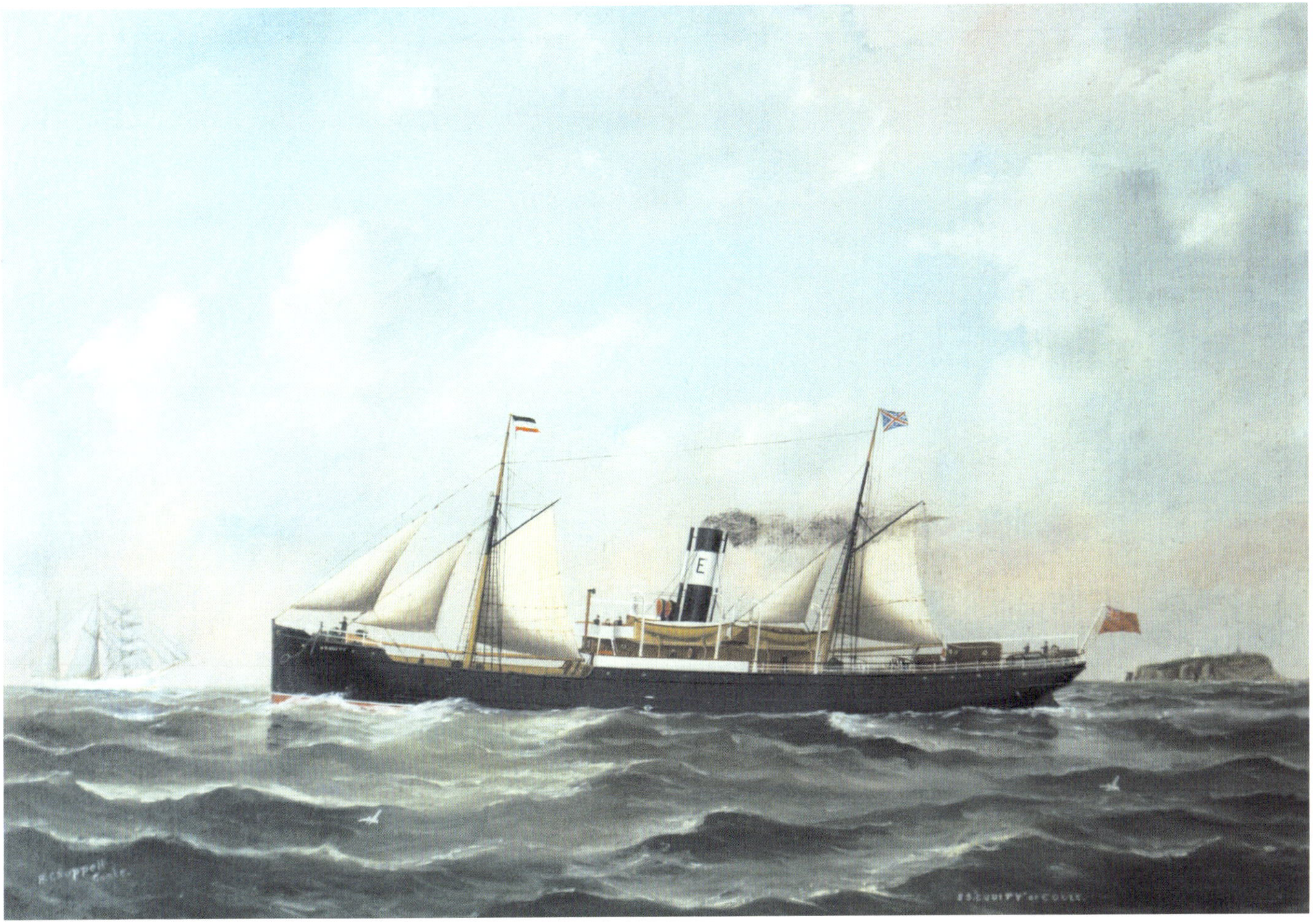

Goole Museum and Art Gallery

SS Equity

ON 91317; Iron steamship; built 1888 by Earle's Co., Hull; 837 tons gross; 226.7' x 32.4' x 13.7'.

SS Equity was built in 1888 for the Co-operative Wholesale Society for use on their Goole – Hamburg service. The society operated a number of steamships that ran services to the continent. The names of these vessels, Equity, Liberty and Unity expressed the principles of the society. In 1906 these ships were sold to the Lancashire and Yorkshire Railway Company. In 1914 Equity was interned at Hamburg for the duration of the war. Renamed Myra, the ship was used on the Hamburg – Kiel – Finland route. The vessel was returned in 1918 and was in operation until 1931 when it was sold to be scrapped.

Seen in the distance in the painting is a white-hulled sailing ship, possibly one of the Danish vessels that Chappell became familiar with in Goole.

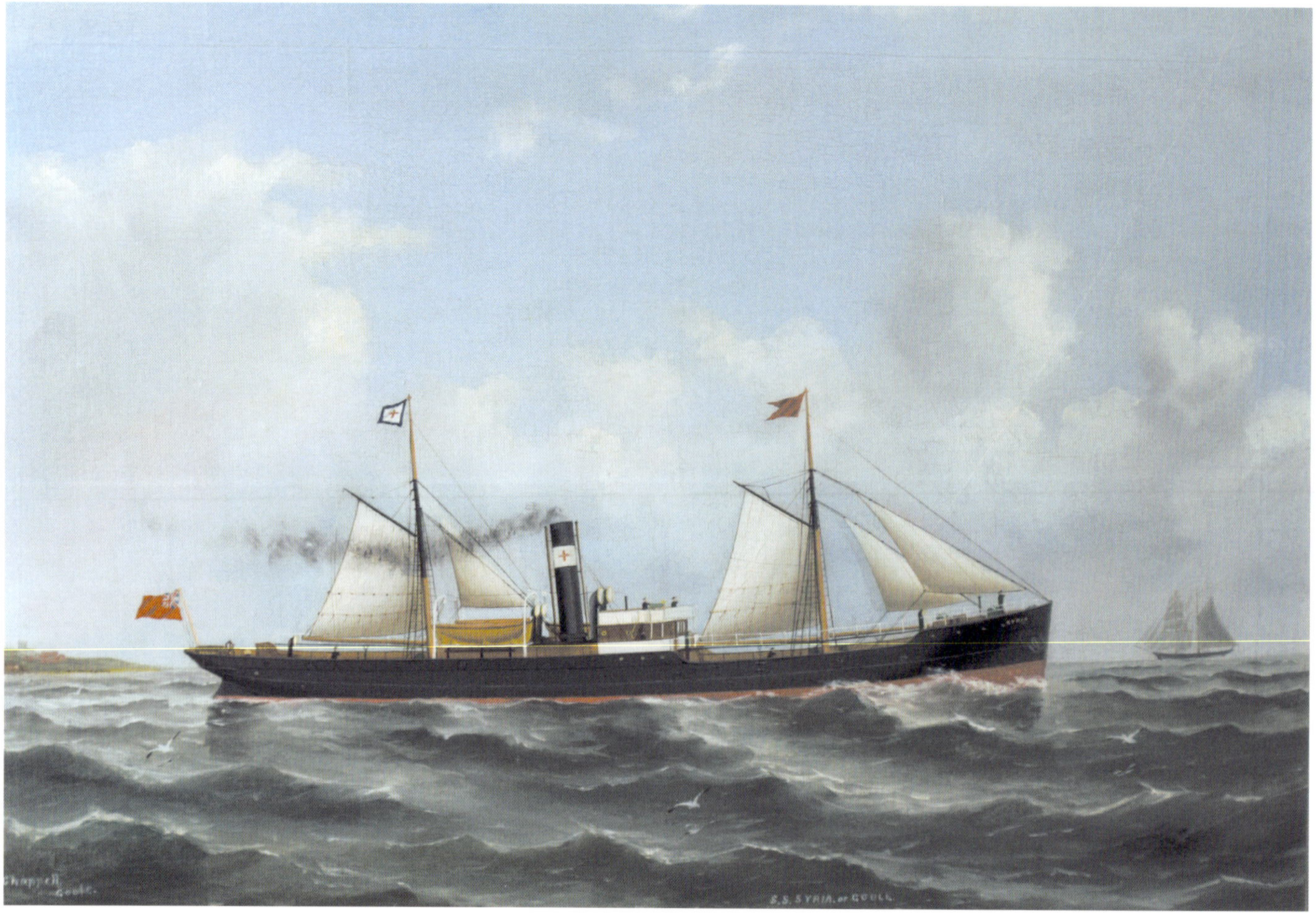

Goole Museum and Art Gallery

SS Syria of Goole

Built 1898 by Earls Company of Hull for Bennett Steamship Co. Ltd.; 750 tons gross; 210' x 31' x 13.6'; reg. Goole.

Humber based steamships operated regular services from Goole, Hull and Grimsby to such ports as Amsterdam, Antwerp, Dunkirk, Ghent, Flushing, Hamburg, Rotterdam, Aarhus, Bruges, Copenhagen, Danzig, Lubeck, Stockholm, Zeebrugge and St Petersburg.

Besides passengers these steamships carried all manner of goods including livestock. It was not unusual to see a flock of geese from Aarhus being driven down the street in Goole.

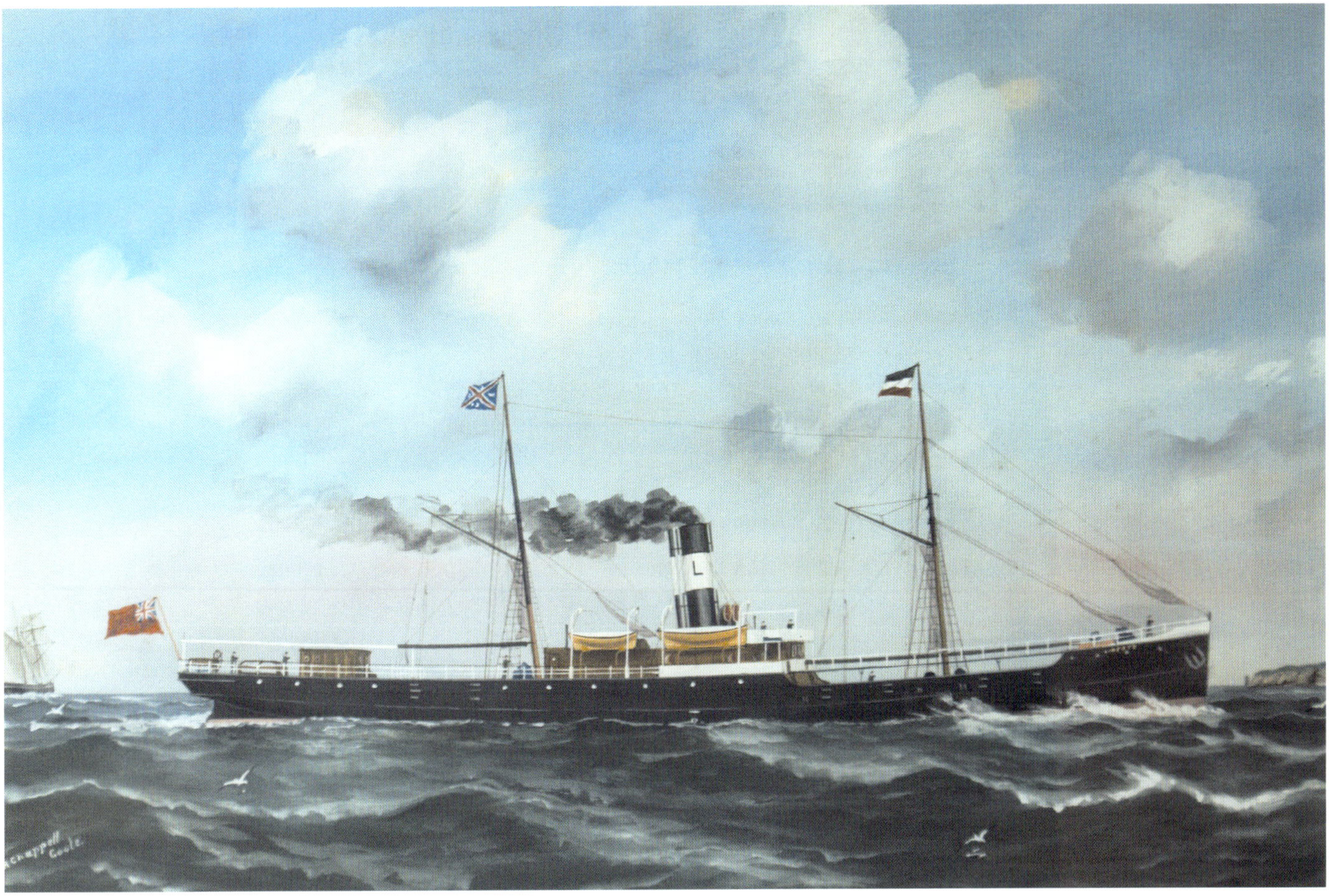

Goole Museum and Art Gallery

SS Liberty of Goole

Steel schooner; built 1890 by Earls Co. Hull; 895 gross tons; 225' x 33.1' x14.1'; reg. Goole.

SS Liberty started service in 1890, with the Co-operative Wholesale Society on the Goole - Hamburg run. In 1906 she was bought by the Lancs and Yorks Railway Company. In these two portraits of the Liberty Chappell shows her in the Co-operative Society's colours. The ship lasted until 1931 when she was broken up in Sunderland.

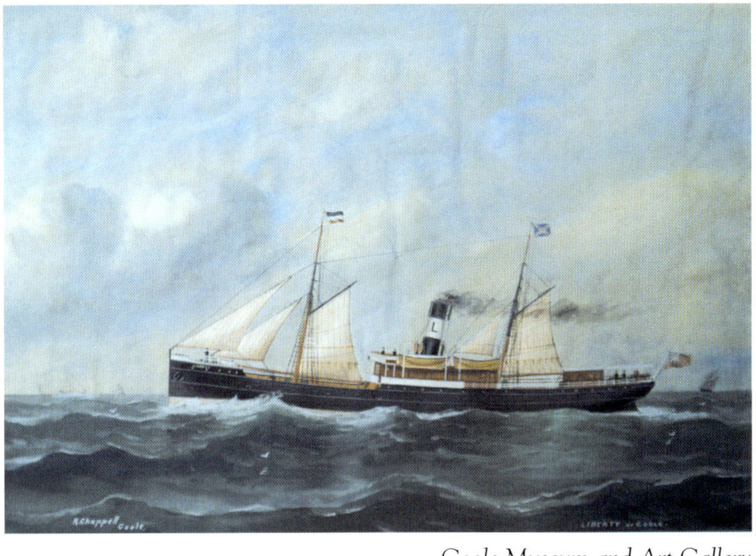

Goole Museum and Art Gallery

Coastal Steamships

The relationship between steam-powered and sailing vessels is not a simple one, and was inevitably controlled by economics. In the coastal trade steamships did not simply replace or take away the trade of sailing vessels. Certainly before the end of the century, and to some extent until the First World War, sail and steam vessels existed side by side in several fleets.

The main advantage of steam-powered vessels was that they were not as dependent on favourable weather as sailing vessels, and were less difficult to operate against strong tides. However, because of the fire risk iron hulls were most suitable for steam-driven vessels, but at that time it was far more expensive to build a ship from iron than from timber. In the early years of steam engine development engines were less efficient. Sailing vessels were less costly to build, and although always dependent on the wind, the wind at least was free. Shipping companies were not just in competition with each other, there were also the growing road and rail networks to compete with.

An interesting feature in many of Reuben Chappell's paintings of coastal steamships, is that most of them had open steering bridges. Conditions aboard must have been extremely harsh. Well into the 20th century ships were being built with their steering bridges open to the elements. It seems incredible that it was not until the 1930s that enclosed wheelhouses commonly came into use in this class of vessel. Like the sailing ships they were crewed by just a few men, their coal fired boilers usually powered a two cylinder steam engine.

There is relatively little recorded of these small ships, although once they would have been a regular sight around the British and European coasts. They were not large vessels, because like the sailing ships they had to get in and out of small harbours and ports and were regularly seen on the Humber and in the clay ports where Reuben Chappell painted them. His paintings of these steam-powered cargo ships are unique records of part of our maritime history. Once commonplace, they did their job and disappeared to the breakers virtually unnoticed.

"Conditions were hard in the 1920s and an able seaman got about £2. 16. 0. a week out of which he provided his own food and bedding, often a sack of straw from a local farm. Food was anything that could be cooked quickly in a frying pan. Two or three men often put money into a food kitty and took it in turns to buy rations when in port".

When Reuben Chappell encountered steam coasters in the clay ports, it is likely that they would be unloading a cargo of coal before loading china clay. The difficulties arising from discharging coal prior to loading china clay are obvious. It "required constant vigilance on the part of the owners, captain and crew to insure that any coal remaining in the hold was carefully cleaned out before the china clay was loaded, otherwise there would be black specks in the paper and the contract to carry clay would be lost." *Steam Coasters* by C.V. Waine.

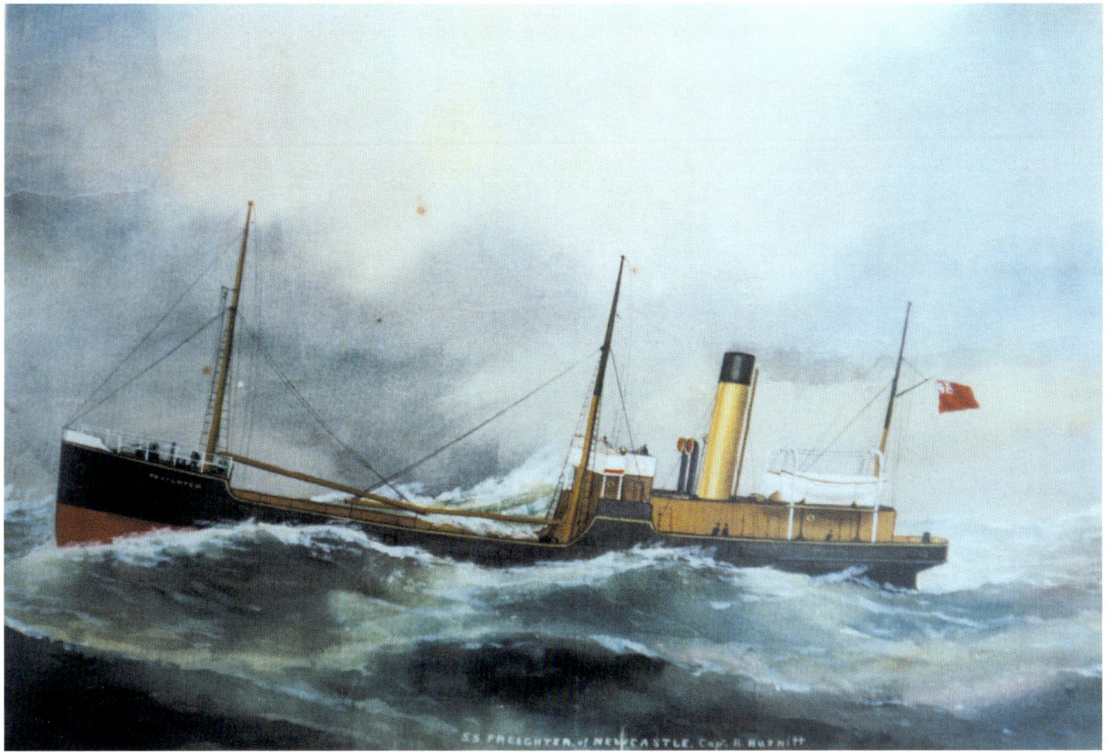

Freighter of Newcastle detail — *Private Collection*

Dirty British coaster with a salt-caked smoke stack,
Butting through the Channel in the mad March days,
With a cargo of Tyne coal,
Road-rails, pig-lead,
Firewood, ironware, and cheap tin trays.

From Cargoes by John Masefield

SS Freighter of Newcastle

ON 127085; steel screw steamer; 8' x 25.1' x 8.8'; Capt. Burnitt; owned by "T" Steam Coasters Ltd. of Newcastle; managed by Robinson Brown & Co, Newcastle; launched Oct. 1910 Smith's Dock Company Middlesborough; code signal HRVS129; Ex-'Liscannor' Ireland; reg. Newcastle.

Reuben Chappell painted at least two versions of this ship at different times.

There were many companies managing small steam coasters around the country. Prior to World War One, one of the main operators was Robinson Brown & Co who managed "T" Steam Coasters. Their ships were employed carrying both household coal and bunker coal for the drifters in East Coast Scottish ports. They also carried packed herrings to the Continent.

These smaller steamships were also well suited to the harbours of Cornwall and the South West where they worked in the coal and clay trade.

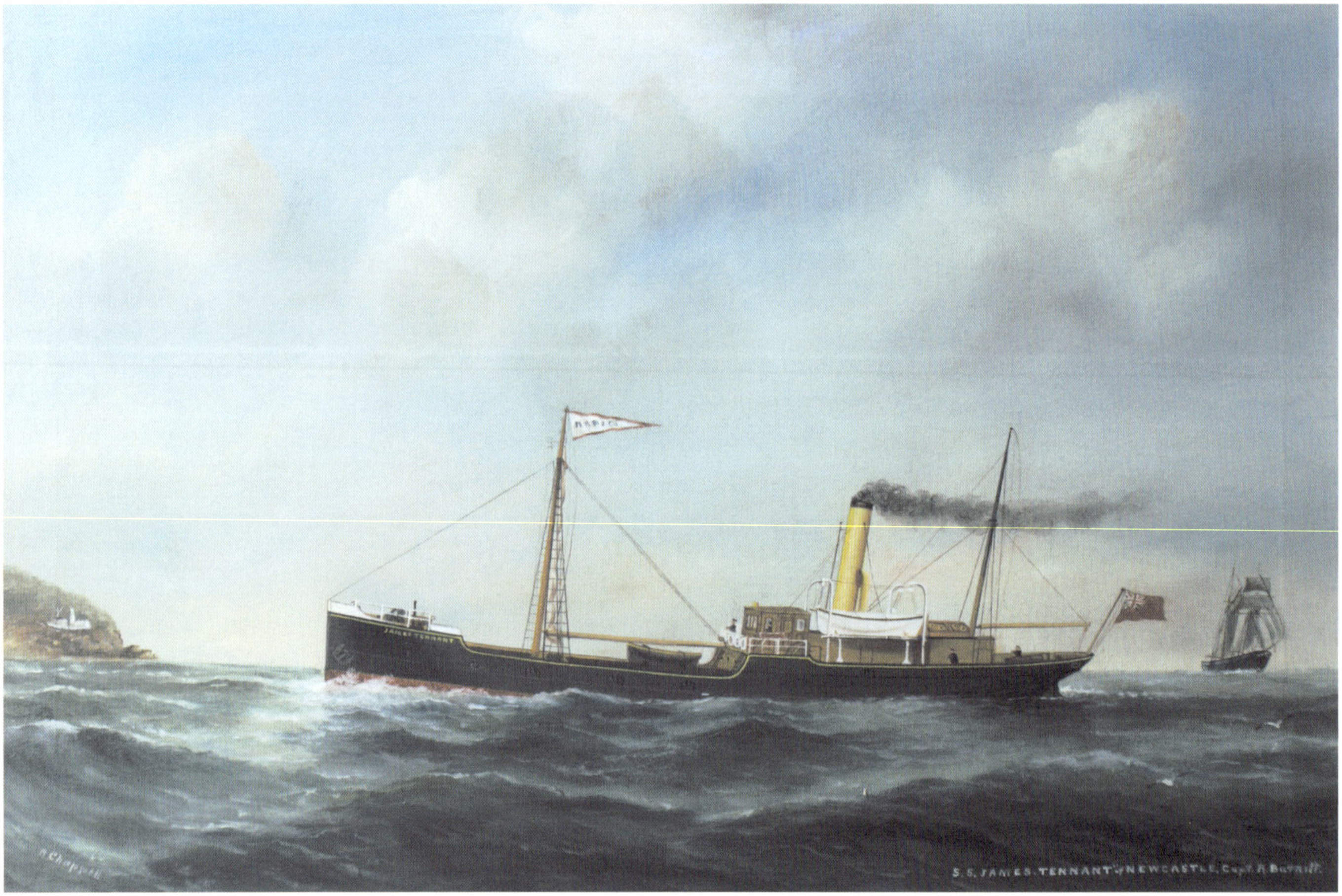

Goole Museum and Art Gallery

SS James Tennant of Newcastle

ON 101833; steel-screw steamer; built 1893 by Mr Wood of Skinner & Co of Newcastle; 203 tons gross; 120' x 20.1' x 9.0'; 2 cylinder 50 RHP; owner "T" Steam Coasters of Newcastle; managed by Robinson Brown of Newcastle; reg. Newcastle.

A pair of fair-and-foul-weather paintings of SS James Tennant which was built in 1893 for "T" Steam Coasters, managed by Robinson Brown. In the painting the ship is shown with an enclosed wheelhouse which did not become a general feature until well into the 20th century.

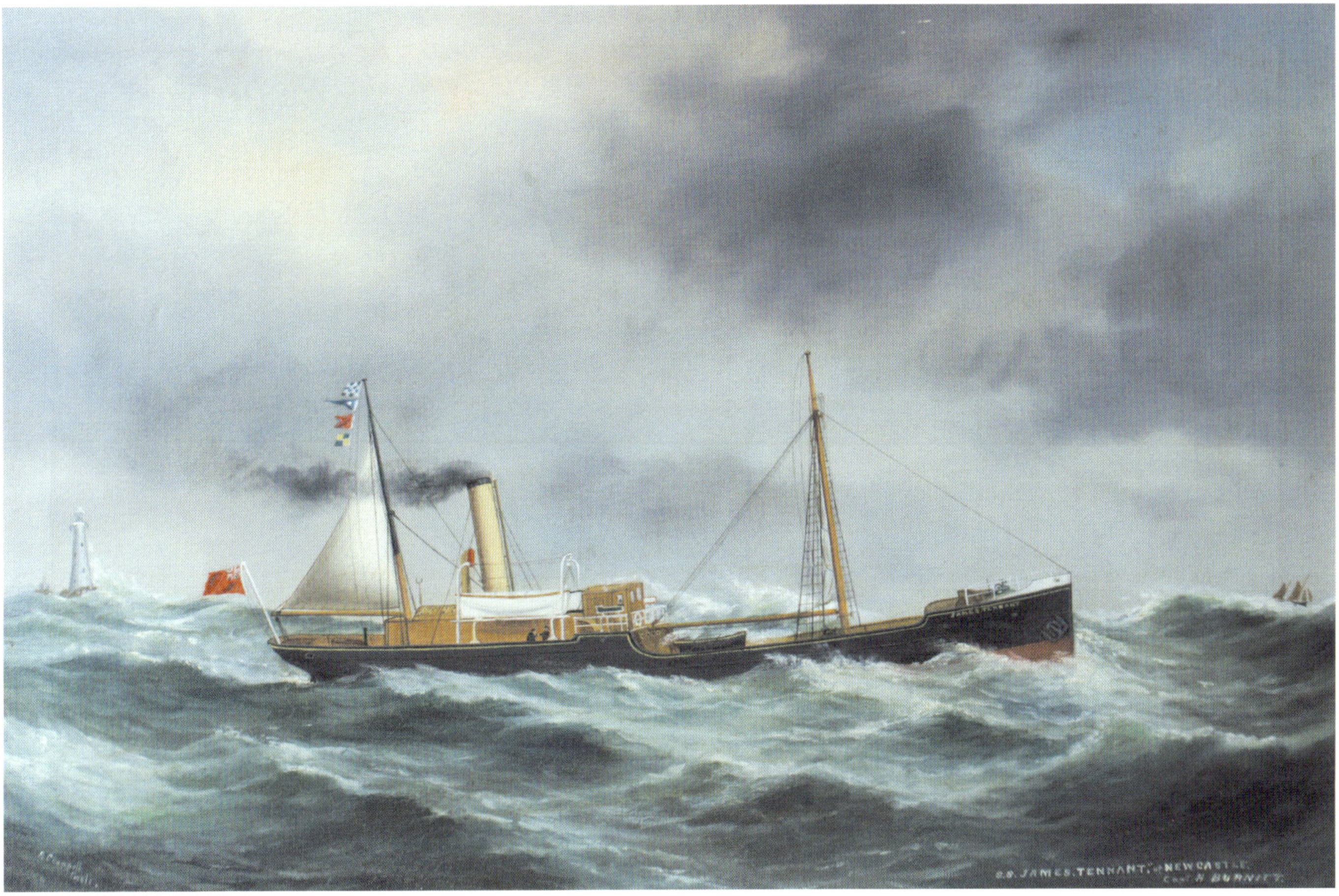

Goole Museum and Art Gallery

SS James Tennant of Newcastle

No photograph or painting could convey the sound or smell of these ships; the steady beat of the steam engine and the evocative smell, a mixture of coal-smoke and steam, hot metal, oil and grease belong to a bygone age.

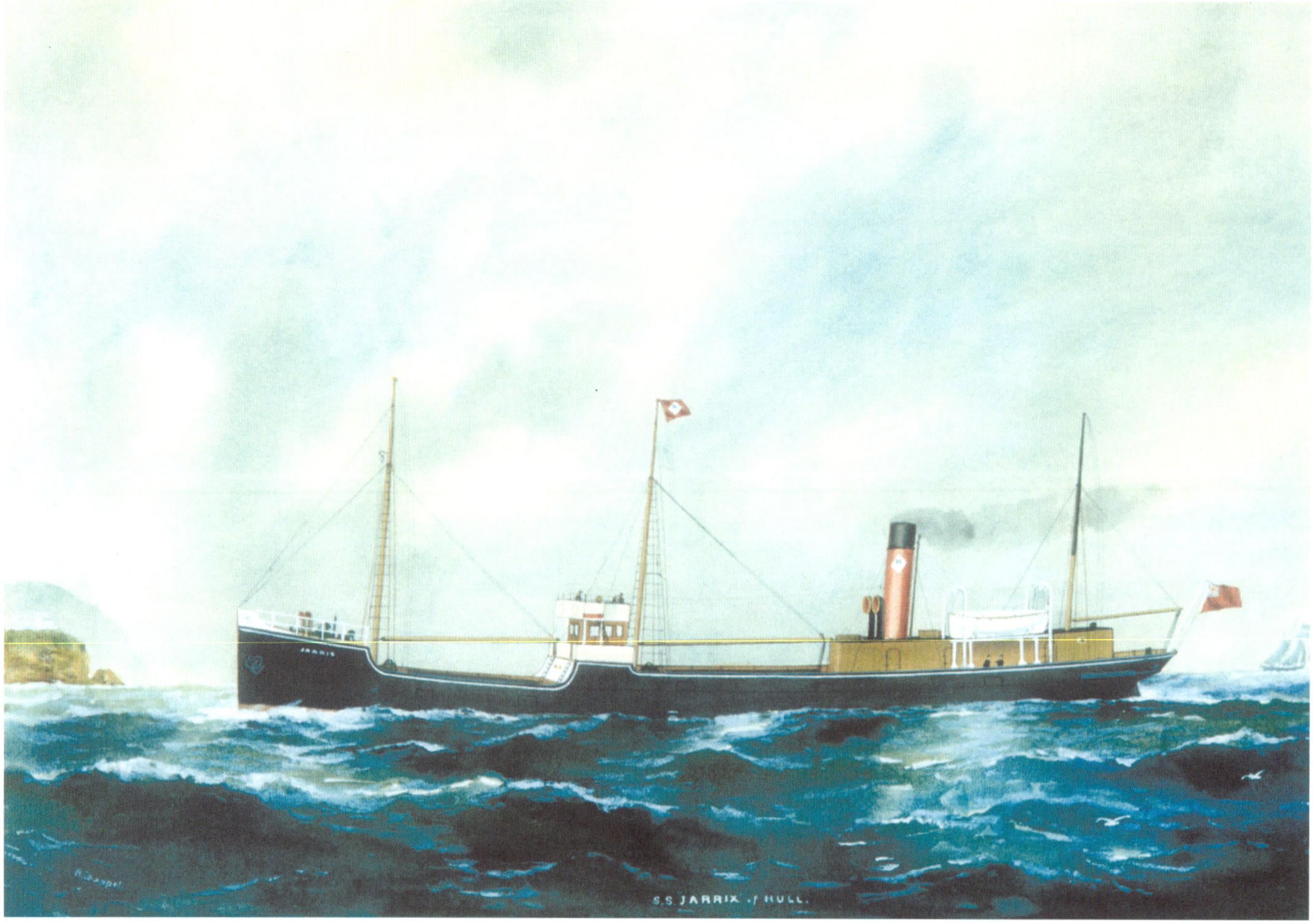

Courtesy of The British Mercantile Marine Memorial Collection

SS JARRIX OF HULL

ON 139308; Steel-screw three-masted schooner; built 1917 in Selby by Cochrane & Sons; 429 reg. tons; 150.2' x 24.6' x 11.0'; 3 cylinder 69 RHP engine; owners Humber Steam Coasters; reg. Hull.

Jarrix was one of the many steamships of between 300 and 800 g.r.t. owned by Robert Rix & Sons of Hull, a company which had been engaged in the coastal trade since the 1880s. It incorporated the suffix 'rix' into the names of its vessels from the 1910s onwards. Among the cargoes that these ships would have carried to ports throughout Scotland would have been cattle feeds produced in Hull, often in the form of compressed slabs.

Employed throughout her life primarily in the coal trade, SS Jarrix disappeared from record during the Second World War.

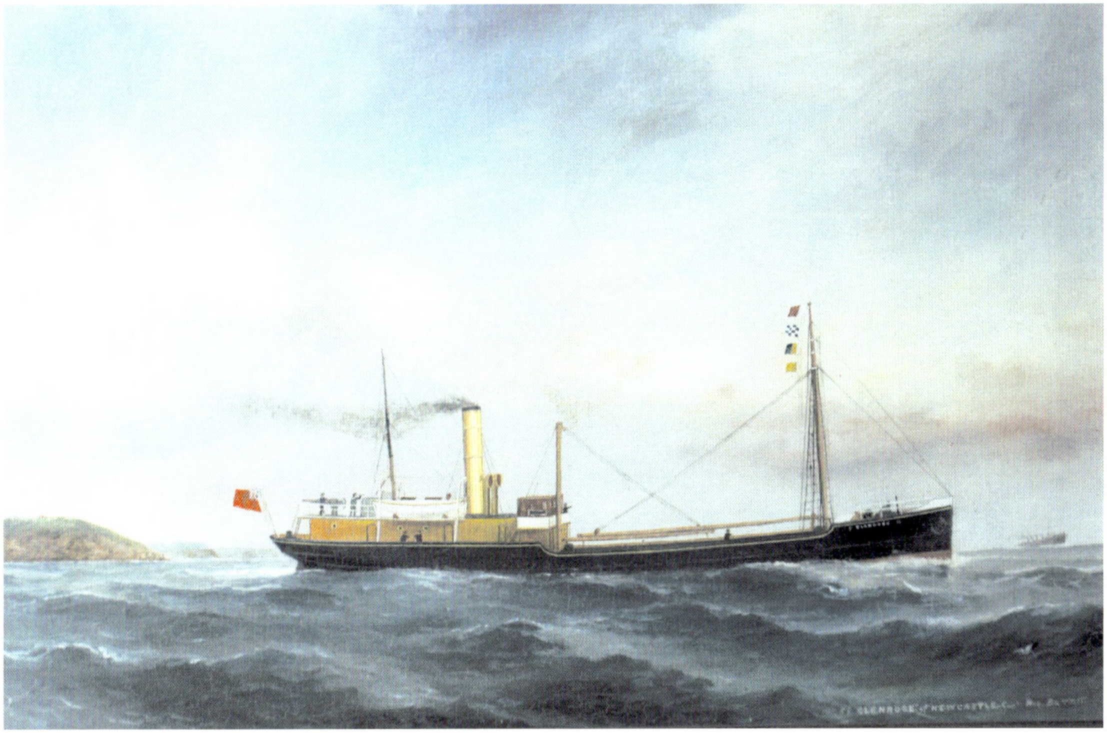

Goole Museum and Art Gallery

SS Glen Rose

ON 125448; steel; built 1908 by Hepple of South Shields; 286 gross tons; 125' x 22.6' x 9'; owners Glen Coasters Ltd; reg. Newcastle.

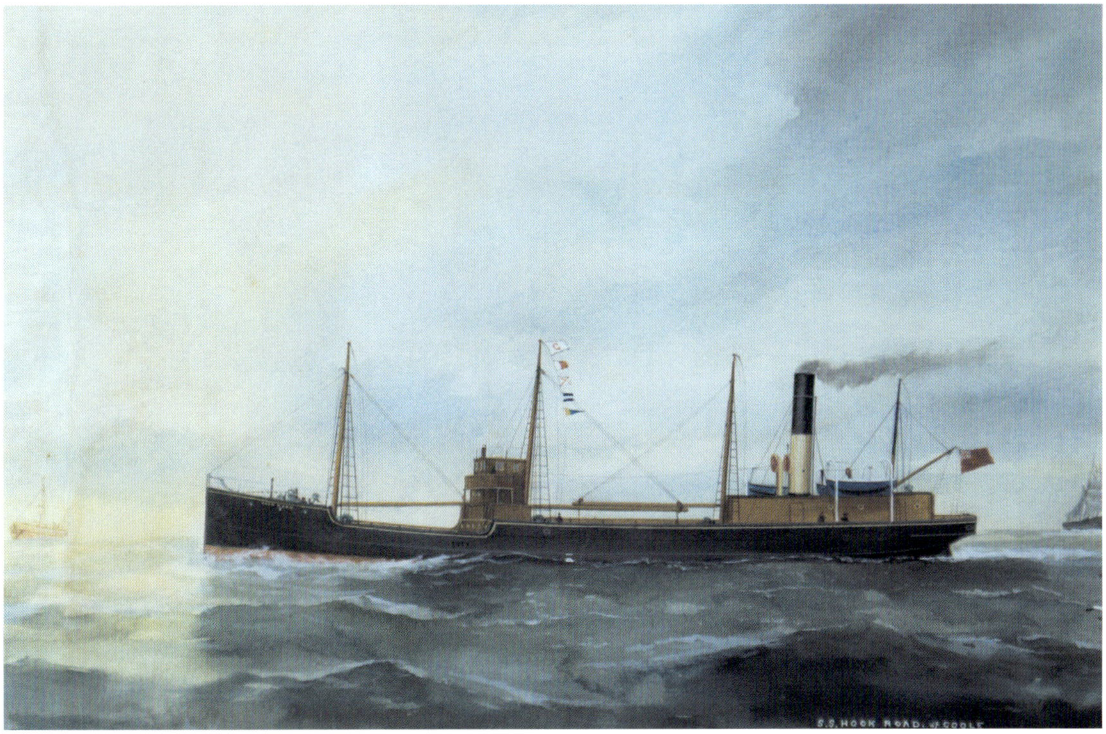

Goole Museum and Art Gallery

SS Hook Road

ON 133014; steel hull; built 1912 R. Williamson & Son of Workington; 811 gross tons; 186.3' x 29.4' x 12.4'; 3 Cylinder 85 RHP engine; owners Goole & Hull Steam Towing Co; reg. Glasgow.

Danish Ships

The maritime history of Denmark, with its tradition of building wooden sea-going trading vessels goes back to the pre-Viking era. In the 19th century, in what is known as the great age of sail, and into the early 20th century, Denmark was an important maritime nation. The merchant sailing vessels that were built there represented shipbuilding traditions which had been refined during the course of many centuries.

Ships from Denmark carried cargoes from destinations all around the North and South Atlantic and to the Mediterranean. A typical voyage for a vessel might have been with timber from Sweden or Finland to Scotland or Ireland, from there with general cargo or in ballast to Newfoundland in Canada. From Canada ships would sail with dry salt cod to the Mediterranean, and there load salt and general cargoes for the South American ports. The salt was used in the leather industry for curing hides which were loaded aboard the ships along with a cargo of coffee for the return voyage to Europe.

Of course, like other European ships, Danish vessels carried a wide variety of cargo but the ships came to Goole for coal and to Fowey, Par and Charlestown specifically for china clay, and the principal cargo they brought with them was Baltic timber.

It was in these ports that the masters and crew of these vessels would have encountered Reuben Chappell and commissioned paintings of their ships. These paintings were taken back with them to their home ports, where they were framed and became valued possessions of the household.

Many of these paintings have found their way to museums. The Danish people are clearly proud of their maritime history which is today celebrated by the presence of some splendid maritime museums which contain large numbers of Reuben Chappell's portraits of ships that are particular to the region. In the background of the paintings Reuben Chappell has shown features that the ships would have passed on their voyages to Britain.

Of particular interest are the Holm Petersen Maritime Museum in Troense and the Marstal Maritime Museum on the island of Ærø. Also on this island is the Museum of Ærøskøbing, and in Northern Denmark, the Helsingor Castle Museum.

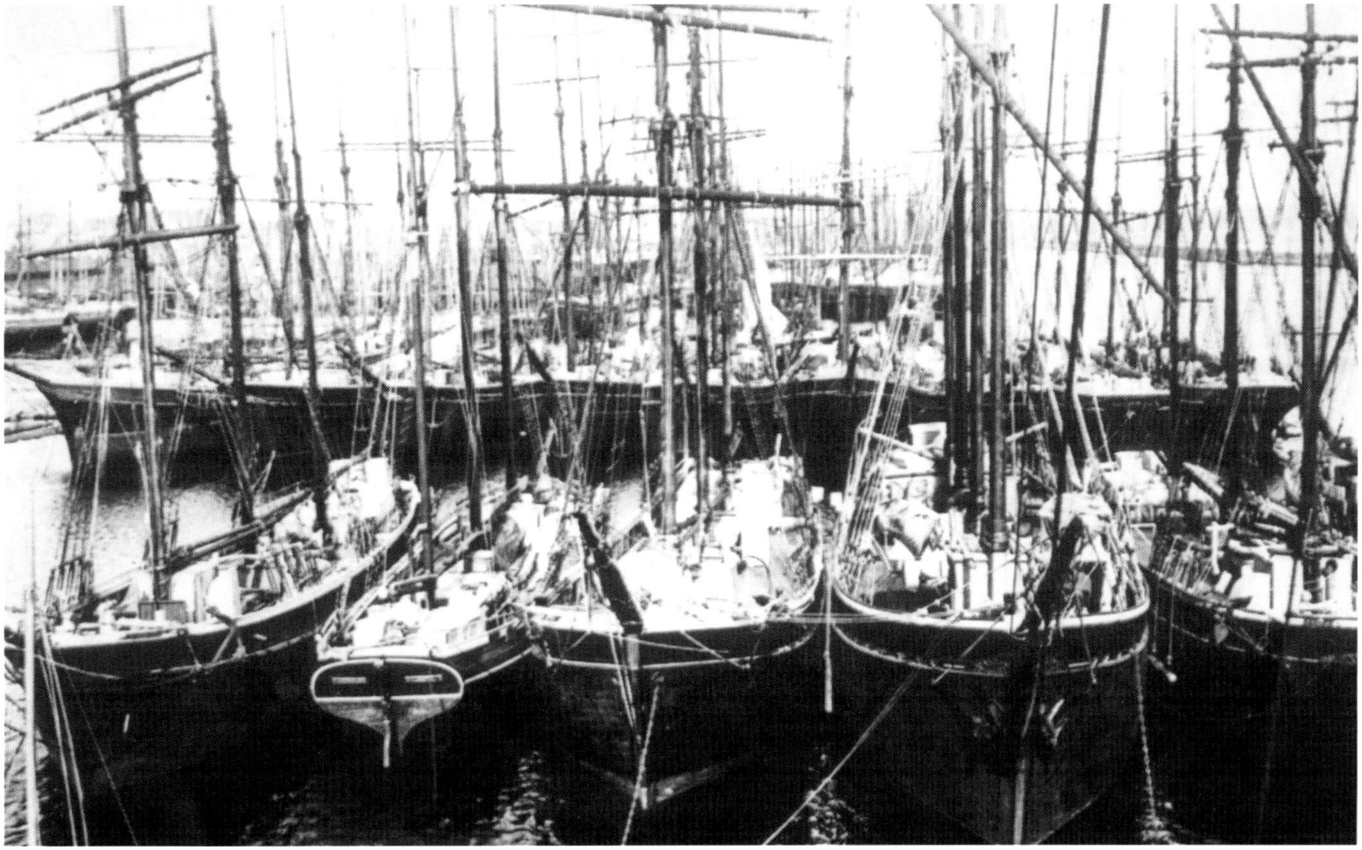

Ships in Marstal harbour February 1922 *Marstal Søfartsmuseum*

Marstal is still a significant seaport and a principal town on the island of Aerø. The middle of the 19th century saw an increase in world trade, and by 1851, 200 sail trading vessels were registered in Marstal. By the turn of the century 320 sail and steam cargo vessels were registered there. In those days Marstal ships and seamen were sailing all over the North and South Atlantic, the North Sea and the Baltic, carrying goods to and from many countries.

During the First World War Danish, Swedish and Norwegian vessels had to have their names and national flags painted prominently on their ships' sides to show their neutrality, otherwise the German warships would sink them. Despite this 41 sailing ships and one steamer were sunk, and more than 60 seamen from Marstal lost their lives.

In Marstal there is an extensive Maritime Museum. Amongst the many ship portraits by artists from all over the world, are 29 by Reuben Chappell. Besides paintings there are over 200 ship models, and many artefacts, including figureheads, connected with its maritime life. The following paintings and photographs are from their collection.

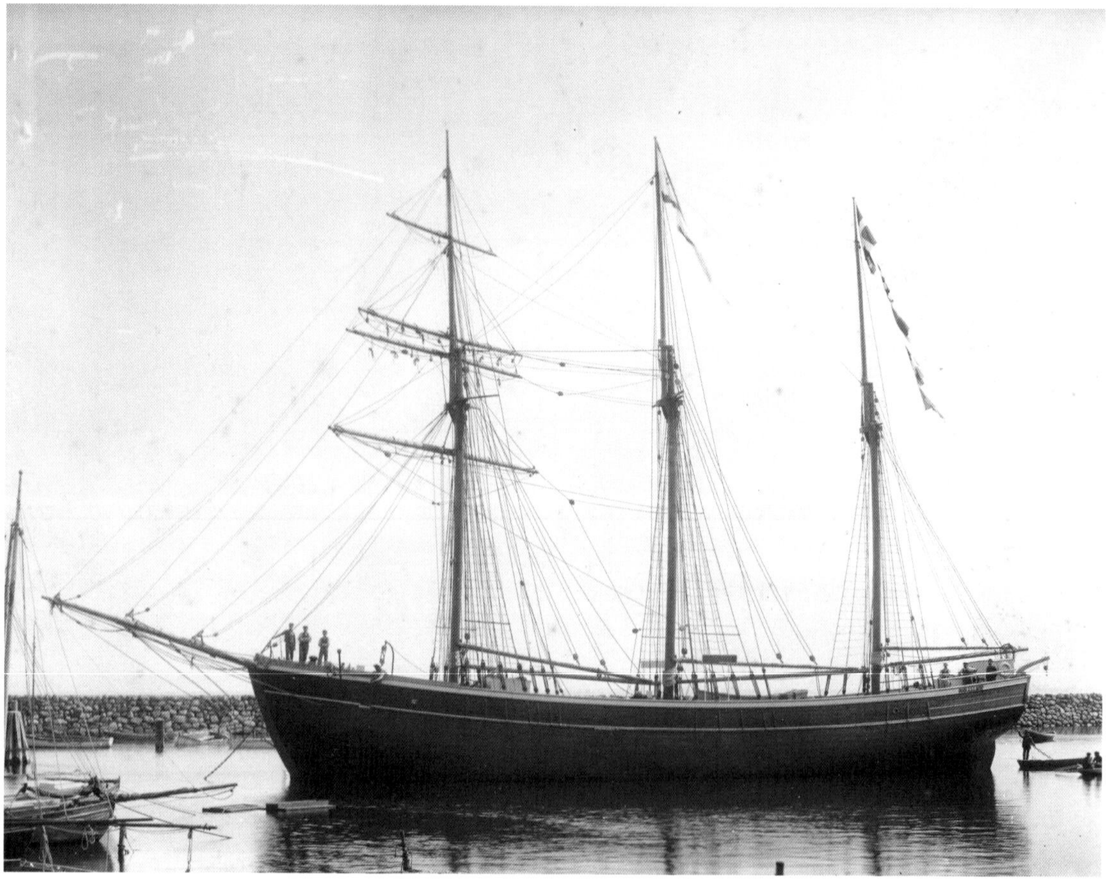

Ruth in harbour, Marstal — *Marstal Søfartsmuseum*

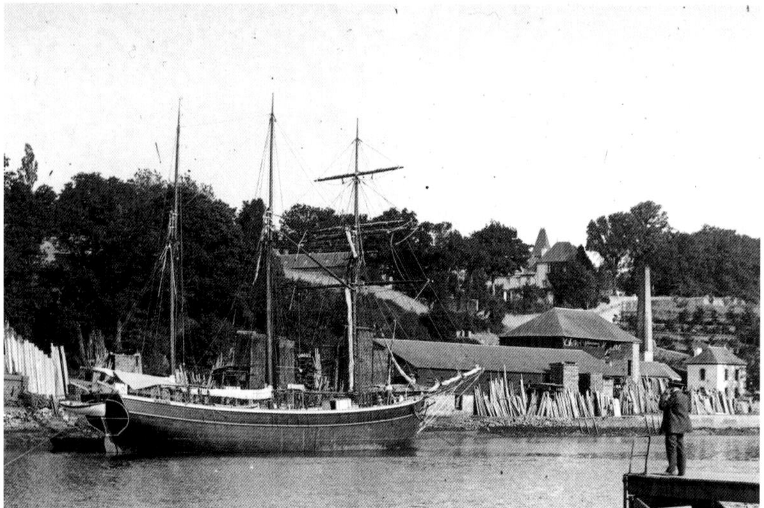

Unloading at St Goustan, the Netherlands, July 1902 — *Marstal Søfartsmuseum*

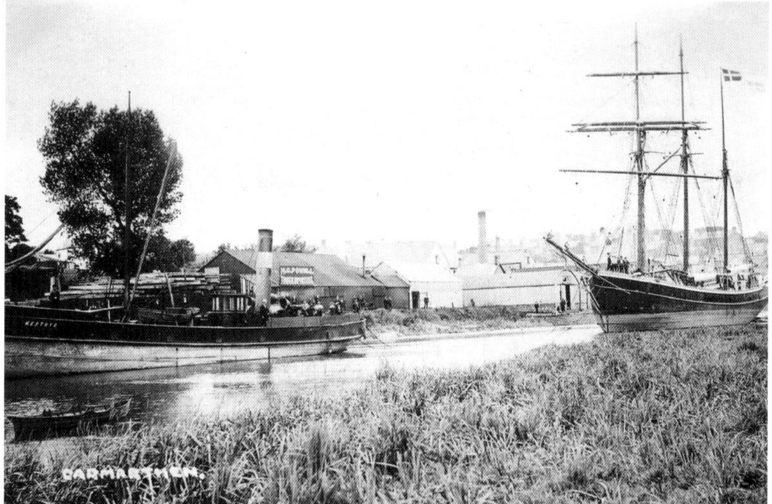

Ruth in channel, Camarthen — *Marstal Søfartsmuseum*

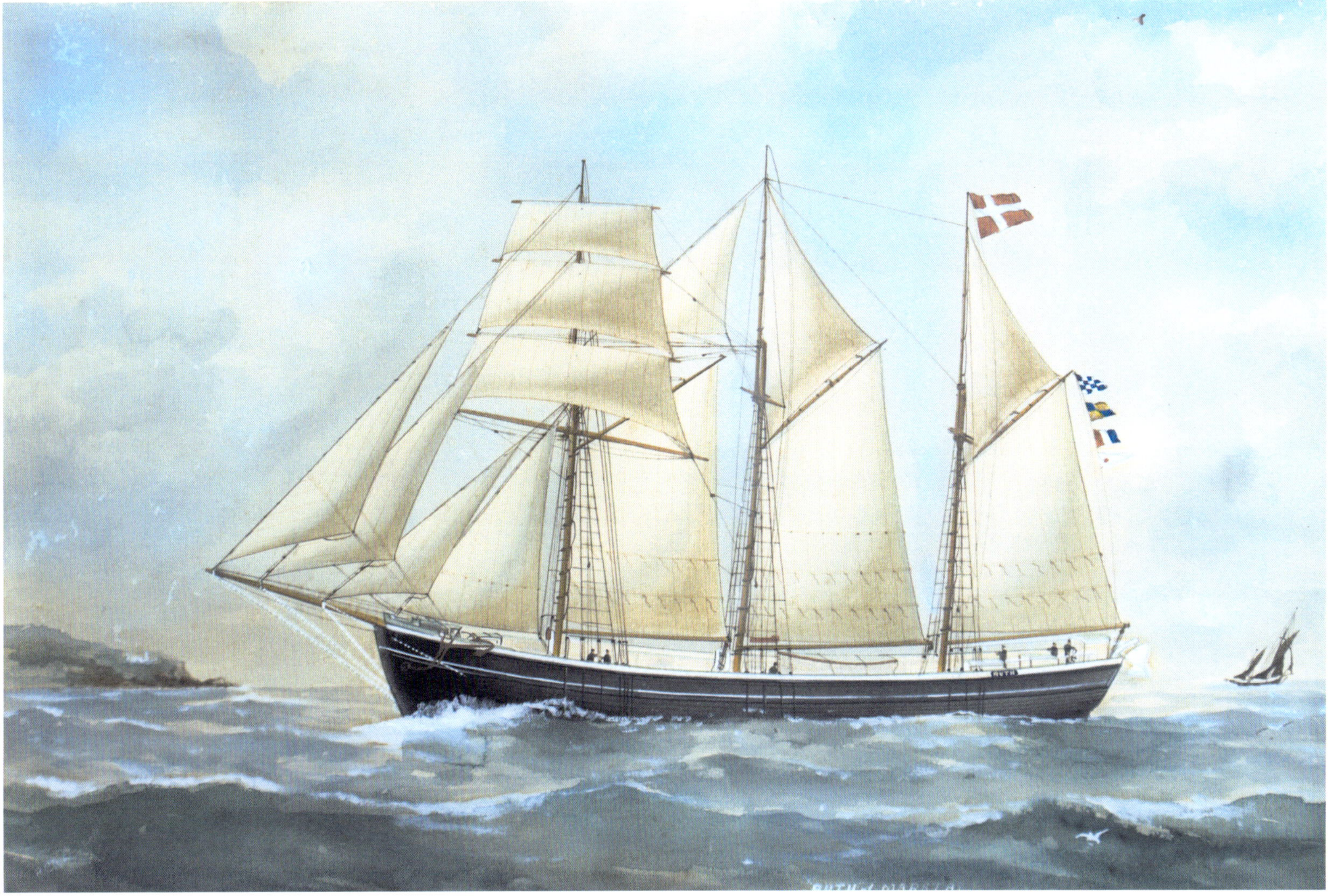

Marstal Søfartsmuseum

RUTH OF MARSTAL

Three-masted topsail schooner; built 1901 in Marstal by Johan Arnt Petersen; tonnage: 172 brt. 116 nrt.; Capt. Hans Nielsen Hansen; call sign: NLTD; reg. Marstal.

In this fair-weather portrait Chappell shows the three masted topsail- schooner Ruth approaching land, a tan-sailed vessel in the distance. Ruth is flying the Danish flag as well as her code signal flags. Her bow is typical of the traditional Danish design.

On 4th December 1910, whilst sailing from St John's, Newfoundland with a cargo of fish oil she disappeared in mid Atlantic and was lost with all hands.

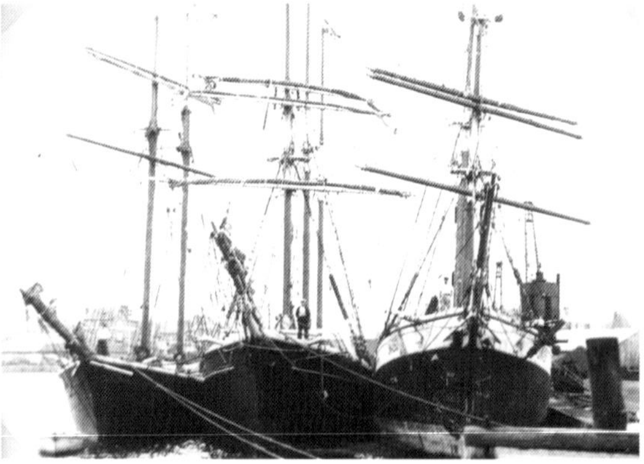

Dana in St Malo *Marstal Søfartsmuseum*

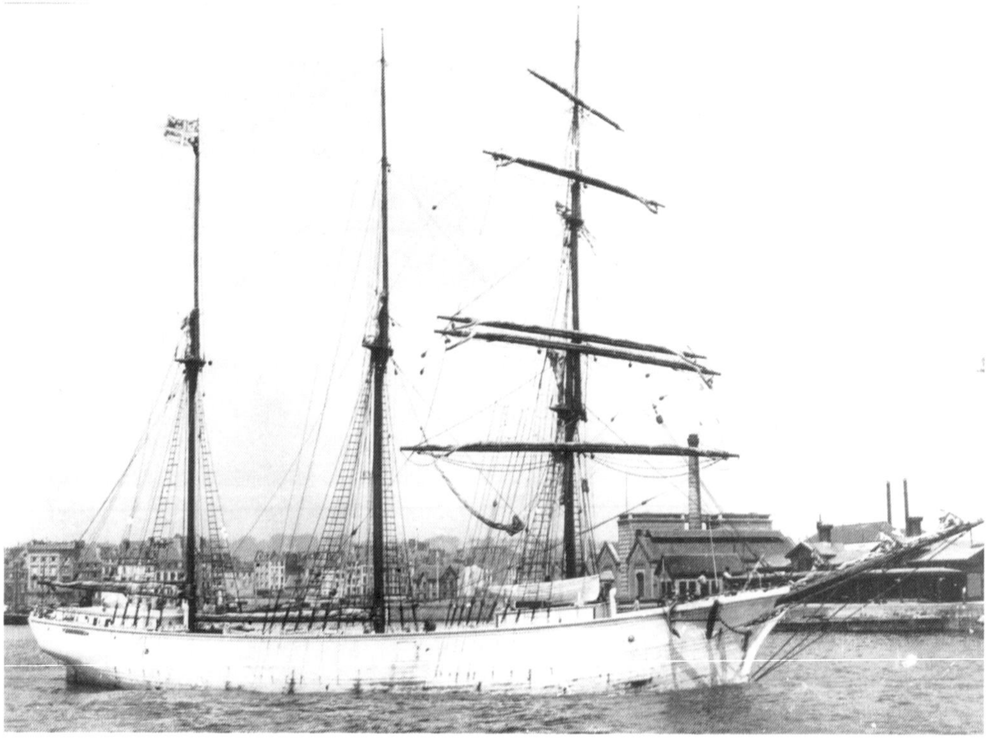

Dana in Le Havre *Marstal Søfartsmuseum*

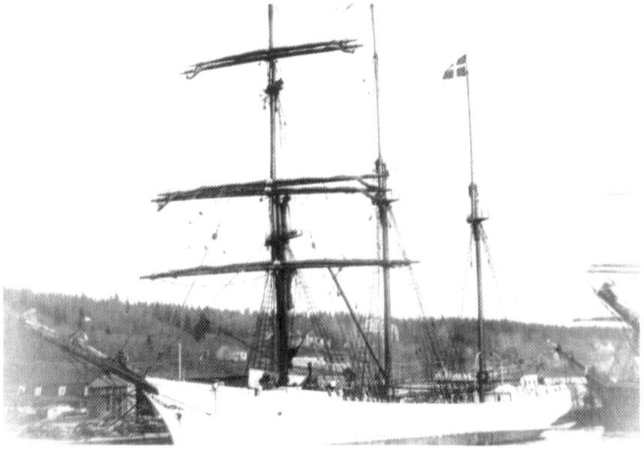

Dana in Nordic harbour *Marstal Søfartsmuseum*

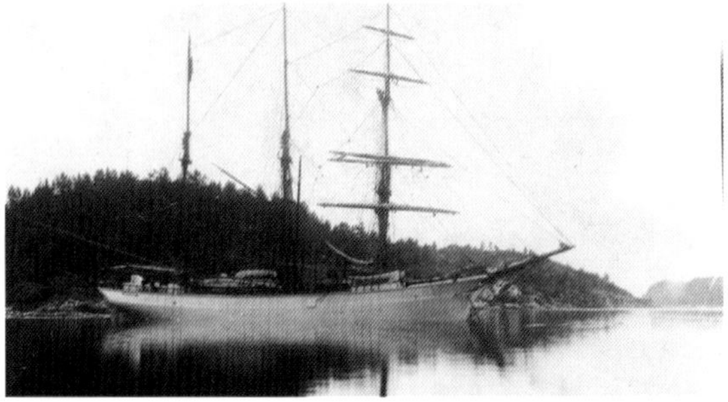

At anchor in a Norwegian fjord *Marstal Søfartsmuseum*

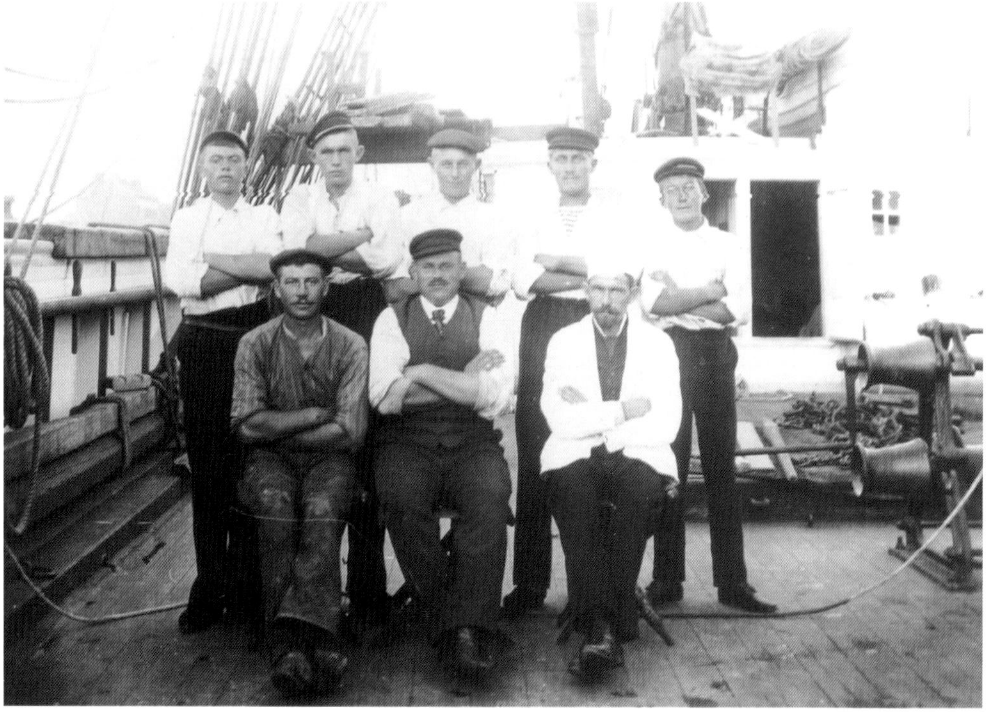

Crew of Dana, Le Havre *Marstal Søfartsmuseum*

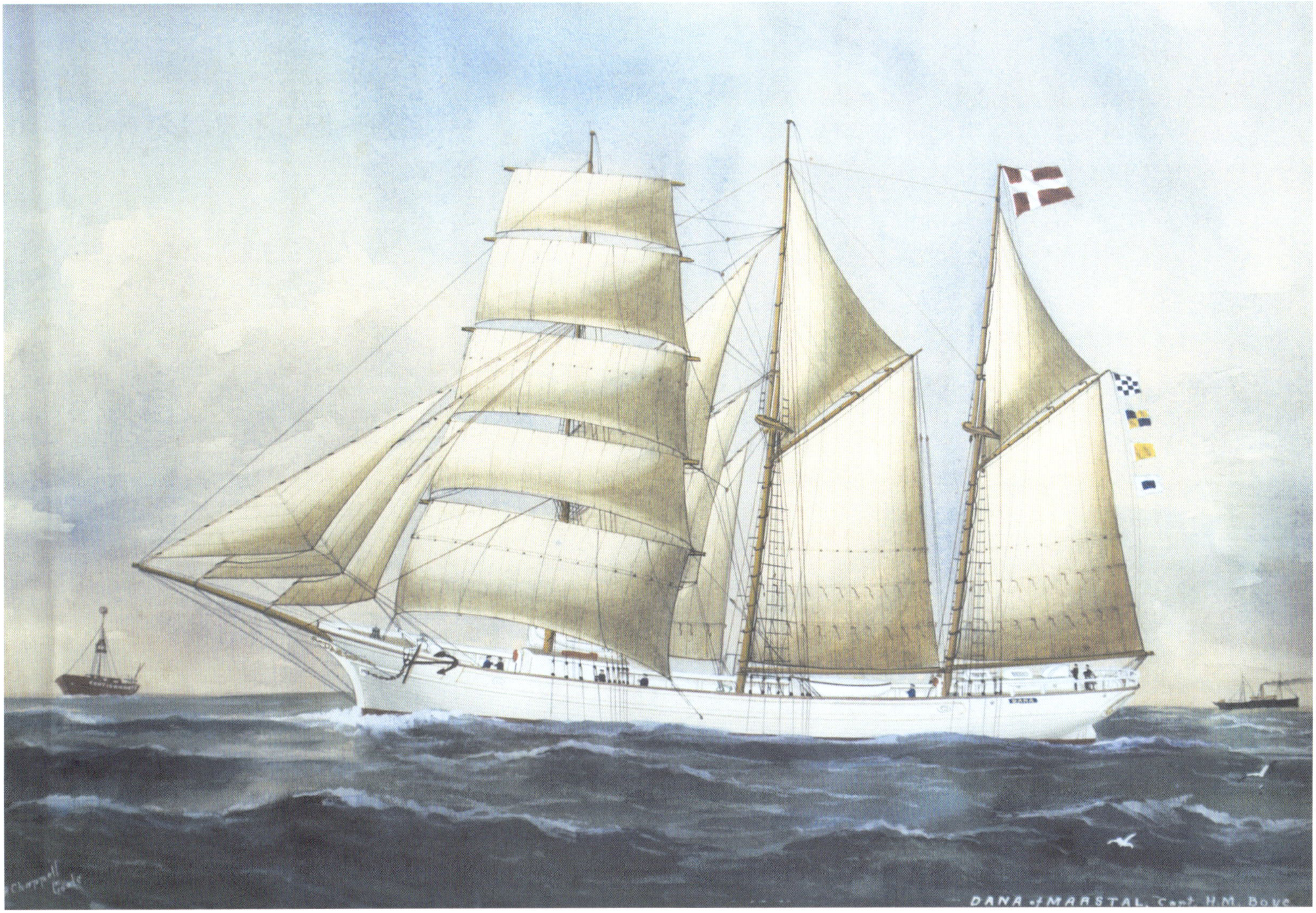

Marstal Søfartsmuseum

DANA OF MARSTAL

Built 1901 in Tvedestrand, Norway by Wrolsen; tonnage: 364 brt 333 nrt; Capts: Andr Carlsen, R. E. Petersen, R. Albertsen; owners: H. M. Petersen, E. B. Kromann, Herman C Boye. Call sign: NLQS. reg: Marstal.

Chappell shows this elegant barquantine at sea in full sail. She is passing a lightship which probably marked dangerous sandbanks off Kent, and would have been a feature of their journey to Cornwall from Denmark. A steamship is seen on the horizon. As ever, there is much detail in the painting, particularly in the sails and rigging of the ship. The small ties on the sails are the reef points for shortening sail in strong winds.

Dana was sold in 1915 to Helsingor and was lost in the North Sea in the same year.

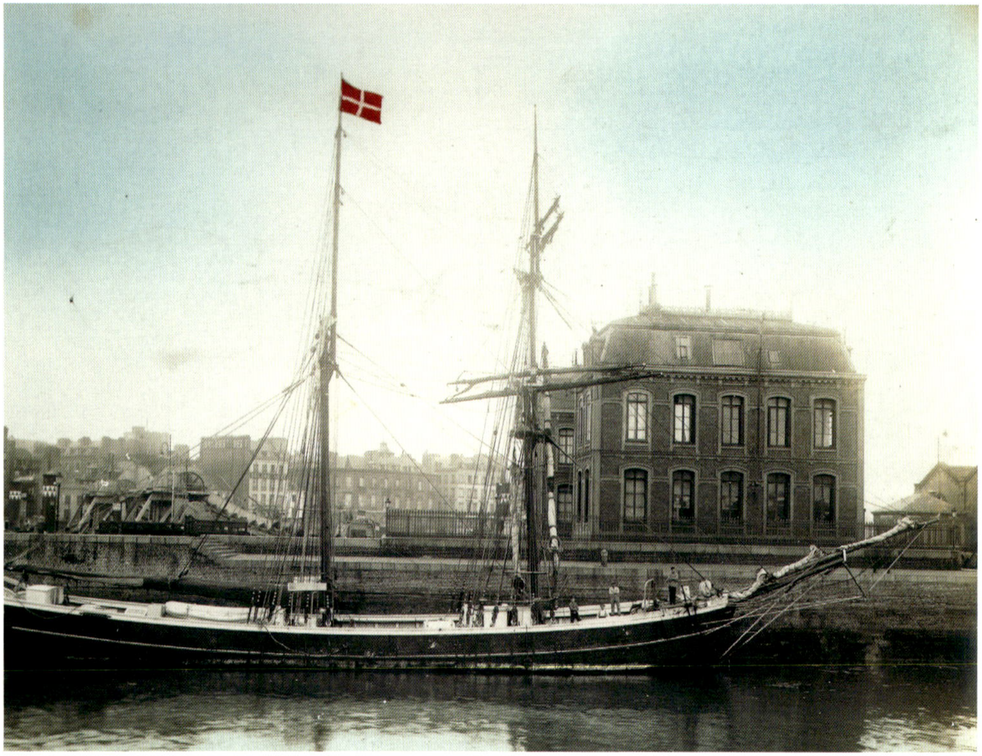

Dannebrog *Marstal Søfartsmuseum*

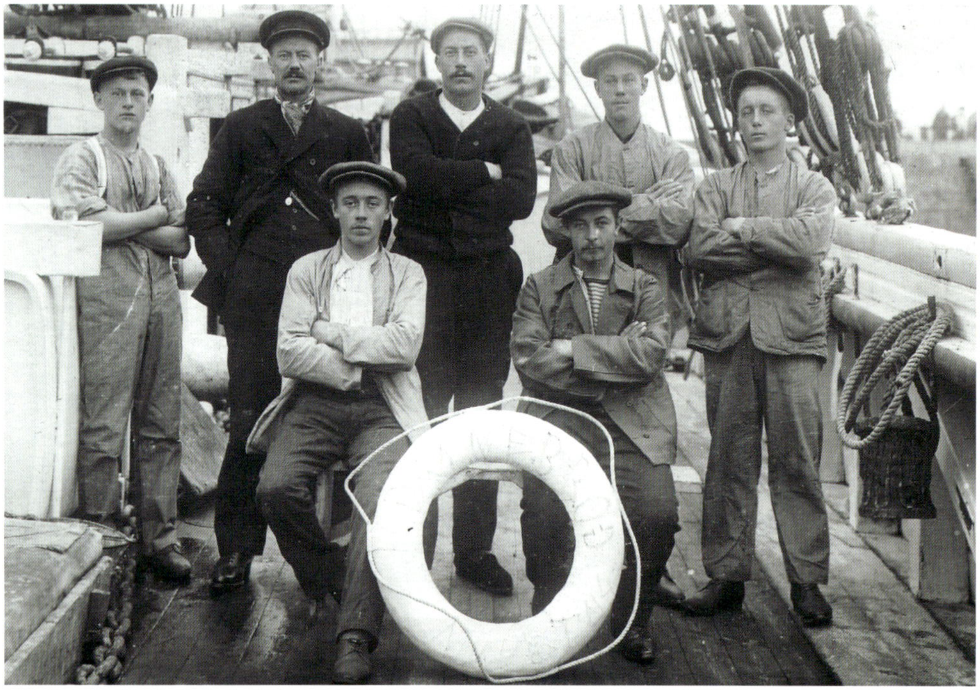

Crew of Dannebrog *Marstal Søfartsmuseum*

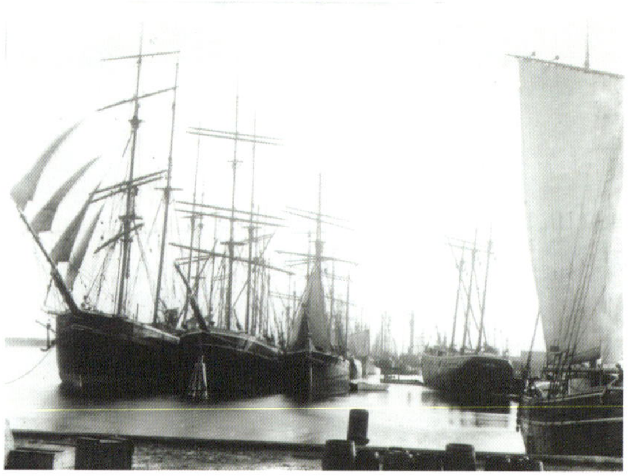

Lay ups. Dannebrog in the harbour at Marstal 1898
Eden and Dannebrog

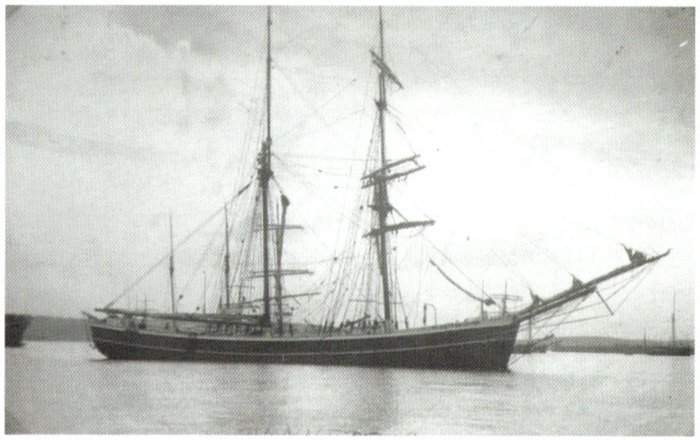

Dannebrog at anchor

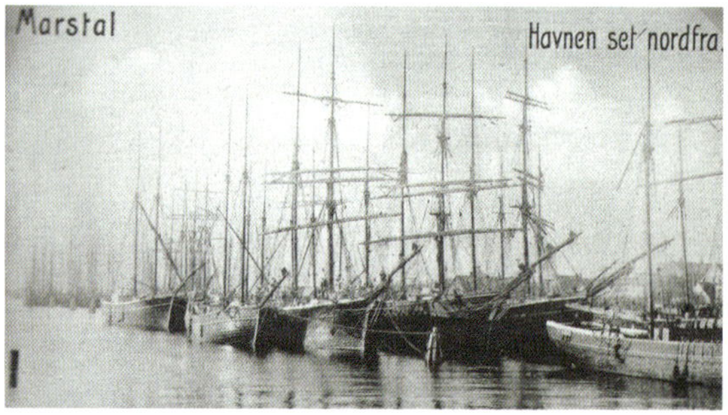

Lay ups. Dannebrog in harbour, Marstal 1898

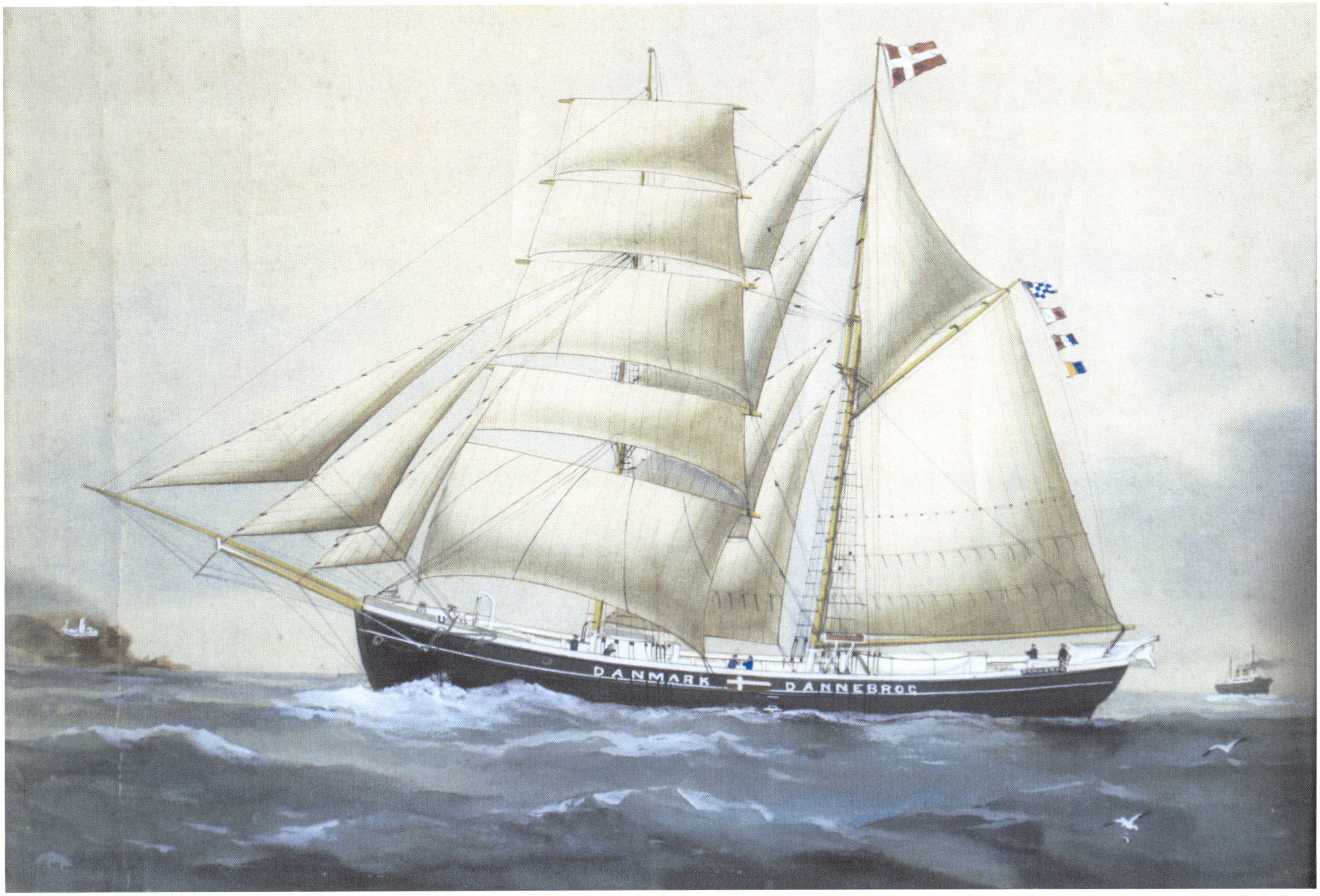

Marstal Søfartsmuseum

DANNEBROG OF MARSTAL

Built 1896 by Johan Arnt Petersen; 155nrt; Capt. Peter H Bager; owner Hans Christiansen; call sign: NHTK; Reg. Marstal.

This painting shows the brigantine Dannebrog in fine weather and full sail. Chappell painted her during the First World War when the Danish ships had their name and country painted on their sides to show their neutrality. In spite of this measure a number of ships were sunk by German warships and submarines. Dannebrog was lost in a gale in the Atlantic in 1916 when sailing from Reykjavik to Liverpool with a cargo of fish. On the 21st December she was struck by a large wave and two men were injured, one of them, the Captain, Peter H. Bager, later died of his injuries. Dannebrog suffered a leak and was abandoned. The crew were saved by the SS San Francisco and were put ashore in Lerwick. The wreck of the Dannebrog was later burnt.

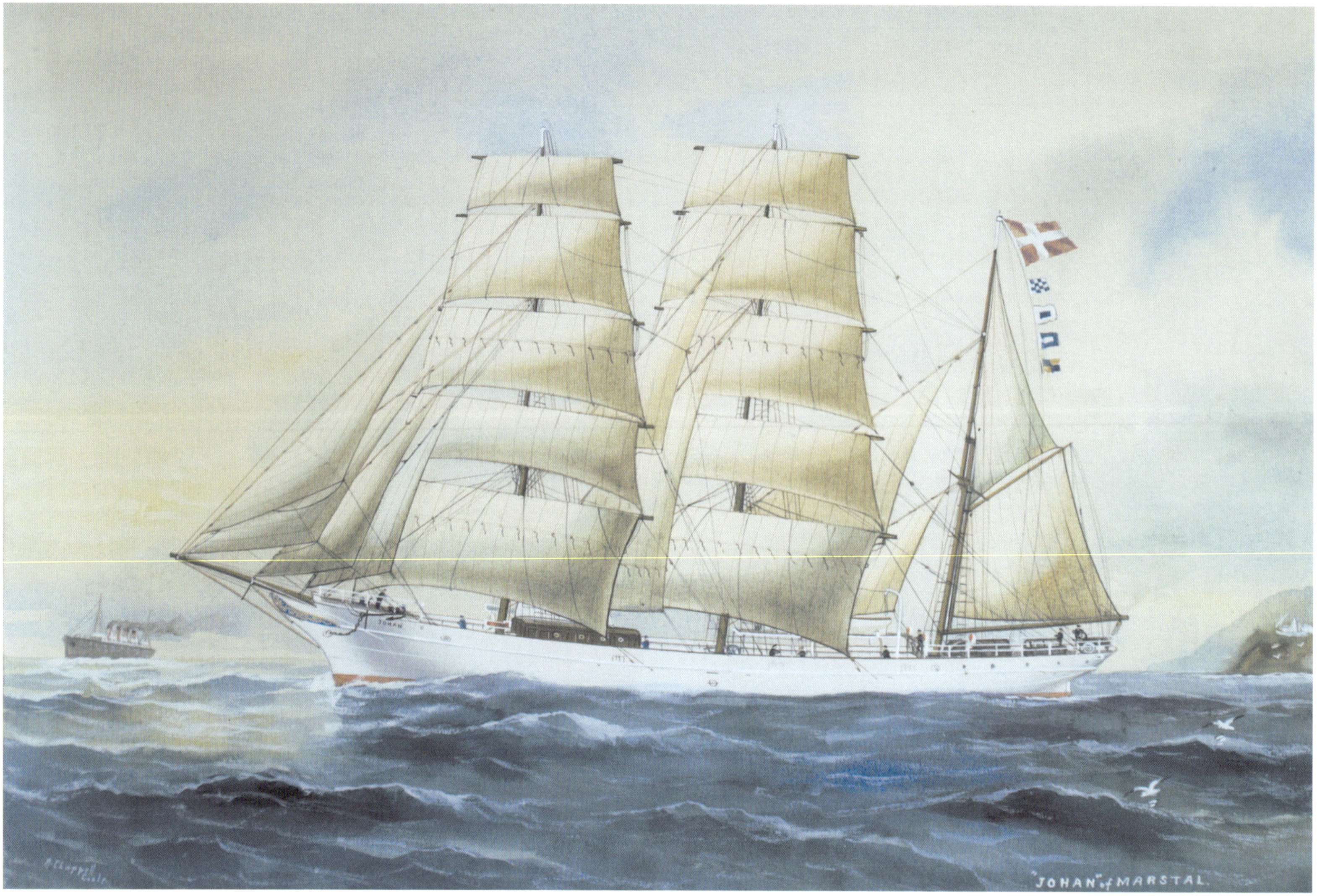

Marstal Søfartsmuseum

Johan of Marstal

Barque; tonnage: 828 brt 793 nrt; Capt. O. Boye; owner R. K. Bager; call sign NSPL; reg. Marstal.

Johan is a larger vessel than most of the ships that Chappell painted. The barque is shown, passing the coast in full sail on what appears to be a fine evening. In the distance is a four-funnelled steamship, a liner heading up the channel.

Johan was built in Glasgow at Russell & Co. in 1883. She was bought in 1913 for Marstal. She was sunk in the English Channel while travelling from Montego Bay, Jamaica to Le Havre with a cargo of timber.

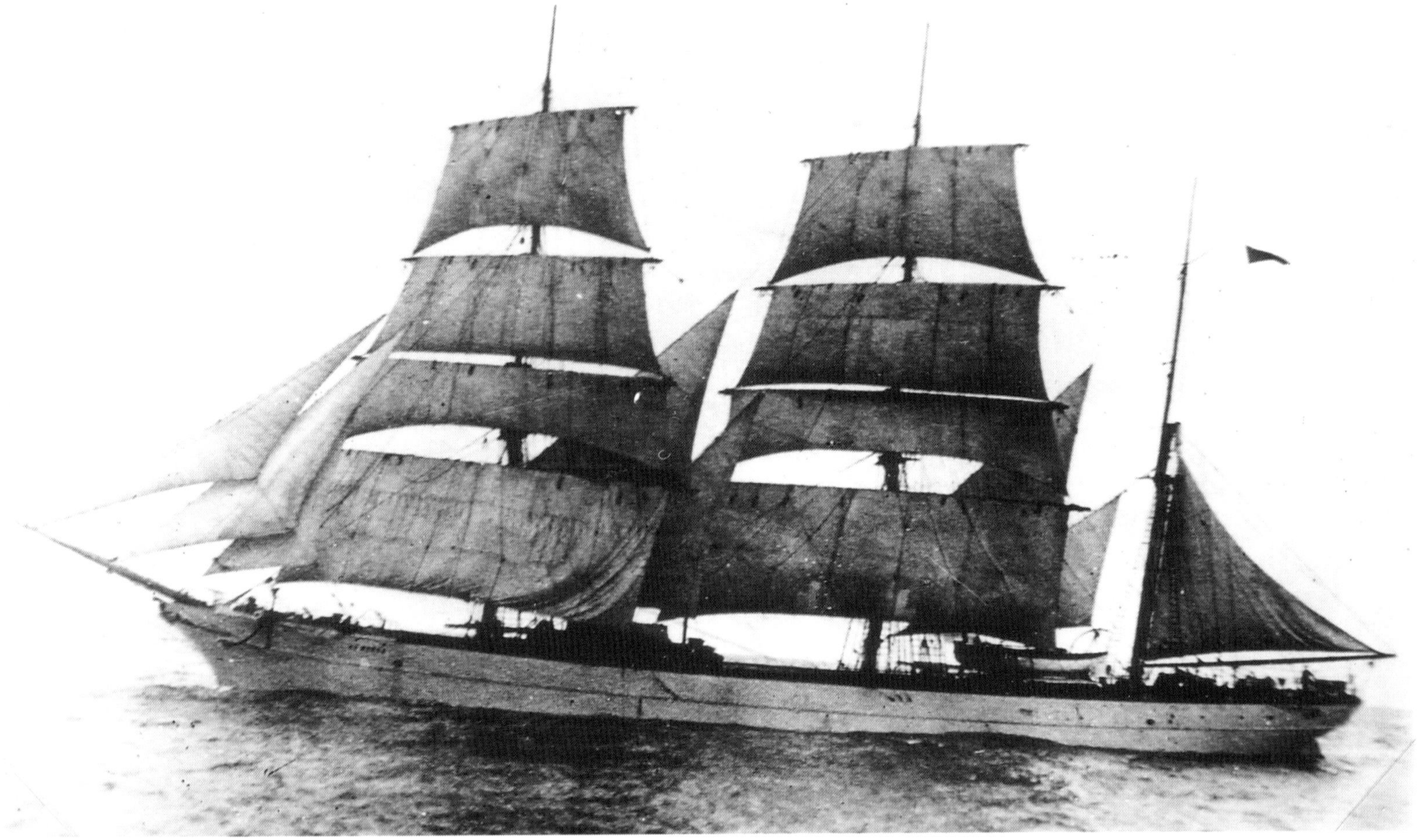

Johan under sail — *Marstal Søfartsmuseum*

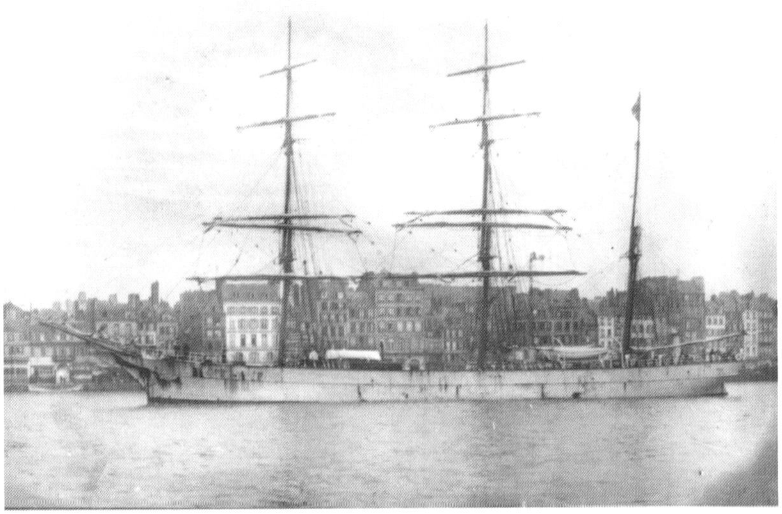

Johan in Le Havre — *Marstal Søfartsmuseum*

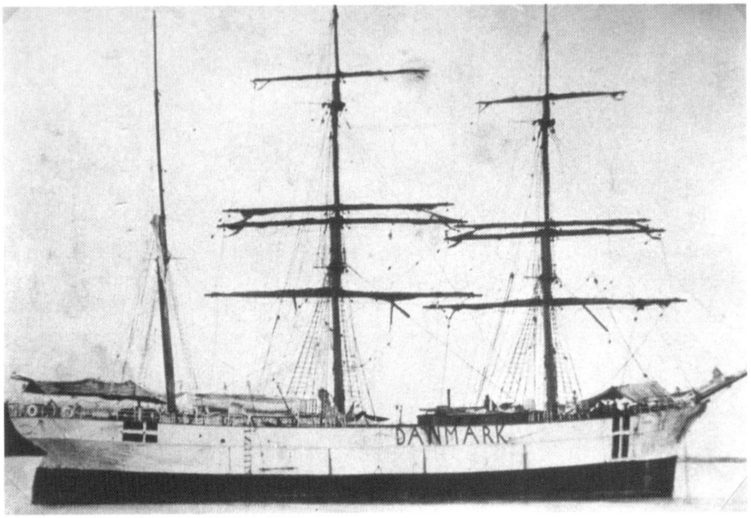

At anchor in Montego Bay, Jamaica — *Marstal Søfartsmuseum*

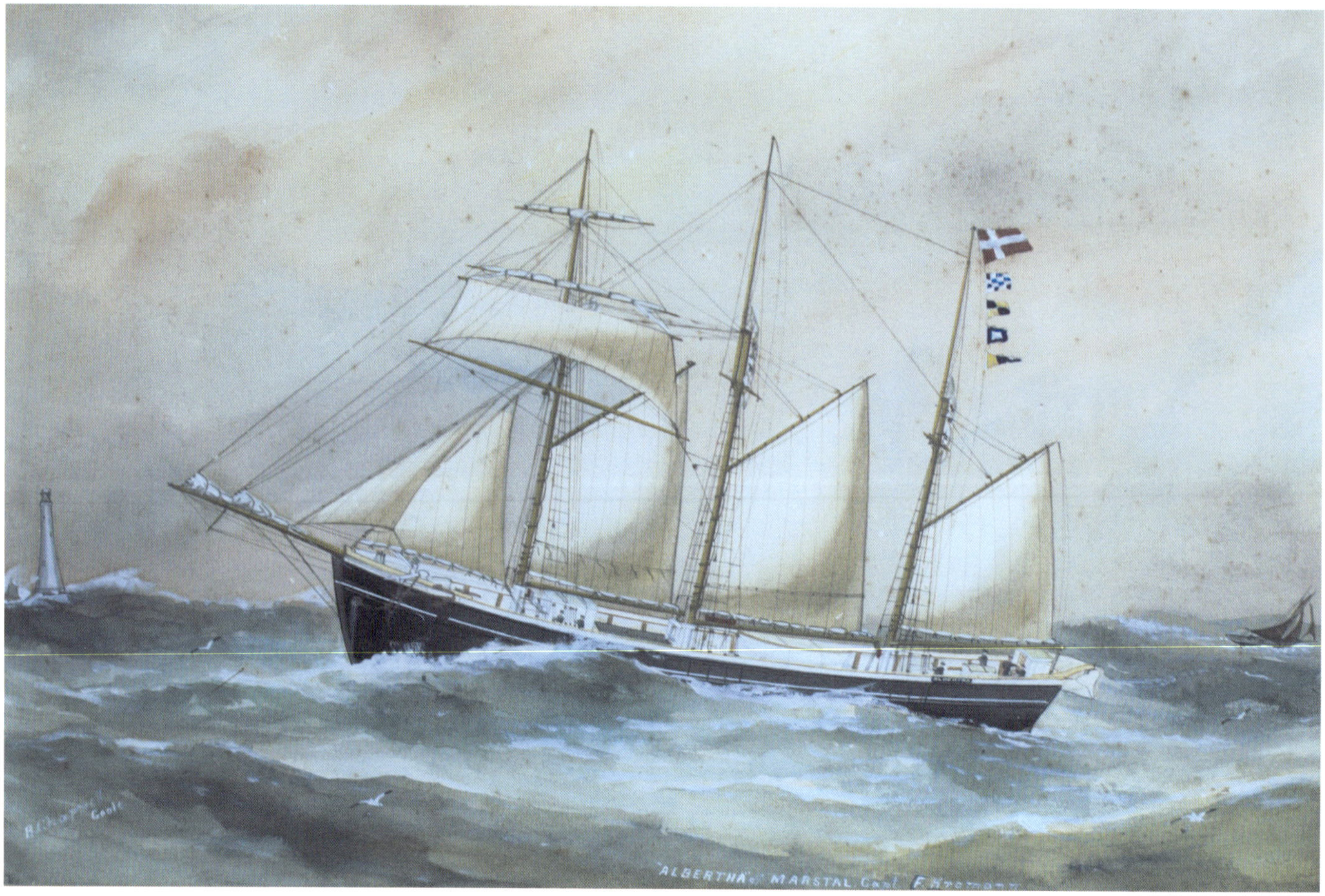

Marstal Søfartsmuseum

ALBERTHA OF MARSTAL

Built 1901 by Neils Hansen; tonnage 170 brt, 142 nrt; owner H. J. Bager; Capt. F. Kromann; call sign NLPG; reg. Marstal.

A foul-weather painting which shows the three-masted vessel Albertha passing the Eddystone light. Albertha is carrying reduced sail in heavy weather. The curved bow and the ship's boat hung at the stern are typical of these Danish vessels.

Albertha was lost on 15th August 1917 in the North Sea. She was sailing from Liverpool to Copenhagen when she was sunk by a German U-boat. The crew were saved.

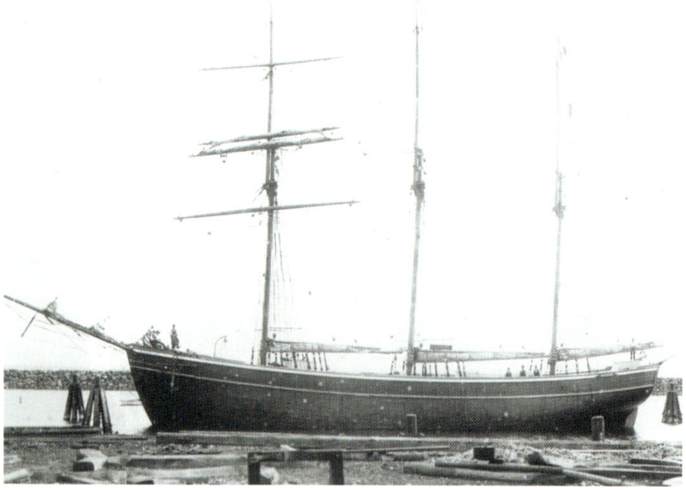

The Albertha in Marstal — *Marstal Søfartsmuseum*

Below, details of Danish vessels from Reuben Chappell's sketch books.

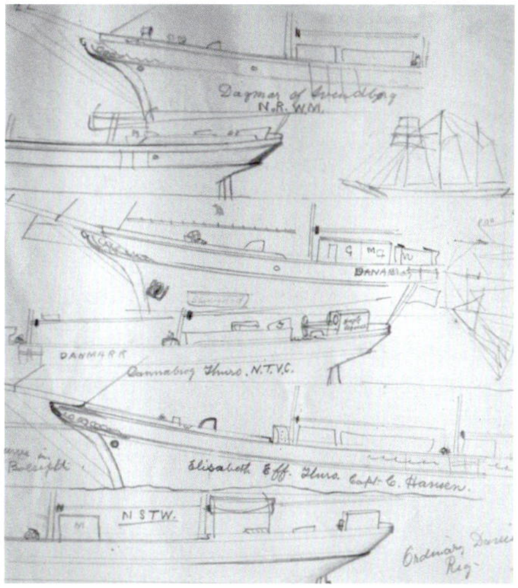

Private Collection

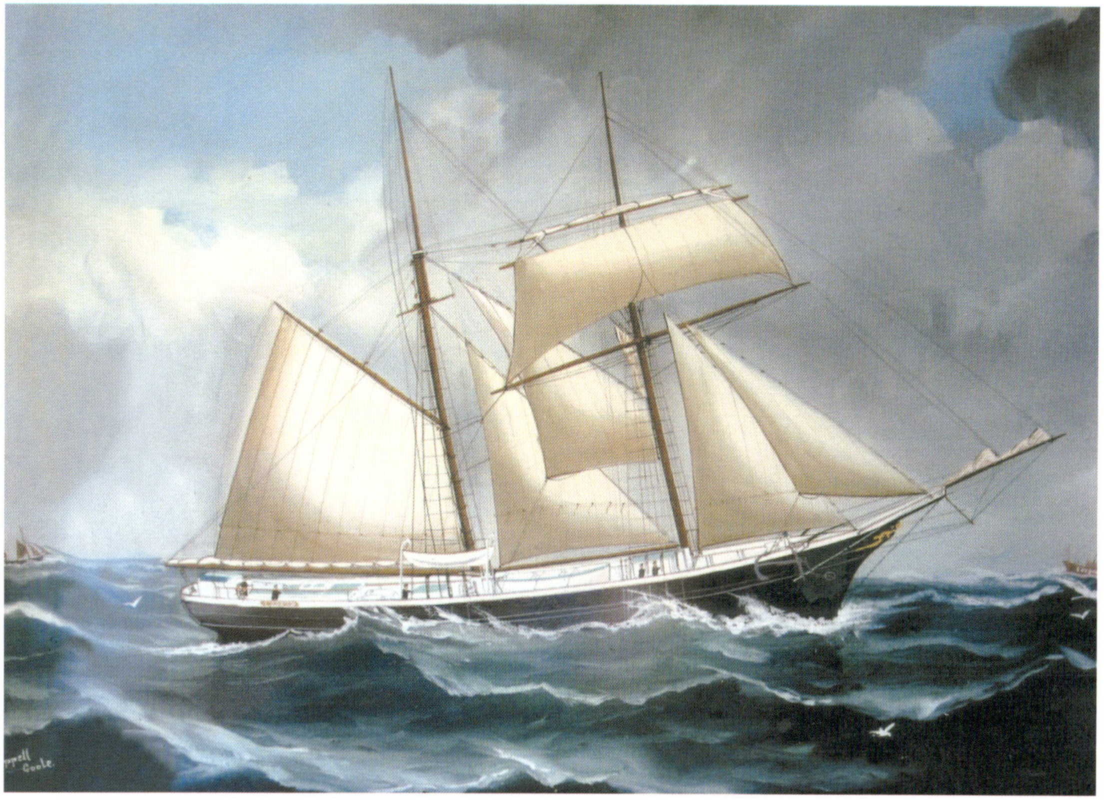

Museum of Ærøskøbing

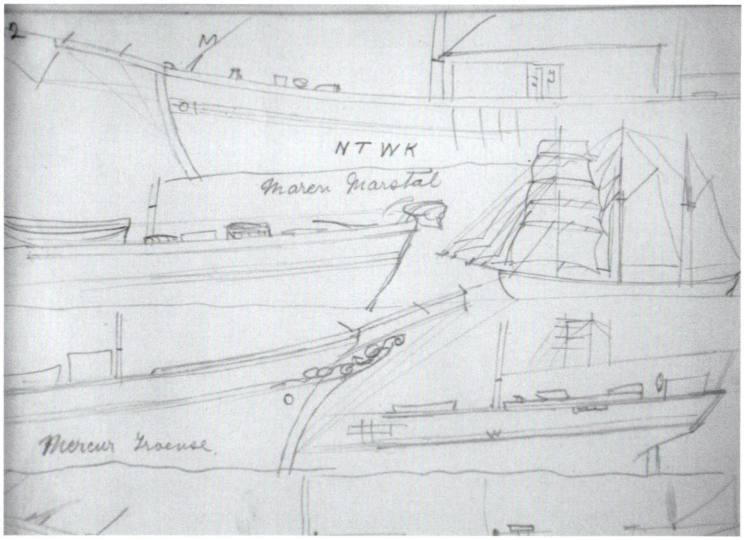

Private Collection

MAGDA OF ÆRØSKØBING

Many of Reuben Chappell's paintings have suffered from fading over the years, perhaps caused by the quality of the materials he used, or, more likely, by the paintings being exposed to direct sunlight causing some of the colours to fade. It is often the skies which are affected most. However, in this painting the sky and cloud effects are in particularly good condition, giving an indication of what has been lost in some of the other paintings, and why Reuben Chappell was admired for his liquid seas and skies.

Magda sails past a lightship into dark and troubled weather, but there are still patches of blue sky which give a sense of hope for the journey.

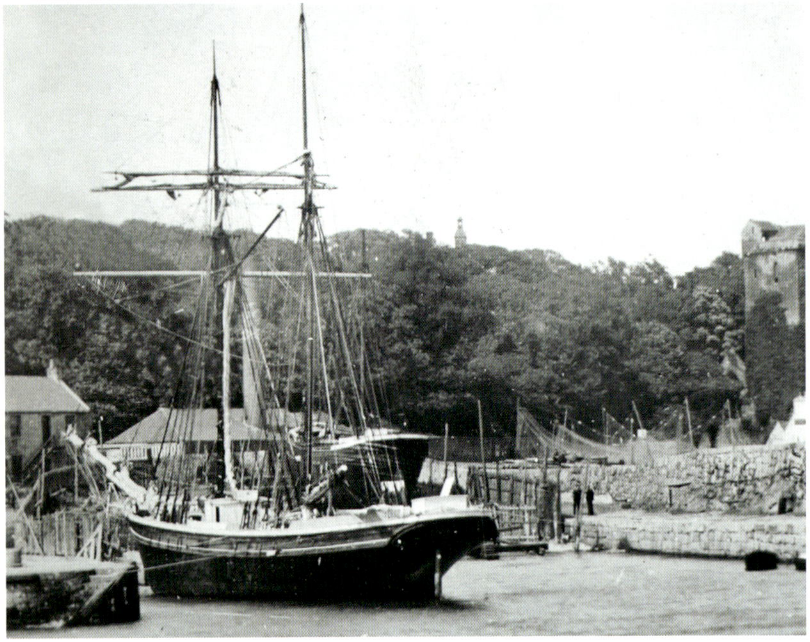
Carl

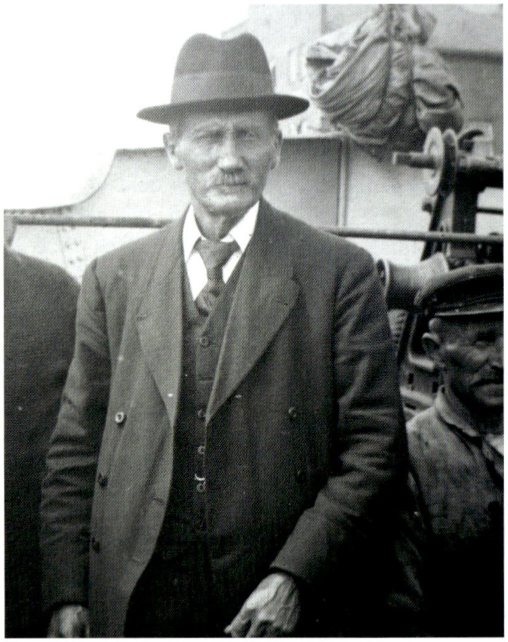
Captain Christian Lindegaard (The King).

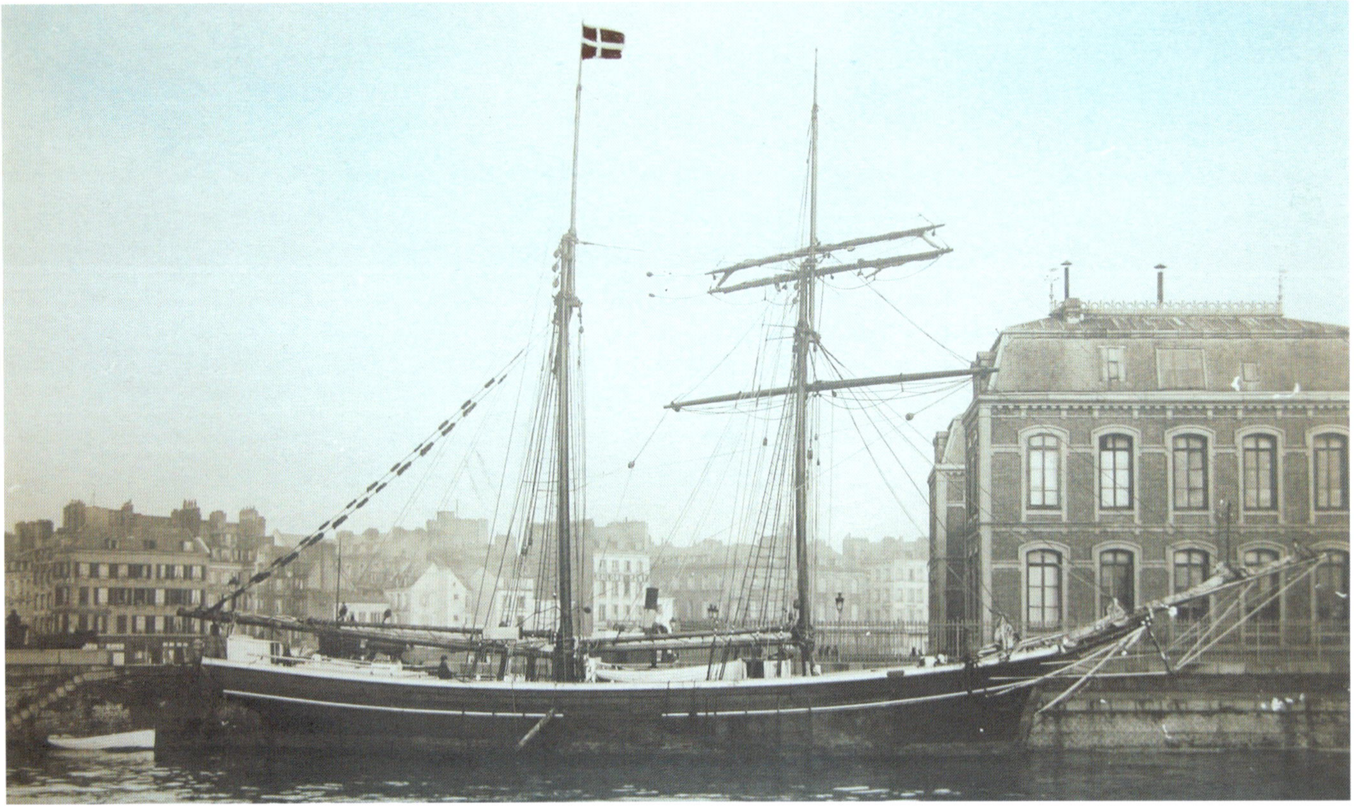
Carl in port

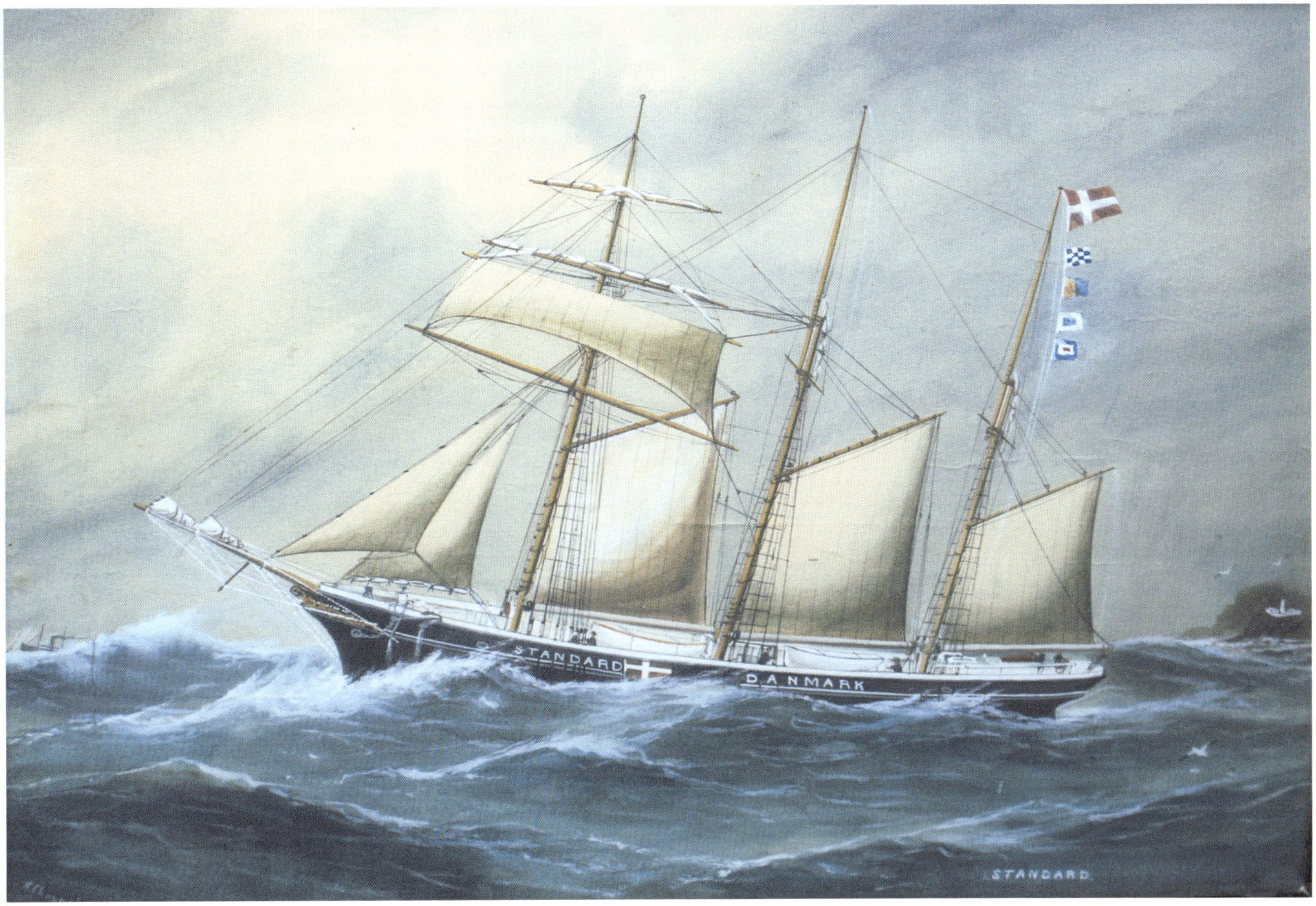

Troense Søfartsmuseum

STANDARD

Built 1899-1900 in Thurø

Standard traded in the North Sea and Baltic Sea with voyages to Canada. The last journey was from Fowey with china clay to Kirkcaldy in the Firth of Forth. During the First World War Danish ships had their names, nationality and the Danish flag painted prominently on their sides to show their neutrality. In spite of this the vessel was sunk by a German U-boat on 20th January 1917. The crew took to the ship's boats and reached the shore alive.

Reuben Chappell painted both fair-and-foul-weather versions of this elegant three-masted schooner with a clipper bow.

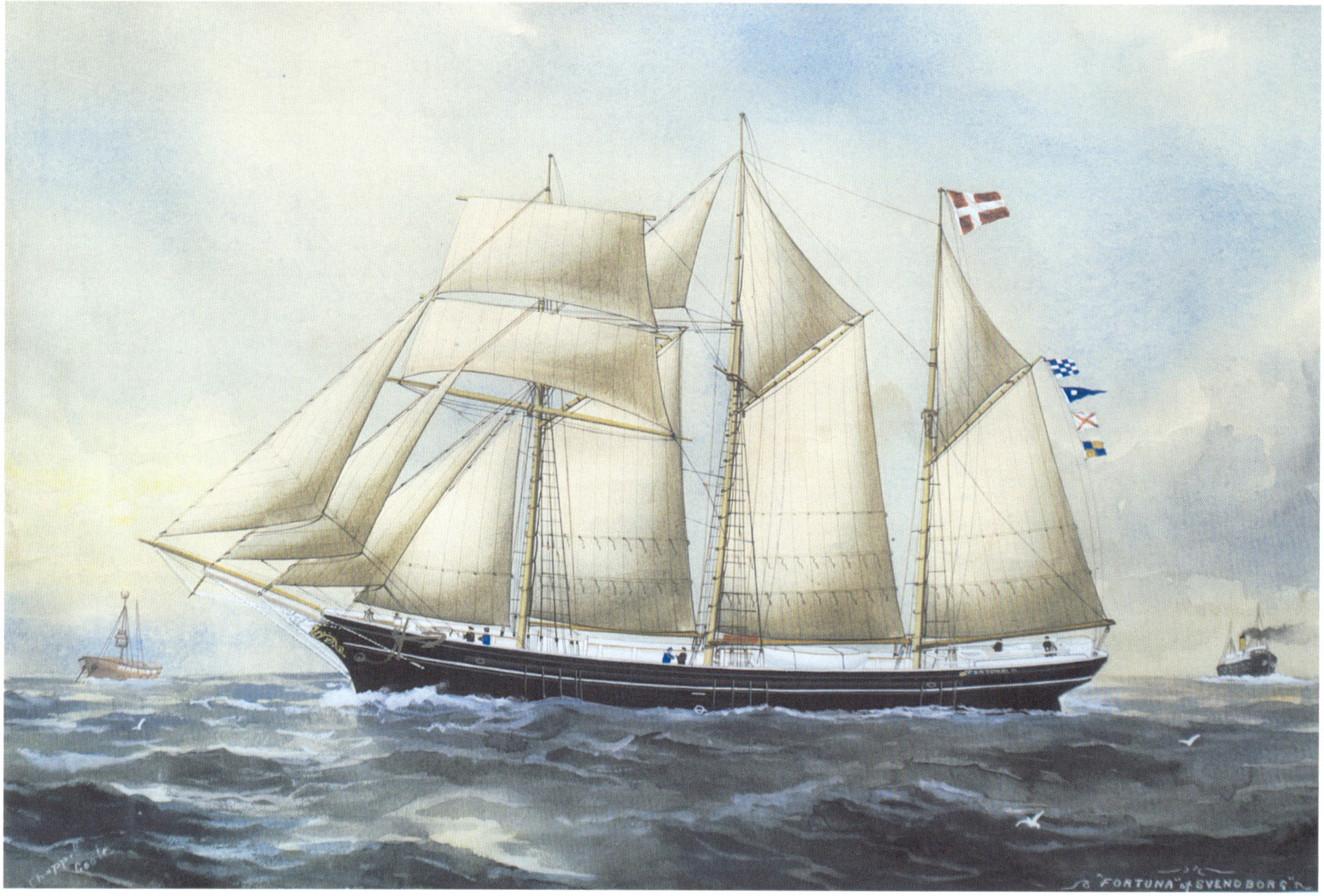

Troense Søfartsmuseum

FORTUNA OF SVENDBORG

Three-masted schooner; built 1892 at Ring Andersen shipyard, Svendborg.

Fortuna of Svendborg traded successfully under Danish ownership until 1933 when she was sold to Swedish owners.

The figurehead represented good fortune and is now preserved in Gothenburg. Reuben Chappell has depicted her about to pass a lightship, one of the features that ships sailing from Denmark to Cornwall would have passed off the south coast of England.

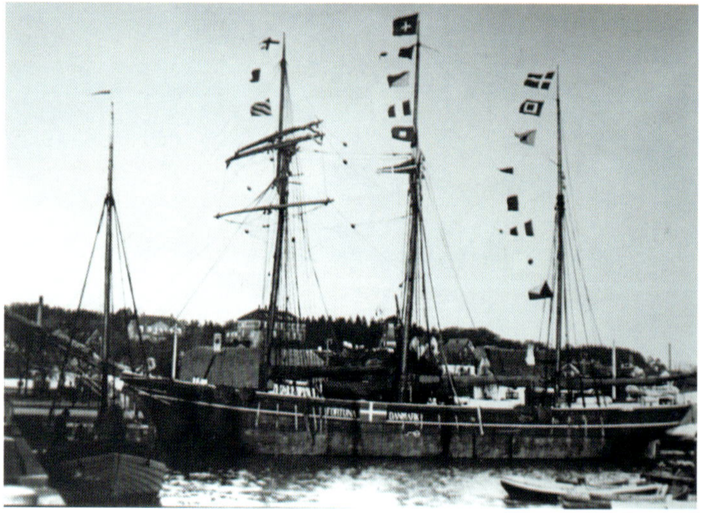

The Fortuna, Svendborg *Troense Søfartsmuseum*

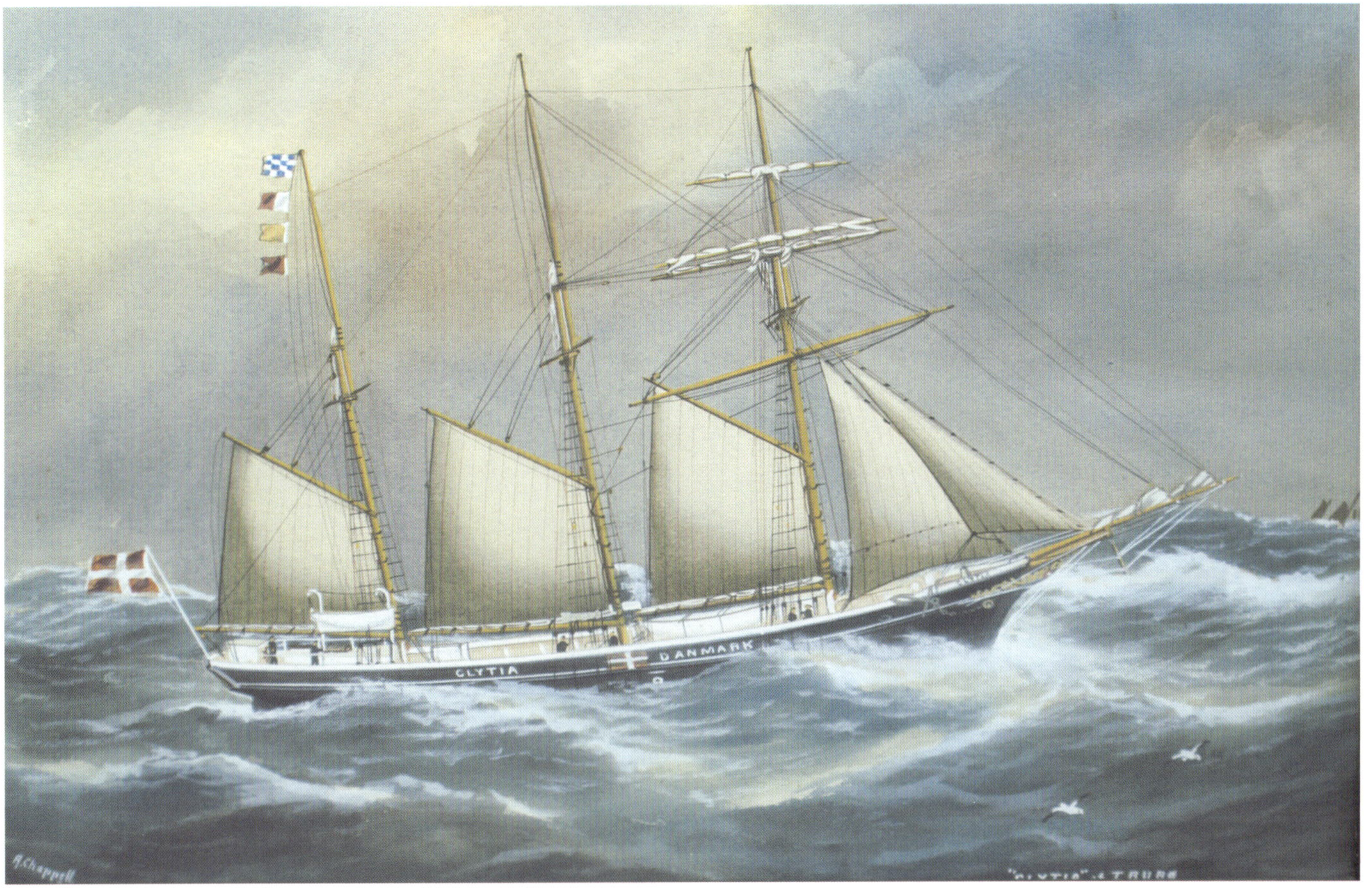

Troense Søfartsmuseum

Clytia of Thurø

Three-masted schooner; built 1896 in Thurø by N. P. Petersen

In this painting Chappell shows Clytia with reduced sail in a strong wind. Another sailing vessel is just visible on the horizon. The name and flag on the side indicate that the painting was made during the First World War. For many years she carried timber, sailing to Canada during the war, and afterwards Clytia worked in the Baltic and North Sea. She had several owners but kept her name until 1960 when it was changed to Holbaek. She later caught fire and sank.

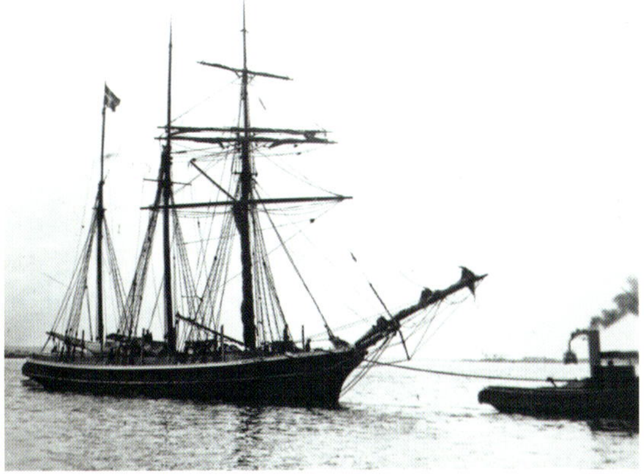
Under tow with steam tug Troense Søfartsmuseum

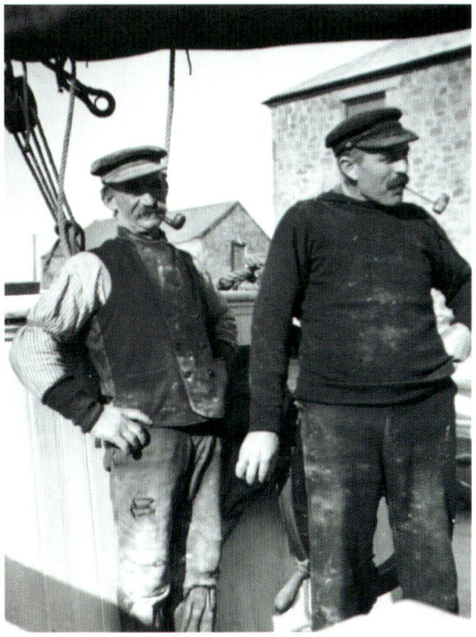
Crew of the Clytia Troense Søfartsmuseum

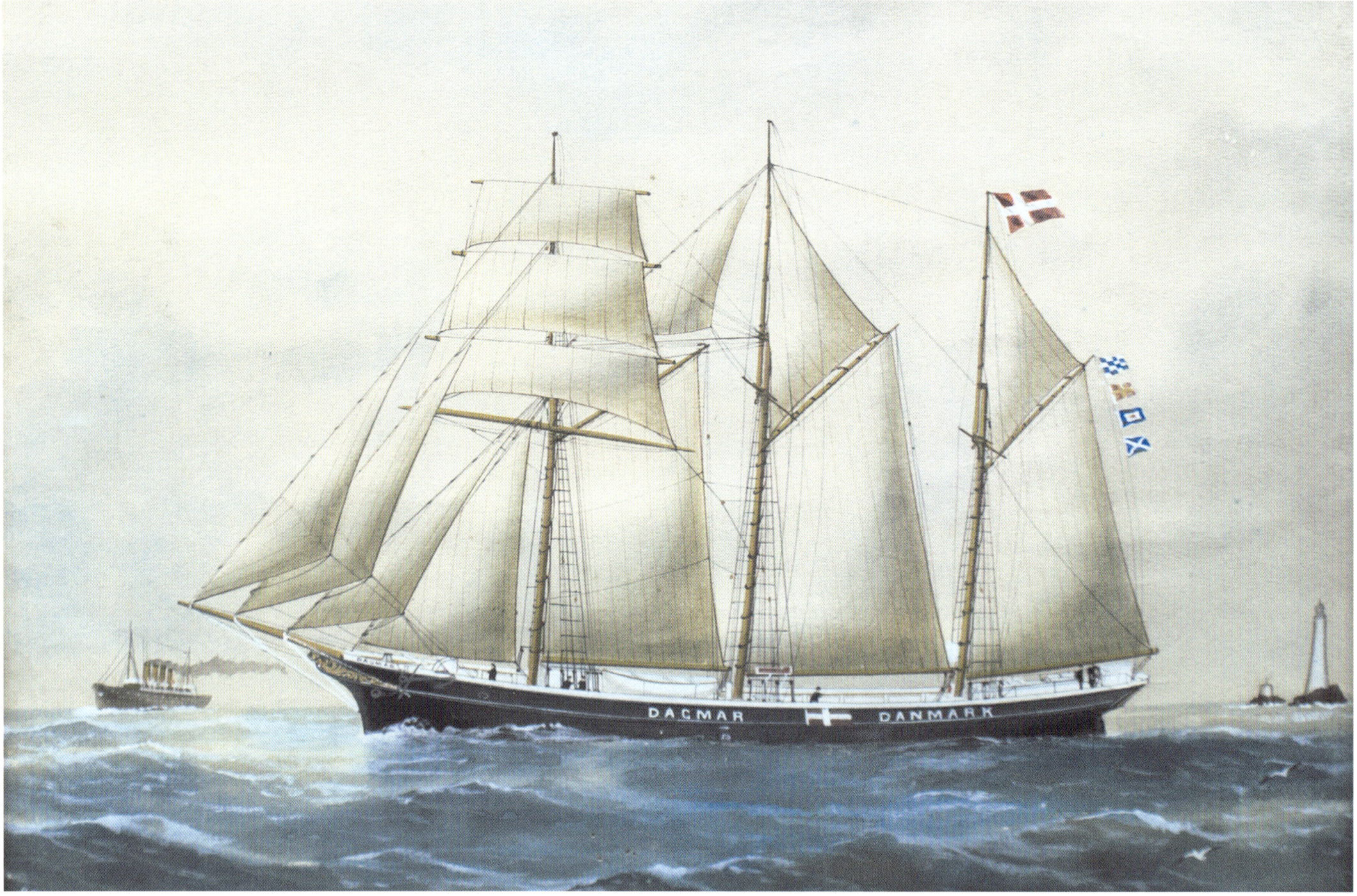

Troense Søfartsmuseum

Dagmar of Troense

Three-masted schooner; built 1911 -12 in Thurø by J Ph. Jorgensen

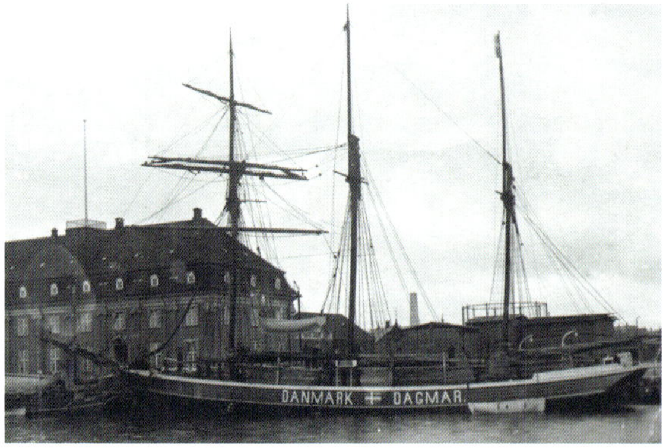

Dagmar in Port *Troense Søfartsmuseum*

For many years Dagmar worked the North Sea and Baltic and carried animal food from Bordeaux to Sweden. On the night of 8th/9th January 1925, she was run down by the barque Oakhurst in the English Channel, off the Isle of Wight. She sank within half an hour and the crew were rescued by an English steamship which landed in Portsmouth.

Painted during the First World War Reuben Chappell has shown Dagmar passing the Eddystone Light, as the ship would have done on the voyage to Cornwall from Denmark and back. The Eddystone, a small and very dangerous rock, lies some 14 miles S/SW, of Plymouth and 40 miles east of Start Point, and the lighthouse features in many of Chappell's paintings and was clearly an important feature of a voyage from Denmark.

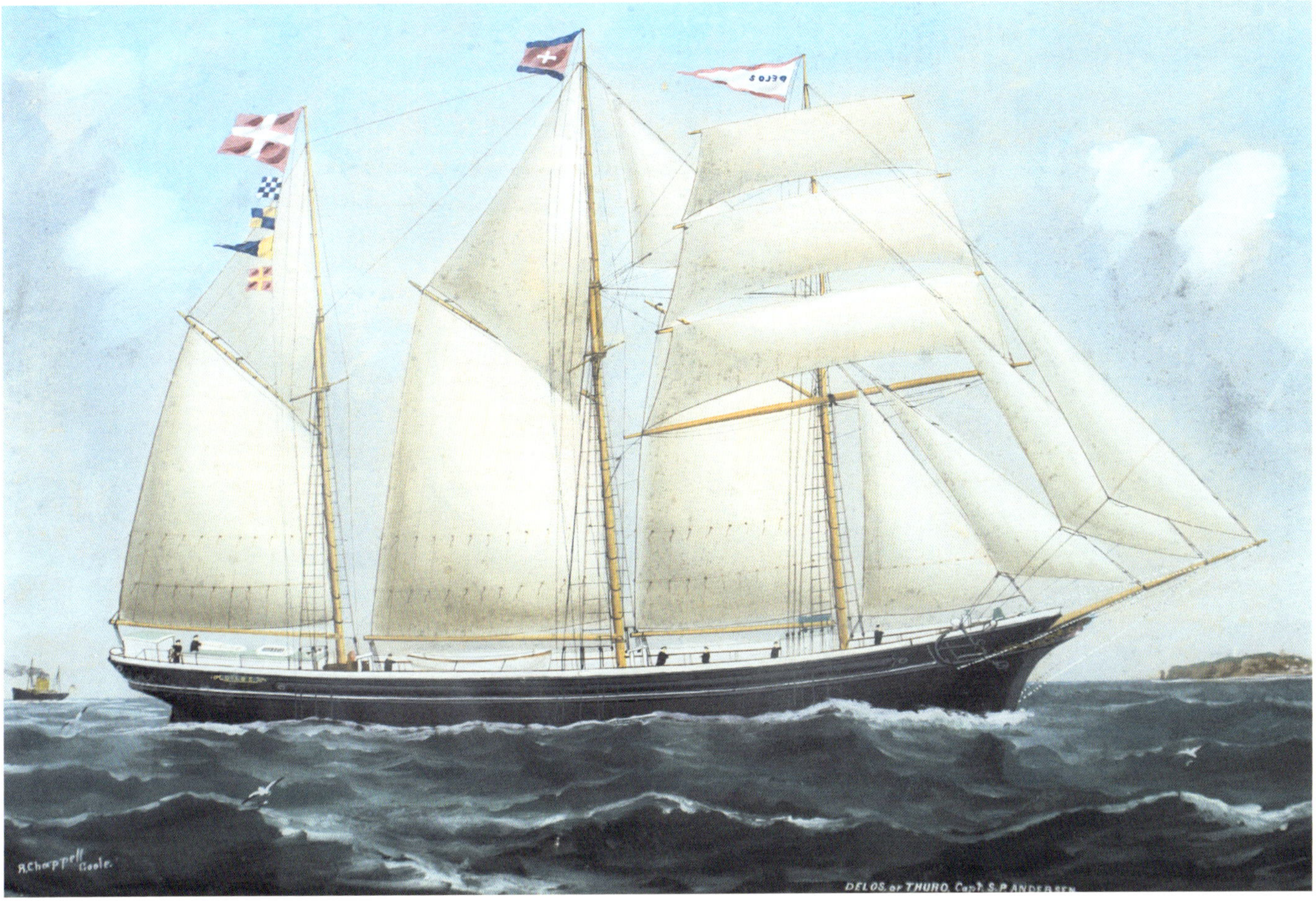

Troense Søfartsmuseum

Delos of Thurø

Three-masted schooner; built 1901 at Ring Andersen shipyard, Svendborg; Captain. S. P. Andersen.

The Ring Andersen shipyard in Svendborg where Delos was built is still operating, repairing and refitting sailing vessels. Delos sailed in the North Sea and the Mediterranean, and was still working until 1945 when, on 8th November she was grounded outside Helsingeland. Only one of the six crew survived.

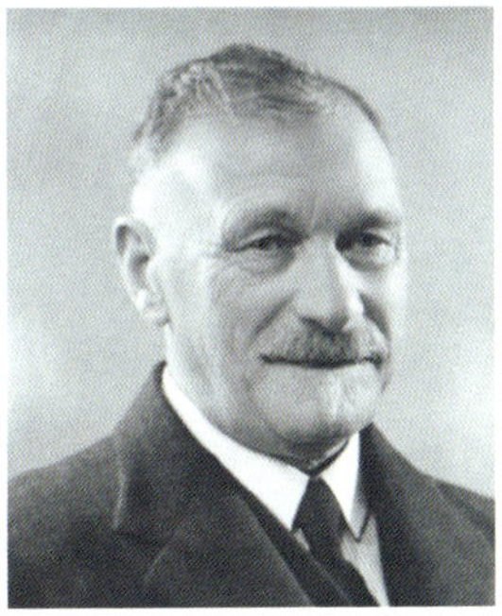

Captain SP Andersen

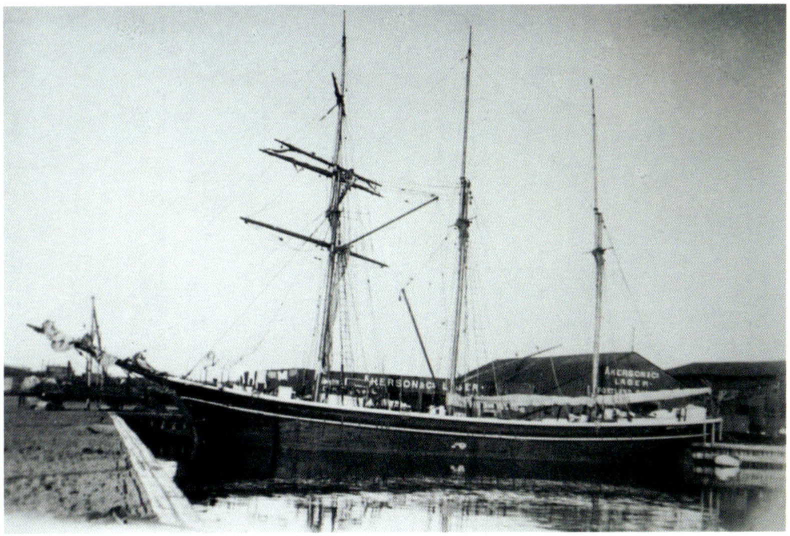

Delos of Thurø

Troense Søfartsmuseum

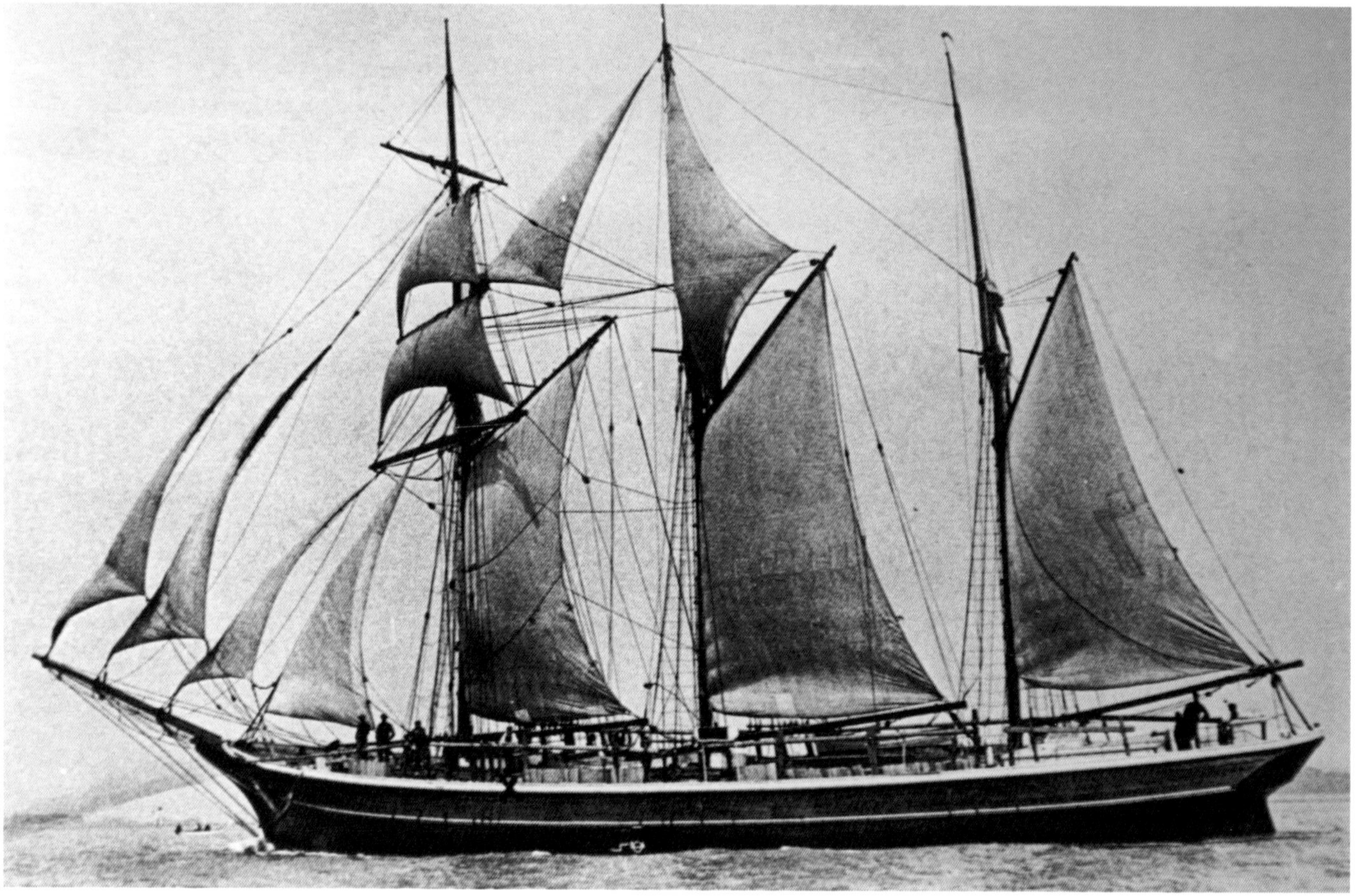

Lindhardt in full sail — Troense Søfartsmuseum

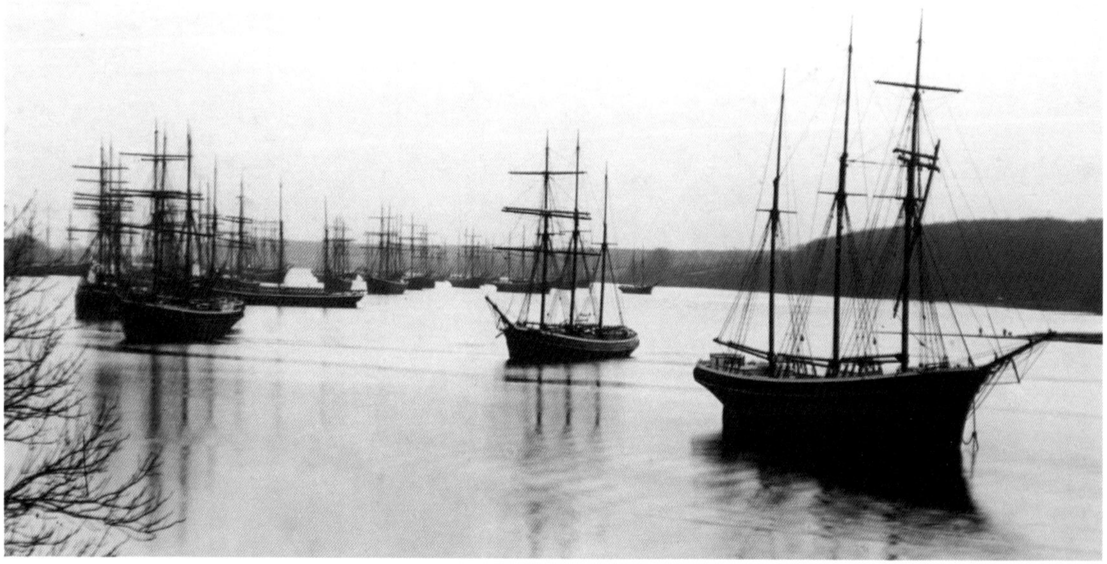

Ships at anchor, Thurø — Troense Søfartsmuseum

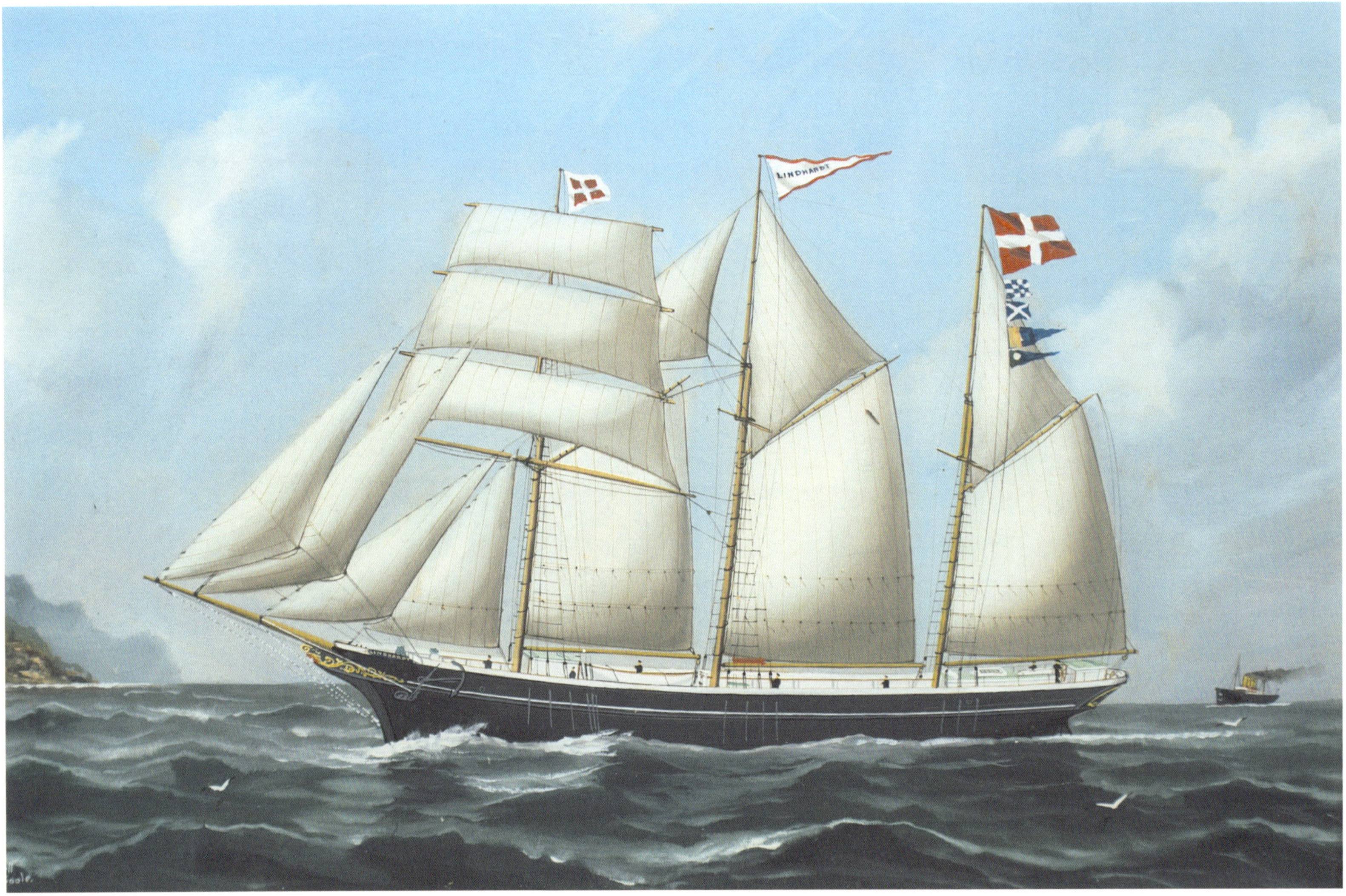

Troense Søfartsmuseum

Lindhardt of Thurø

Three-masted schooner; built 1902-3 by C. Bom

Lindhardt is known to have traded in the North and Baltic Seas as well as voyages to Reykjavik in Iceland. She was sunk by a German U-boat in the North Sea in 1917. The cargo was within the war restrictions, so the Germans granted compensation, admitting it was unintentionally hit.

Reuben Chappell shows the vessel passing Start Point on their voyage to the clay ports.

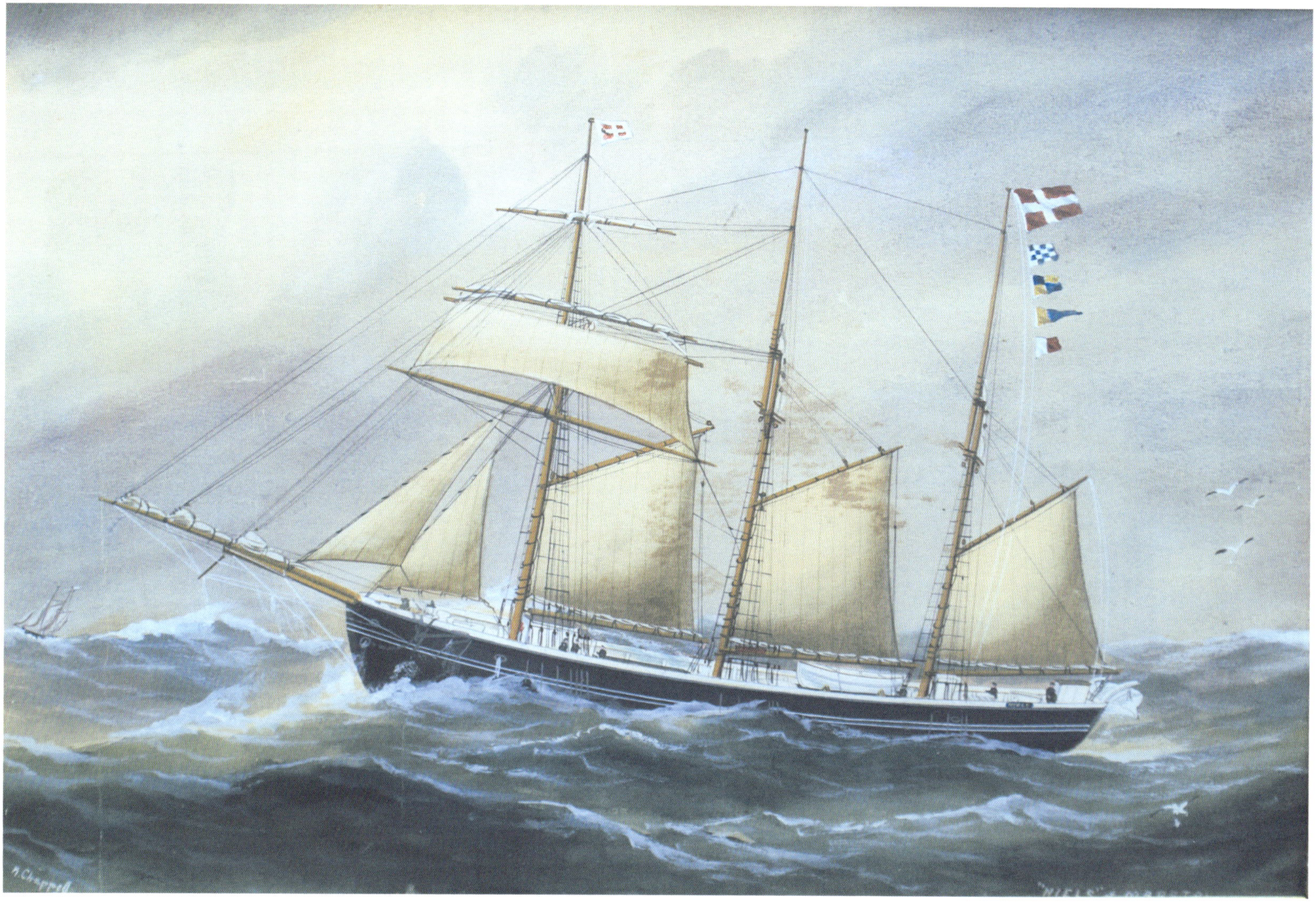

Troense Søfartsmuseum

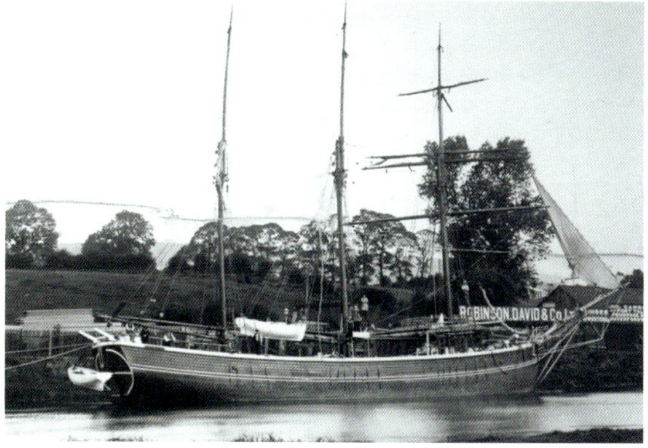

Niels in Welsh harbour *Troense Søfartsmuseum*

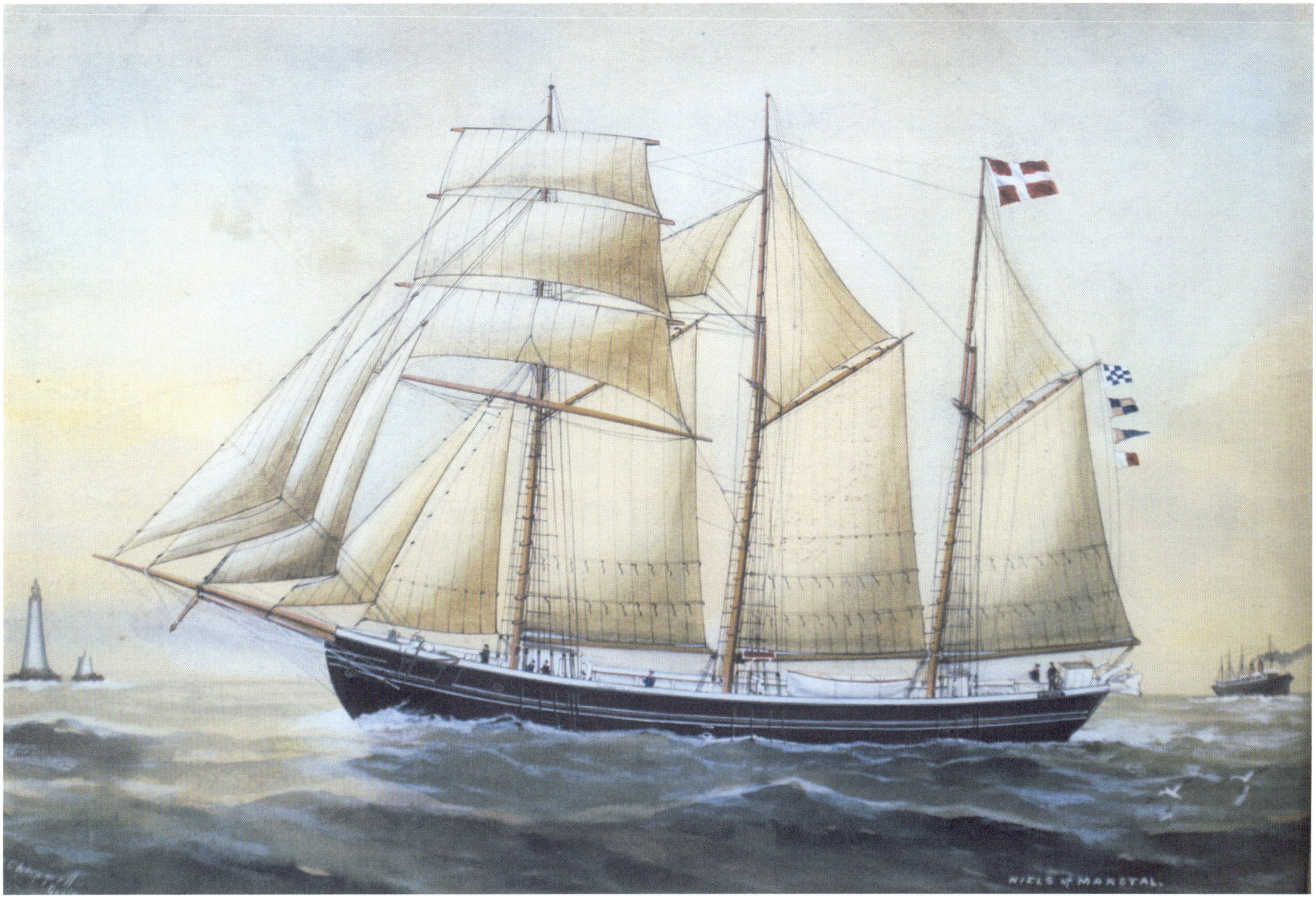

Troense Søfartsmuseum

NIELS OF MARSTAL

As was often his practice, Reuben Chapell shows Niels of Marstal in a pair of fair-and-foul-weather paintings. The hull shape, with its curved bow, is typical of traditional Danish sailing ship design of the period. The fine-weather painting shows the Niels passing the Eddystone on her return voyage to Denmark.

West Country Ships

Reuben Chappell witnessed and recorded the zenith and decline of the great days of commercial sail. At the same time he recorded the rise of steam and oil powered vessels. His paintings show a part of our maritime history that has now largely gone for ever.

Just a few of the ships that Reuben Chappell painted have survived to the present day. One or two of those have been painstakingly restored and cared for by people who love them. The Kathleen and May at Bideford, and the Bessie Ellen based in Plymouth, are two such West Country sailing ships. Some of the traditional Humber vessels have been restored by the Humber Keel and Sloop Preservation Society, and in Denmark several ships have survived and are still sailing. But for the most part they have gone, either lost at sea or abandoned when they became unprofitable, wooden ships left to rot in the mud of some quiet creek, and steel vessels broken up for scrap metal. Not only have the ships gone but also the culture and the way of life that produced and used them.

It is important to realise the spirit of enterprise that drove men to invest sufficient money to commission the building of a new ship, and to sink their wealth in a speculative venture the success of which was always dependent on weather.

Ships were sometimes family or company owned, or were owned by one individual, possibly the master and a number of shareholders. There were 64 shares, and profits were divided according to the number of shares owned. When things went well returns could be good, but this was always an unpredictable business. Ships required constant maintenance, refits and repairs, in addition to the cost of wages of master and crew. There were times when they had to wait while a cargo was found, and then there was always the possibility that the ship could be damaged by collision, dismasted in a gale, or worse, sometimes ships simply disappeared at sea with everything lost, ship, cargo and men.

In time there developed a system of insurance for these ships, ship owners forming a mutual association. Every member registered, and paid two or three percent of the value of each ship. If a vessel was lost, each member made a contribution, the sum depending on the value of the ships they had covered. The system needed enough vessels to spread the risk. These mutual associations were an integral part of the shipping business and had regulations regarding the standards of ship maintenance and the qualifications of ship's masters.

In the West country, the ships were built in harbours, creeks, coves, estuaries and on riversides and beaches all around the coast, by skilled men using timber that was available to them. Trees from farms and estates were purchased and felled. Cut into transportable pieces, they were loaded on to horse drawn timber wagons to be carried to the boatyard. A great deal of timber was also imported from Europe, from Canada and especially Scandinavia. Pieces were selected and stored until sufficiently seasoned to use. During the seasoning process

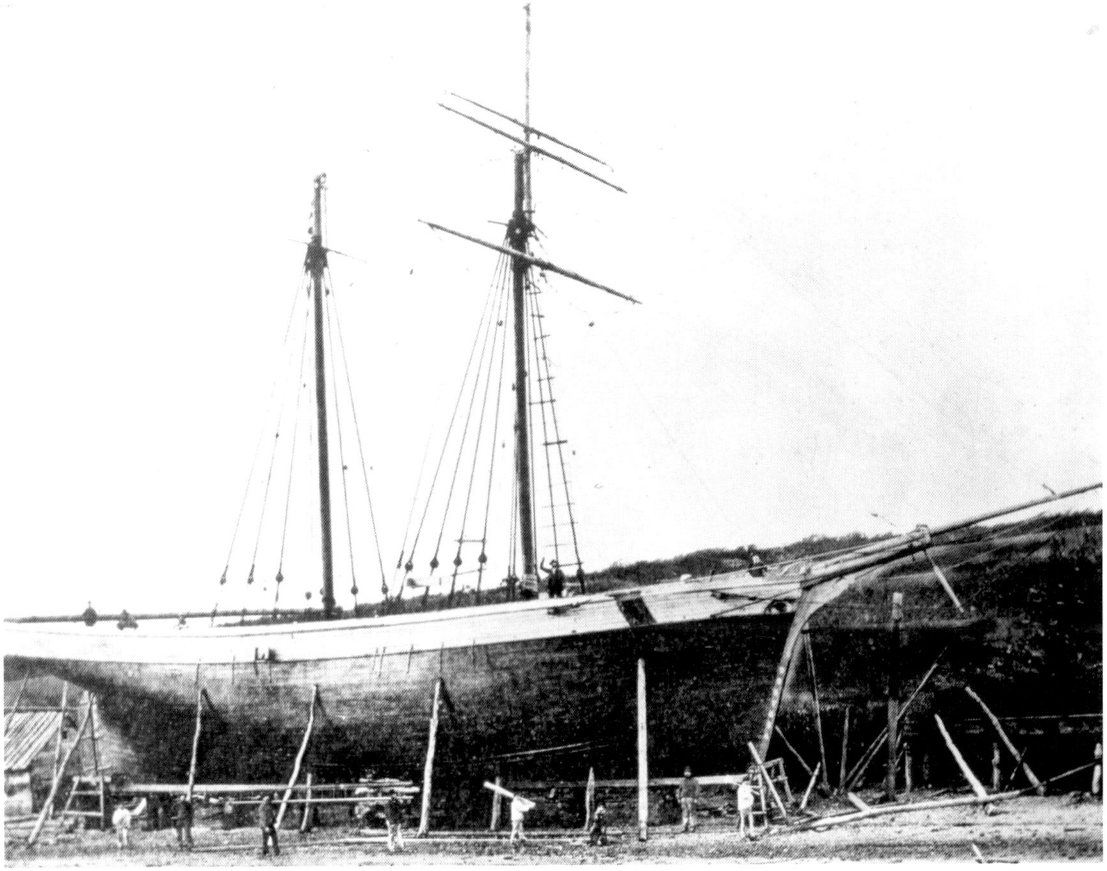

Building the schooner Louise at Clements Yard, the Gannel, Newquay *Royal Cornwall Museum*

large pieces of timber were stacked in a way that allowed air to circulate. Sometimes timber was buried in mud, or left in a river for a number of years.

After seasoning the required pieces were then sawn with a pit saw, a large saw worked by two men, one man in a pit and the other on the surface. Every piece of timber used in a ship was sawn by hand in this way. Bigger yards had several pairs of sawyers.

The keel was laid and the lines of the ship laid out by eye, by the experienced master shipbuilder who worked to a design agreed with the owners. In the larger shipbuilding yards the design, showing the lines of the ship, was expressed in the form of a small scale model of half the hull, and the measurements of the model were scaled up to build the ship.

First the bow and stern posts and then the cut ribs were joined to the keel. Then the ship's planks were attached, the masts stepped, and deck added. The planking had to be caulked to make the ship water tight, and then the hull was tarred. At about this stage of completion the vessel was launched, providing an occasion for celebration.

The ship had to be rigged with spars, gaffs, booms, ratlines etc., and the sails, which had been made specially

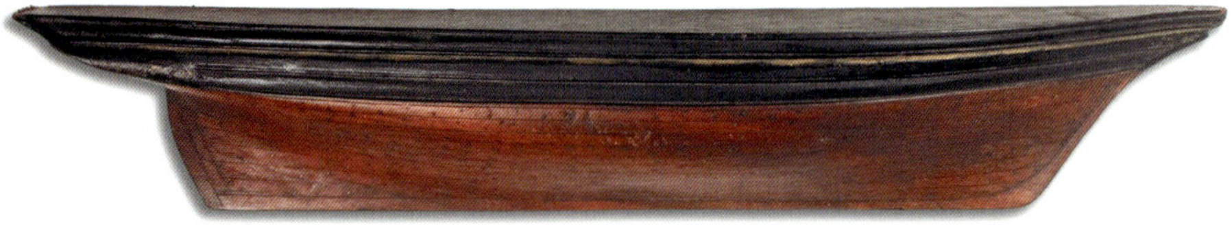

Half model of a Bideford Fruit Ship circa mid 19th Century.

Private Collection

for the ship by the sail-maker, were fitted. Anchors and chains were forged in the foundry, and the ship's fittings made in the blacksmith's shop. The building of the ship required the very best skill for at sea she would have to withstand the worst of weathers, and if there was a weakness the sea would find it.

If the ship was going 'Deep Water,' that is outside 'Home Trade' waters, the hull would have to be sheathed. Below the waterline a layer of tar-soaked felt was covered with copper or yellow metal to protect the hull timber from wood boring beetles. It was said that without sheathing one trip to tropical waters or to the Mediterranean might ruin the hull.

During the building of first-class vessels, surveyors would call at the shipyards to inspect the shipbuilder's work. They could, and did, condemn parts of the work and insist that they were rebuilt. When ready the ship would finally be inspected and be registered with Lloyds, the best being classed A1 or A1+.

There were hundreds of shipbuilders located in the West Country. Some of the more notable ones were W. Date of Kingsbridge, John Stephens of Fowey, C & J Clements of Newquay, Massey of Portreath, N. Schoble of Malpas, Harveys of Hayle, Samuel Moss of Par, K.P. Harris and the Cook brothers of Appledore, and F.J. Carver of Bridgewater.

A suitably skilled master and crew would obviously be essential. The qualifications for masters differed, those sailing in sqare-rigged vessels needing to be more qualified than those in tfore and aft-rigged vessels. The captain, mate and crew were usually local men from the port where the ship was registered.

Finding suitable cargoes to carry from port to port was a business in itself, involving brokers who were able to 'fix' a cargo. Some of the brokers became ship owners, for example John Stephens of Fowey, who built a highly successful business as a broker, ship owner and ship builder. His business became known as 'The Company of Little Ships'. His ships were of the highest standards, always well maintained and so were held in high regard by merchants seeking the best ships for their cargoes.

As to where trade might take a vessel, Basil Greenhill in his book 'The Merchant Schooners Vol 1' gives a vivid description by tracing the voyages of one of John Stephens's ships, the 75' schooner Isabella. "On the 10th May 1899, she sailed from Fowey to Cadiz in ballast, and there loaded salt for Newfoundland; from Newfoundland she sailed to Viassa with fish. She crossed to Newfoundland again, loaded, and sailed for Oporto. Once more she returned to Newfoundland and once more she came back across the Atlantic to Oporto. From there she sailed for Fowey, and she arrived at her home port on 28th November, having accomplished the voyage to the peninsula and back, and six crossings of the Atlantic in six months and eighteen days. This schooner, it will be remembered, was just 75' long and her crew consisted of four men, her master John Stephens's grandson, and three other men from Fowey."

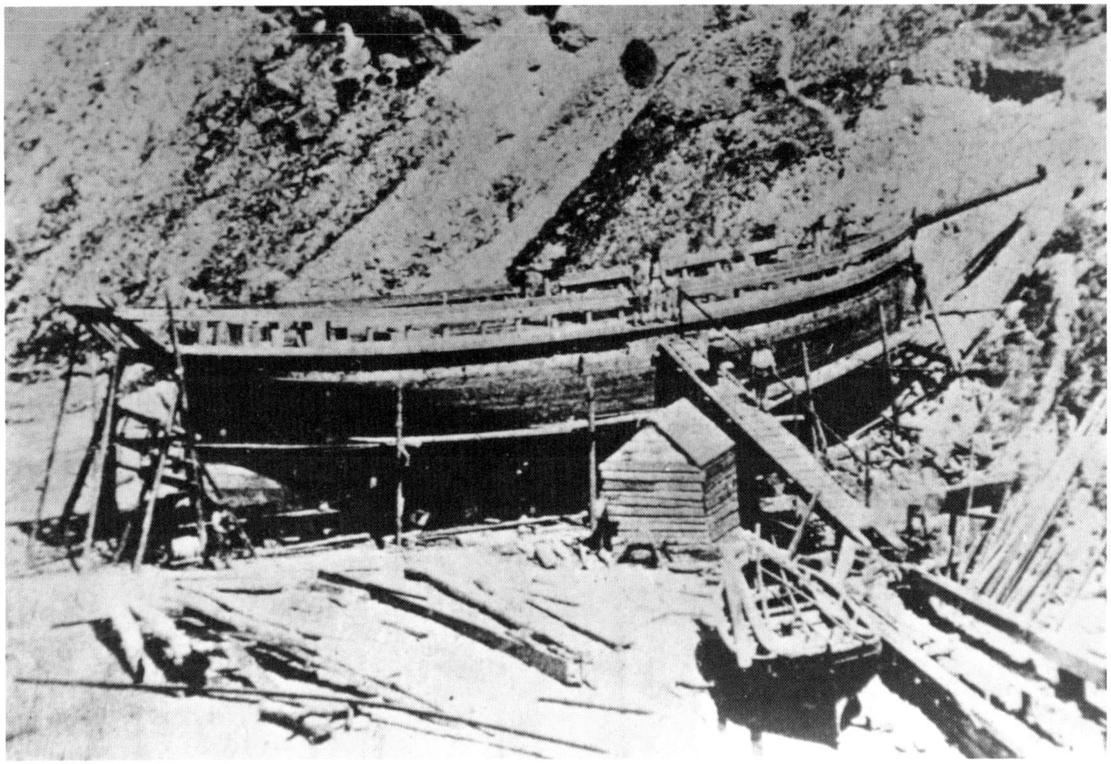

Trevellas under construction, St Agnes *Richard Gillis Collection*

To have made so many voyages in such short a time seems almost incredible, yet in those days such voyages were not unusual. 75' is small for a schooner but they were usually under 100'. They had to be small to sail in and out of small tidal harbours.

At the time, shipping was the best and most efficient means of transport. Until the latter part of the 19th century the rail networks were poor or non-existent, and road transport was slow, difficult and uncomfortable. Transport by sea, in spite of all the difficulties and dangers involved, was still the most efficient means of moving goods.

Naturally, around the coast communities grew - towns and villages, most of whose inhabitants' livelihoods were dependent in some way on maritime trade. A great deal of all this enterprise and industry remains largely forgotten. Little has been written or recorded of the way of life surrounding these little ships. This makes Reuben Chappell's contribution all the more important, though as he rarely dated his pictures it is unlikely that he himself would have been aware that the paintings he was producing would come to have historical value.

Although steam vessels were becoming more common, before the First World War a large amount of the coasting and short sea trade was still being handled by sailing vessels. These vessels, distinguished by their sail layout, sloop, ketch, schooner, brig, brigantine, barque and barquentine would have been common sights around the coast in the 19th century. Thousands of ships were built and their trade took them around the shores of the British Isles to the Baltic and European ports. They carried all manner of goods: coal, salt fish, fruit, china clay, cement, slates, bricks, gravel, scrap metal, pilchards, fertiliser, salt, phosphate, farm produce, livestock, cowhides, grain and stones, etc. All the cargoes were loaded and unloaded by hand.

In the coasting trade around the British Isles, these vessels did the work that road and rail transport do today. But many of these small sailing vessels went far from the British Isles. There were regular crossings and established trade links with North and South America. One of the principal transatlantic routes was to Canada, in the Newfoundland dry salt cod trade which employed a large number of European ships, amongst which many were from the West of England. Of course, sailing ships were entirely dependent on the weather and in favourable conditions they made surprisingly fast passages. The voyage from St John's in Newfoundland to Britain, for example, could take as little as 13 days. In poor weather the same journey might take three months. As a rule the owners did not expect word of a schooner's arrival until 25 or 30 days had elapsed on an eastward passage, and 45 or 50 days on a westward passage. The voyages across the Atlantic often followed a triangular course. Ships from the West Country often took wine, salt or general cargo over to Newfoundland, dried cod from there to the Mediterranean, then returned to Britain with dried fruit from Italy or Greece. The salt cod they carried to the Mediterranean was caught by Canadian fishermen on the fishing banks, off the coast of Nova Scotia and Newfoundland.

The schooners generally carried four or five men drawn from the area around their home port. Conditions aboard contrasted strongly with the graceful lines of these vessels. At sea all the work aboard was done by hand, from hoisting the anchor, to setting the sails and pumping water from the bilges. This required a great deal of effort and often needed most of the crew, day and night, and in all weathers. A coal stove in the galley was used for cooking, but in rough seas it was often impossible to get hot food for several days. In port the crew were kept busy loading and unloading cargo.

"Life consisted mainly of unrelenting hard work, often done in considerable discomfort and danger. Long working days were unavoidable, and there was very little leisure and certainly no holidays as we know them today. There was always something to do, scraping, painting, rigging and sail repairs and so on. When in the port the crew usually dealt with the cargo, discharging and loading. When at sea there were usually sail adjustments to be made, day and night, often needing all the hands to take advantage of the wind, and make the fastest possible passage."

Bainbridge, George. *The Wooden Ships and the Iron Men of the Cornish China Clay Trade*. Charlestown Estates Ltd. 1980.

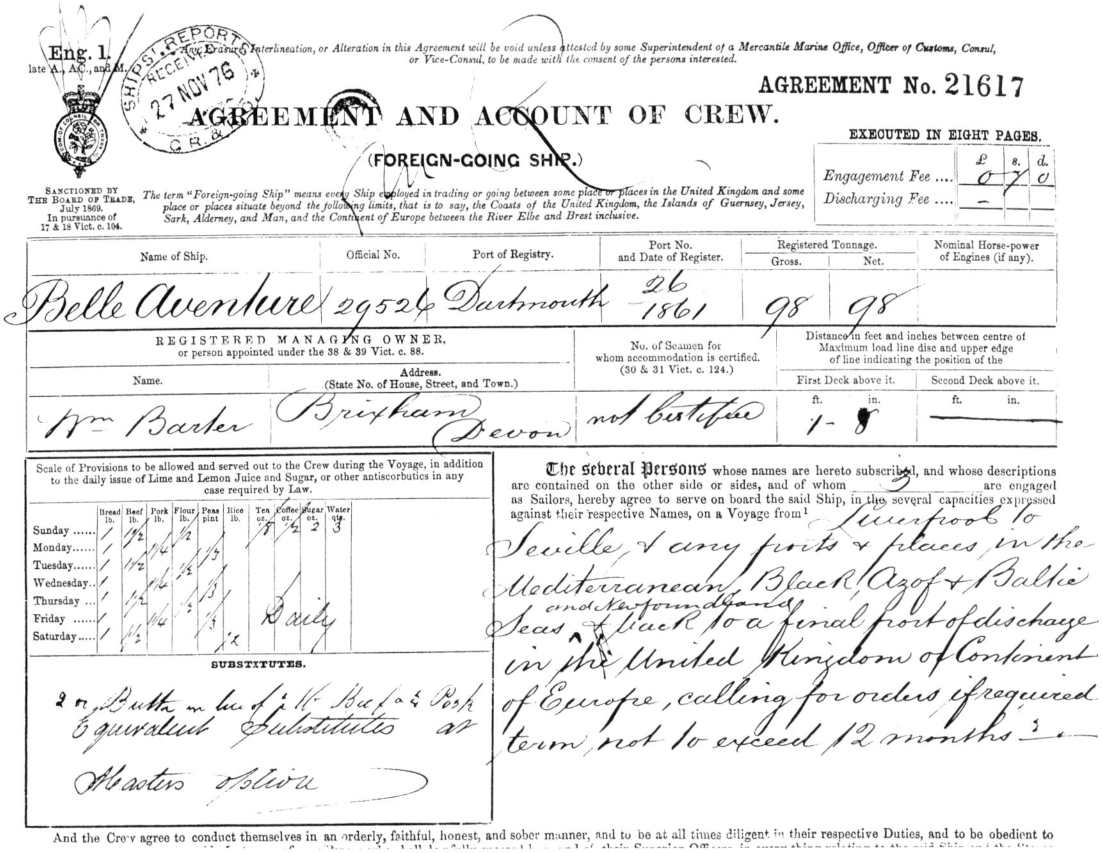

Eng. 1.
late A., A.C., and M.

SHIPS' REPORTS RECEIVED 27 NOV 76 G.R. &

Any Erasure, Interlineation, or Alteration in this Agreement will be void unless attested by some Superintendent of a Mercantile Marine Office, Officer of Customs, Consul, or Vice-Consul, to be made with the consent of the persons interested.

AGREEMENT No. 21617

AGREEMENT AND ACCOUNT OF CREW.

(FOREIGN-GOING SHIP.)

EXECUTED IN EIGHT PAGES.

	£	s.	d.
Engagement Fee	0	7	0
Discharging Fee	–		

SANCTIONED BY THE BOARD OF TRADE, July 1869. In pursuance of 17 & 18 Vict. c. 104.

The term "Foreign-going Ship" means every Ship employed in trading or going between some place or places in the United Kingdom and some place or places situate beyond the following limits, that is to say, the Coasts of the United Kingdom, the Islands of Guernsey, Jersey, Sark, Alderney, and Man, and the Continent of Europe between the River Elbe and Brest inclusive.

Name of Ship.	Official No.	Port of Registry.	Port No. and Date of Register.	Registered Tonnage. Gross.	Registered Tonnage. Net.	Nominal Horse-power of Engines (if any).
Belle Aventure	29524	Dartmouth	26 1861	98	98	

REGISTERED MANAGING OWNER, or person appointed under the 38 & 39 Vict. c. 88. Name.	Address. (State No. of House, Street, and Town.)	No. of Seamen for whom accommodation is certified. (30 & 31 Vict. c. 124.)	Distance in feet and inches between centre of Maximum load line disc and upper edge of line indicating the position of the First Deck above it. ft. in.	Second Deck above it. ft. in.
Wm Barker	Brixham Devon	not certified	1 – 8	——

Scale of Provisions to be allowed and served out to the Crew during the Voyage, in addition to the daily issue of Lime and Lemon Juice and Sugar, or other antiscorbutics in any case required by Law.

	Bread lb.	Beef lb.	Pork lb.	Flour lb.	Peas pint	Rice lb.	Tea oz.	Coffee oz.	Sugar oz.	Water qts.
Sunday	1	1½		½			⅛	½	2	3
Monday	1		1¼		⅓					
Tuesday	1	1½		½						
Wednesday	1		1¼		⅓					
Thursday	1	1½		½	⅓					
Friday	1		1¼		⅓					
Saturday	1	1½				½	Daily			

SUBSTITUTES.

2 oz Butter in lieu of 1 lb Beef or Pork Equivalent Substitutes at Masters option

The several Persons whose names are hereto subscribed, and whose descriptions are contained on the other side or sides, and of whom 5 are engaged as Sailors, hereby agree to serve on board the said Ship, in the several capacities expressed against their respective Names, on a Voyage from[1] Liverpool to Seville, & any ports & places, in the Mediterranean, Black, Azof & Baltic and Newfoundland Seas, & back to a final port of discharge in the United Kingdom or Continent of Europe, calling for orders if required term, not to exceed 12 months.

And the Crew agree to conduct themselves in an orderly, faithful, honest, and sober manner, and to be at all times diligent in their respective Duties, and to be obedient to

THE AGREEMENT AND ACCOUNT OF CREW

These are fascinating historical documents which the owner, master and each member of the crew were required to sign. The agreement covered the terms and conditions of employment and laid out a general outline of the duration of the voyage which they were undertaking. In this agreement of 1876 for the Dartmouth schooner Belle Aventure the men who are being engaged as seamen "hereby agree to sail on board the said ship in the several capacities expressed against their respective Names, on a Voyage from Liverpool to Seville and any ports and places in the Mediterranean, Black, Azof and Baltic seas and Newfoundland and back to a final port of discharge in the United Kingdom or continent of Europe, calling for orders if required, term not to exceed twelve months." "and the crew agree to conduct themselves in an orderly, faithful, honest and sober manner, and to be at all times Diligent in their respective Duties, and to be obedient to the lawful command of the said master" etc.

The men were paid at the end of the voyage in order to discourage desertion. This vessel probably sailed to Seville for salt which would have been carried to St John's, Newfoundland where it was used in the production of dry salt cod, the cargo that would be brought back to Europe.

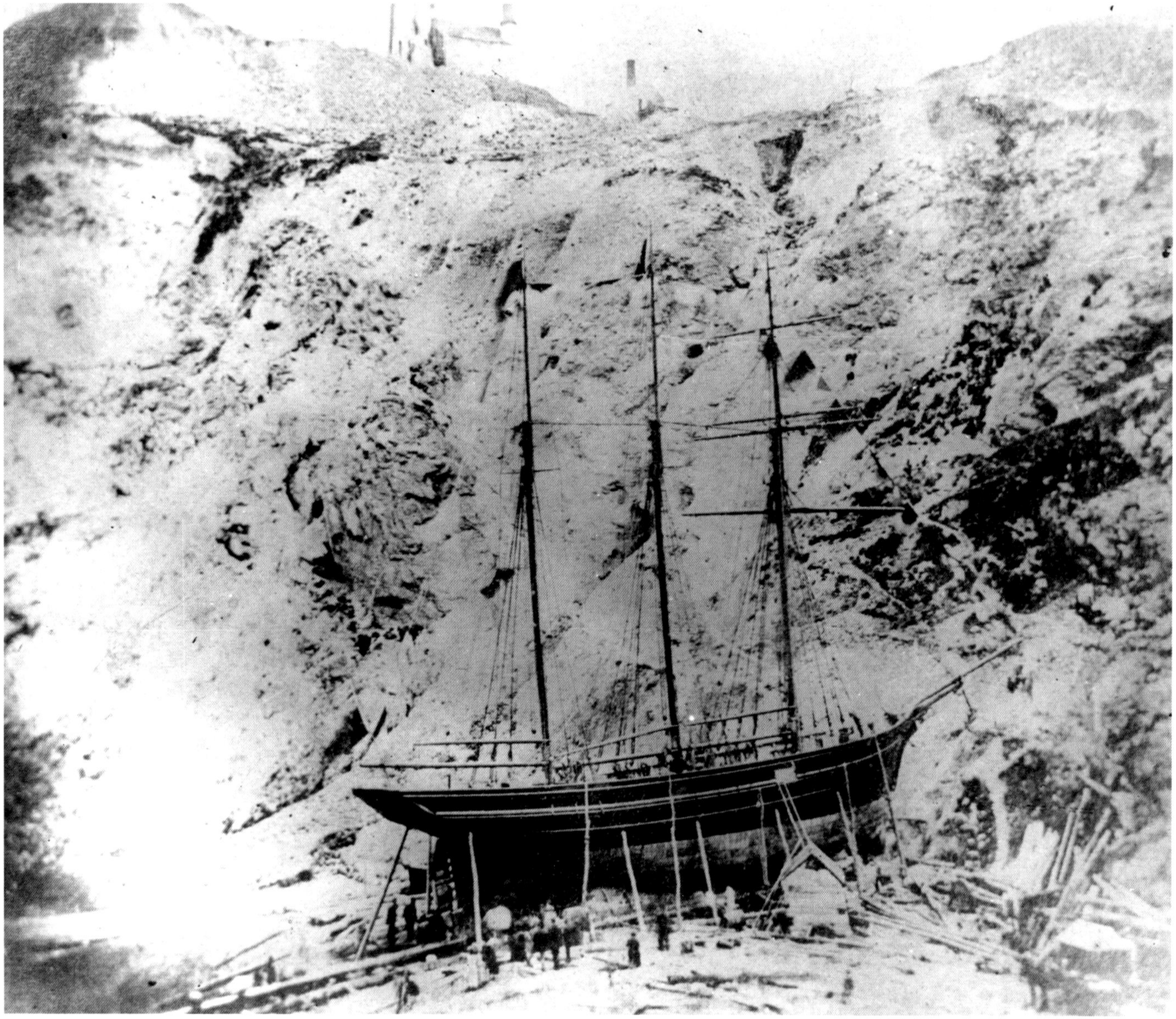

Trevellas ready for launching, St Agnes. Note the mine buildings at the top of the cliff. *Royal Cornwall Museum*

TREVELLAS

ON 68864; three-masted schooner; built 1876 by M.T. Hitchens, St Agnes; 128 gross tons; 97.0' x 22.3' x 11.4'.

Ships were built in some unlikely places, but the yard of M. T. Hitchens at the bottom of a cliff in Cornwall must be unique. Hitchens was a ship owner and builder from St Agnes, and he built several other ships on the site on the foreshore of Trevaunance Cove right under Goonglaze Mine. St Agnes, launched in 1873, Goonglaze in 1874, and Lady Agnes in 1877. At this time St Agnes has a harbour, since destroyed by the sea.

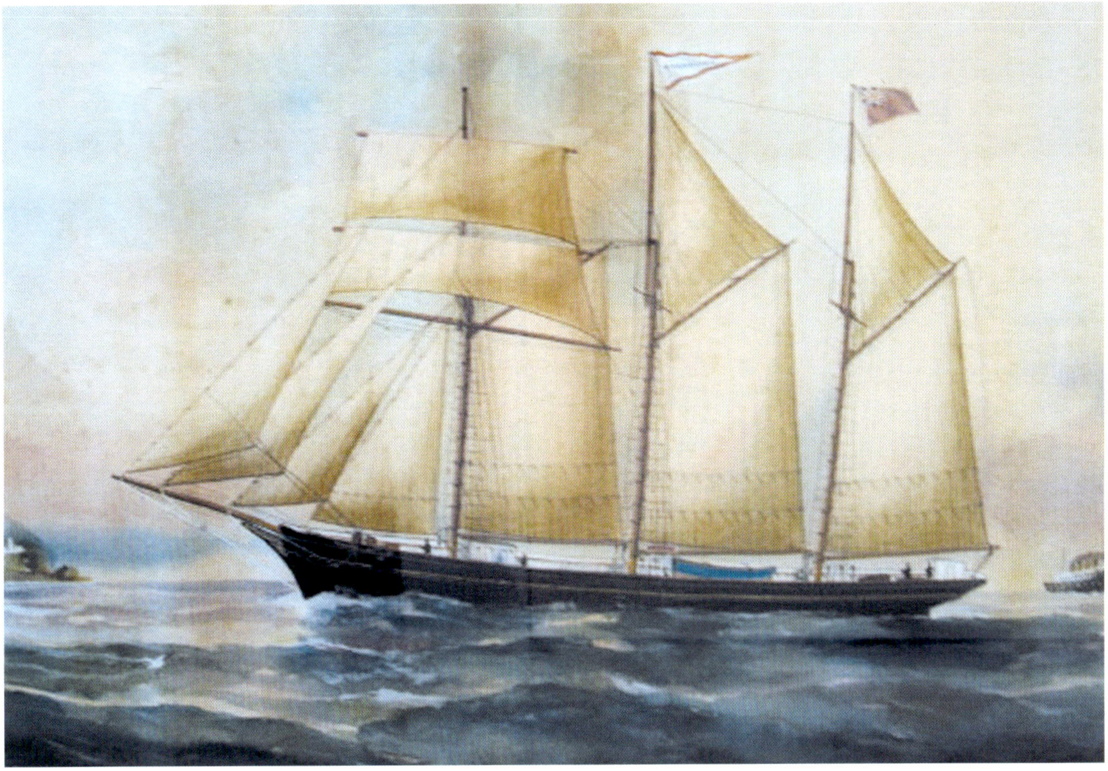

Goole Museum and Art Gallery

Trevellas was intended to trade deep sea, as she was copper sheathed. The vessel was launched in July 1876 fully rigged and needed only her sails to be ready for sea. For many years she sailed from Fowey, and was renowned as a very fast ship. With Katie Cluett and Result, Trevellas was known as "the fastest of all the schooners of the narrow seas" *The Merchant Schooner,* Basil Greenhill.

In 1929 Trevellas was sold to Irish owners and fitted with an engine. In November 1930 she sailed from Port Talbot to New Ross, Ireland, with coals. "A few days later" some wreckage, identifiedas hers, was found on the Hat & Barrel Rocks, Bristol Channel.

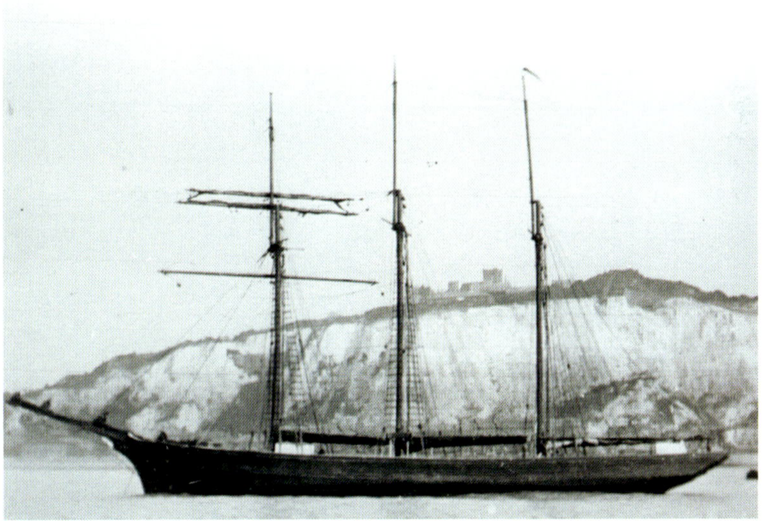

Trevellas at anchor off Rochester *Royal Cornwall Museum*

KATIE OF PADSTOW

ON 80410; pitch pine on oak; built 1881 by John Cowl Padstow; 100 tons; 88.9' x 22.9' x 7'3'.

Katie was built as a replacement for another ship also called the Katie, ON80401 launched in 1878; unfortunately she foundered off Land's End in April 1881.

The second Katie, again built by John Cowl for Thomas Jenkins of Newquay, was launched in Padstow in 1881. Always considered a fast and beautiful ship, she sailed a few times to Newfoundland for dry salt cod and also carried slate to the Continent. Newquay was at that time a thriving port and many ships were owned there. Ships from Newquay regularly carried cargoes of pilchards to the Mediterranean.

Katie remained in Newquay until 1930 when she was sold to Clunes and Co of Par and was employed sailing regularly out of Par to the Thames and Runcorn with china clay. This continued until the Second World War, during which time she was managed by John Stephens becoming part of his 'Company of Little Ships.'

From 1931 Katie was commanded by the well known Capt. W R Cort. Originally from the Channel Islands, he was a very experienced seaman, but always in sailing ships. Katie had been fitted with an engine, and her topsails removed, but the engine proved to be more trouble than it was worth and was removed in 1935, and the topsails reinstated. So for a few years she became the last sailing cargo schooner without an engine in Europe. Because of this, in 1939 Katie was banned from the English Channel, and worked the west coast up to Scotland carrying coal. On one such voyage during the war she was attacked by a

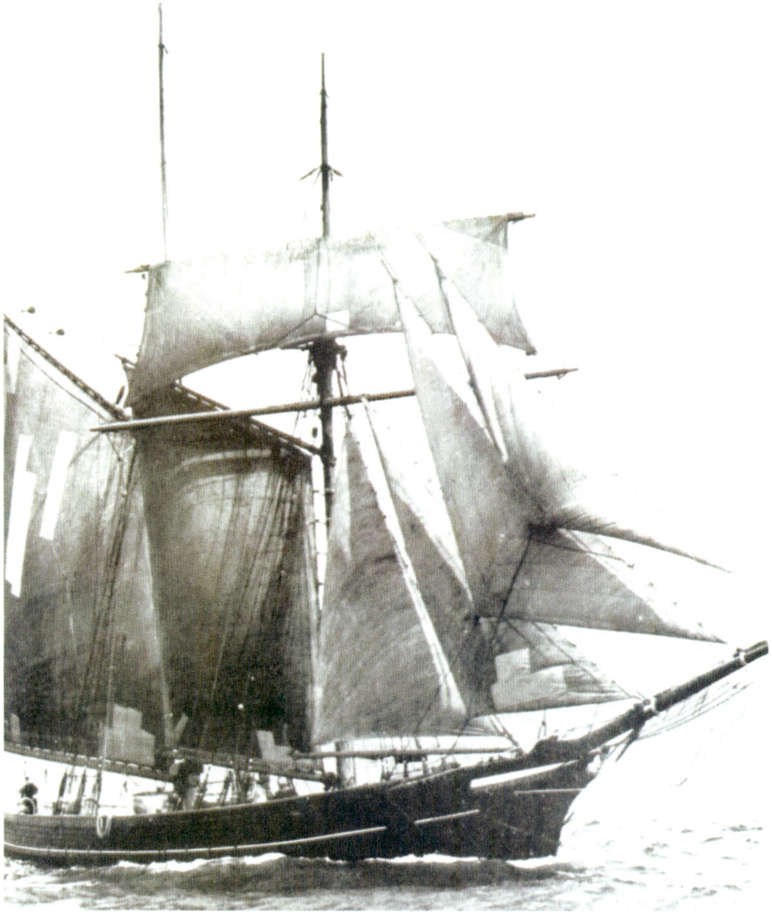

Katie of Padstow — *Richard Gillis Collection*

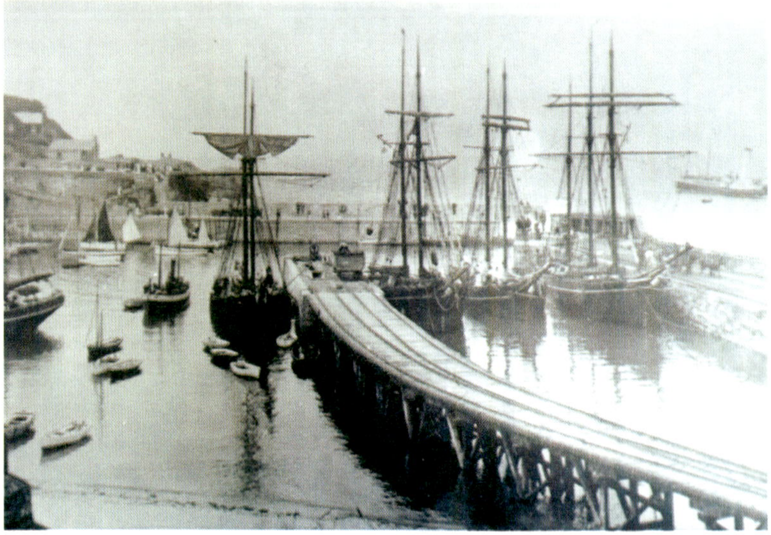

Schooners Hettie, Fairy Maid, Katie and Emma in Newquay harbour — *Richard Gillis Collection*

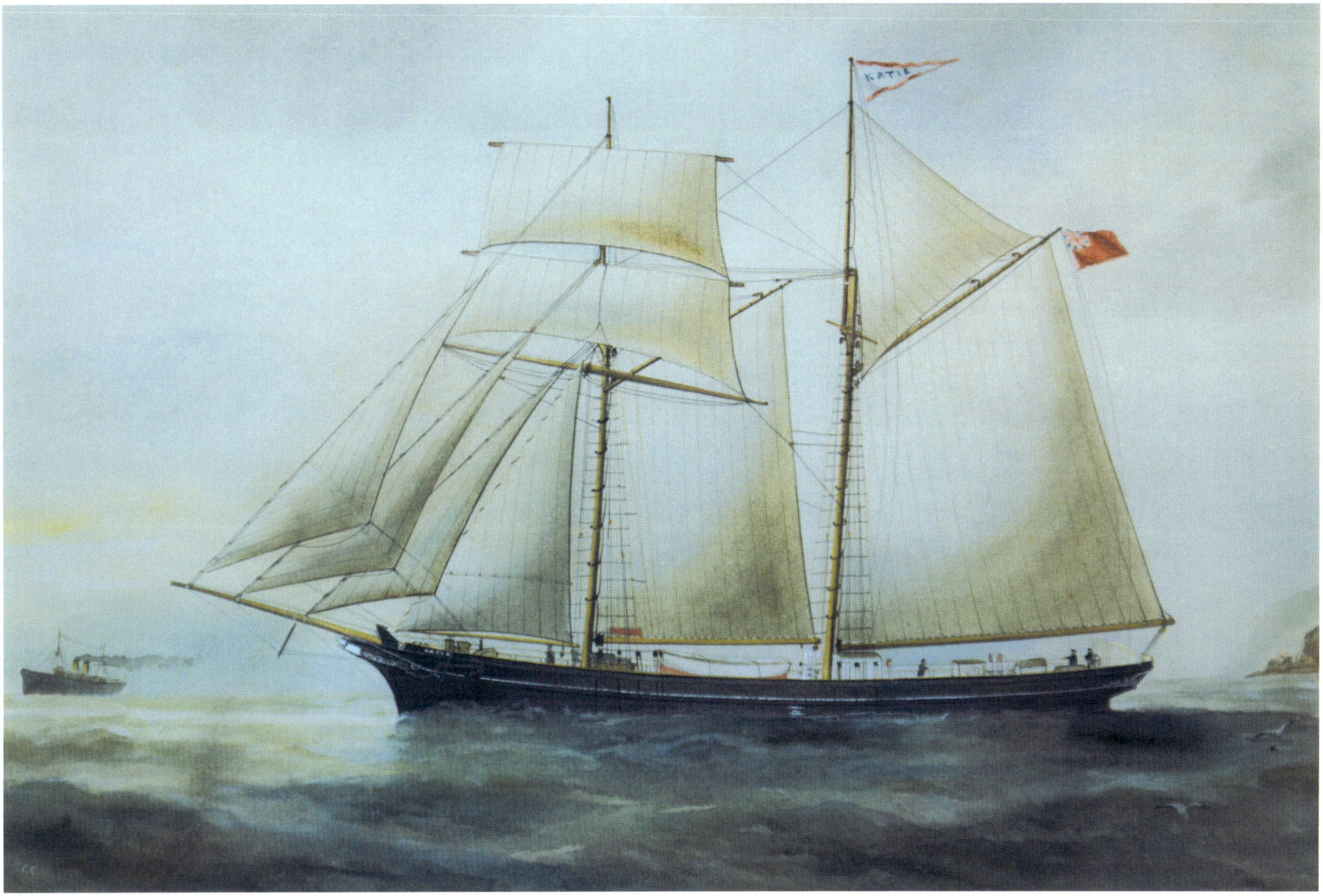

Private Collection

German plane while off the Isle of Man. After this incident she was laid up in Par. After being refitted, she was sold to Danish owners in 1947.

In 1970 Katie was discovered in poor condition in Copenhagen and a society was formed to bring her back to Cornwall and refit her. Unfortunately while being towed from Denmark to Cornwall she sank off the German coast.

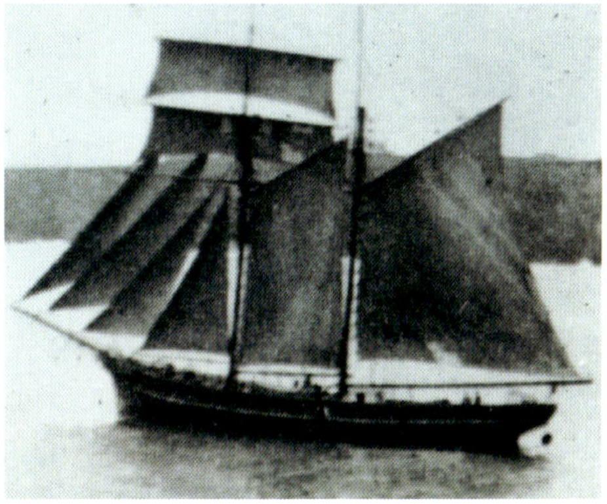

Katie off Newquay *Richard Gillis Collection*

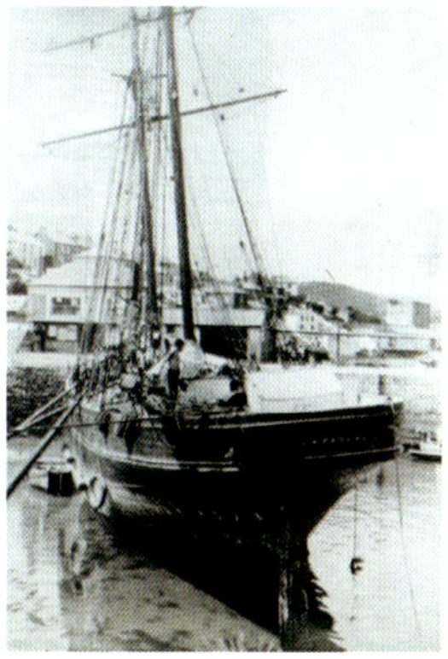

Katie in port
Richard Gillis Collection

Pilchards

While many of the West Country ships were involved in the salt cod trade from Newfoundland, others, particularly in Cornwall, carried salted pilchards which had been caught by local fishermen. The pilchard, in abundance in late summer, is a member of the herring family, and West Country ships took them salted in barrels to the Mediterranean countries.

The Seine Fishery

The history of the Cornish fishing industry has been shaped by the abundance of one particular fish, the pilchard. Pilchards were caught either in drift nets from the luggers, or by seine nets, using two large rowing boats, a method unique to Devon and Cornwall.

There was a major pilchard fishery in St Ives, and overlooking St Ives Bay is the Huers Hut. From there, during late summer, a constant lookout was kept for the pilchard shoals, their presence marked by a characteristic red brown patch of their oil on the water. When a shoal was spotted the huer gave the call 'hevva!' (they are here!) This call would summon the fishermen who manned the seine boats. The huers guided these rowing boats, manned by six or seven men, by signalling from the shore, and the fishermen shot the seine net around the shoal. This was a scene of great excitement for people watching, as in a short time many tons of fish could be encircled.

Pilchard Drivers

The other method of catching pilchards was from fishing boats. The west Cornwall pilchard drivers were rigged with lug sails

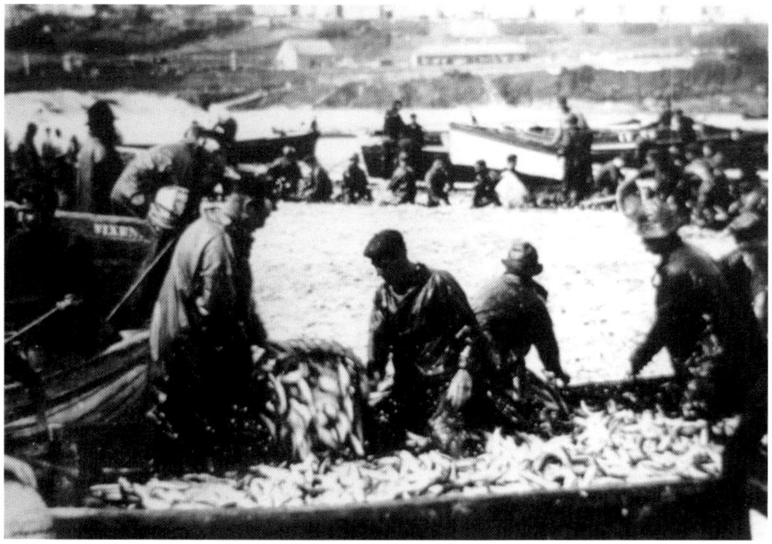

Seine fishermen with pilchards, St Ives — *Private Collection*

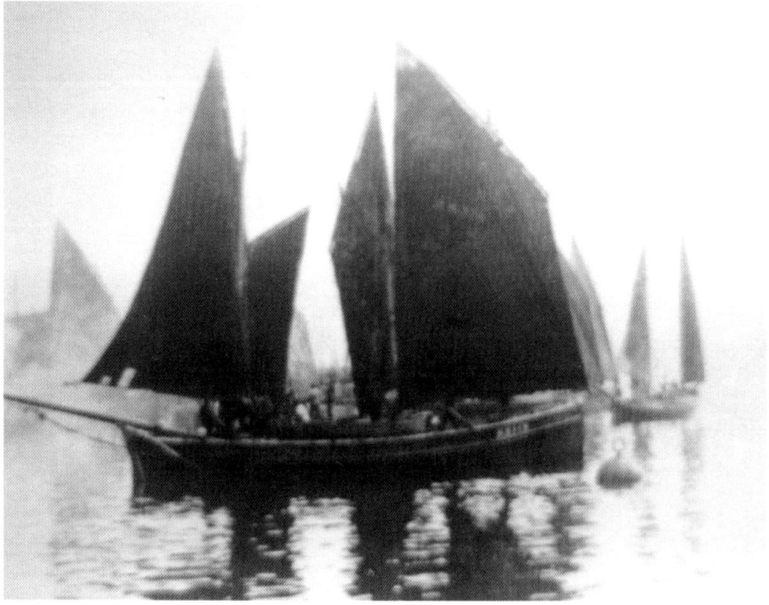

St Ives fishing fleet — *Private Collection*

and distinctive outriggers at the stern. They worked around the coast of Cornwall with drift nets which were shot at dusk. The boat and the nets which hung down in the water like a curtain, drifted along with the tide. During the night the fish that swam into the net were caught by the gills. In the early morning, or when the net was full, the fishermen hauled it over a roller on the starboard side of the boat. They shook out the fish onto the deck, while the cleared net was being stored in the net room.

Although some were sold fresh, whichever method of fishing was used, most of the fish were taken to curing cellars. Here they were salted for thirty or forty days before being packed into barrels by women and children. Each barrel, known as a hogshead, contained four and a half hundredweight, about three thousand fish. Once packed, the barrels were taken to the harbour by horse and cart and loaded aboard ship to be taken to the Mediterranean. Their destinations were primarily Spain, France and Italy, to supply a market created by the Catholic tradition of meat-free days. On their return voyage the ships brought cargoes of dried fruit, olive oil, wine and salt.

In 1869 St Ives alone had 260 seine nets, and in the year 1870 43,000 hogsheads of cured pilchards were exported from there. This was an extraordinary amount of fish, and even though this was an exceptional year, it gives some idea of the capacity of the industry at the time. Virtually the entire community of the fishing village was in some way involved in the industry. It was certainly a time when St Ives smelled of fish, rather than fish and chips. The Reverend Francis Kilvert, on a visit to Cornwall, noted in his diary: "The vicar of St Ives says the stench there is so terrific as to stop the church clock."

A few miles up the coast from St Ives is Newquay. There was also a large pilchard fishery there and the Huers Hut still stands overlooking the bay. Several ships were owned there, and each

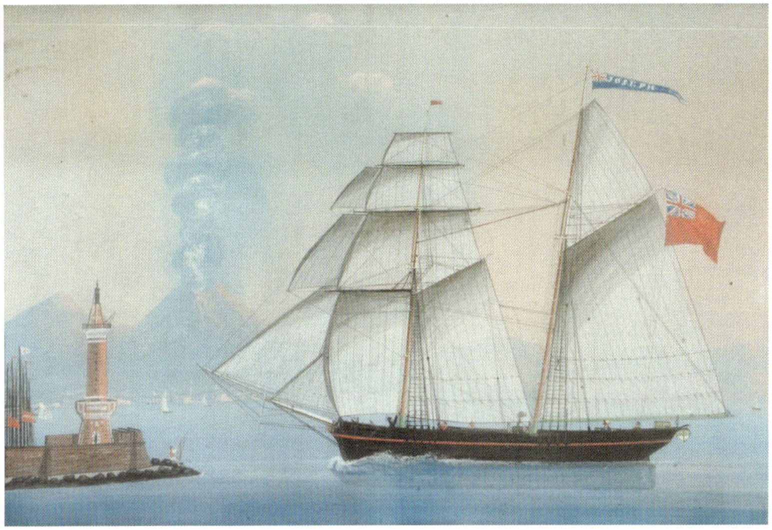

Joseph and Mary of Truro. Michalé Funo, Naples *Private Collection*

year a number of vessels from both Newquay and St Ives carried cargoes of pilchards to the Mediterranean.

When the ships visited some of the Mediterranean ports, the master and crew might well have encountered an artist showing examples of his ship portraits and, like Reuben Chappell, offering to undertake a commission to make a portrait of their ship. Such pierhead painters are known to have operated in many of the Mediterranean ports. Several were known to have worked in Marseilles and Venice, but Naples, in particular, became well known as a centre for ship portrait painting.

Often topographical details were included in the background, for example, particular buildings in Venice, and in many of the Naples paintings Vesuvius can be seen smouldering in the distance. These paintings were brought back to their homes by the seamen and were a lasting momento of their voyage and their ship. "Pictures of Vesuvius, always in full eruption, decorated the front rooms of many cottages in nineteenth century Newquay and St Ives. Many of these paintings of west country schooners in full sail in the Bay of Naples, still exist, pictures made by Italian artists for a few shillings and brought home to adorn Cornish firesides for generations." Basil Greenhill, *'The Merchant Schooners' Vol 1.*

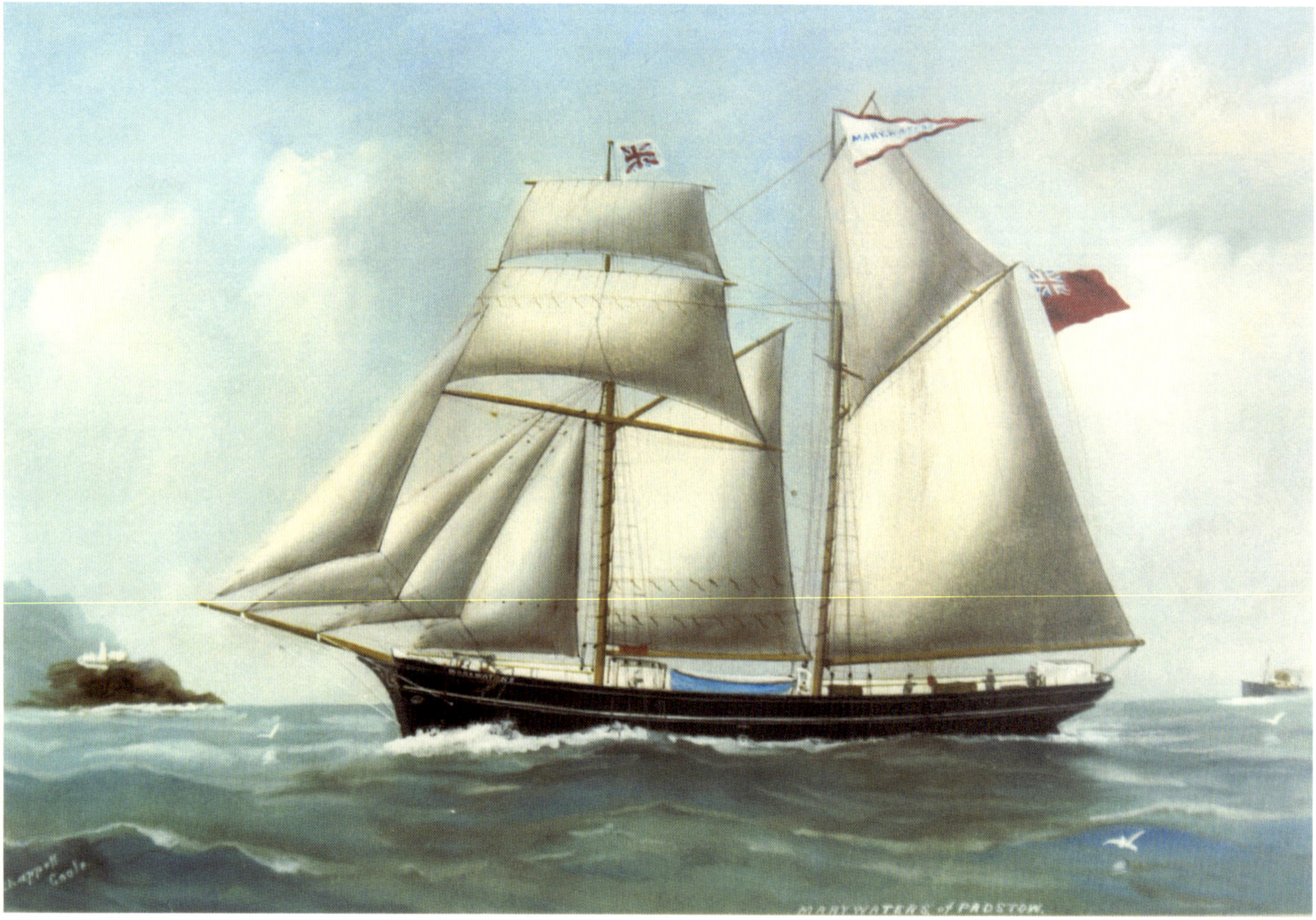

Private collection

Mary Waters of Padstow

O.N. 69464; schooner; built 1875 in Padstow by C. Rawle; tons 116 gross.

This elliptical sterned schooner was registered at Padstow and was owned by Joseph Waters of Port Isaac. In 1910 the vessel was bought by J. Daniel of St Ives, and in 1918 she was bought by John Renouf of Jersey.

Her crew of five was rescued on 3rd October 1923 by the Tenby lifeboat as she dragged anchor towards rocks, and the ship was saved next day. She was lost on 13th April 1925 having sailed from Par with china clay. The vessel became stranded at Ardrossan, but the crew were saved.

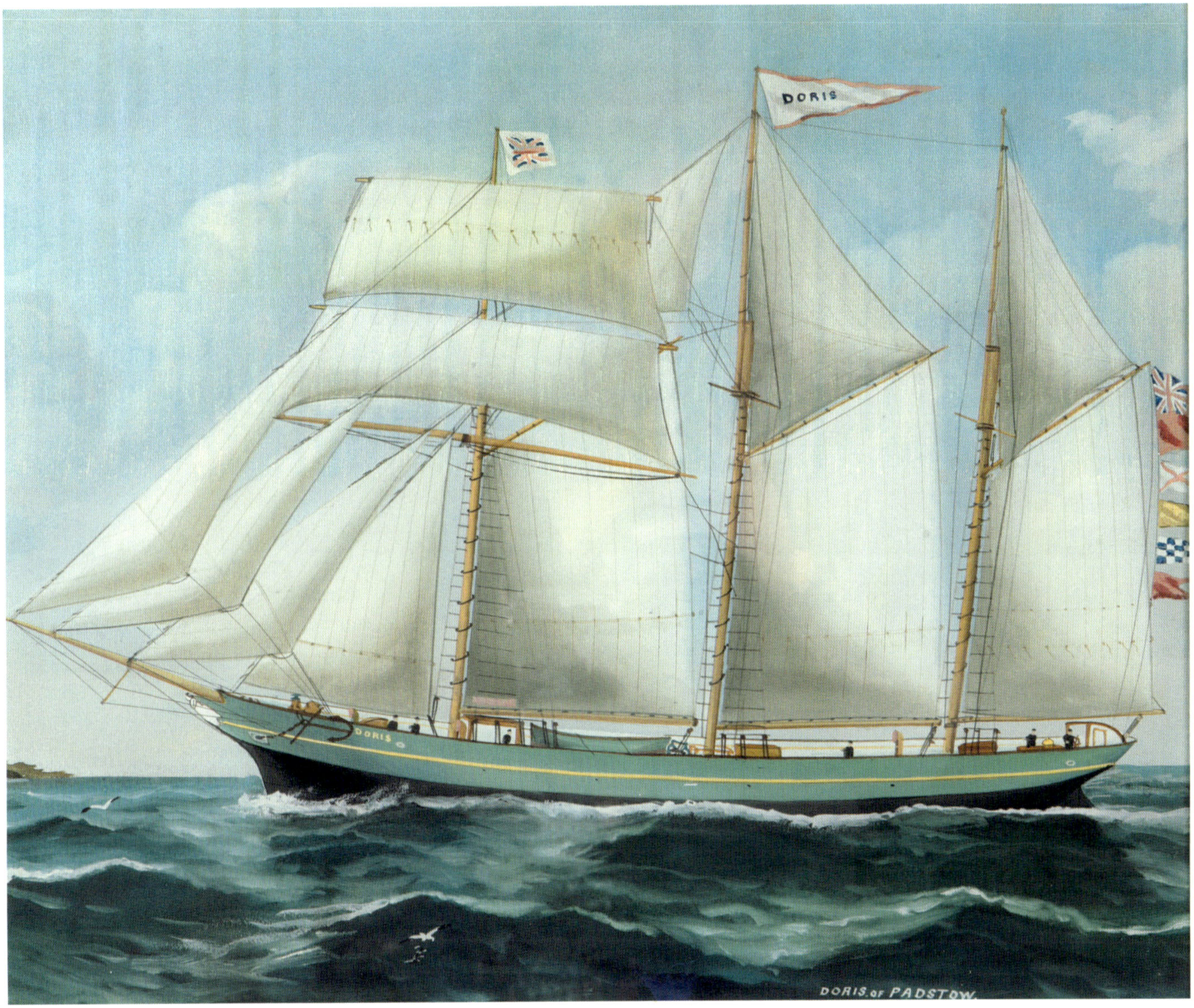

Padstow Museum

Doris of Padstow

O.N. 84985; steel three-masted schooner with an elliptical stern; built 1904 by R. Cock & Sons, Appledore; tons 137 gross; 98.8' x 22.5' x 9.4'; reg. Padstow.

The Padstow registered three-masted steel schooner Doris was owned by William S. Allport and other shareholders from the area. At the time Allport, obviously an important ship owner in Padstow, owned four other vessels: the Ariel 132 tons, the Bessie 99 tons, the Kinnard 120 tons, and the Lord Devon 98 tons.

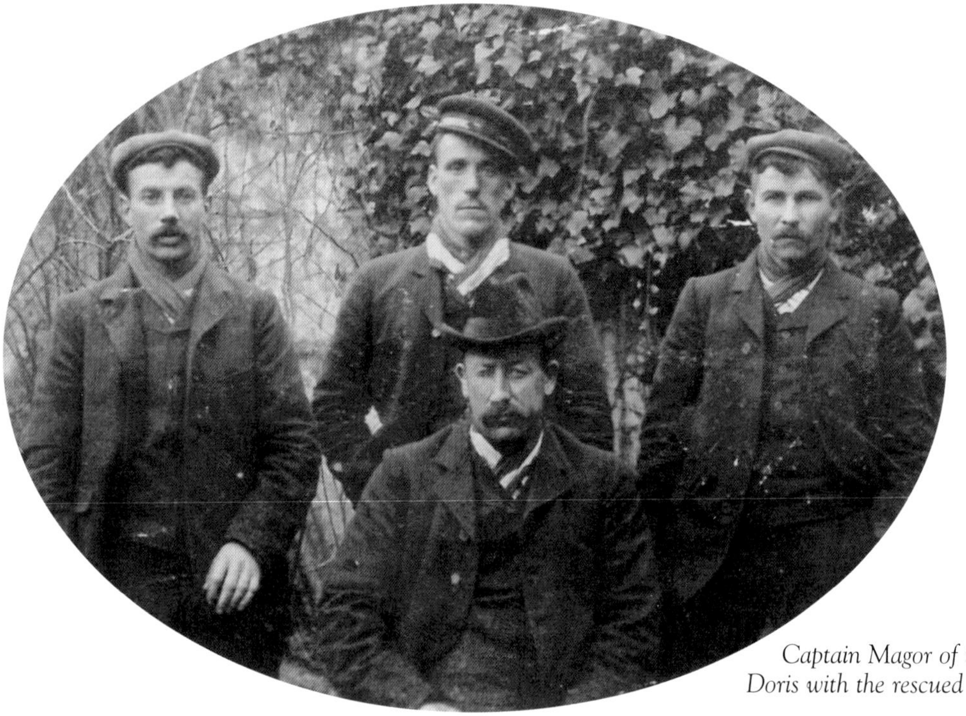

Captain Magor of the Doris with the rescued crew 1907

Padstow Museum

His ship Doris was wrecked in a force ten gale off the coast of Holland on 14th December 1907 while sailing from Plymouth to Ghent with china clay. Captain Magor and three crew members were saved in a dramatic rescue, but one man, the cook, was lost.

The archive of Padstow Museum tells the tale of the loss of the Doris. Articles in the Royal Cornwall Gazette, 19th December 1907, Dutch Newspaper reports, and the personal recollections of a lady who was a child living in Flushing, Holland, at the time of the wreck, report the dramatic rescue attempts of the crew.

Having grounded on sandbanks off the coast of Zeeland in a north-westerly gale, the hull of the ship was under water. The captain, Thomas Magor, the mate and three crew members climbed into the rigging. They had been there for more than twelve hours and the Flushing lifeboat had made several unsuccessful attempts to reach them, but the heavy seas made this impossible. However, a local seafaring family called Schroever who owned a heavily-built sailing boat bravely decided to attempt a rescue. Before setting sail Father Schroevers asked his sons and fifteen year old grandson whether they were prepared to go out in such a gale. They agreed and prayed to God to bless their enterprise. They were able to rescue the Captain, mate, and two seamen, all suffering from exposure. Crowthers, the ship's cook who was on his first voyage

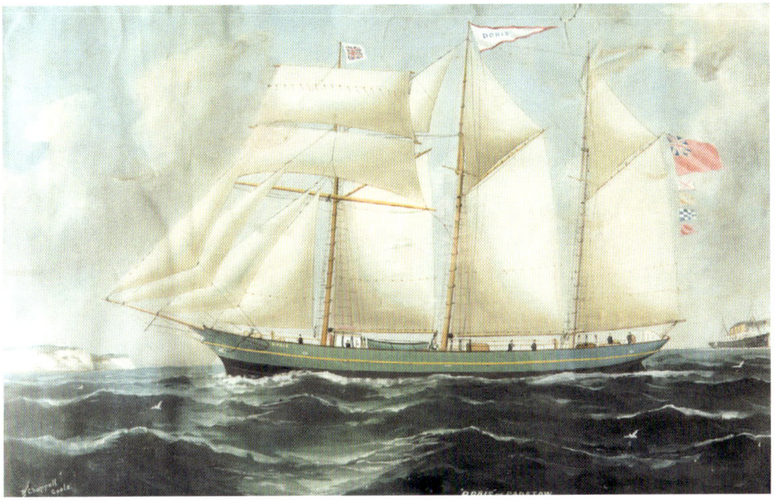

Doris of Padstow depicted passing white cliffs. The present owner found this painting discarded in a chicken shed when he was nine or ten years old.

Private Collection

Below, the Schroever Family of Vlissingen who rescued the crew of the Doris 1907

Padstow Museum

was 'so benumbed with cold and exposure that he had let go his hold and was drowned.' The rescue was an act of true humanity which astounded the people of both Great Britain and the Netherlands. Their heroism was widely recognised and a 'Doris' fund in aid of seamen in need was founded in their honour.

Padstow Museum is in the centre of the town, a short distance from the harbour. There are paintings, models, tools and photographs which relate to the town's rich nautical history as well as a display on the famous 'Obby-Oss.'

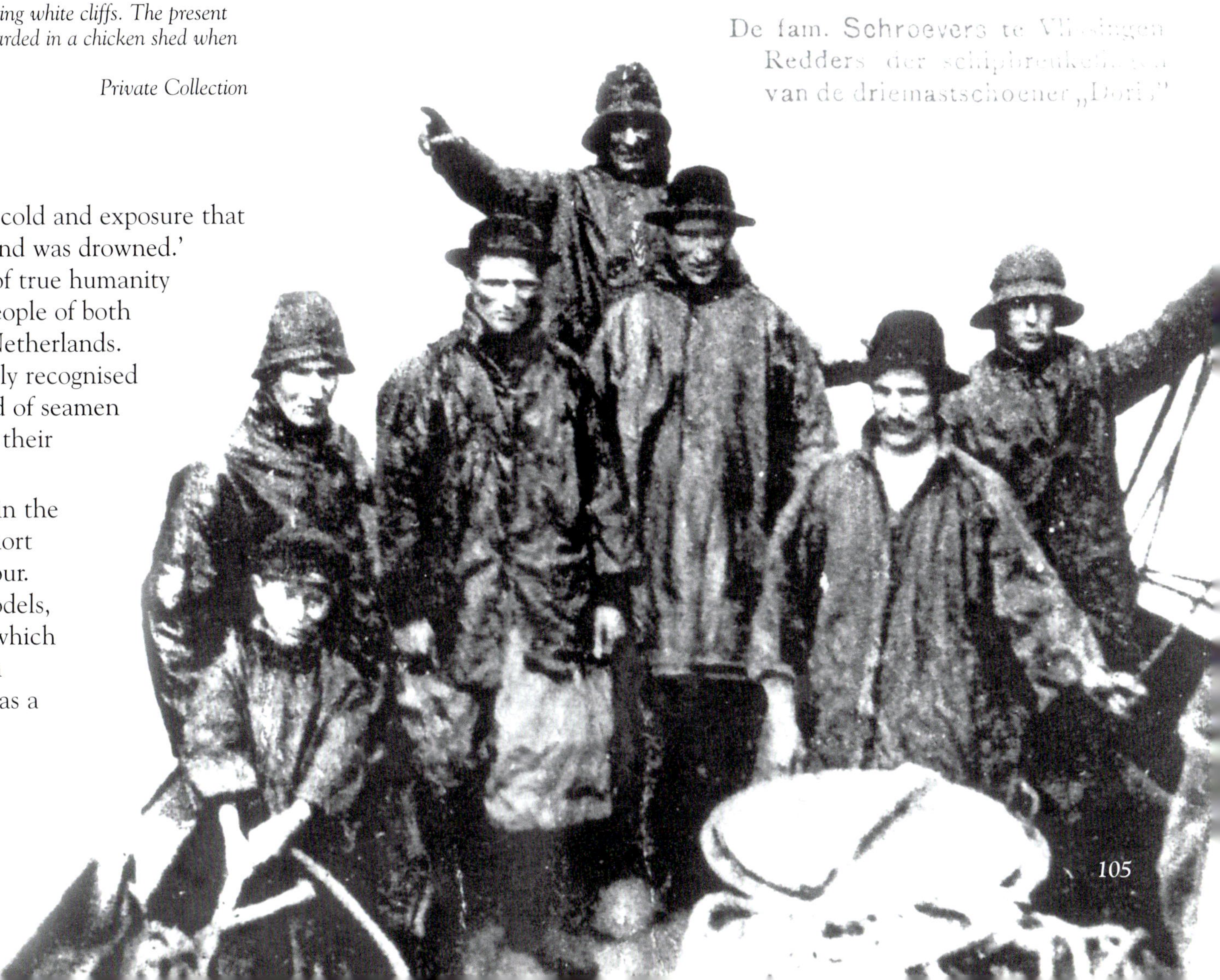

Guiding Star

ON73582; wooden schooner; built 1875 by Banks Junior, Kilpinpike, Yorkshire; 106 gross tons; 81.4' x 22.4' x 11'.

Guiding Star was a wooden schooner with an elliptical stern and was for many years engaged in the Newfoundland trade. While off the coast of Labrador in 1885 the vessel was badly damaged in a gale. Guiding Star was registered in Padstow until 1920 when she was sold to Plymouth.

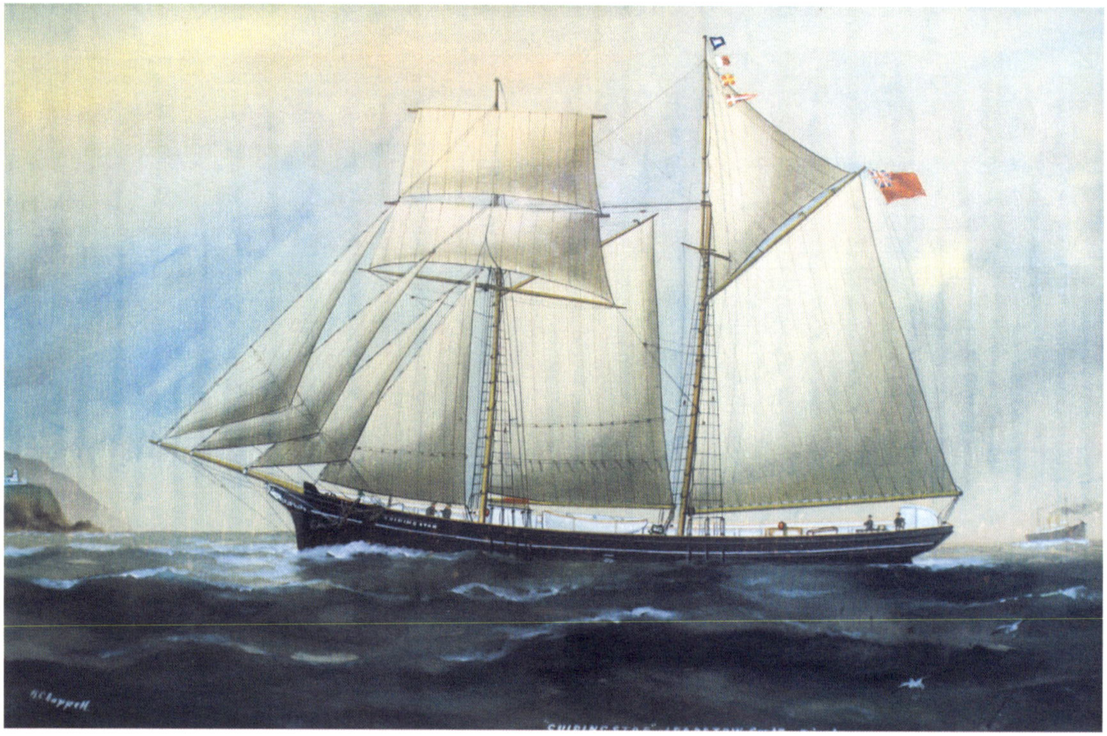

Royal Cornwall Museum

Following a gale the schooner was abandoned and washed ashore on the coast of Wales on Christmas Eve 1926.

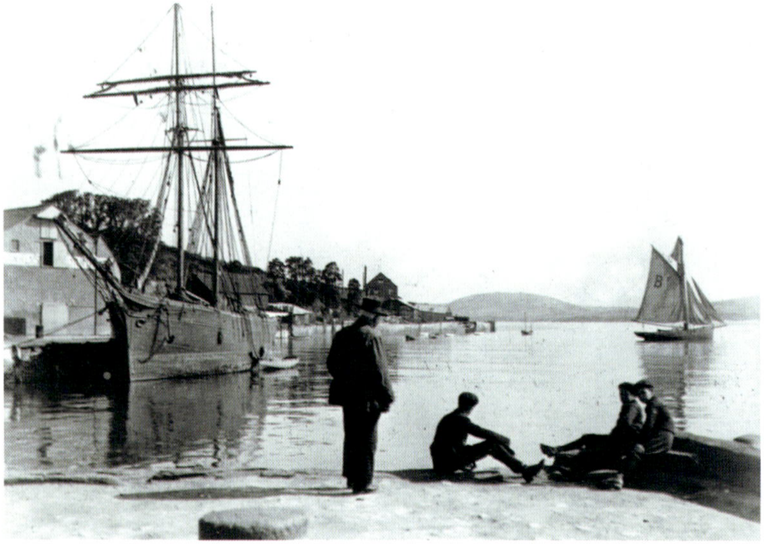

Guiding Star against the quay, Padstow. *Padstow Museum*

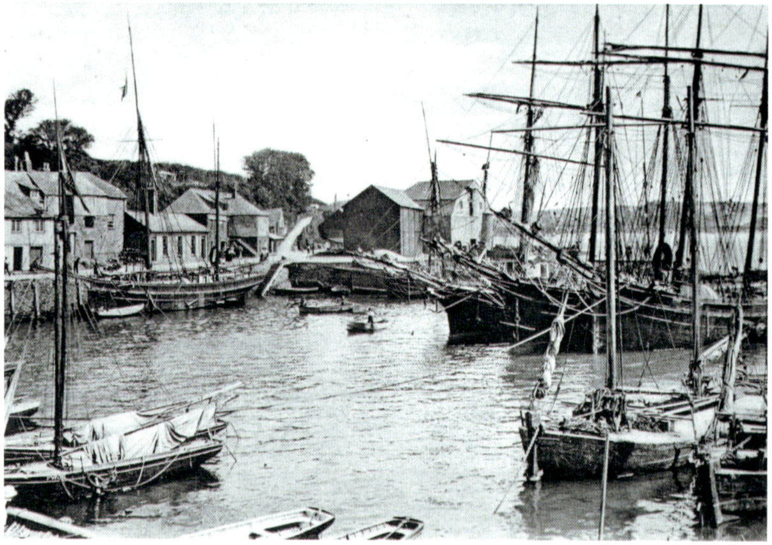

Padstow Harbour turn of the century postcard. *Padstow Museum*

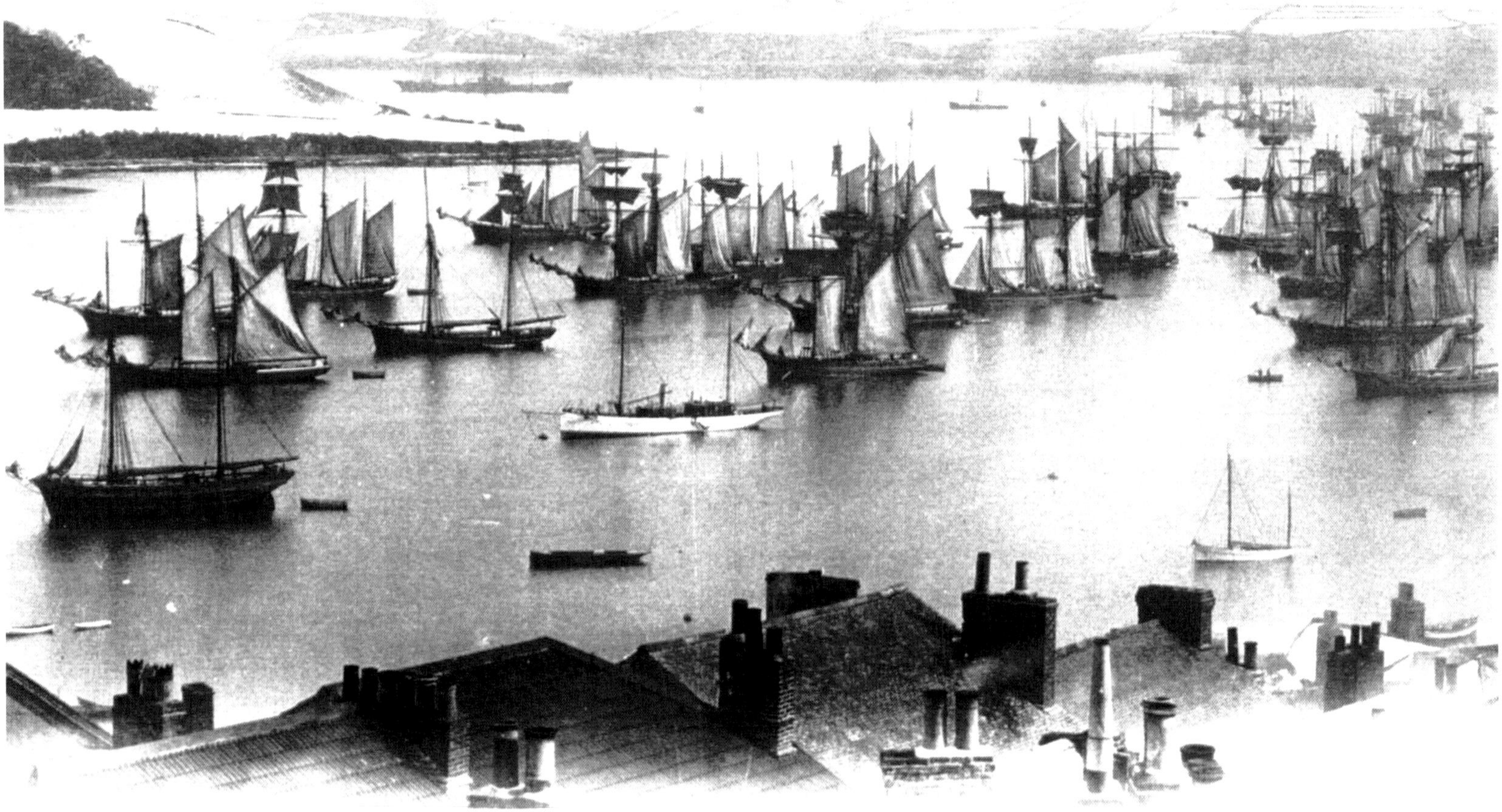

The Great Blizzard 1891. (This photograph shows Falmouth Roads packed with ships that had come into the port to seek shelter). With bitterly cold easterly hurricane force winds and driving snow the blizzard claimed over 200 lives, most of which were at sea. 63 ships were known to have been lost between Goodwin Sands and Scilly.

The Royal Cornwall Polytechnic Society

FALMOUTH

Falmouth is the third largest natural harbour in the world and the principal port of Cornwall. It is the first significant port of call for vessels returning to British waters via the Western Approaches. Before the invention of radio many vessels arriving or leaving British waters would be sent to 'Falmouth for Orders.' There they would receive information concerning their destinations, where they should load and discharge cargoes, etc.

A sheltered, deep water anchorage, Falmouth grew to cater for the maritime trade. Here there were docks which could service wood and iron ships, and pilot services were available for larger vessels. The town revolved around shipping, many businesses catering for ships and seamen, chandlers, sail and rope makers, nautical instruments and charts, ships stores and a great many public houses.

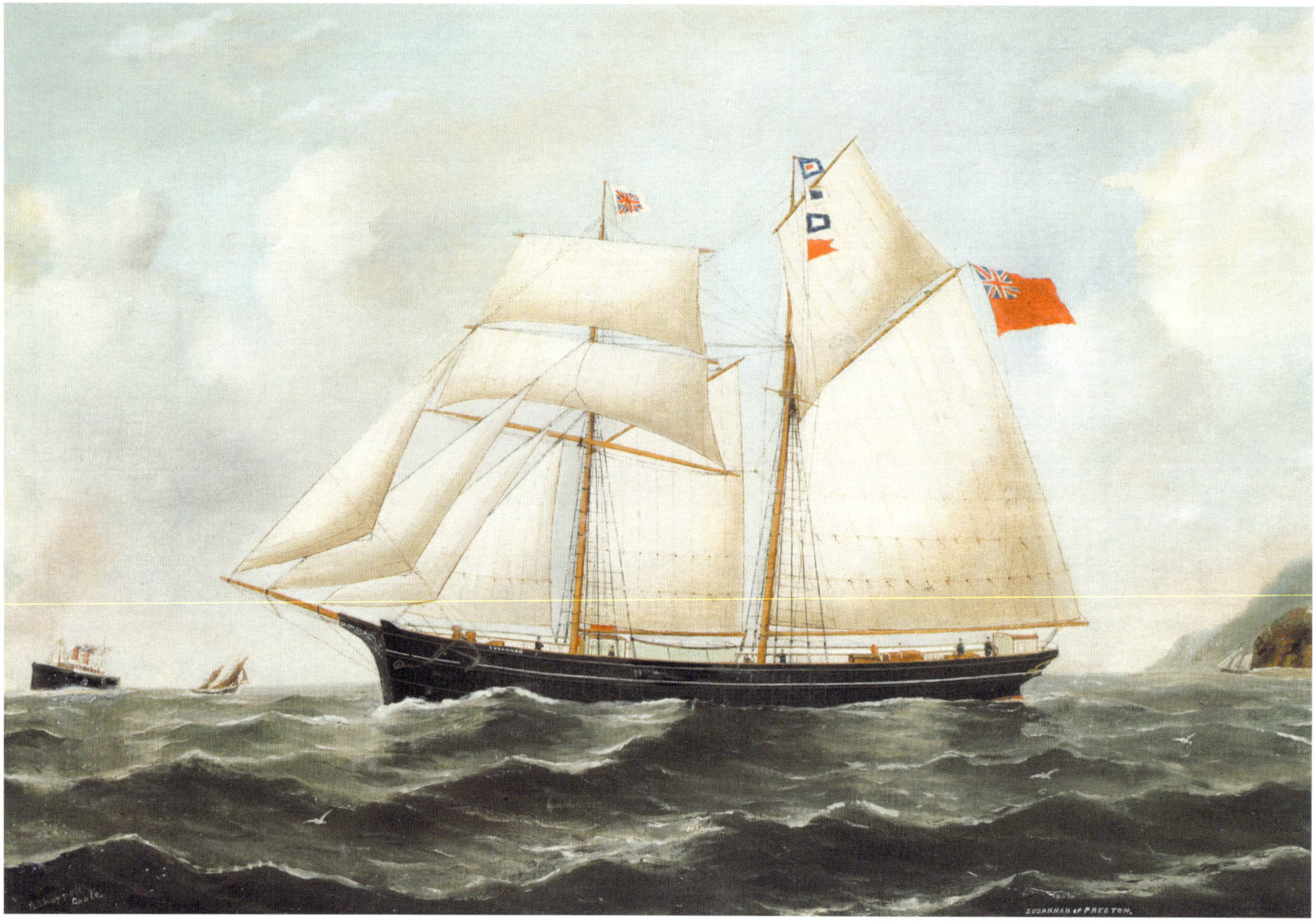

Private Collection

Susannah of Preston

ON62775; signal WSPB; built 1873 Ardrossan by Barr. 115 gross tons; 88.8' x 21.9' x 10.5'.

Falmouth was visited by ships from all over the world, but there were also a considerable number of vessels registered and trading from there. It was a town of ship-owners and seamen and two of them, Captain William Bate and his brother Captain Sidney Bate, obviously valued the work of Reuben Chappell, as over the years they commissioned a number of paintings from Chappell of the ships they commanded. William and Sidney Bate came from a well known seafaring family originally from Port Isaac. Their father was a master mariner and several of his sons became well known sea captains in Penryn, Falmouth and Port Navas.

William Bate lived for many years in Penryn, a tough, fit and active man, still getting around on his bicycle in his eighties. He started his career in sailing ships and commanded several, Susannah of Preston, Amis Reunis, Mary Waters, Queen of the Chase amongst them. He ended his days commanding steamships. The steam coasters SS Irish Coast and SS Cornish Coast were the last ships in his command. During the First World War two of his ships, including the Susannah, were sunk by German submarines.

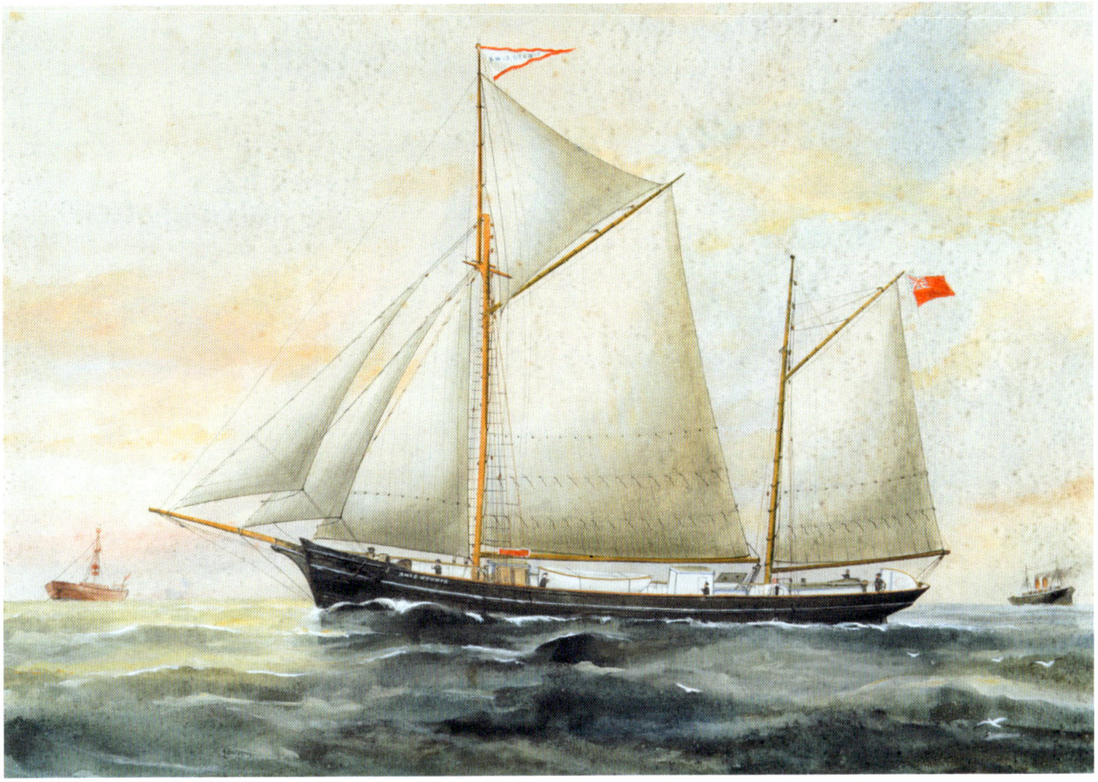

Private Collection

Amis Reunis

ON 137204; built 1883 "France". 74 gross tons; 72.2' x 20.3' x 8.1' reg. Falmouth

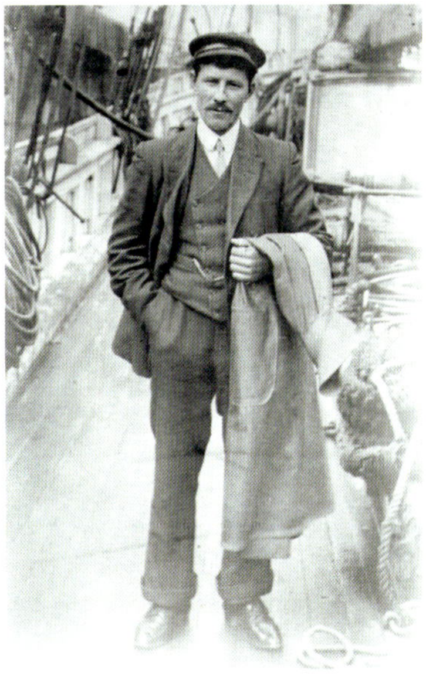

Captain Willliam Bate aboard his ship in Penryn

Private Collection

Before the first world war a significant amount of the coasting and short sea trade around Britain was still being handled by sailing vessels. Many of these were West Country schooners, with their combination of square and fore-and-aft rig, giving manoeuvrability as well as a good sail area. Well into the 1930s there was still quite a fleet of West Country schooners working mainly in the coal and china clay trades.

West Country Ports & Harbours

The following are some of the ports and harbours around the west country which were operating in the 19th century. In many of these places there were yards where ships were built and repaired, and vessels were locally owned and registered. They were often busy places with ships coming and going with cargo. Besides the places mentioned below there were also numerous coves and beaches where, in fair weather, vessels grounded, and at low water unloaded and loaded cargo.

Poole, Swanage, Weymouth, Bridport/West Bay, Lyme, Exmouth, Topsham, Exeter, Teignmouth, Torquay, Brixham, Paignton, Dartmouth, Salcombe and Kingsbridge, Plymouth and ports on the Tamar, Looe, Fowey, Par, Charlestown, Pentewan, Mevagissey, Falmouth, Penryn, Porthleven, Penzance, Newlyn, St Ives, Hayle, Portreath, St Agnes, Newquay, Padstow, Boscastle, Bude, Hartland Quay, Clovelly, Appledore, Bideford, Barnstaple, Ilfracombe, Lynmouth, Minehead, Watchet, Bridgewater, Weston-Super-Mare, Bristol.

ADELAIDE

ON 58295; built 1869 Padstow by Tredwen. 180 gross tons 106.0' x 24.3' x 12.7'.

Besides having to face the natural dangers associated with the sea, during the first world war merchant ships, sailing vessels included, were attacked by the German warships, particularly submarines. Sidney Bate's ship was also attacked by a German submarine, and he asked Reuben Chappell to record the event in a painting. This painting depicts what must have been a very dramatic moment in Capt. Bate's life. While sailing in the English Channel a German submarine surfaced and the crew of the schooner Adelaide were ordered to leave their vessel and had to row away in the ship's boat. As the painting shows, the submarine opened fire on Adelaide and she was dismasted. The Germans would not waste an expensive torpedo on such a small vessel, so the ship was either sunk with shellfire or a scuttling charge placed aboard. If the crew were lucky they were ordered to leave the ship beforehand. On this occasion Adelaide sutvived and was re-rigged as a schooner. During the First World War German submarines accounted for the loss of a great many merchant sailing ships in this way, and they were particularly active in the waters around the West of England. Clearly Capt Bate and his crew lived to tell the tale and were eventually picked up by another

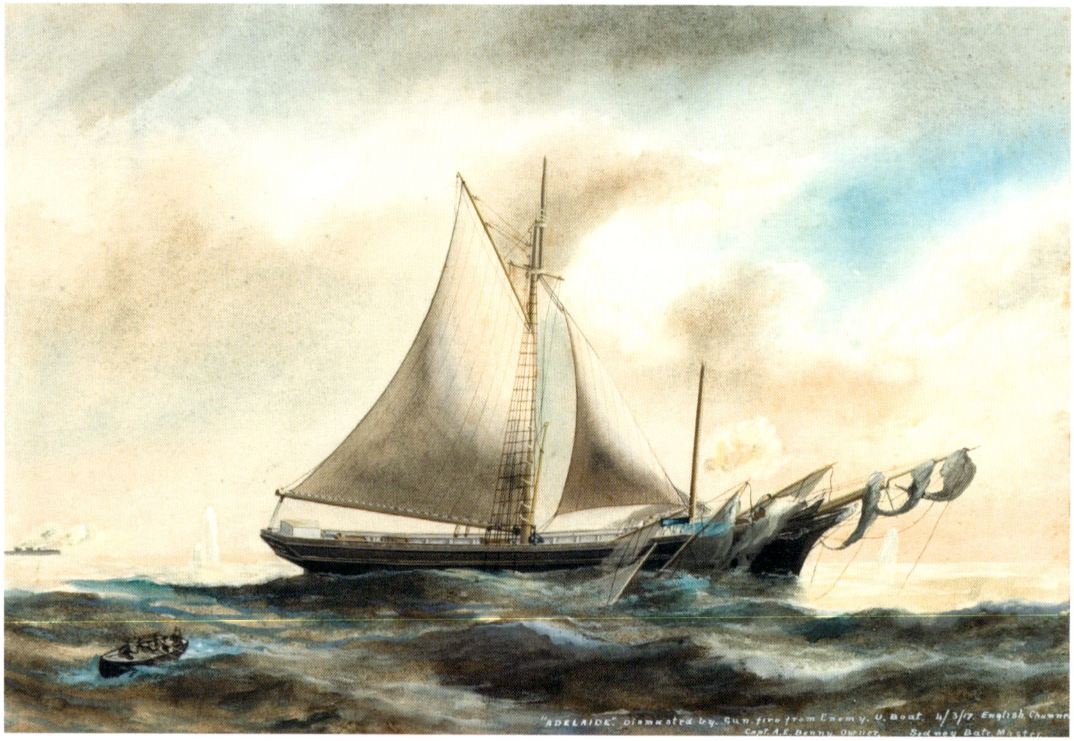

Adelaide dismasted by gunfire from enemy u-boat 4/3/17 English Channel *Private Collection*

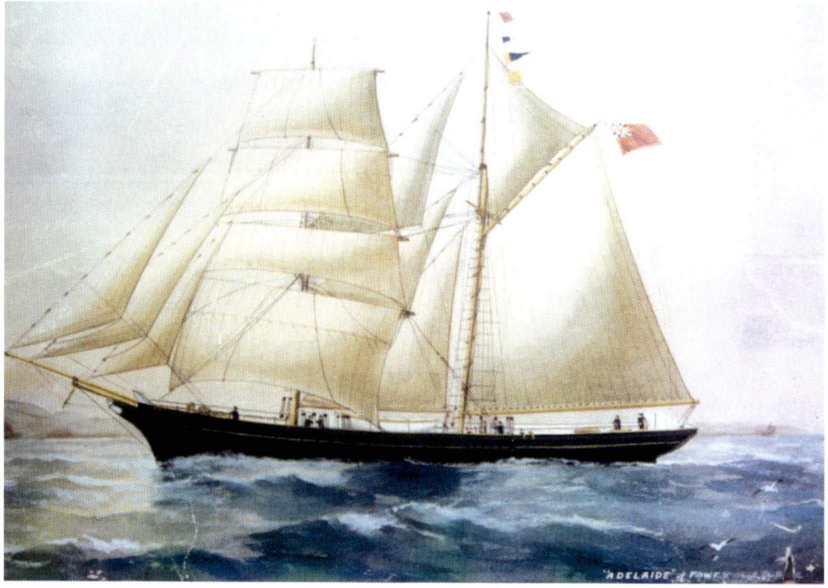

Private Collection

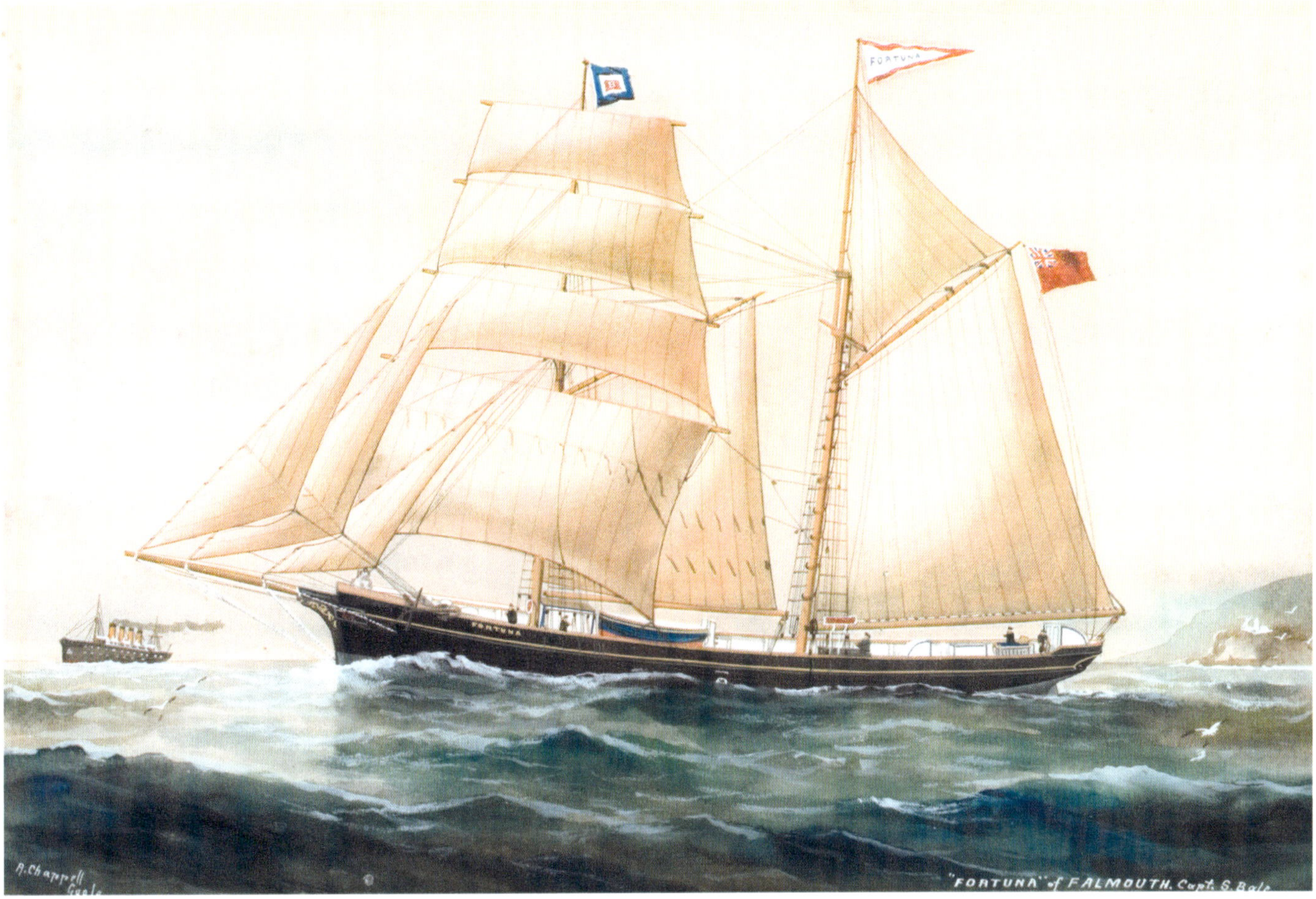

Private Collection

Fortuna of Falmouth

ON 98456; built 1892 Emsworth. 131 fross tons 100' x 24.3' x 7.8'

ship but many of the crews of the small unarmed merchant ships were not so lucky. Another ship he commanded was the brigantine Fortuna of Falmouth which was sunk by a u-boat in 1916. He also commissioned a painting of her from Reuben Chappell.

Captain Sidney Bate eventually became Captain of the steam tugs associated with Falmouth Docks.

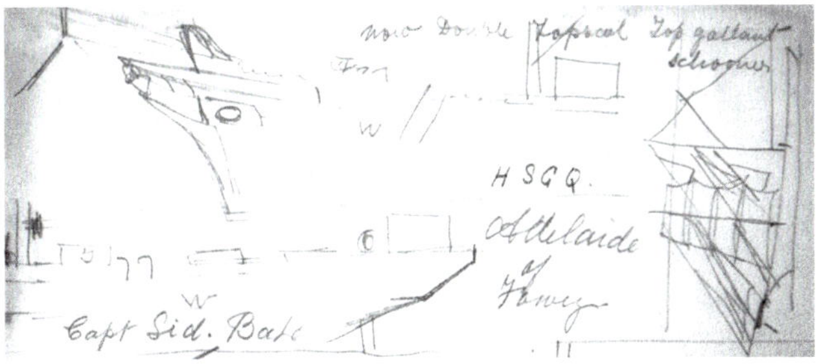

Sketches for Adelaide

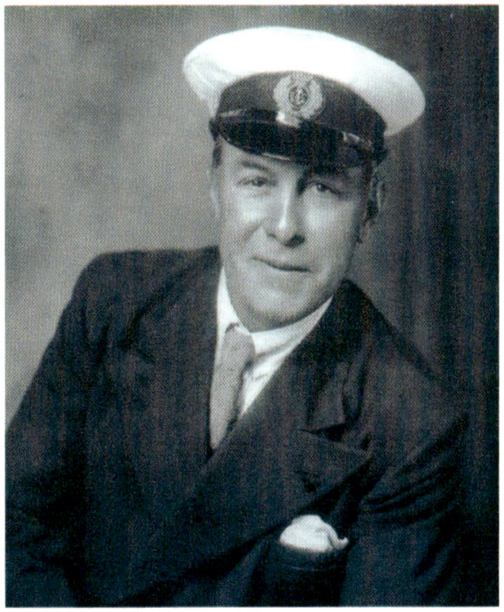

Captain Sidney Bate *Private Collection*

Alice Williams

ON 22780; built 1854 by Bevans of Llanelli;131 gross tons; 83.1' x 23.2' x 11.8'; signal code JNQD.

This wooden topsail schooner traded for nearly three quarters of a century. Alice Williams was built in Wales and launched in 1854 to be registered in Falmouth in 1855. She was engaged in the coastal and home trades carrying coal and ore. She also made voyages to Scandinavia, Northern Spain and France with cargoes of coal, ore and timber. From 1885 the ship carried china clay and granite from Par and Pentewan. During this period a member of the ship's crew bought the painting from Reuben Chappell but it was not painted for him; it had been commissioned by the captain of the vessel, but on seeing the picture he decided not to buy it. The seaman, the present owner's father, decided that he would have the painting himself, but as his earnings at the time were only 'thirty shillings per month all found' there was not much, other than the painting to take home for his month's work.

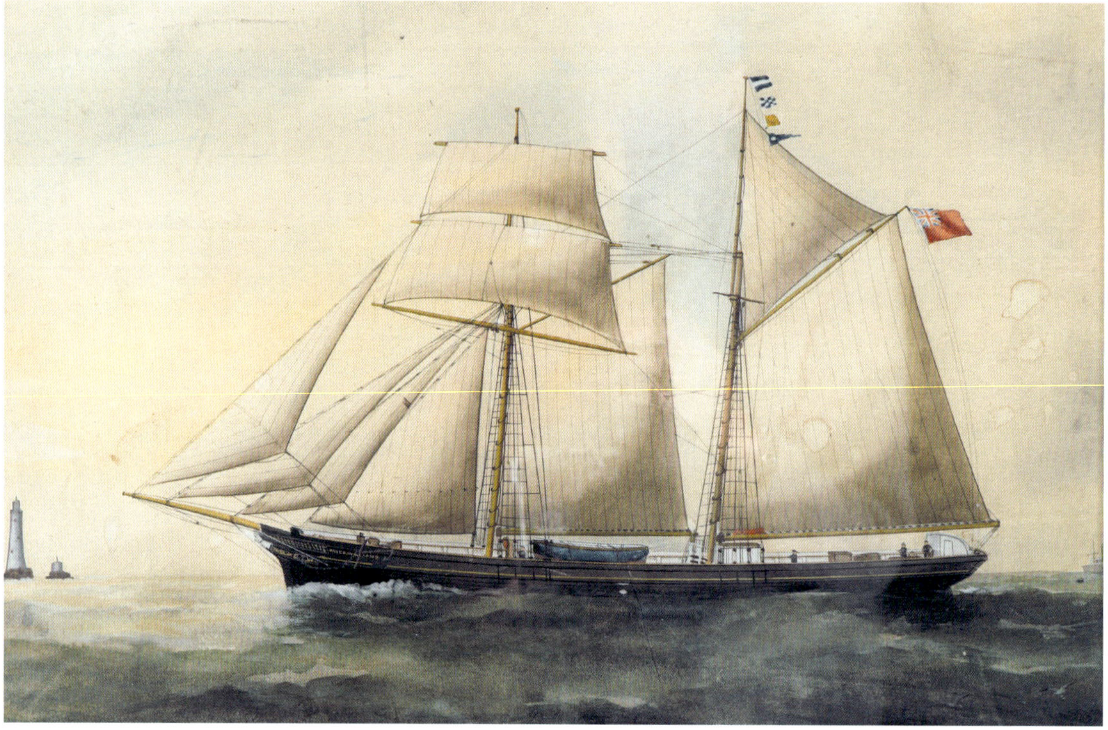

Private Collection

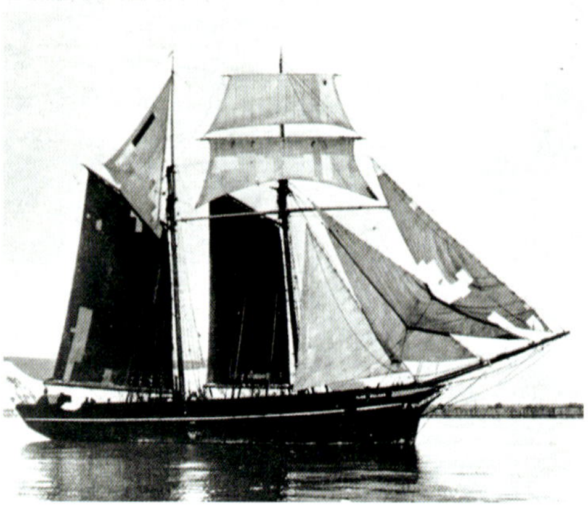

Alice Williams *Royal Cornwall Museum*

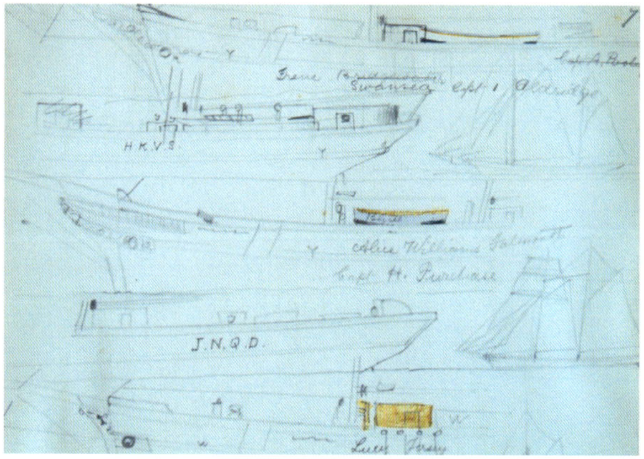

Sketchbook details of Alice Williams *Private Collection*

Understandably, his wife was rather annoyed with him.

In February 1928 Alice Williams was caught in a storm in the Irish Sea, and, leaking badly, she was abandoned by her crew off Milford Haven. The crew were taken off by a trawler, but the schooner did not sink and was eventually washed ashore on the southern side of the island of Skokholm. Her cargo of steam coal proved very useful to the inhabitants, and for many years the ship's figurehead has stood on the island where the schooner was wrecked. The island is now a bird reserve.

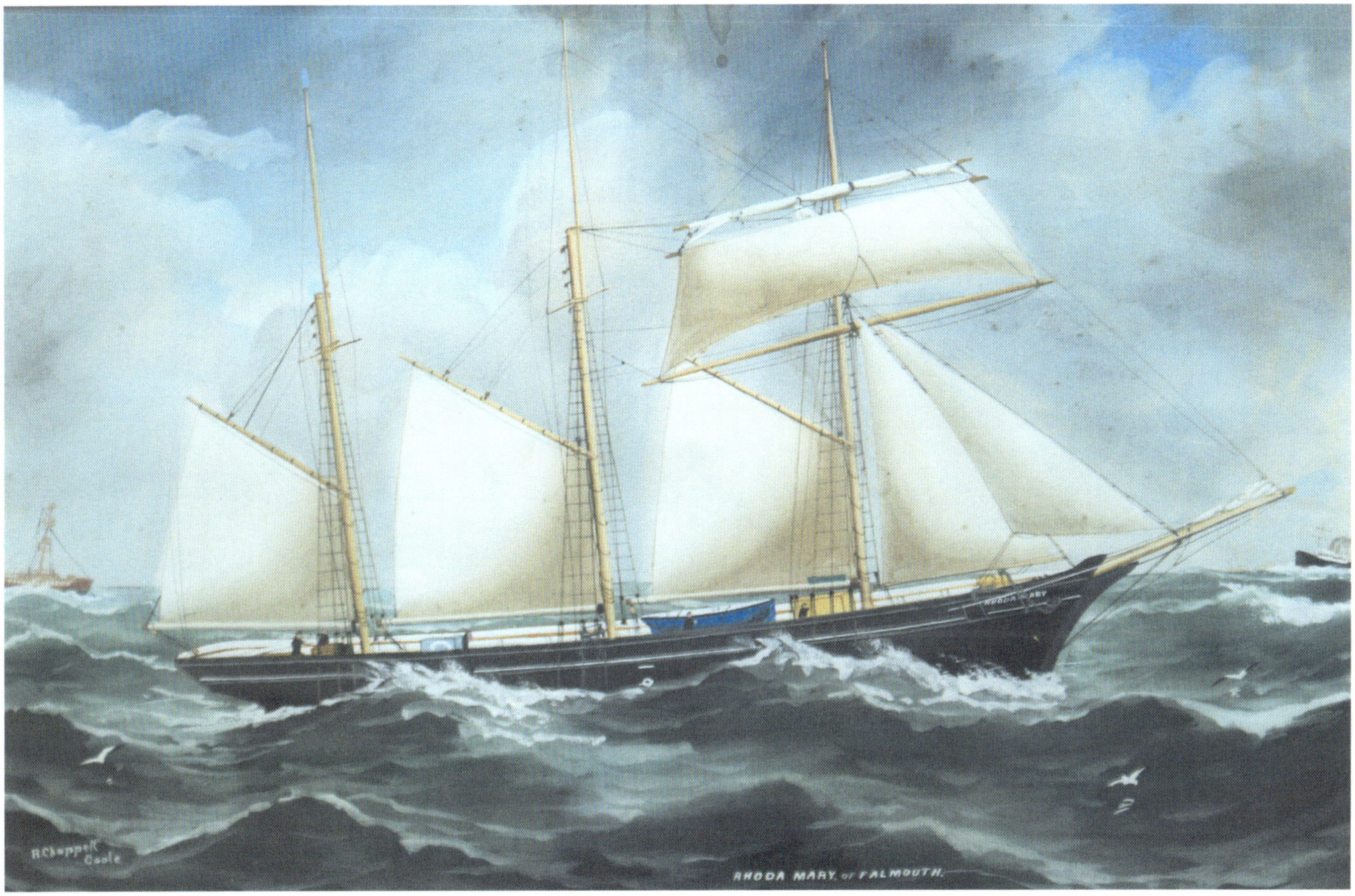

Private collection

Rhoda Mary of Falmouth

ON62036; wooden three-masted schooner; built 1868 converted 1898 by Stephens of Point; 130 tons gross; 101.2' x 21.9' x 11.5'; owned by S.T. Westlake & Co; reg. Falmouth.

Rhoda Mary was one of the fastest merchant vessels of her era. She was built in 1838 as a schooner and later converted to three masts for easier handling. She had a deep narrow hull which was designed for fast sailing. Rhoda Mary had English oak frames, American grey-elm keel, Baltic red pine plankings and yellow pine decks. For many years her owner and master was S. T. Westlake of Falmouth and she sailed from Charlestown and Par with china clay returning with coal.

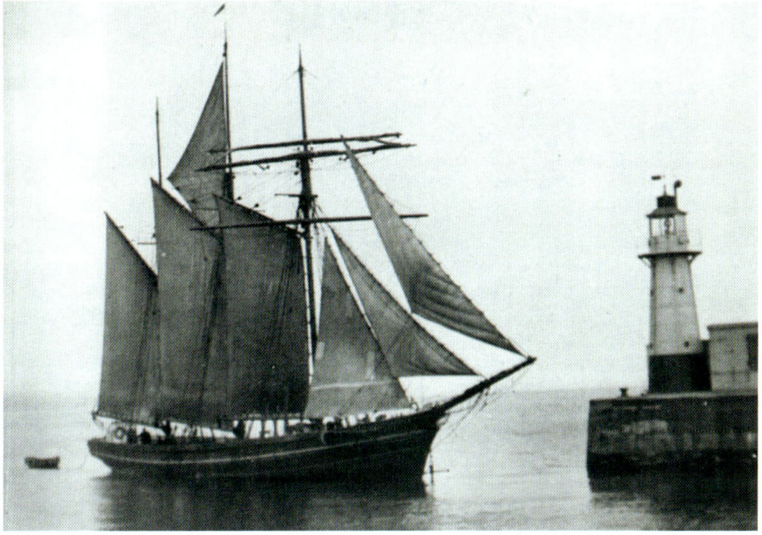

The Clay Ports

Ships from all over Europe came to the Cornish ports of Par, Fowey, Pentewan and Charlestown; they came primarily for kaolin, known as china clay, which was found in the St Austell-Bugle areas of Cornwall.

Kaolin had been found in China many centuries ago and for a long time was used by the Chinese potteries to produce white porcelain. Their white ceramics were highly valued, and their production method was a closely guarded secret. It was not until the mid eighteenth century that deposits were found in Cornwall by Plymouth chemist William Cookworthy. English potters such as Josiah Wedgewood had for many years been trying to make white ceramics without success, so the discovery of of this clay was of great interest to them. It became known as china clay.

An important industry grew in this area, and many people were employed in extracting, refining, drying, packing and transporting the clay. Clay and sand were excavated and washed, and the clay was separated in settling tanks. The waste sand was discarded in conical piles which became such a feature of the landscape that they became known as the Cornish Alps. After processes of settling and refinement the clay was thickened enough to be cut into blocks which were dried. In the early days the clay was carried in heavy horse-drawn wagons to the ships, and needed to be packed in substantial casks. Of the china clay ports, Fowey and Par are still busy with good-sized ships carrying china clay. Millions of tons of clay pass through these ports each year.

Pentewan harbour was the most westerly of the clay ports. In its day a significant amount of clay was exported from there. It had the advantages of having a narrow gauge railway which ran from St Austell and a spacious dock in which vessels could turn around before leaving. However, shipping declined there,

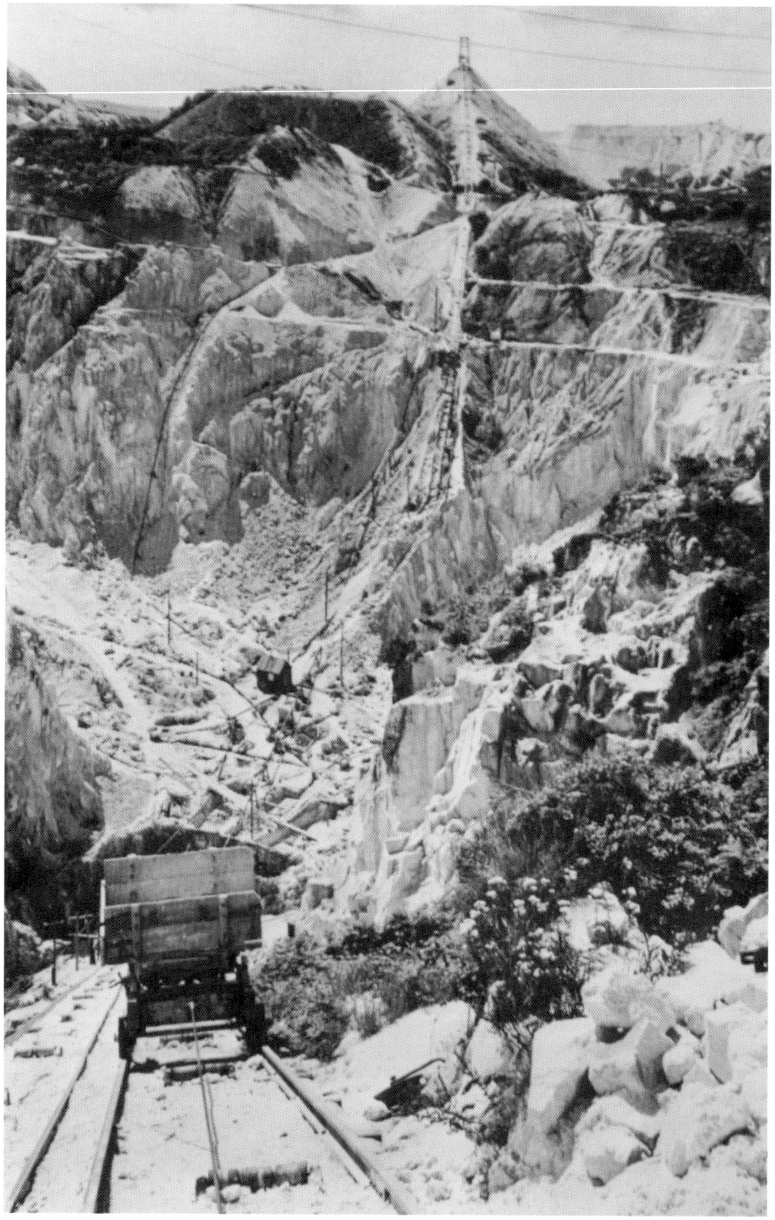

Cornish Alps *China Clay Museum*

and the last cargo-carrying vessel left the port in 1929.

Charlestown is the oldest of the clay ports and is one of the places where Reuben Chappell would have encountered seamen who might commission a painting of their ship. Charlestown is not a large harbour and it is difficult to believe how busy it was a hundred or so years ago. Yet these two photographs of 1914 show the activity that was taking place then. The number of sailing vessels in these photographs show just how many were still working until the First World War. On most days it was possible to cross the harbour by walking from one boat to another.

Charlestown harbour is also a dock. The gates could be shut shortly after high tide, keeping the water in and allowing the vessels to remain afloat when the tide went out. This enabled cargoes to be loaded and unloaded efficiently. There developed a system of tramways and chutes which could put the china clay straight into the holds of the waiting vessels.

An important cargo which came into Charlestown was Welsh coal, used to fuel beam engines which drove pumps in the tin mines and clay pits. Also, Danish vessels brought Baltic timber, some of which was used in the mines and clay pits. This timber was also in demand for shipbuilding. There were several shipbuilding yards in the area including those of John Stephens, well known broker, shipbuilder and ship owner, whose fleet became known as The Company of Little Ships.

There were three coopers in Charlestown, employing up to 40 men until the late 1940s. They made large casks for high quality china clay, casks for salted pilchards, and wet barrels for beer, salt meat and vinegar.

Dock workers would go home to lunch black from the dust from the coal they had unloaded in the morning, and return home again in the evening white from the china clay they had

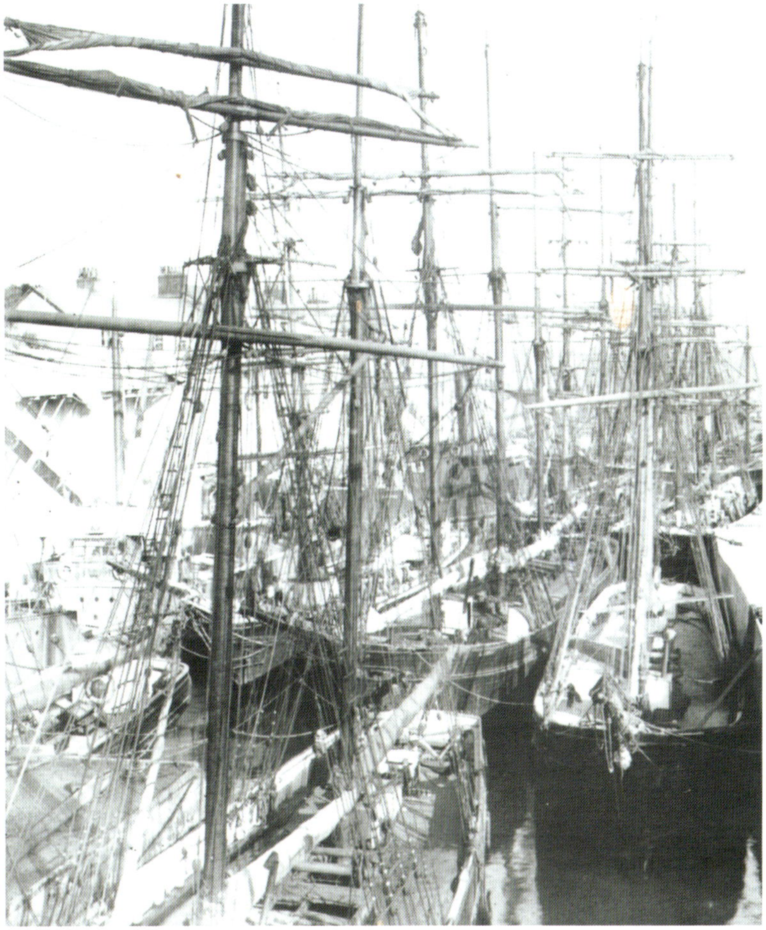

Charlestown Harbour *China Clay Museum*

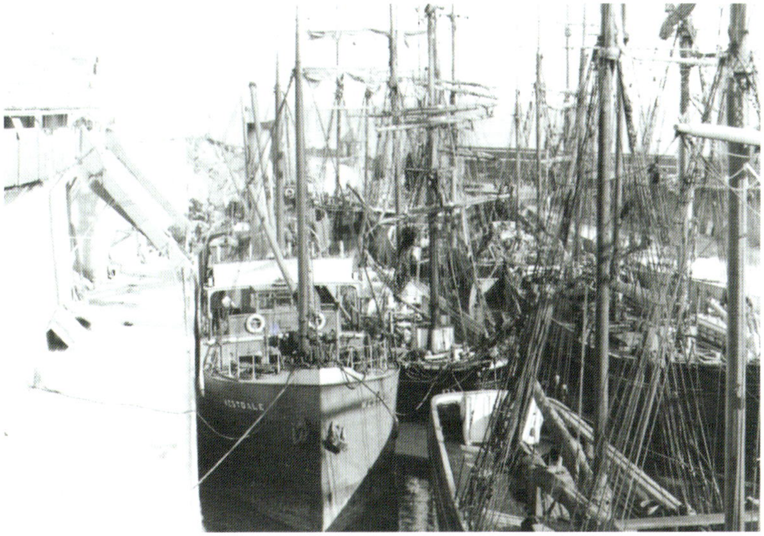

Loading clay, Charlestown Harbour *China Clay Museum*

been loading in the afternoon. A large amount of this trade was to Runcorn where the clay was taken to the Potteries via the canal system.

The following excerpt gives an insight into the life and conditions aboard a steam ship engaged in the coal and clay trade. "From Falmouth we sometimes went to Fowey and loaded china clay occasionally for France or Holland but mostly for Runcorn. This was a dirty trade, together with the coal which was full of greasy black dust which penetrated everywhere during both loading and discharging. Then the holds had to be brushed and washed out scrupulously clean before loading the china clay which was used for making pottery and cosmetics. The china clay was loaded by tipping it into the hold down a chute from a 10 or 12 ton wagon, a cloud of white dust covered the ship whilst this was in progress and a coat of dust about half an inch thick settled over the whole ship." *Old Time Steam Coasting*. Owen G Spargo Thomas H Lawson, Waine Research Publications

Reuben Chappell lived in Par and he could see the docks from his home. Par harbour had been built in the 1850s. It was originally constructed for the shipping connected with local mines and stone quarries, but as these declined china clay became the major export. Many thousands of tons of china clay still pass through Par docks each year. When Reuben Chappell lived there it was a very busy port with many vessels coming and going and he would have been a familiar figure on the quayside.

Another port that Reuben Chappell visited was Fowey, a few miles to the east of Par. The town is situated on a deep-water natural harbour in a sheltered position and is still used by ships carrying china clay.

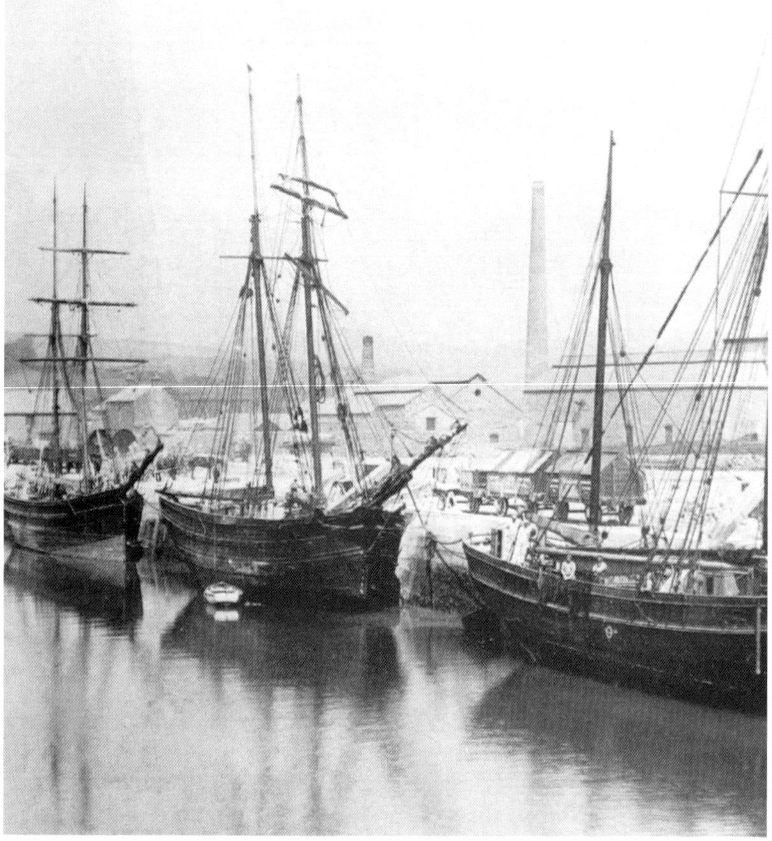

Par Harbour schooners loading china clay — *China Clay Museum*

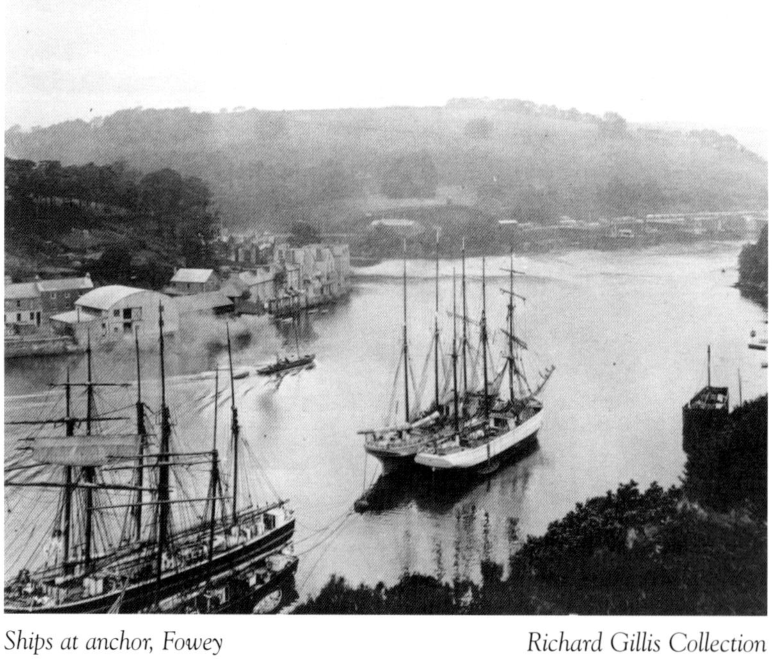

Ships at anchor, Fowey — *Richard Gillis Collection*

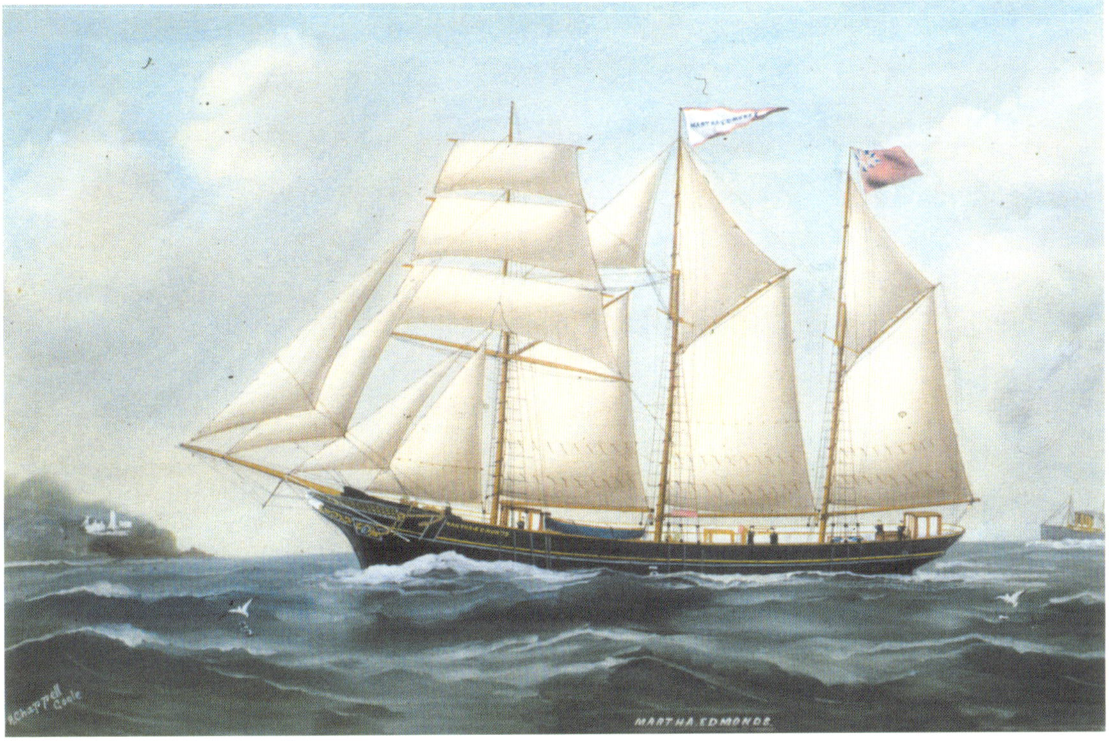

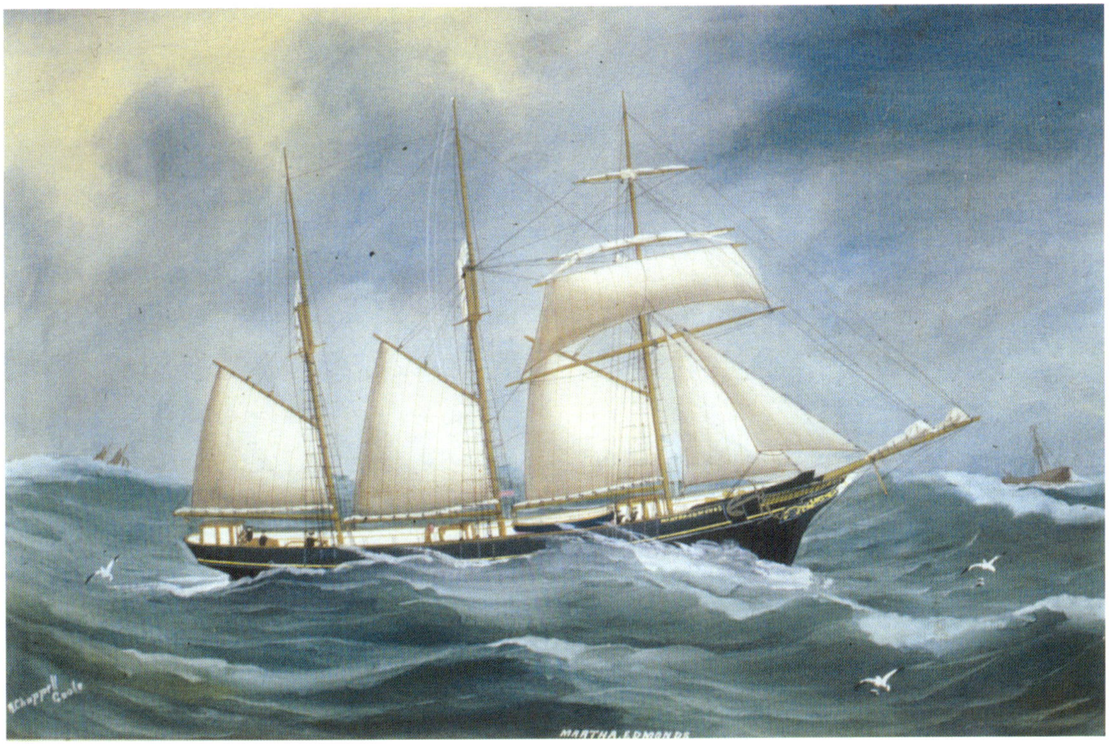

MARTHA EDMONDS

ON 60768; built 1873 by Jones of Milford; 186 tons net; 102.7' x 23' x 12.8'. code signal LWNR.

Martha Edmonds was built as a brig in 1873 in Milford, and was yellow-metalled in 1879. She was sold to J. Clunes of Par in 1878/9 whose family had extensive interests in local shipping affairs, and she worked from Fowey. In 1901 she was converted to a three-masted top sail schooner, and in 1909 she came under the management of Edward Stephens of Fowey. During the First World War, on the 20th August 1915, while on a voyage from Rouen to Seville carrying silver sand she was sunk by gunfire from a German submarine 125 miles off the Lizard. Later the crew were picked up by a Swedish steamer.

Martha Edmonds. A fine and foul-weather pair of paintings

Private collections. Photographs courtesy of Parker Gallery, London

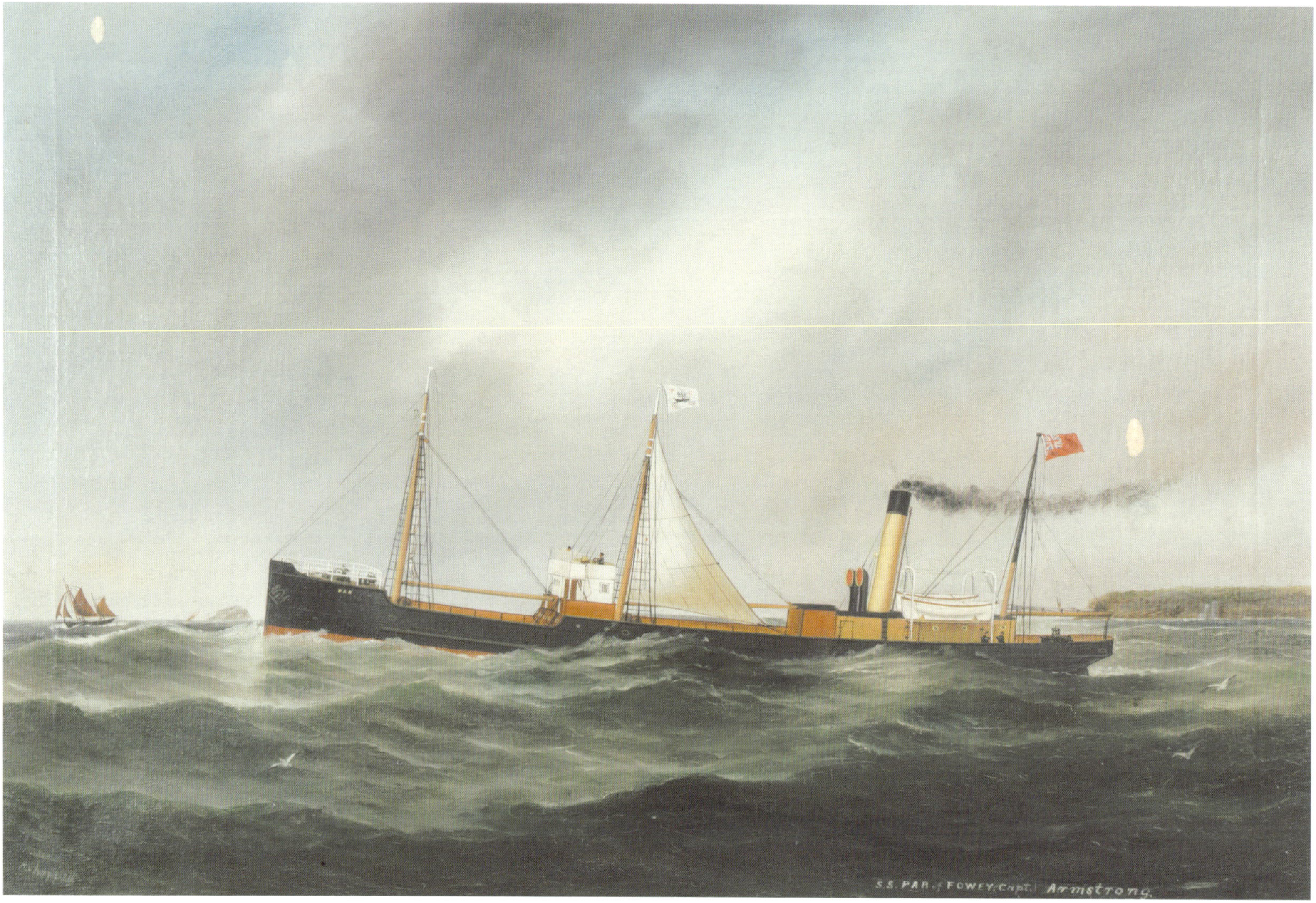

SS Par *Private Collection*

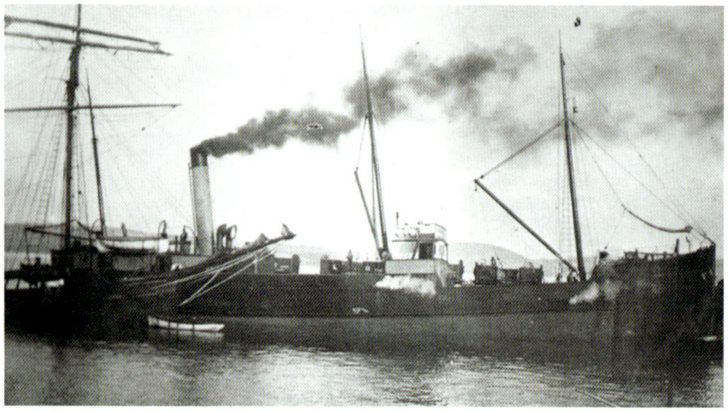

SS Par in Padstow *Richard Gillis Collection*

SS Par of Fowey & SS Foy of Fowey

SS Par ON95739; steel screw; built 1902 Paisley; 436 gross tons; 155.5' x 27.0' x 10.6'; 88 hp engine; owners The Par SS Co.

SS Foy ON116062; steel screw; built 1902 Workington by R. Williamson & Son; 354 gross tons; 136.4' x 23.8' x 9.0'; 2 cylinder 69 hp engine; owners The Fowey SS Co.

Captain Jim Armstrong was born in County Antrim and at the age of twelve went to sea as a cabin boy in the barquentine Indian Queen, captained by his father. This was the beginning of his life at

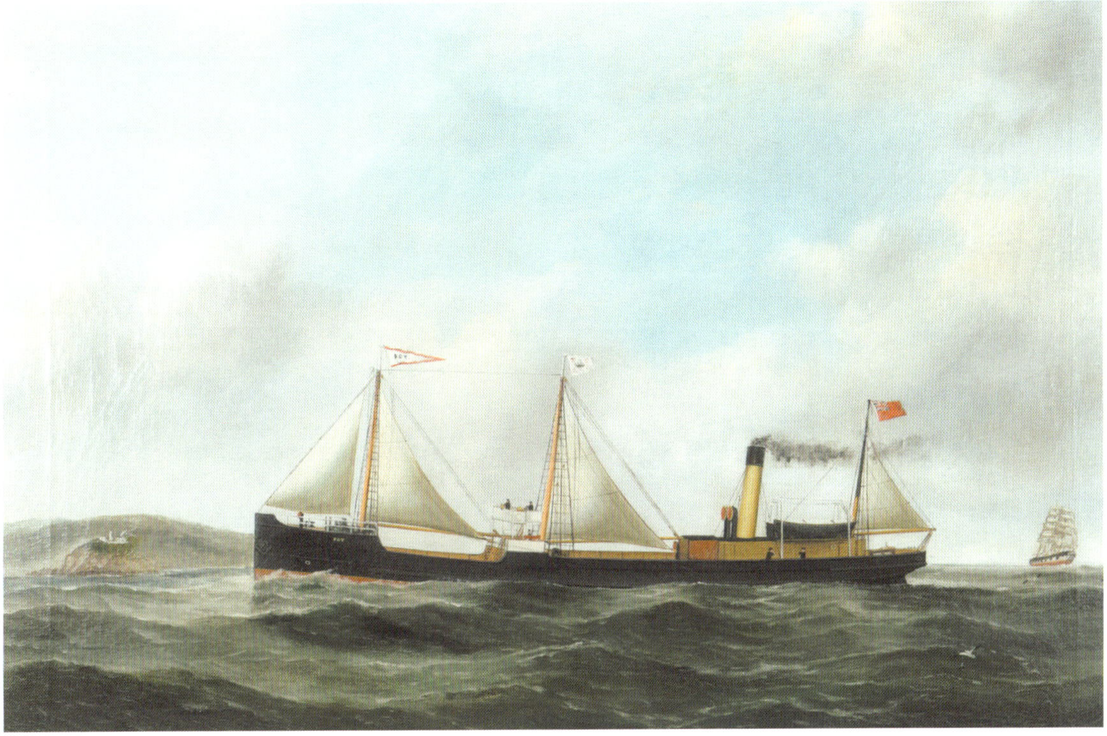

SS Foy *Private Collection*

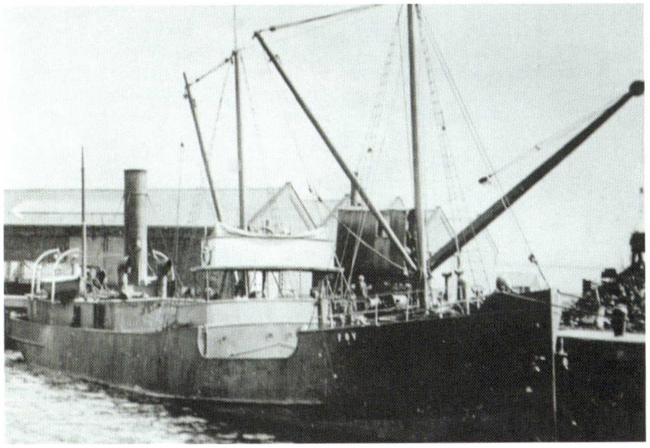

SS Foy *China Clay Museum*

sea, and he went on to become a master in both sail and steamships, and was also a Liverpool pilot. He married a Mevagissey girl and settled in Cornwall, becoming a well-known figure in Par. For many years he commanded two well known Par ships, the SS Par and the SS Foy, both owned by the Toyne and Carter company of Par. It was during this time that Captain Armstrong commissioned his friend Reuben Chappell to make oil paintings of the vessels. Captain Armstrong later became the captain of the Par tug Treffry which was employed towing vessels both sail and steam in and out of the port of Par. At that time there could be as many as seventeen ships unloading and loading cargo in the port at the same time.

Captain Armstrong's granddaughter, together with her mother, took some sea trips aboard one or two of the ships her grandfather commanded. She recalled that on some of the voyages the weather was so bad they were shaken out of their bunks.

As well as carrying cargoes of china clay, SS Par and SS Fowey regularly carried coal.

S.S. Deerhound

ON 87030; iron screw schooner-rig steamer; launched Forrest & Son, Limehouse, London 1882; 420 tons gross; 159.5' x 24' x 12.2'; two cylinder compound engine; owned 1886 Walker & Howard of London, and 1905 Toyne & Carter of Fowey.

This vessel would have been very familiar to Reuben Chappell as she was based in Fowey and used to carry china clay. He has shown her with her full set of sails as well as steam power as she makes her way eastward up the English Channel past the white cliffs. During the First World War the government took the more modern ships for war service, but SS Deerhound which came from an older mid-engined class continued to trade throughout the First World War.

The silhouette of an interesting transitional period vessel is seen on the horizon astern of her.

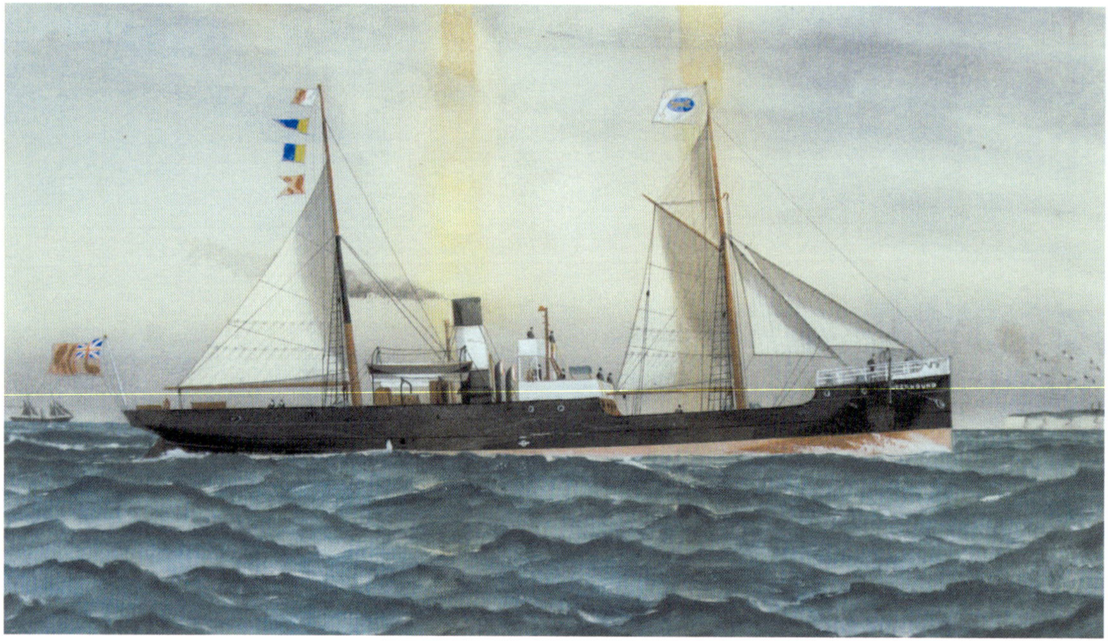

Private Collection

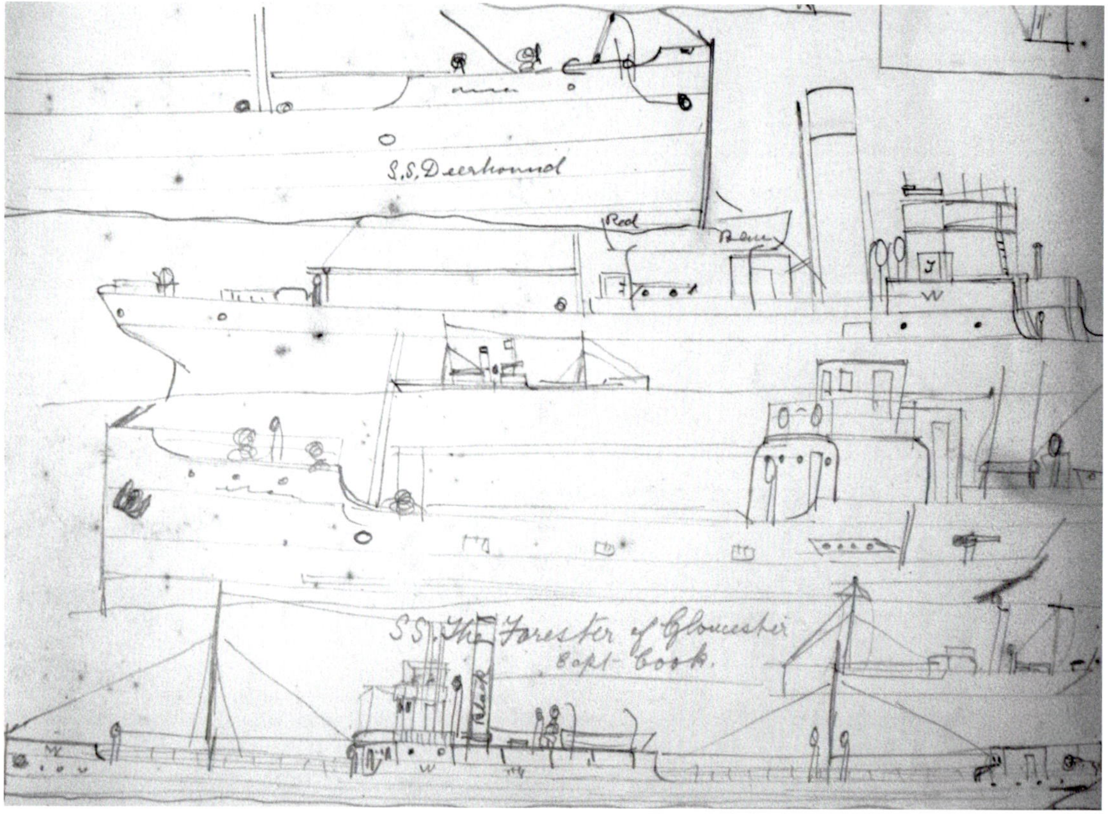

Sketchbook drawings of steamships including the Deerhound *Private Collection*

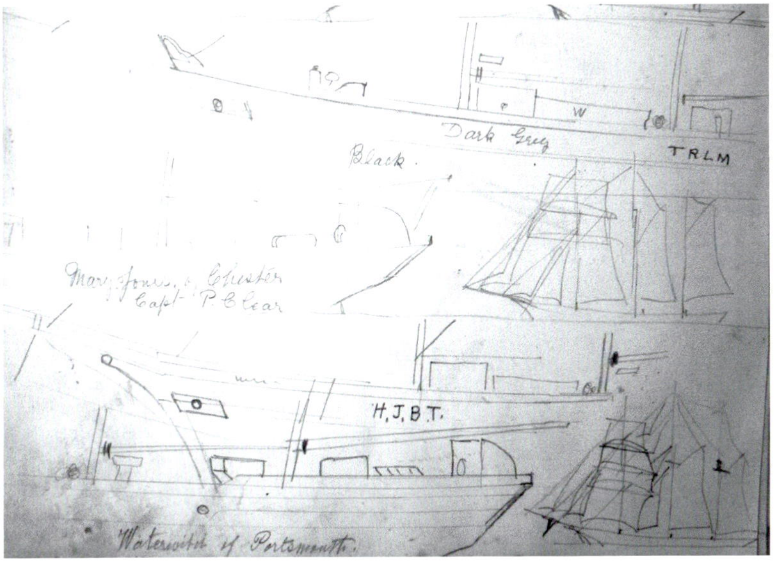

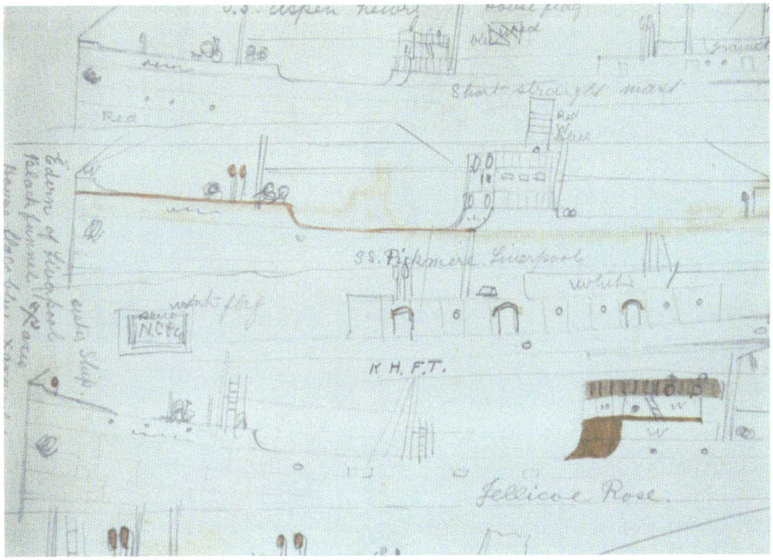

SKETCHBOOKS

Having secured an order for a painting, Reuben Chappell would make drawings and notes of details of the vessel in a sketchbook. Clearly he had enough information here and in his memory, to produce the finished painting. Chappell's knowledge of his subject must have been considerable. For the most part he would only have seen the vessels when they were alongside the quay with their sails furled.

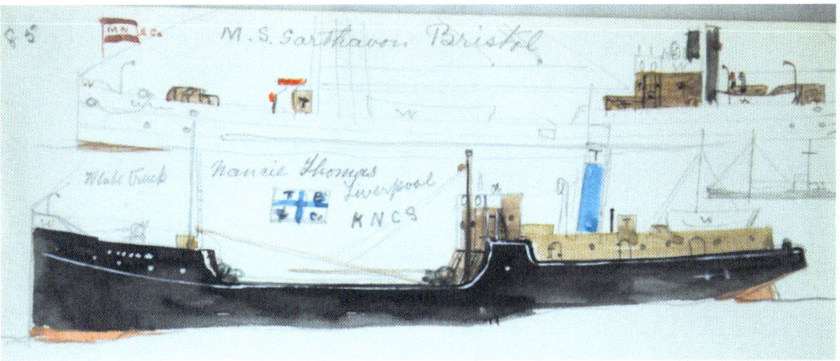

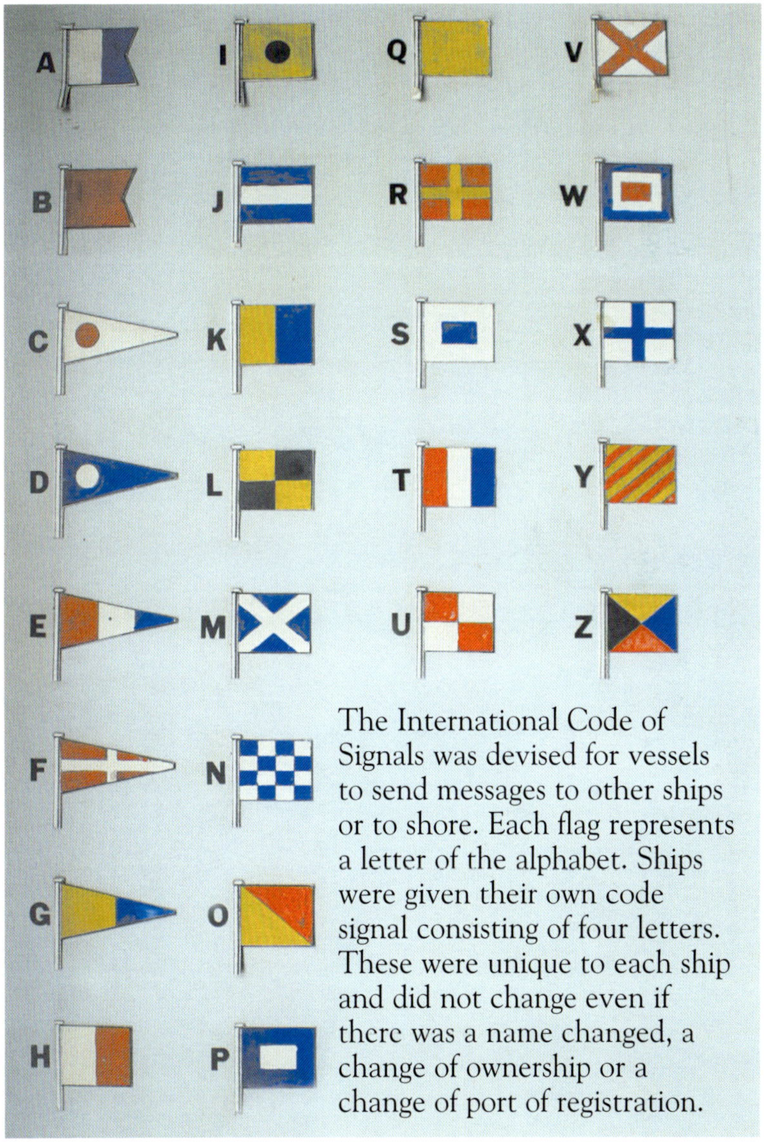

The International Code of Signals was devised for vessels to send messages to other ships or to shore. Each flag represents a letter of the alphabet. Ships were given their own code signal consisting of four letters. These were unique to each ship and did not change even if there was a name changed, a change of ownership or a change of port of registration.

International Code of Signals with amendments 1857-1931

The North Atlantic Cod Trade

Along the eastern seaboard of Canada and north America were, until recent times, rich fishing grounds on offshore shelves known as banks, the most well known of which are The Grand Banks. Since medieval times these areas were known for their abundance of fish, especially cod. The banks are the meeting place of several important ocean currents, the Labrador Current, the St Lawrence Current, and the Gulf Stream. From early times fishermen from the Basque region of France and Spain fished here and later the fisheries were exploited by other European countries. These fishermen had to return to their native shores with their catch, and to preserve it they salted the fish aboard their boats, at sea.

As settlements grew along the shore, the cod was caught by American and Canadian fishermen just off their coast and later on the offshore banks. Schooners were built which were about 60 - 80 ft in length and crewed by 10 - 12 men. From the fishing schooner small rowing boats known as dories were launched. They were worked by one or two men who would either jig for cod with hand lines or set longlines with hundreds of baited hooks which they hauled, cleared, baited and reset throughout the day, returning to the schooner to unload their catch. Aboard the schooner the freshly-caught cod would be gutted, the head and backbone removed and the flesh cleaned. The fish was then dispatched to the hold where it was packed with a layer of salt between each layer of fish. The salt would draw the moisture from the fish and preserve it for many months. Working in this way a fishing schooner would usually stay at sea for two or three months before returning to shore with her catch.

Life aboard these ships was hard and it was a particularly dangerous occupation for men in the dories, for besides the rough seas and swells of the North Atlantic this was an area of frequent dense fog, and many men lost their lives by getting lost in the fog, when attempting to return to their ship. Others drowned when their 15 ft dories, overloaded with fish, became swamped, the men in their heavy oilskins standing no chance in the freezing waters.

When the schooners returned to shore the fish would be washed, laid out and dried in the sun. This was a labour-intensive process which often involved women and children who had to bring in all the drying fish every time there was a chance of rain. Given good weather the drying process would take between one and two weeks. Salting and drying the cod was a very effective way of preserving it, and provided that it was kept dry it could be stored for many months. Fish laid out to dry in the sun was a conspicuous feature of the many small settlements and harbours along the coast. Competition led to the development of faster ships as it was important to travel to and from the fishing grounds as quickly as possible. So the fast fore and aft rigged fishing schooners evolved, in time influencing the design of European vessels.

In the 19th century merchant sailing ships from all over Europe came to the settlements in Newfoundland and eastern Canada for cargoes of dry salt cod. Particularly prominent in this trade were vessels from Wales, south west England and Denmark. They brought salt and general cargoes and returned across the Atlantic with their holds full of dried cod which would go to the ports of Europe, especially to the Catholic countries of the Mediterranean where there was a practice of eating fish on Fridays. St John's in Newfoundland became the principal centre of the salt cod industry where the visiting ships would have dealt with companies such as Job Brothers & Co. For three centuries this was a very successful company primarily concerned with importing goods for sale on the local market and the exportation of dry salt cod to diverse foreign markets.

The voyage across the Atlantic and back was a considerable undertaking, and most ships in the cod trade were small, between 80 and 100 ft, and had crews of three to six men. The winter crossings in particular would have been extremely demanding on both ships and men.

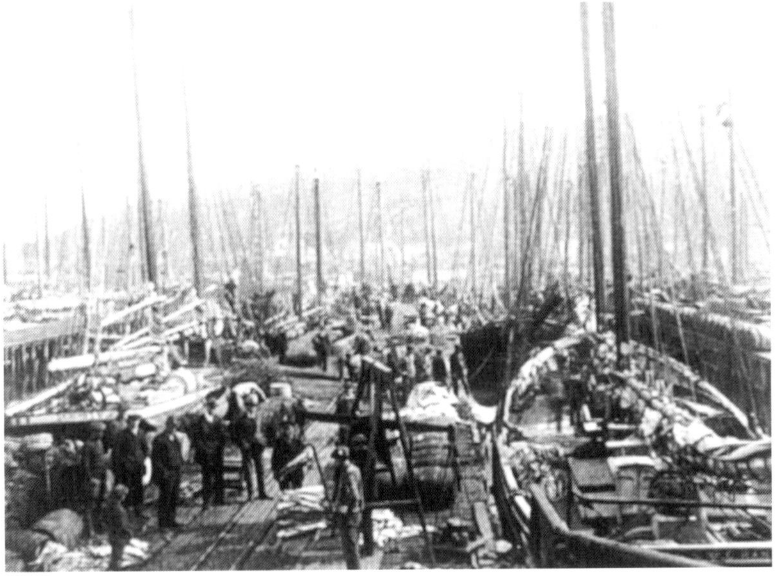

A forest of masts and trading vessels, St John's Harbour, early 20th century.
Maritime history archive Memorial University Newfoundland. PF-010

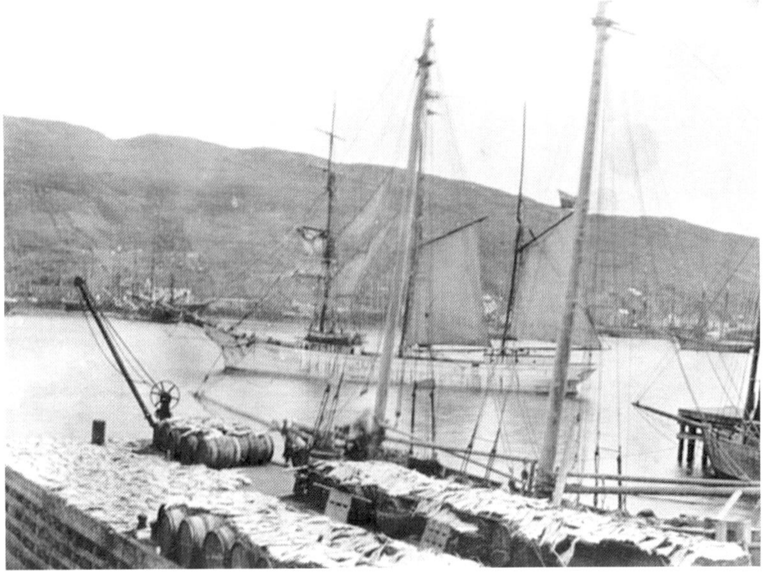

Cod fish spread for drying at Job Brothers & Co. St Johns.
Maritime history archive Memorial University Newfoundland. PF-315.178

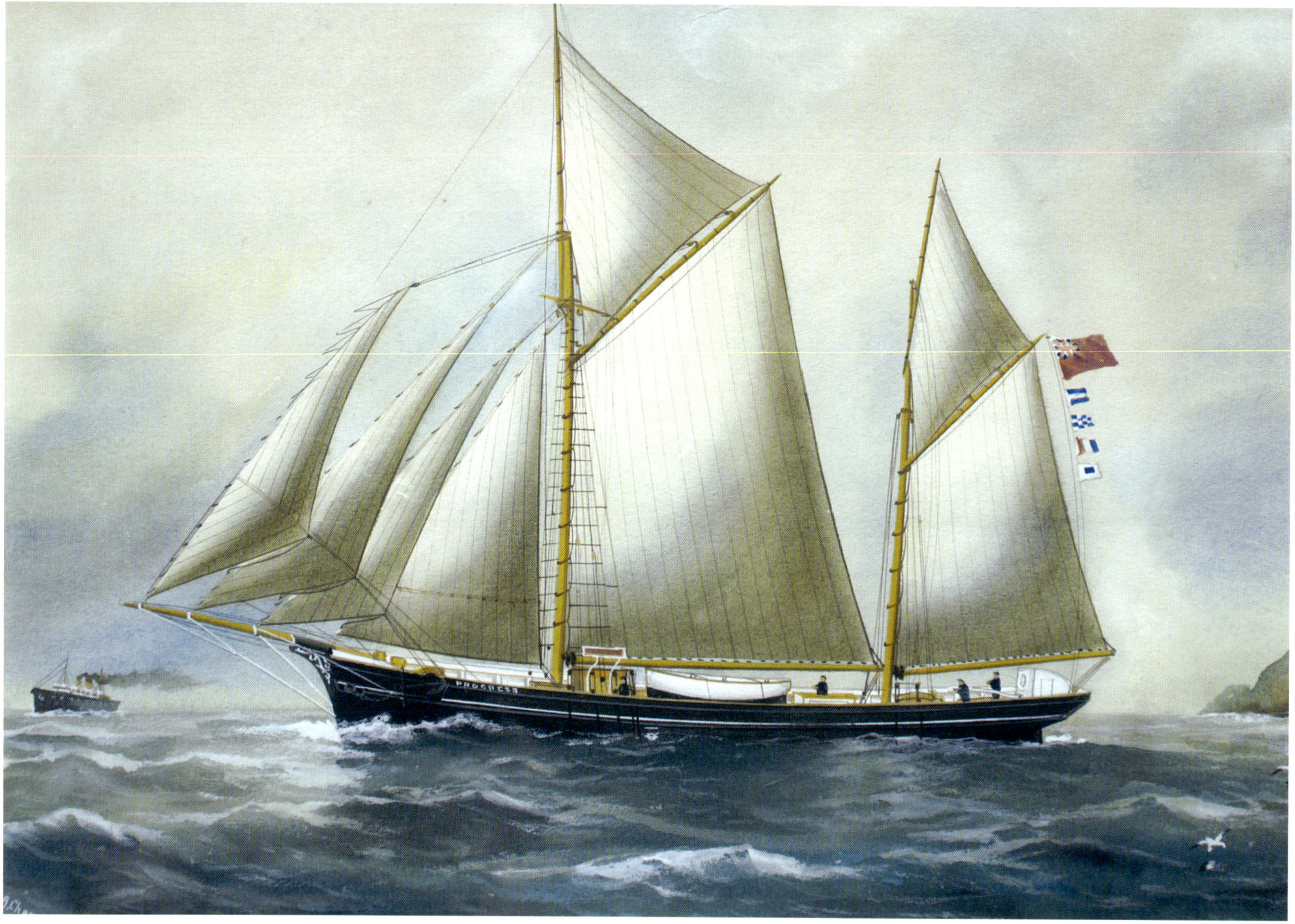

Progress of Bideford

ON 86466; wooden ketch; launched 1884, W. Date, Kingsbridge; 85 gross tons. 80.2'; signal JNTS.

The West Country ketch Progress was well known for 75 years. She was built for the North Atlantic trade to Newfoundland and sailed there for nineteen years, making four Atlantic crossings each year. This extraordinary record exemplifies the sort of voyages these vessels undertook. It is said that during this time Progress, unusually, never lost a member of her crew, and only once suffered serious damage - when hove to for 30 days during a gale. On another occasion she is said to have made passing contact with an iceberg, and on yet another to have

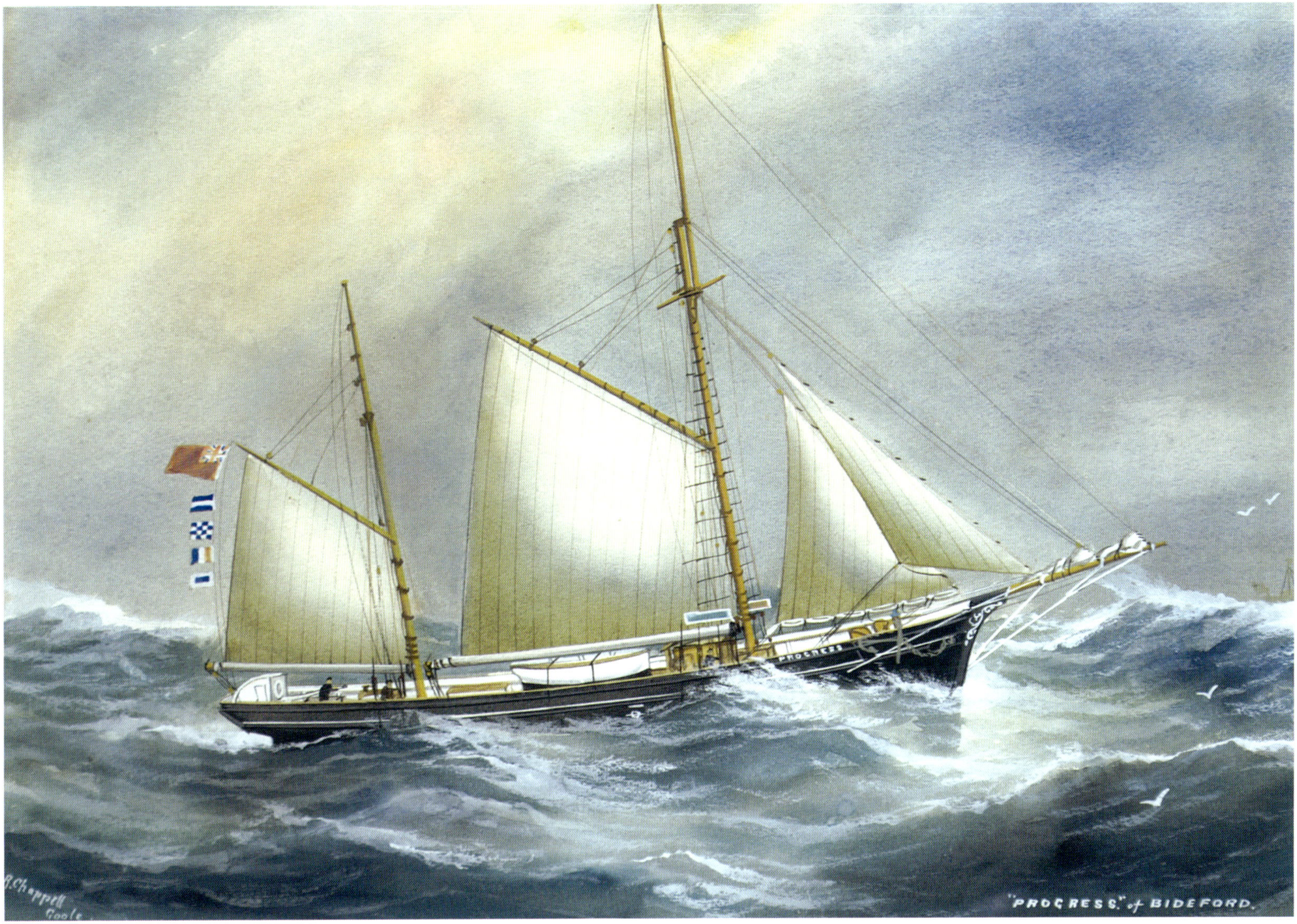

sailed from Newfoundland to the English coast in fourteen days. Progress's voyages to Newfoundland were for cod. Cod caught off the coast by Canadian and American fishermen, was cleaned and salted aboard their fishing schooners. At the end of the fishing trip it was taken ashore and then dried in the sun. The fish drying stages were a feature of every creekside settlement in Newfoundland. Over the years hundreds of sailing ships and thousands of men were involved in this trade.

Progress of Bideford was built by W Date & Sons of Kingsbridge, one of the greatest of the West Country builders of small sailing ships. The Date family started shipbuilding in Kingsbridge early in the 19th century and continued until its last years.

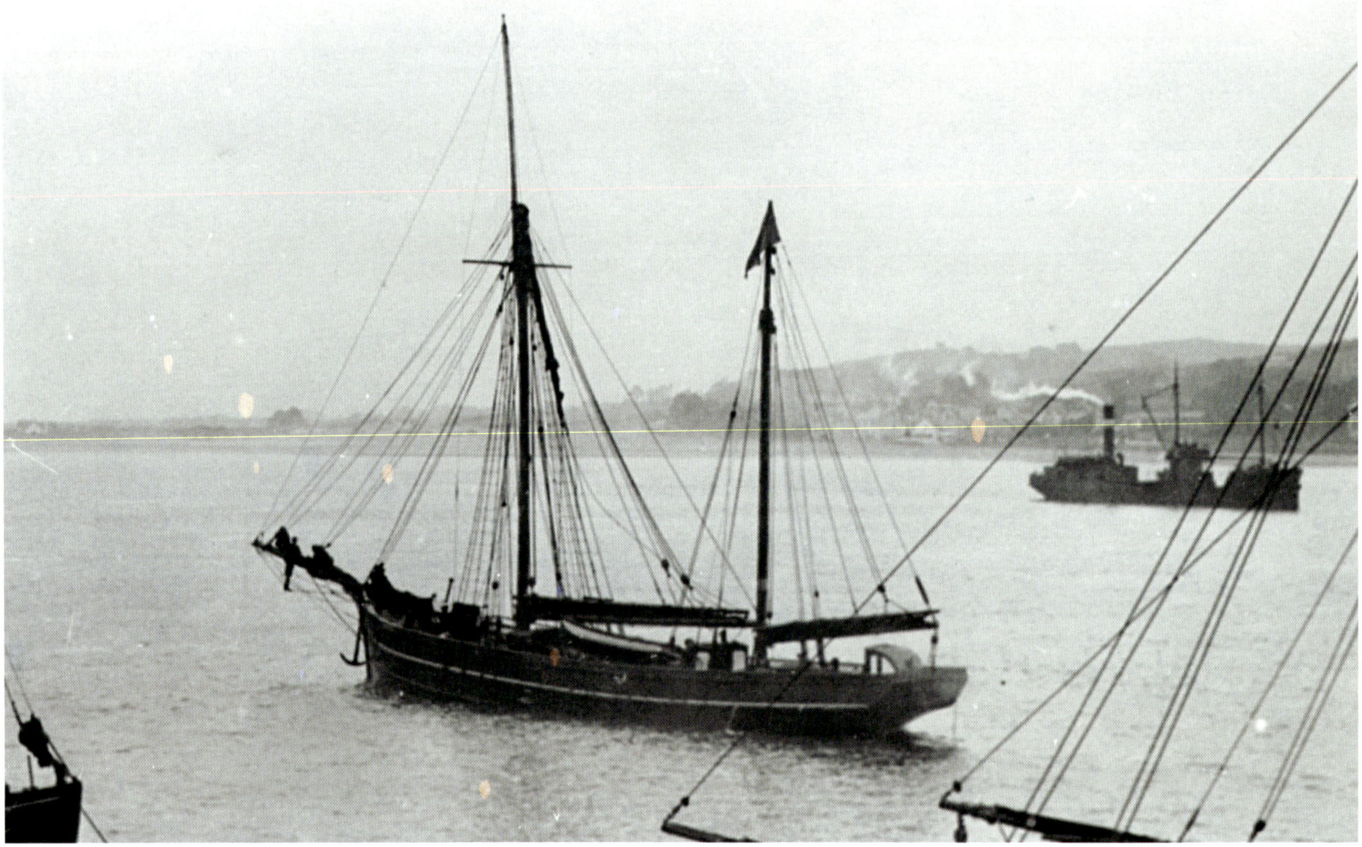

Progress of Bideford and passing steamship at Appledore. *Royal Cornwall Museum*

Following the decline in the trade to Canada, Progress was employed in the coasting trade. In 1919 she was fitted with a motor and converted to wheel steering, and in World War Two she was requisitioned as a barrage balloon vessel at Falmouth.

After years as a hulk Progress was refitted by the Harris brothers at Appledore and returned to sea as a ketch in 1950 when she resumed work in the coasting trade carrying road stone, scrap metal, cement, coal, concrete blocks etc., until July 1954, when bound for the West Indies she was seriously damaged by a storm and has since been lying at Milford Haven.

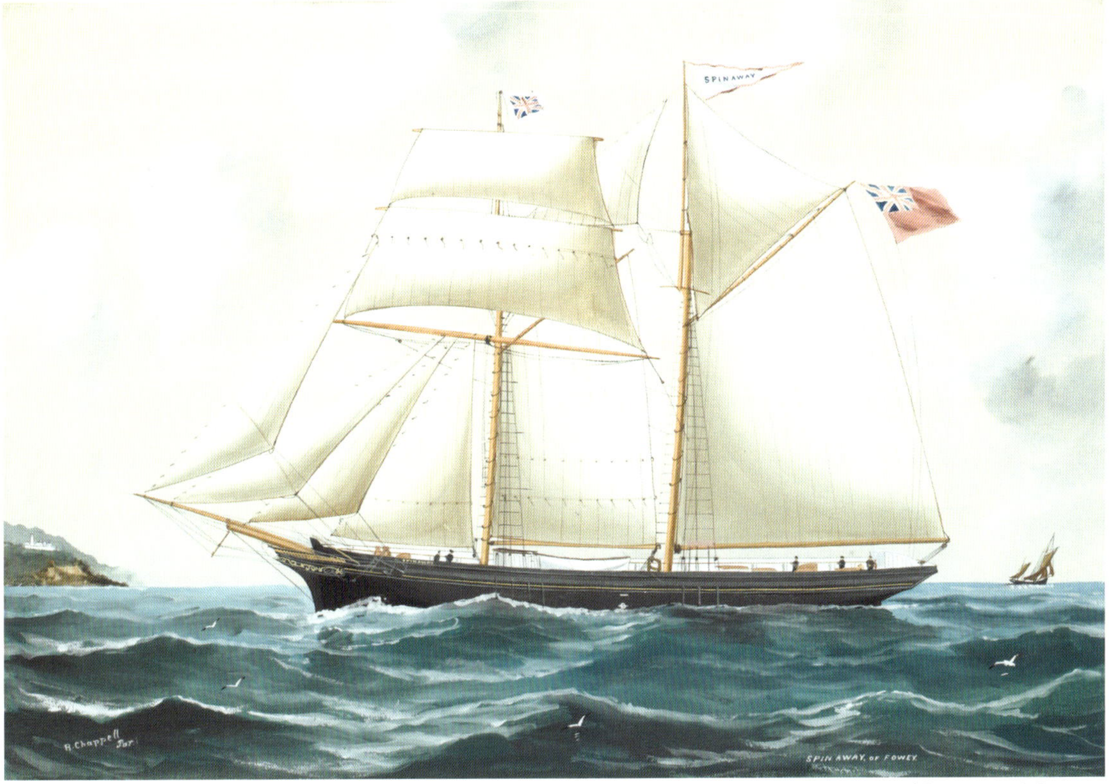

National Maritime Museum

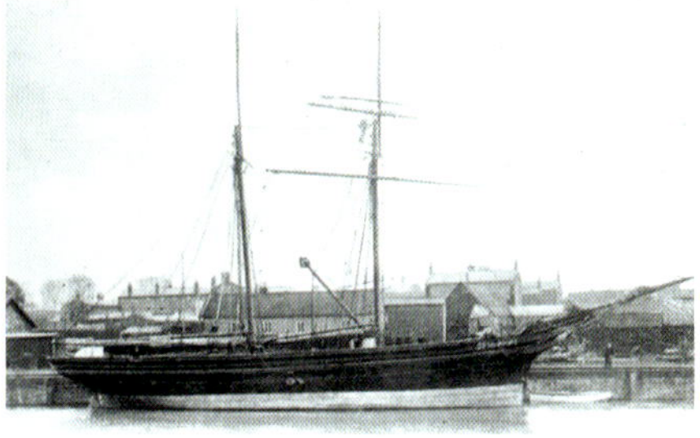

Spinaway Royal Cornwall Museum

SPINAWAY OF FOWEY

ON 77360; wooden schooner; built 1887 by John Stephens of Fowey; 95 tons gross; 83.2' x 20.4' x 10.5'; owners E. Stephens; reg Fowey.

Spinaway, a fast and beautiful little schooner was one of John Stephens's Company of Little Ships. In 1895 she sailed from St John's to Oporto crossing the north Atlantic in fifteen days. In the winter of 1911-1912 a series of gales swept the north Atlantic, among the worst gales on record at the time. Ships were being driven into shelter for weeks, and many vessels were wrecked. On the 28th October 1911 Spinaway left Trepani, Italy with salt for Newfoundland. She had a crew of five and passed Gibraltar into the Atlantic a month later. For the next two months she fought continuous gales and bad weather. She was within 600 miles of the Newfoundland coast when she suffered damage to her rigging.

Captain Rundle turned about and headed back across the Atlantic towards Britain. One day after her supplies had run out she reached Fowey.

Captain Rundle was in command when Spinaway was sunk by submarine gunfire 45 miles north west of Cape Finisterre on December 26th 1916.

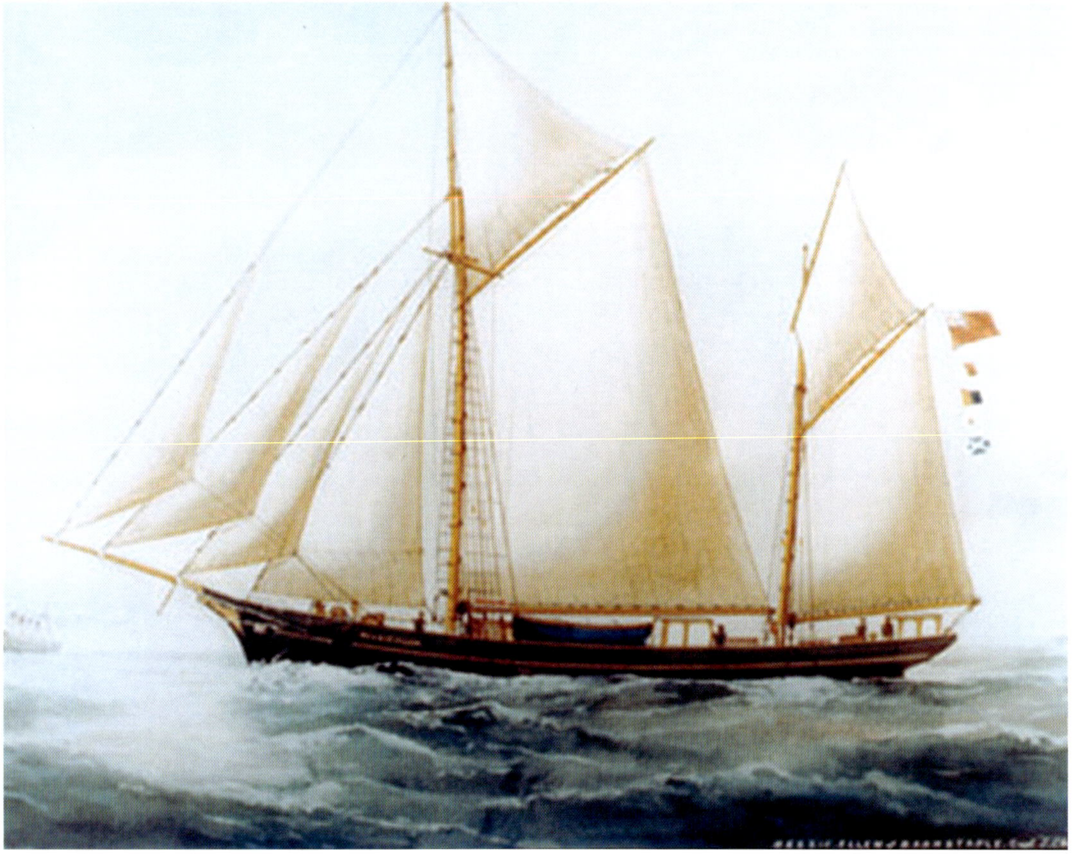

Private collection

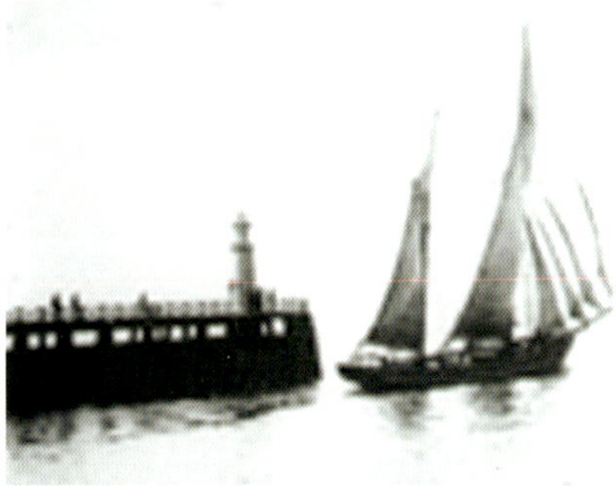

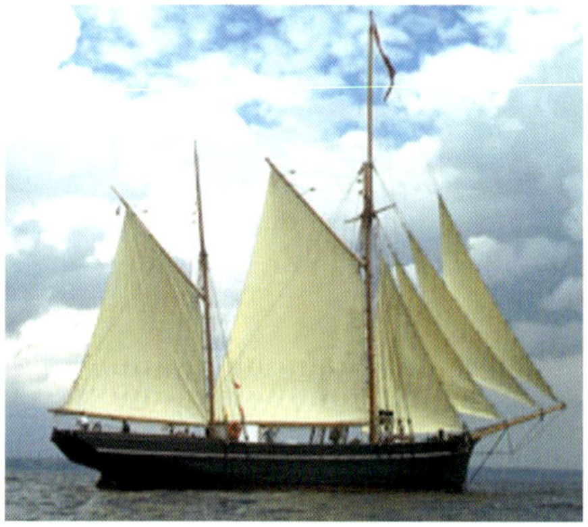

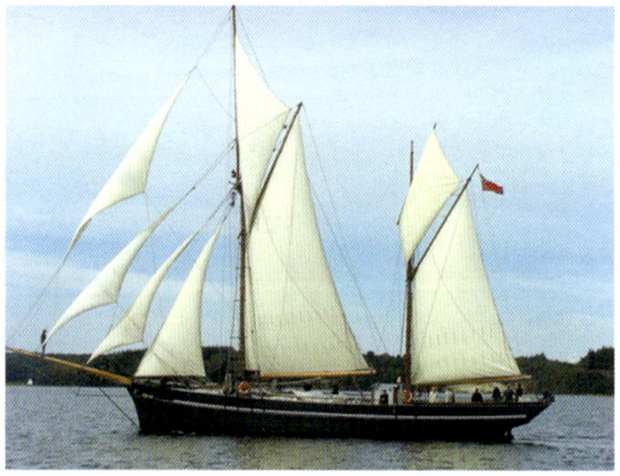

Bessie Ellen

ON 45671; wooden ketch; launched January 1907, W. S. Kelly of Plymouth; 77.4'; 79 gross tons; Captain J. S. Chichester; owned by Mrs B. G. Chichester of Braunton; signal HKCM; reg. Barnstaple.

For most of her life Bessie Ellen was engaged in the coasting trade. She worked around Newport, Swansea and also the Bristol and English Channels. For many years she was involved in the coal trade from South Wales to North Devon. In 1916 Bessie Ellen was sailing down the Welsh coast in company with the schooner P. T. Harris. During the voyage the pair were caught in a squall, the P. T. Harris vanished and was never seen again.

A Widdop engine was installed in 1922 salvaged from the Bideford ketch Heather Bell. In April 1947 Bessie Ellen was sold to Denmark and remained there until she was found in a disused state by her present owner. She is one of the few ships that Reuben Chappell painted that have survived. She is now based in Plymouth. Her present owner has spent several years refitting her since she found her in Denmark. The current photograph of her sailing shows just how accurate Chappell's paintings were.

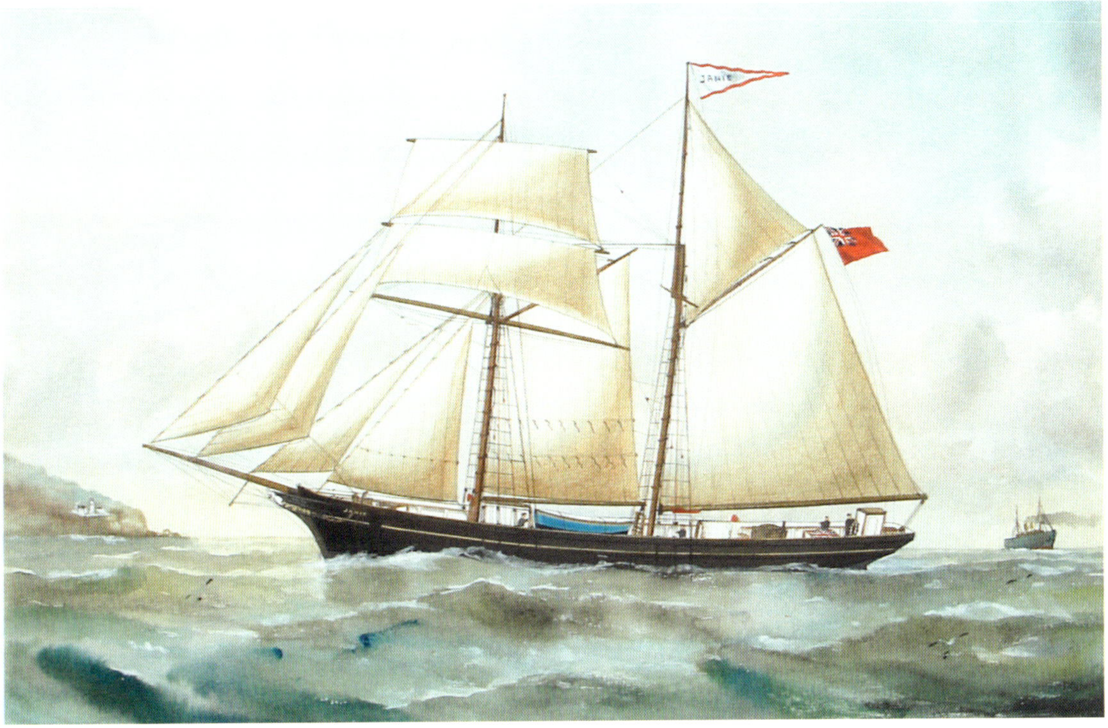

Private collection

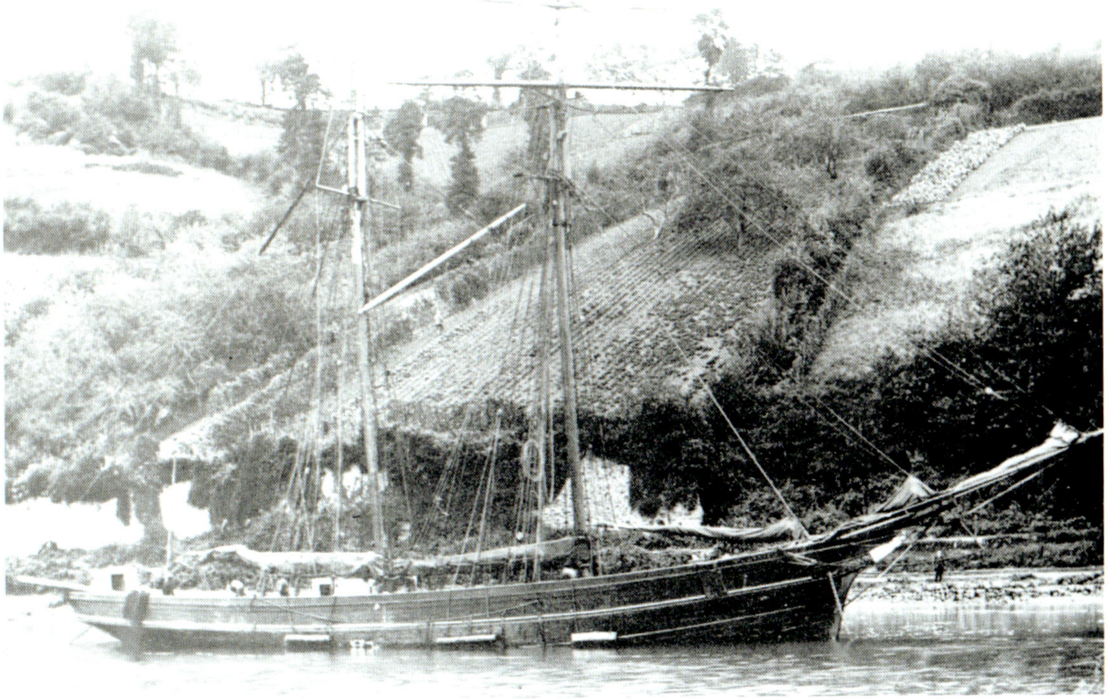

Janie on the Tamar near Calstock — *Royal Cornwall Museum*

JANIE OF TRURO

ON 77425; schooner; built 1876 by Nicholas Scoble of Malpas; 134 net tons; 82.0' x 22.7' x 11.6'; owners R. S. Hitchens & Co of Truro.

Janie of Truro was employed in the Newfoundland and South American fish trade. She sailed from England to Newfoundland and then with salt cod to Brazil, and from there to the Rio Grande for hides which were carried to Plymouth or London. Janie was a fast ship. It is said that she sailed to Oporto from Plymouth in ten days, and returned in the same time, and that she loaded cargo in Plymouth which was discharged in London in less than a week.

The Fruit Trade

The great fruit trade ports were those of the South Hams of Devon, Dartmouth, Brixham and Salcombe. This trade lasted from about 1840 until about 1870 with occasional cargoes into the late 1890s.

Ships had been built within the shelter of Salcombe estuary for many centuries. The quality and workmanship of the boat-builders of this area attracted buyers from far afield, one of the most famous being W Date and Son of Kingsbridge. The fruit ships were sheathed with strips of copper below the waterline to protect the timber from Teredo worm. The copper also protected the hull from the formation of barnacles and weed, which could affect the speed of the boat.

The fruit ships were employed from November to April in the worst weather of the year. The small fruit schooners, mostly just under 100 tons, forged their way west in ballast and returned with their very perishable cargoes. As much canvas as possible was hoisted by ships returning from the Azores for the fastest passage.

The Orange and Lemon Trade from the Azores and Western Mediterranean was the most important of the fruit trades. The fruit was discharged in London, Liverpool and Bristol. The first boat home had the best price for the oranges and was sometimes rewarded with a fresh set of sails. Oranges from the Azores came wrapped individually in maize leaves and in 1854 sixty million oranges and fifteen million lemons were imported in to London alone. That year there were 240 schooners in the trade.

The number of crew on these ships was kept to a minimum, sometimes only the master, mate and three hands to ensure greater profit. One of the most famous of the Salcombe schooners, The Eleanor, made the Azores and back in 17 days. The West Indies Pineapple Trade began in about 1842 and rapidly increased. By 1854 two hundred thousand pineapples were brought into London each year. There was also the Spain and Portugal Melon Trade and the Currant Trade from the Greek islands. Currants were less perishable than fresh fruit so bigger and slower vessels could be used. Fruit ships operated from Salcombe from about 1840 to the end of the century when the advent of the steamship and improved port facilities meant the decline of the schooner trade. By the end of the century most of the fruit schooners had lost their business to the faster steamships. Some of them were employed in the Newfoundland salt fish trade while many others were employed carrying various cargoes in home waters.

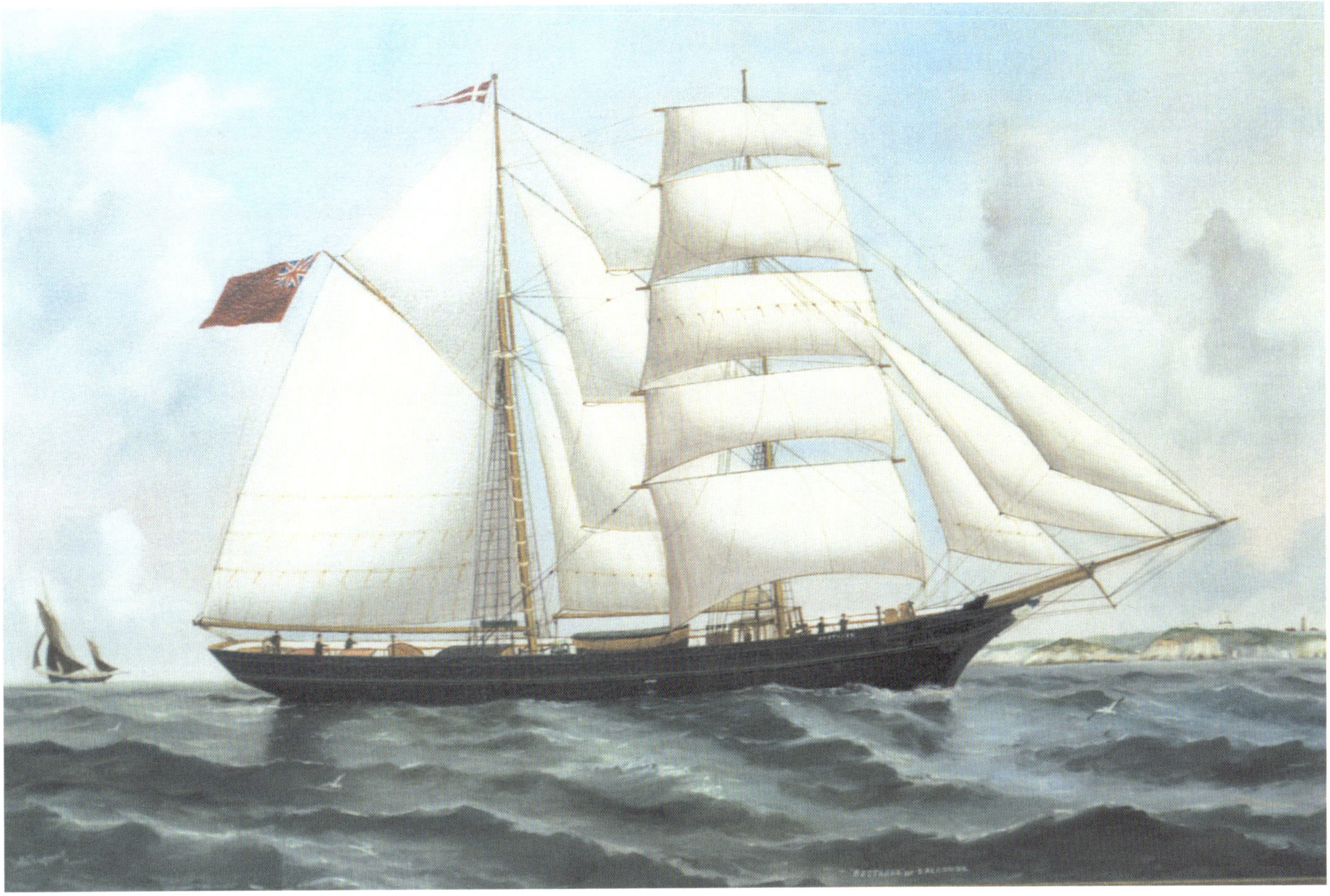

National Trust, Overbecks Museum, Salcombe

RESTLESS

ON 51304; built as schooner changed to brigantine in 1870; built 1865 by W.M. Date, Kingsbridge; 190 tons; 101' x 23.5' x 12.7'; owned by W.R. Beer; reg Salcombe.

This painting of Restless, a famous fruit ship which sailed from Salcombe, is in the Overbecks Museum which overlooks the mouth of the estuary at Salcombe. There is an account book there for the ship which records her voyages from March to November in 1880. Restless sailed to Demerara, from there to New York, across the Atlantic to Belfast, and from there to St Michaels in the Azores, before returning to England. In 1914, in the Thames Estuary, the ship sank after a collision with the steamer Lord Londsborough.

PENZANCE

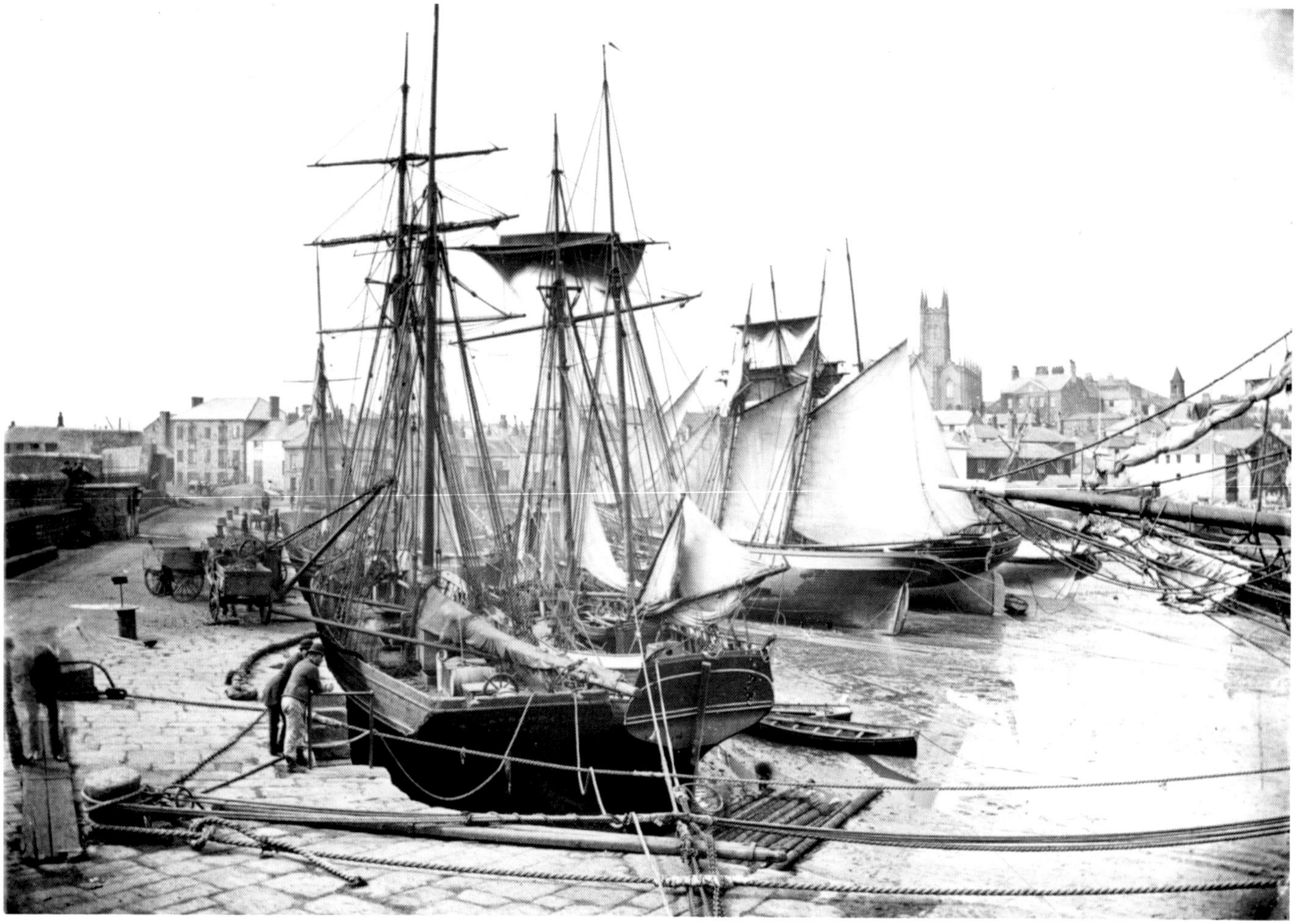

Penzance, the most south westerly port in Britain, developed from a medieval fishing village. In 1845 the size of the harbour was increased with the building of the Albert Pier, and by this time was a busy trading port with a good number of locally owned sail trading ships, some of which were involved in transatlantic and Mediterranean trade. Towards the end of the century the local coal company J. H. Bennetts owned a fleet of steamships.

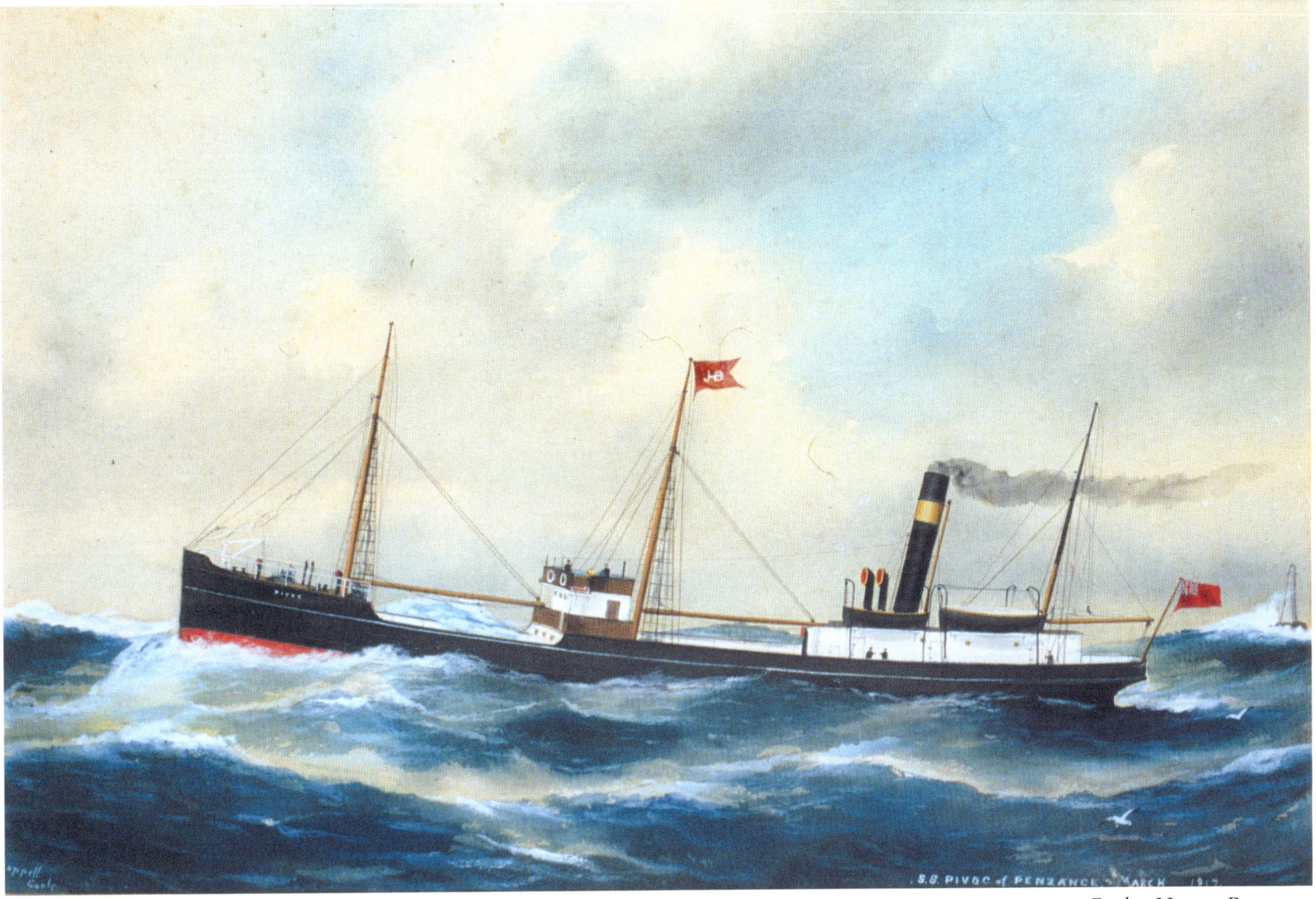

Penlee House, Penzance

SS Pivoc of Penzance

ON 102469; steel three-masted; built 1899 by Irving S & E Co Ltd.; 483 tons gross; 165' x 25.1' x 9.7'; owned by J. H. Bennetts, Penzance; reg Penzance.

Pivoc was the last steam coaster to be registered in Penzance. The ship was owned by J. H. Bennetts, coal importers and merchants.

The name of the vessel is an anagram of the first letters of the company's other ships, Progress, India, Vril, Omerod and Cornubia.

HAYLE

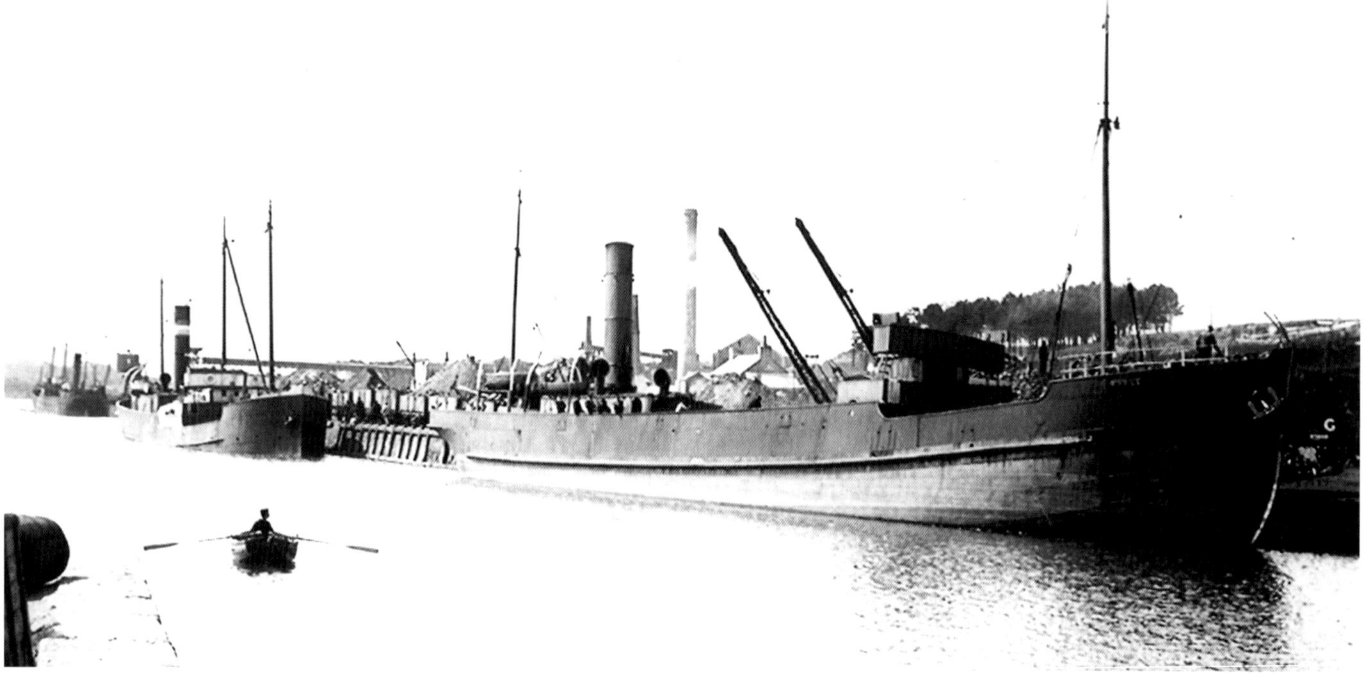

Hayle 1893 ship in the foreground SS Hayle built at Harvey & Co. *Paul Dyer*

The port and town of Hayle on the north Cornish coast grew rapidly in the latter part of the 18th century when local copper and tin mining industries were developing. Coal from Wales was brought in to Hayle to fuel the pumping engines for the mines in the surrounding area. Hayle's two main companies were the Cornish Copper Company and Harvey and Co. The latter was a very large engineering company employing over one thousand men. They were at the forefront of technological development of steam engines in the industrial revolution, and their machinery was used not only in Cornwall but was exported throughout the world.

In the 19th century Hayle had become the most important industrial port in Cornwall. The fleet of coasting sailing vessels which regularly voyaged to and from South Wales became known as 'The Welsh Fleet.' They carried tin and copper ore to Wales to be smelted, and returned with coal. Ships also carried the beam engines, boilers and mining equipment manufactured by Harvey's.

Although the Cornish mining industry declined, Harvey's engineering empire survived. They extended their ship building operations and produced some fine steamships.

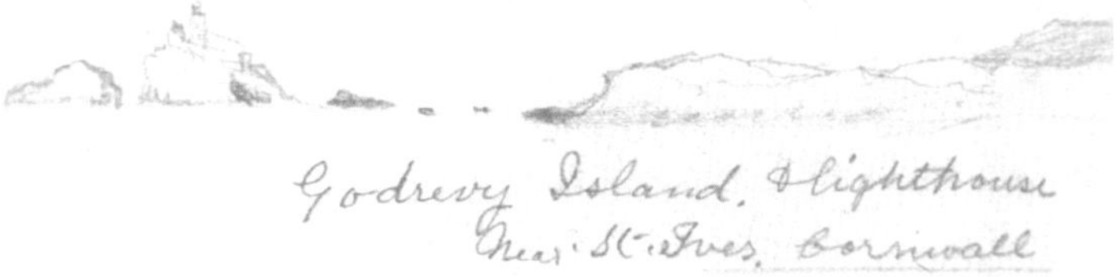

Sketch of Godrevy, near Hayle

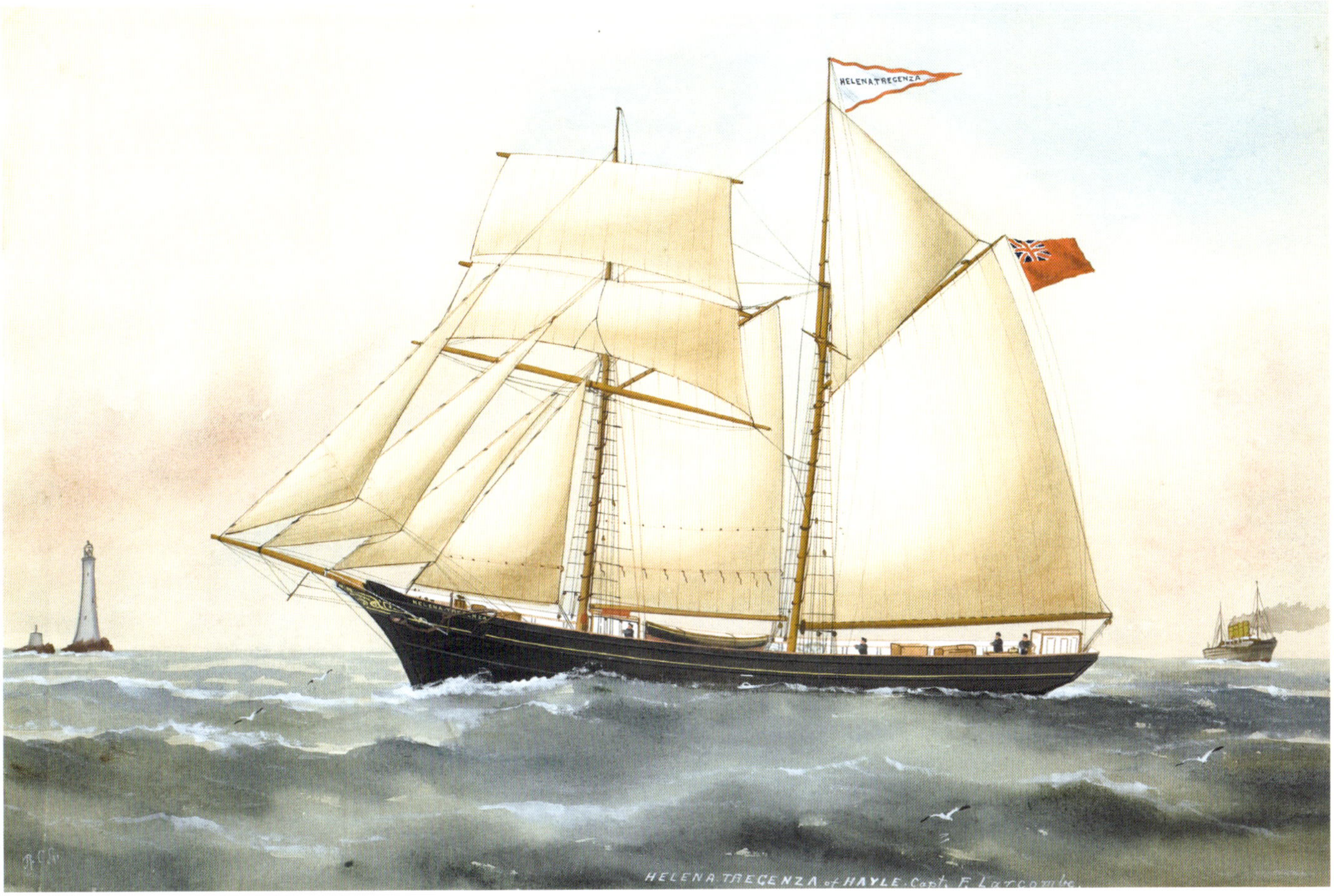

National Maritime Museum

Helena Tregenza of Hayle

ON 58675; wooden schooner; built 1869 by Massey of Portreath; 155 gross tons; 103' x 23' x11.5'; owners J. L. Tregenza of Hayle.

Helena Tregenza, a two-masted wooden schooner, was owned by John Tregenza, and registered in Hayle. She sailed regularly from South Wales to Hayle with coal for the local foundries and mines. In the 19th century large amounts of coal were used to fuel the beam engines which pumped water from the Cornish tin mines.

On 19th November 1894 while engaged in this trade, inward bound to Hayle, she was damaged in a collision. On 16th February 1908, with a cargo of coal from Newport for Charlestown her anchor dragged in a strong SSW gale and she was blown ashore near Charlestown. Fortunately the schooner was refloated with the aid of the Fowey tug.

Helena Tregenza was lost off Trevose in a severe storm on 17th November 1916.

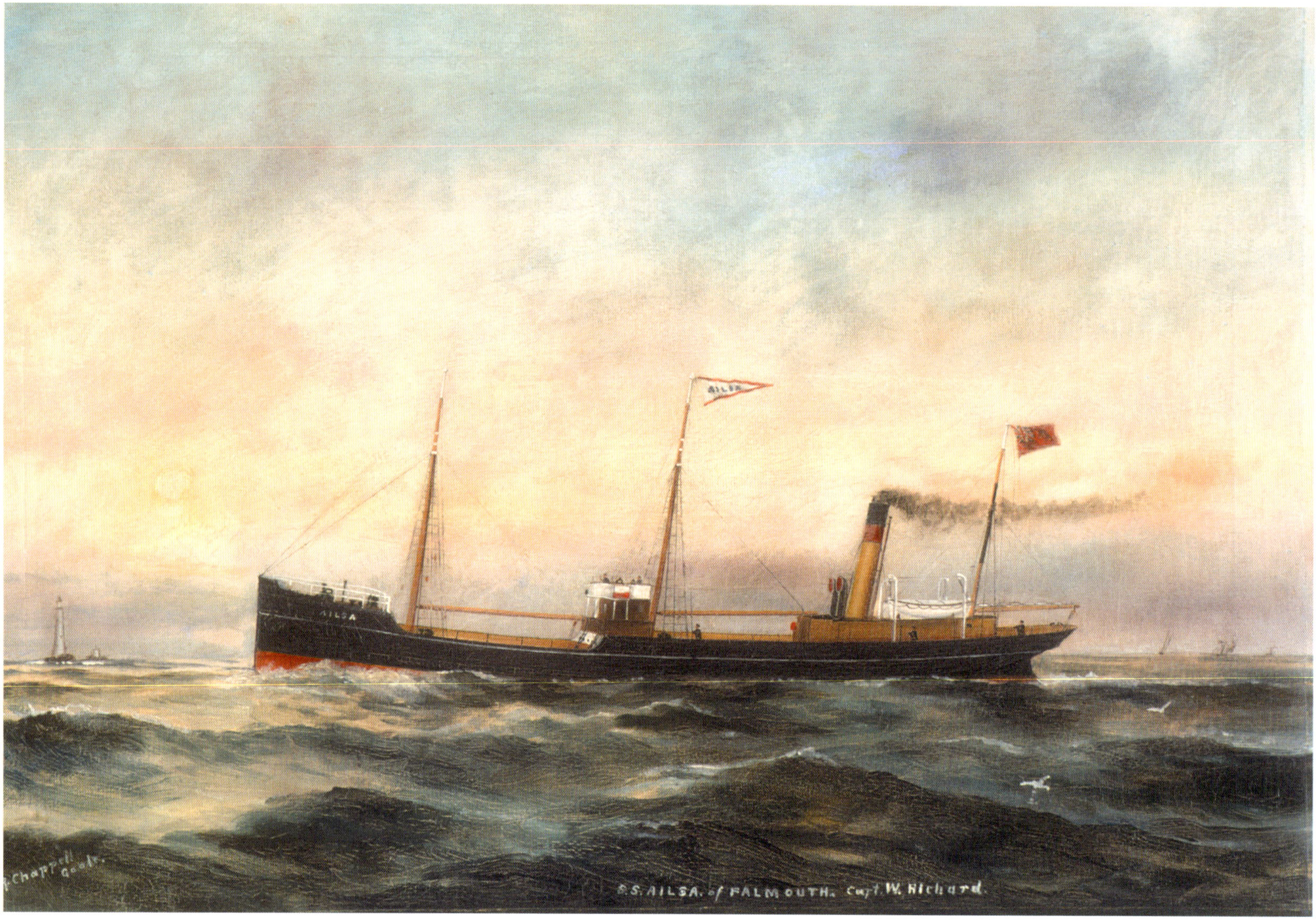

Courtesy of the British Mercantile Marine Memorial Collection

SS Ailsa of Falmouth

ON78735; iron screw steamship; 325 reg tons; built 1894 by Ailsa Shipbuilding Company of Troon for J. Hamilton of Troon; 290.6' x 34.2' x 23.9'; 200HP engine; owned by Atlas Steamship Company; reg Liverpool.

Another steam coaster regularly seen in Hayle was SS Ailsa. She had been bought by the Williams family who were mining merchants. The ship was employed carrying coal from South Wales to Hayle. Ailsa was later sold to Belfast and was scrapped in 1933.

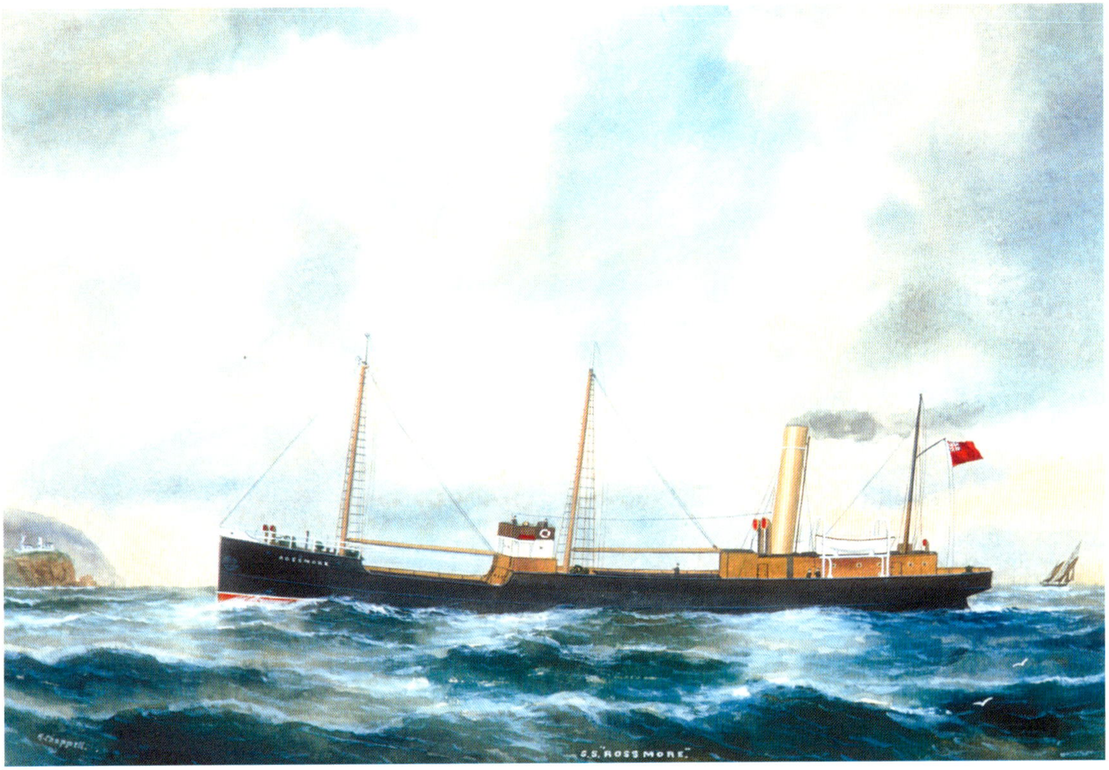

Courtesy of the British Mercantile Marine Memorial Collection

Both photographs from the Clive Carter Collection

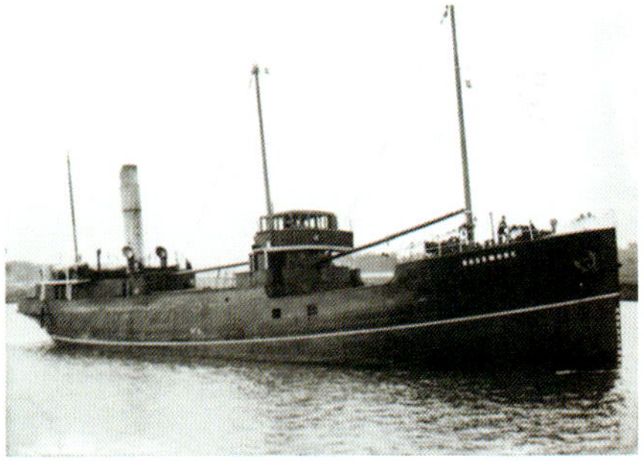

Rossmore in the 1930s

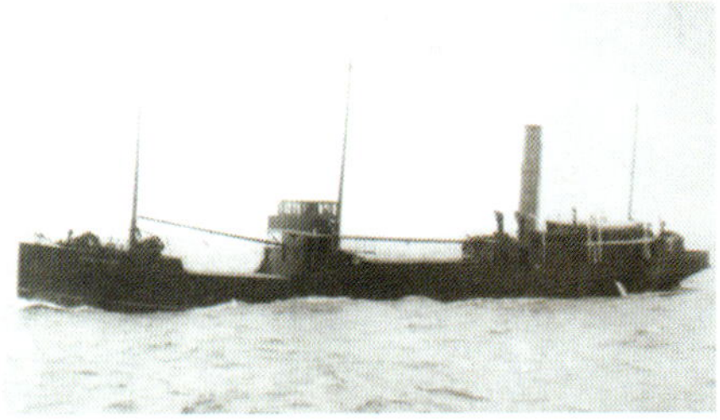

Rossmore in 1928 headed for Barry

SS Rossmore

One of four steam colliers, Taycraig, Abercraig, Marina, and Rossmore bought by the County of Cornwall Steamship Company in the 1930s. Although they remained registered in their previous ports (Glasgow and London) they were manned by crews from Cornish ports. The ships were employed in the general coasting trade but spent most of their time carrying coal to the port of Hayle where it was destined for the Cornish mines and foundries, and Hayle power station. SS Rossmore had the nickname 'clipper of the colliers.'

There is a remarkable story about one of the men connected with SS Rossmore. Having survived two dramatic sinkings on both SS Taycraig and SS Porthcarrack, he was serving as mate on SS Rossmore. By 1941 German bombers were highly active over the Southwest Approaches and the Bristol Channel. On 28th March, SS Rossmore and SS Marina left Hayle in ballast, bound for Barry to collect a cargo of coal. There was a strong wind and quite a sea running, when, just after 8pm, SS Rossmore was attacked by a German plane. There was machine-gun fire followed by a heavy explosion. The mate stayed with the ship until she started to sink. She was almost vertical when at last he jumped into the sea. Fortunately the slower Marina was behind SS Rossmore, and was able to rescue four of the crew including the mate.

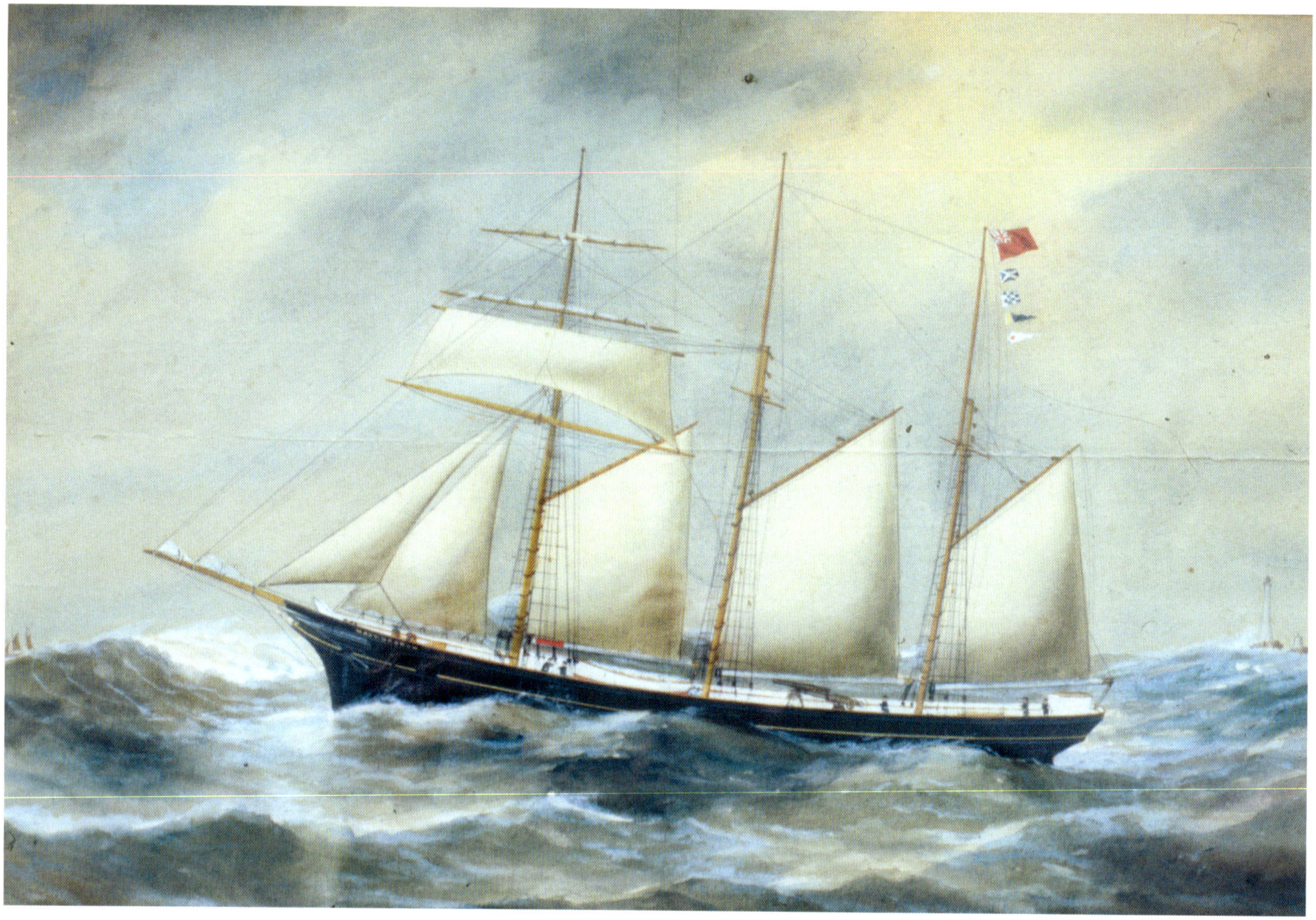

Private Collection

MARY BARROW

ON 93424; wooden three-masted schooner; built 1891 by William Henry Lean, Falmouth; 166 gross tons; 103' x 24' x 10.8'; owned by J. Barrow; reg Barrow.

The schooner Mary Barrow was built in Falmouth for owners in Barrow-in-Furness, and her first master was Captain James Crewdson. In her early years the ship was employed in the Newfoundland cod trade. She also sailed to South America in what was known as the 'Rio Grande' trade, carrying hides and bone-meal from Brazil and Uruguay. It was on one such voyage in 1894 that some of the crew developed yellow fever. During the five week return voyage two of the six crew had died, and two more had contracted the disease.

On 7th January 1908 two three-masted schooners, Mary Barrow and Lizzie J. Wilce, left Swansea with coal. The weather became a strong N'N'Westerly gale, and on 11th January both ships were washed ashore on Porthmeor Beach, St Ives. The crew of both vessels were rescued by the local lifeboat, and several

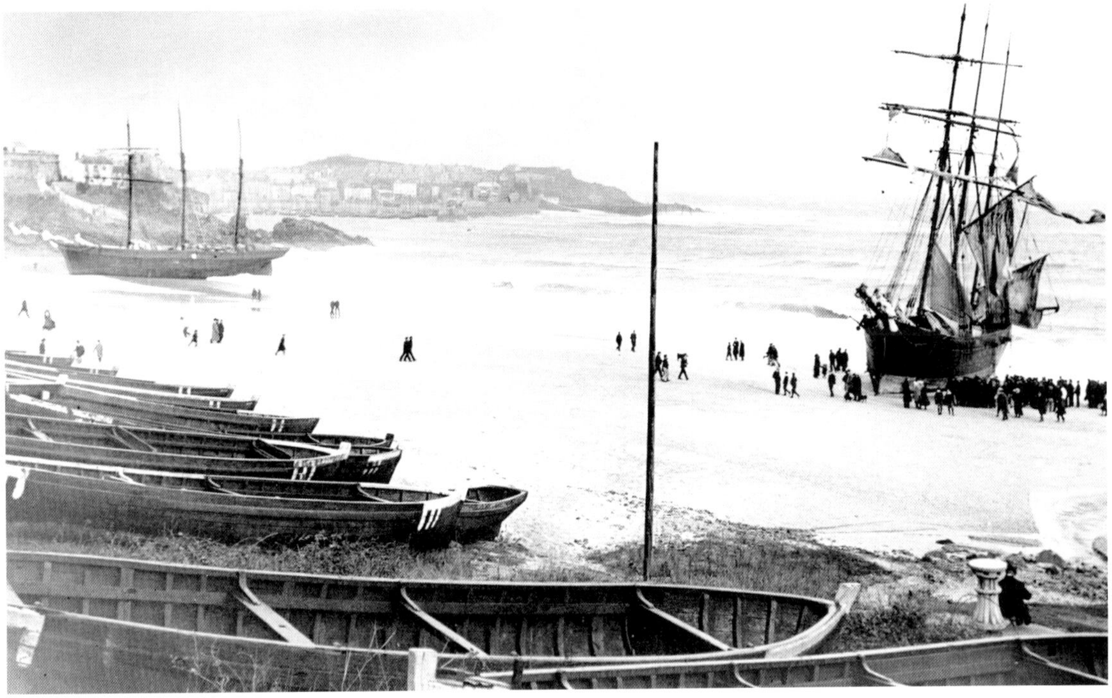

photographs of the event show the vessels stranded together on the beach before being towed off by a steamship. From 1912 Mary Barrow was owned in Newquay, and until 1930 she was employed in the china clay trade. It is likely that during this period Reuben Chappell made the portrait of her. Mary Barrow was employed in the 1930s carrying cement from the Thames to Penzance and Hayle for local authority housing schemes. She was lost in 1938 when, carrying a cargo of coal from Ayr to Truro, she was wrecked on the Calf of Man.

Photographs: The Royal Cornwall Museum

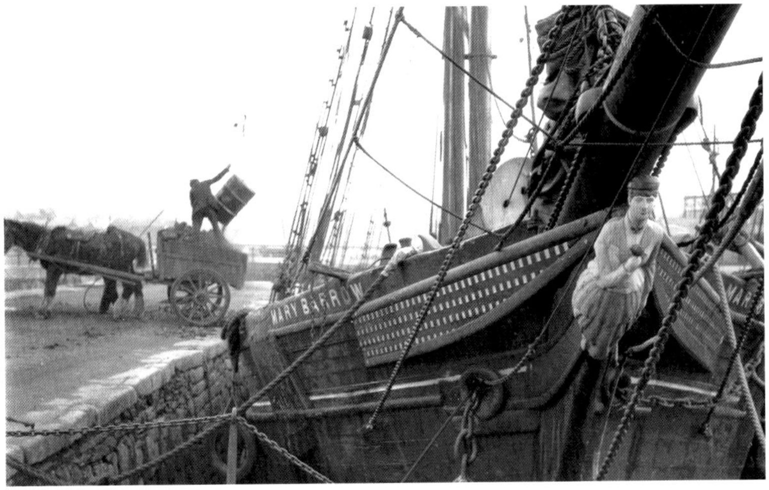

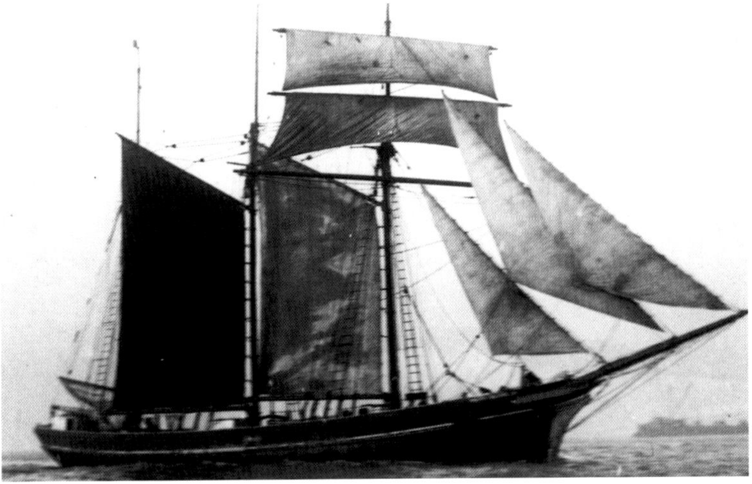

Wales, Liverpool & North West Coast Ships

Maritime trade around the coast of Wales had a special significance, for the landscape of Wales made communication and the transportation of goods difficult. So, as in the West Country, a very strong seafaring tradition evolved. Ships were built all around the coast in ports, small harbours, creeks and beaches. Welsh merchant ships and seamen were highly regarded, and they carried cargoes to and from European, Mediterranean and transatlantic ports. Specific cargoes associated with Wales were the natural resources of the country, coal from South Wales, and slate and copper from North Wales. Many millions of tons of coal were shipped from the ports and harbours of South Wales during the 18th, 19th and early 20th century. The quality of the coal that was mined in the valleys of South Wales was considered to be the best in the world. Thousands of small sail trading ships were employed carrying coal from the larger ports of Cardiff, Barry and Swansea and the many smaller ports around the coast, not only to British and European ports, but all over the world. Foreign-going ships would take coal out and return with a variety of cargoes including copper from south America. Welsh coal was taken to ports in Cuba, Venezuela, Australia and Canada. Welsh coal ports were very busy places with thousands of ships involved. In the 19th century there were over one hundred shipping agents in Cardiff alone.

The inland mountainous area of North Wales is particularly noted for fine quality slate. This was quarried and brought down to the coast, often by narrow gauge railway. Many ships sailed from the ports of Barmouth, Porthmadog, Caernarfon, Port Penrhyn and Beaumaris with cargoes of Welsh slate. These ports all had shipbuilding yards, and built some fine and noteworthy vessels. Porthmadog in particular produced a series of ships which became known as the Western Ocean Yachts, noted for their speed and elegant lines. During the eighteenth and nineteenth centuries thousands of cargoes of Welsh slate were exported to ports throughout Europe, and some across the Atlantic to America and Canada.

On the north coast of Anglesey in Porth Amlwch, created to handle the export of copper extracted from the nearby Parys Mountains, there was an extraordinary mining business which at one time employed many people. Today it is difficult to imagine the huge amount of industry and maritime activity that has taken place there over the years. As trade increased the harbour was improved and quays were constructed. There was smelting there, ships called for copper ore, and as the port developed, shipbuilding began.

There is a strong Cornish connection with Amlwch as the families who managed the mines came from Cornwall. The Cornish were regarded as the best hard rock miners in the world. Many ships were built in this tiny port. One of the builders was Captain William Thomas who built some very elegant vessels, timber and iron sailing ships and iron steamships. Some of his ships were the Elian and the Cymric and her sister ships, all painted by Chappell.

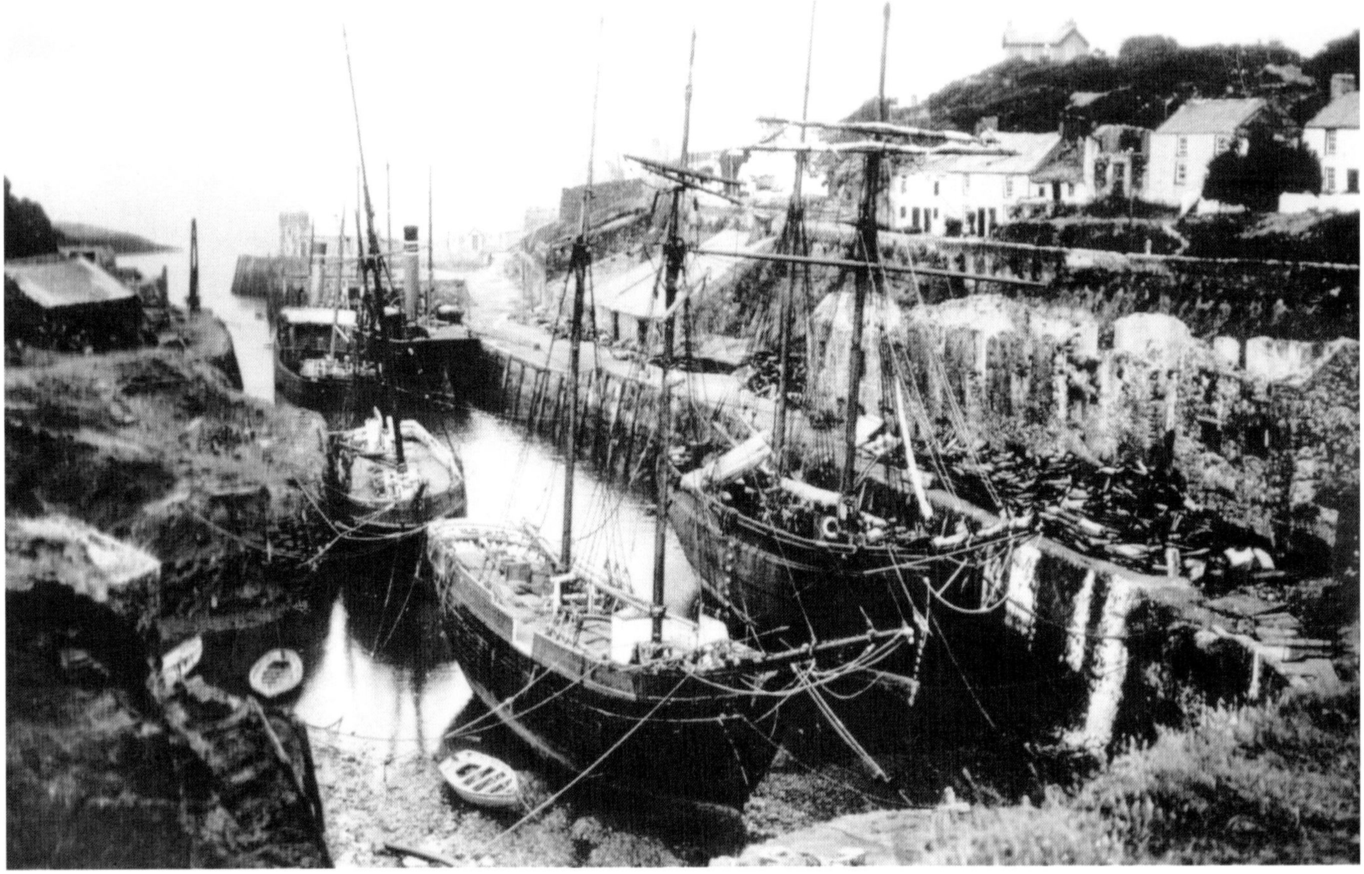

Port Amlwch, late 19th century *Photograph courtesy of Vintage Amlwch*

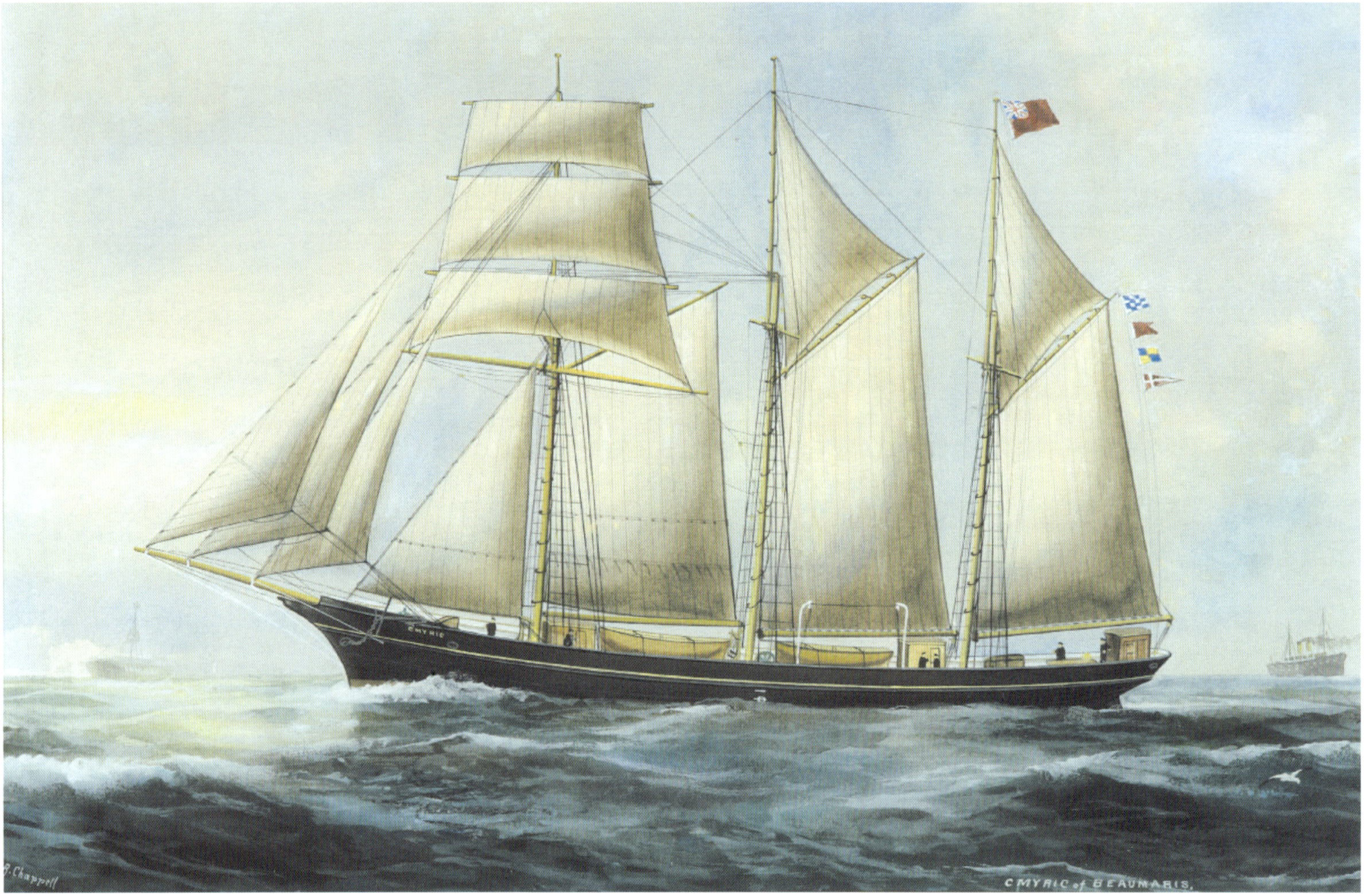

Private collection

CYMRIC

ON 101752; built in 1893 by E. T. Hall at W. Thomas & Sons; 126 tons gross; 123' x 24' x 10.8'; owned by W. Thomas & Sons Amlwch; reg. Beaumaris.

Reuben Chappell would have seen this three-masted iron hull topsail schooner when she visited Cornwall in the clay trade.

Sister ship to Gaelic and Celtic, all three traded from Runcorn to Gibraltar and were in the Rio Grande hide and bonemeal trade. After years of trading in deep water and at home Cymric and Gaelic were sold to Irish owners and fitted with engines. During the Second World War they both ran from Ireland to Portugal. The Cymric was lost during this period when, in 1944 she set off for Lisbon. After being sighted off Dublin she was never seen again.

Q Ships

This painting shows Cymric during the First World War when she was fitted with two guns at the bow.

During World War One many merchant ships, sail and steam, were sunk by German submarines. Sailing ships were easy targets, and it was the submarine's practice to approach them on the surface, sinking the ship with gunfire or by placing a scuttling charge aboard. If the crew were fortunate, they would have been allowed to leave beforehand by way of the ship's boat.

The British government armed a number of steamships, sailing and fishing vessels. In effect they acted as decoys, surprising the submarines by firing on them as they approached. The Q Ships proved to be a valuable part of the allies anti-U-boat campaign and succeeded in destroying at least fifteen U-boats.

Perhaps it was difficult to distinguish between the British and German submarines, for as a Q Ship Cymric was responsible for the sinking of the British submarine J6 in error on 15th October 1918.

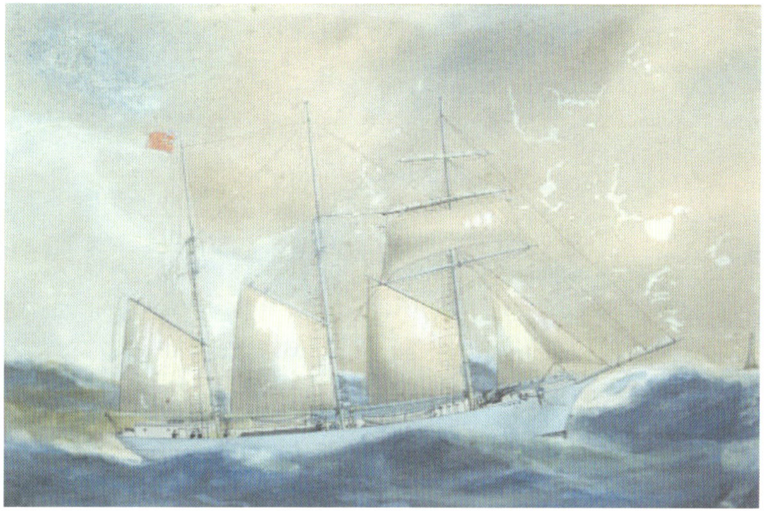

Private collection

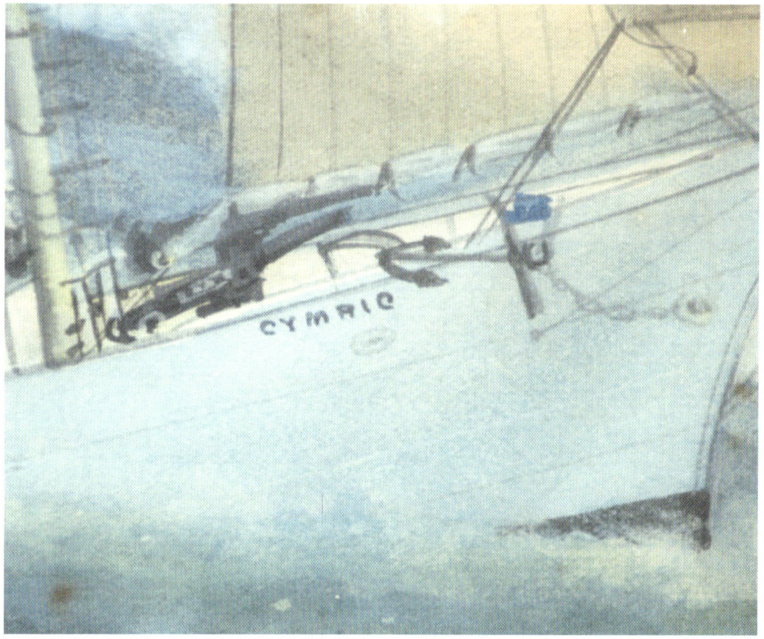

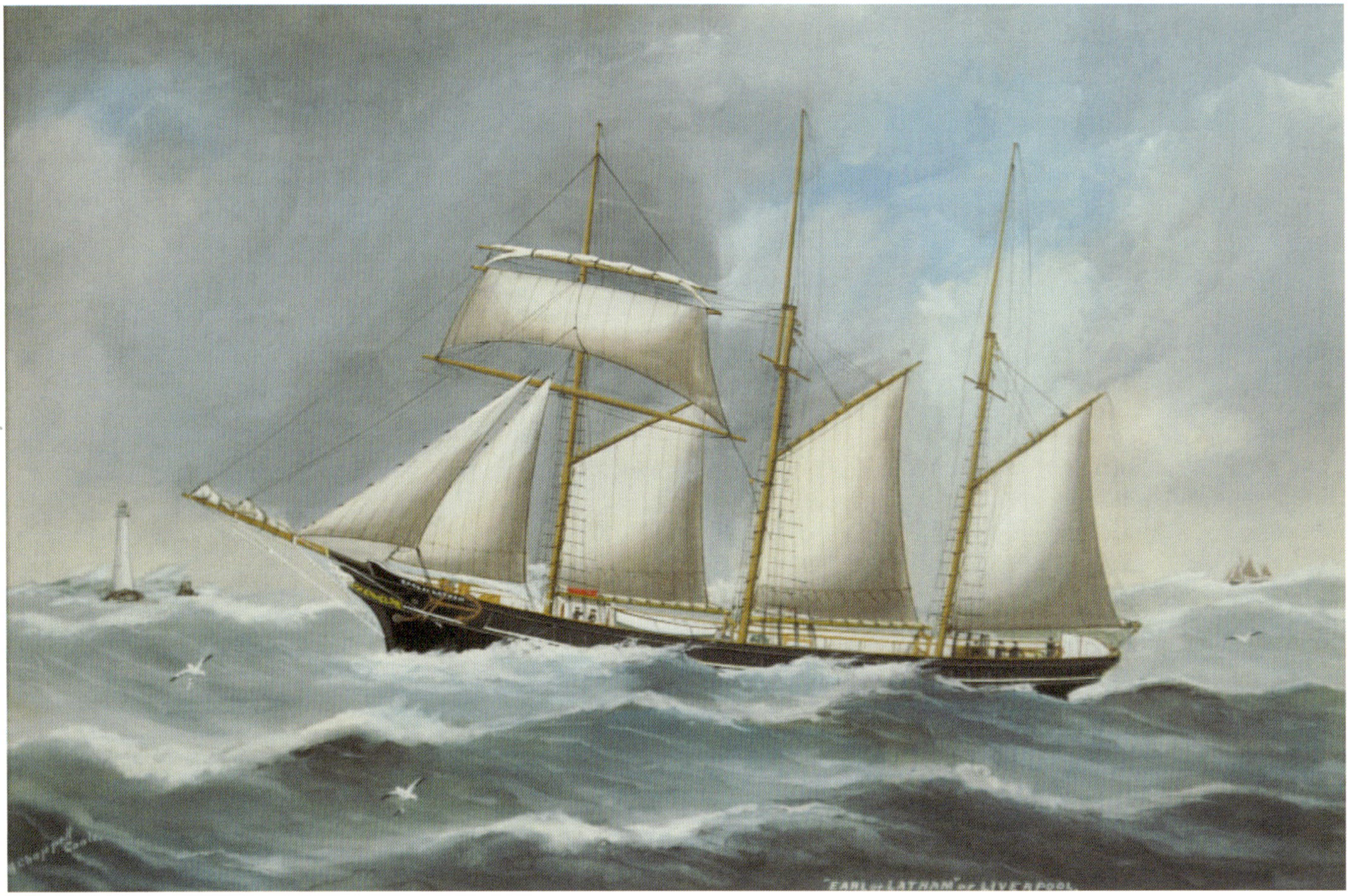

Private collection

EARL OF LATHOM OF LIVERPOOL

ON91172; wooden three-masted schooner; built 1885 by Ferguson & Baird, Connah's Quay; 132 tons gross; 94.5' x 23.2' x 10.4'; owned by G.T. Raynes; reg. Liverpool.

In this painting Reuben Chappell has depicted Earl of Lathom with reduced sail in stormy seas. The Eddystone Light is on the starboard side as the ship heads east up the channel after leaving the clay ports. On the distant horizon a tan sailed ketch-rigged boat is seen.

Work in the Home Trade often brought Earl of Lathom to the West Country. In 1901 she was brought into Penzance on fire with a cargo of scrap metal turnings and borings which would have had an inflammable coating of machine oil. The ship was saved by the local fire brigade. She was less fortunate in 1915 when her sinking was linked to an event that became one of the most dramatic and tragic incidents in the history of the war.

From early in the First World War the British Navy had blockaded the German ports. This was having considerable effect not only on the German war effort, but also on morale and trade in Germany. In response to the blockade the German government had adopted an intensive programme of submarine warfare. Previously there had been rules and conventions regarding attacks on merchant and passenger ships during war, but as the war intensified the Germans adopted a policy of unrestricted submarine warfare. All vessels, including merchant and passenger ships in British territorial water were likely to be attacked.

On 5th May 1915 the U-boat U20, commanded by Kapitanleutnant Walther Schweiger, lay off southern Ireland primarily waiting for British troop ships and supply vessels heading from British ports to the Dardanelles. When the 132 ton schooner Earl of Latham was seen off Queenstown the ship was boarded and inspected by the German crew. The men aboard the unarmed schooner were ordered to leave in the ship's boat, and the U-boat opened fire, sinking the sailing ship. The next day the U20 sank merchant steam ships Candidate; 6,000 tons, and Centurion; 5,495 tons, south of the Conibeg Lightship. On 7th May a large four-funnelled passenger liner was spotted. It was the Lusitania, which, when built in 1907, was the largest ship in the world and had won the Blue Riband for fastest transatlantic crossing several times. Having left New York on 1st May and crossed the Atlantic, she was in sight of the coast of Ireland. The luxurious British Cunard-line ship was sailing under an American flag, and among the passengers were 128 Americans including the multimillionaire Alfred Vanderbilt. With one torpedo from the submarine the liner was hit and following the initial explosion there was a violent secondary blast. The Lusitania went down in 18 minutes, and of the 1,918 passengers 1,155 perished. This caused considerable anti-German feeling throughout the world, and public outrage in America. Although the event did not directly bring them into the war, it did create a climate of public opinion that would later allow America to enter the conflict in 1917.

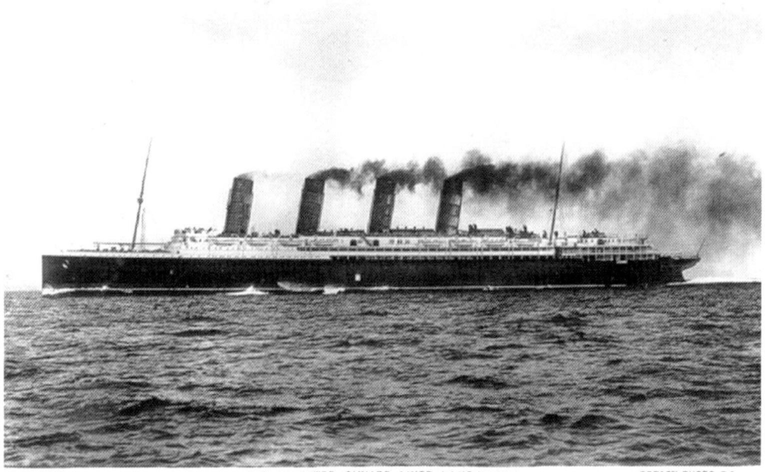

3563 D THE ILL-FATED CUNARD LINER "LUSITANIA." ROTARY PHOTO, E.C.
TORPEDOED AND SUNK BY GERMAN SUBMARINE OFF THE OLD HEAD OF KINSALE, IRELAND.
MAY 7TH, 1915

MARY JONES

ON.44050; built Flint 1863;
113 tons; 93'; signal TRLN.

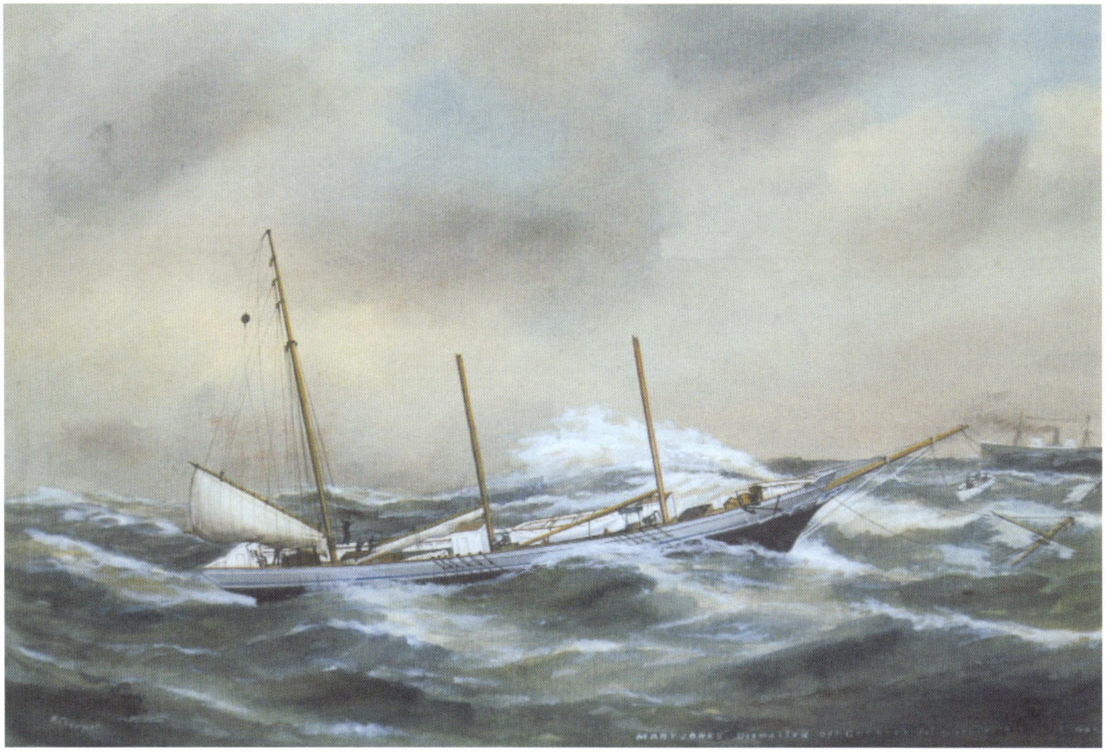

Private collection

In this unusual painting by Reuben Chappell, obviously commissioned to record an event which took place off Godrevy Island on the North Coast of Cornwall on 19th February 1919, Mary Jones is clearly in distress as shown by the signal by her mizzen mast. She is drifting with her fore and main masts broken. The top part of a mast is seen floating at her bow, perhaps acting as a sea anchor. In the distance a steamship waits and a ship's boat is rowed towards Mary Jones. It is known that she was taken into St Ives where she was repaired sufficiently to return to Wales where she was refitted. Probably this painting was commissioned by the captain and no doubt represented poignant memories for him.

Mary Jones was built for the Newfoundland trade in 1863 and registered in Chester. In 1923 she was registered at Bideford and fitted with a motor. By 1928 she was recorded carrying oats, coal and scrap iron. She was considered an elegant vessel with distinctive flared bows. She was later fitted with a 60hp two cylinder Bolinder engine.

In February 1932 she was wrecked off Ramsgate.

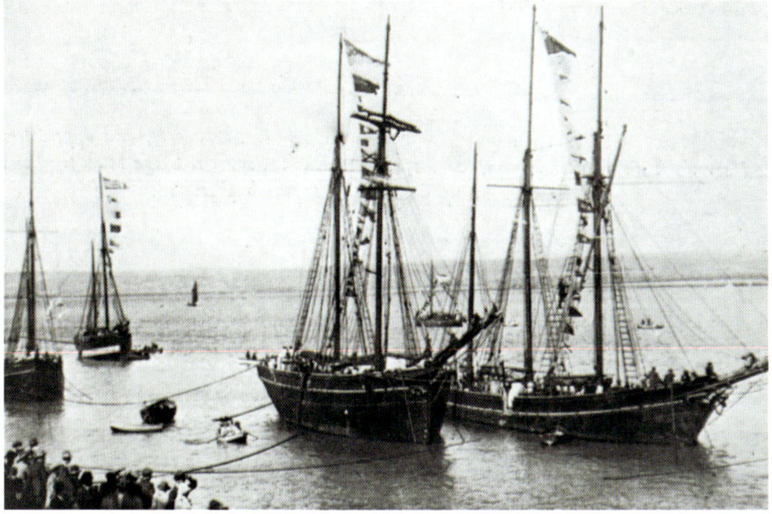

Schooners, John Farley and Mary Jones dressed for regatta day.

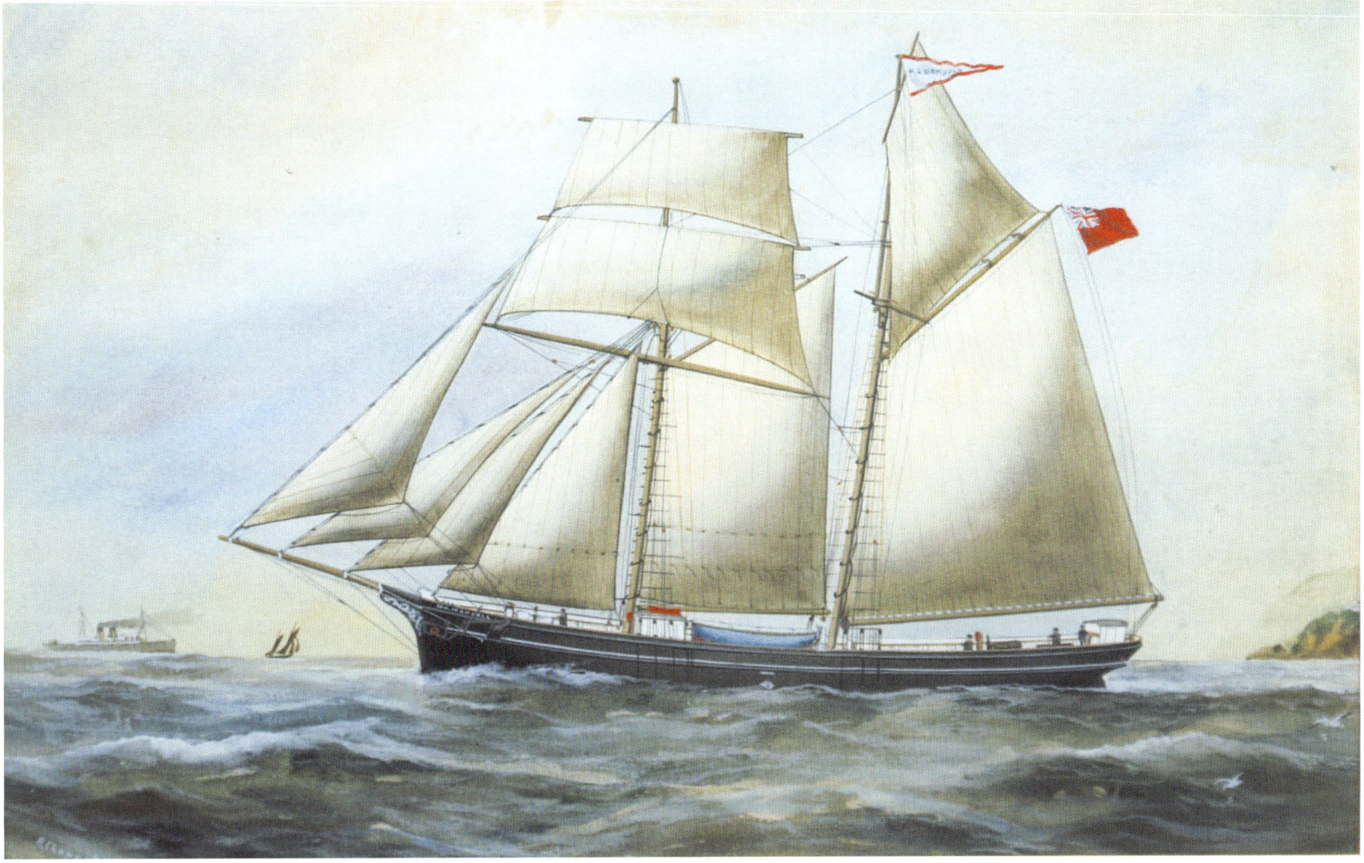

Private collection

Mary Ann Mandall

ON 62701; wooden schooner; built October 1868 by Wilson of Ulverston, ; 112 tons gross; 84' x 20.6' x 10.9'; Signal WMDS; Capt (1916) T. J. Jones; owners W. Postlethwaite; reg. Barrow.

The wooden schooner Mary Ann Mandall was built in Ulverston in 1868. By 1925 the ship was still trading, and was owned by the Reney brothers who had a fleet of ships based at Connah's Quay. Chappell would have seen this ship when she was in the clay trade, and in the painting the schooner is seen off the south Devon coast, with Start Point in the distance.

LIVERPOOL

The river Mersey runs into the Irish Sea. On its banks grew the city and port of Liverpool which became one of the major ports in England. Considerable international trade took place here particularly from America, the West Indies and Europe. Cargoes such as tobacco, timber, corn and sugar were all important imports. From here millions of emigrants crossed the Atlantic and ships from Liverpool were also engaged in the slave trade, from Africa to the Americas. Whaling ships and large shipping lines were based in Liverpool and passenger and cargo ships travelled from here to destinations all over the world. In Liverpool there were several coastal steamship companies whose vessels Reuben Chappell painted when they visited the Humber or the clay ports. Amongst them were those run by Richard Hughes who ran the largest coastal fleet in Liverpool at the time. His company, set up in 1884 with an iron steamer called Primrose, subsequently added so many ships to the fleet that it became known as 'The Welsh Navy.' Many of his ships' names ended in Rose, for example the Gronant Rose, named after his family's home town. Most of his seamen were from North Wales, Anglesey and the Llyn peninsula.

A great many of Hughes's ships carried coal, and as the business expanded they carried coal to France, returning with general cargo. Another major cargo for the Hughes fleet was china clay from Cornwall. This was taken to Runcorn where it was transhipped onto narrow boats to be transported to the Potteries. The canal system joins the Mersey and reaches industrial towns and cities of the North West. The canal system in this part of England is extensive, and it is even possible for canal-borne goods to cross the country via the Trans-Pennine Canal to the Humber and North Sea.

During the First World War most of the Richard Hughes fleet was taken over by the Admiralty and was employed carrying stores to France from Dover and other south coast ports. Throughout his career Richard Hughes had new ships built and bought and sold older ships, but in the early 1930s the elderly Hughes overstretched himself financially, having ordered eleven new ships, and the company collapsed. Within two years Richard Hughes died, but his ships continued trading under new ownership and such was his reputation that his name was valued highly enough to be retained. Many of these ships were attacked and lost during the Second World War, but those that were left traded until the 1950s. Before the Second World War there were a great many ship-owning companies in Liverpool. Labour was relatively cheap and it was not difficult to find men to crew the ships. These extracts give an indication of how hard working conditions aboard were.

'We had continual changes of crew, especially firemen, who found the job too heavy for them. The ship was by then burning 22 tons of coal in 24 hours, which meant that each man had to shovel 7 tons of coal plus ashes a day. The firemen were on a three watch system of four hours on and eight hours off, but after their four hour watch, they spent another hour heaving ashes up from the stokehold. This was done with a hand ash winch and dumping the ashes overboard, so that instead of an eight hour day they were working a ten hour day without overtime. The heat in the stokehold was intense and the noise and vibrations from the Howden fan which was always running flat out, was enough to try the patience of a Saint. It was not surprising that the firemen became dissatisfied, their growls and grumbles no doubt influenced the sailors because we had a considerable turnover of sailors also.'

'At sea everybody including the master worked watches, four hours on and four hours off, a total of twelve hours a day (without meal breaks) and if the ship had entered and left port once or twice during the week, another 20 hours could easily be added to this amount and 100 hours was more often the rule than the exception. Leave and holidays were unheard of; if you wanted leave you got it 'off pay' and with no guarantee of returning to your job, and there were plenty of men on the dole, desperately needing work and ready to take your place.'

Old Time Steam Coasting. Owen G. Spargo Thomas H.Thomason. Waine Research Publications 1982

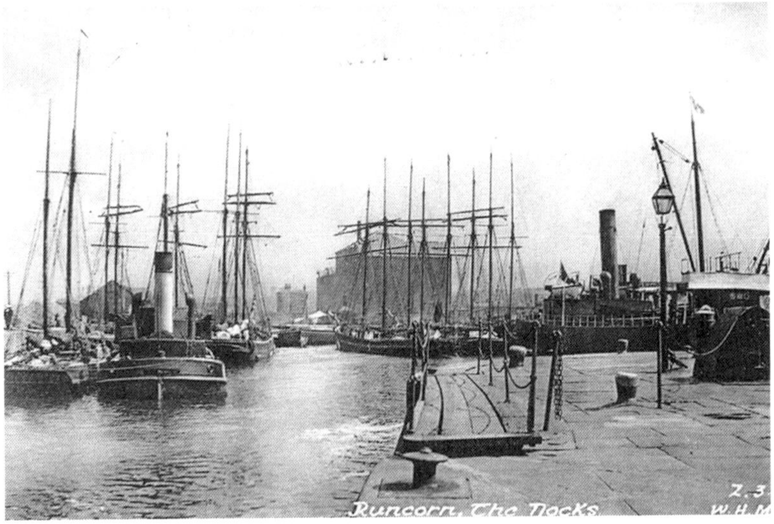

By courtesy of Diane Stanley

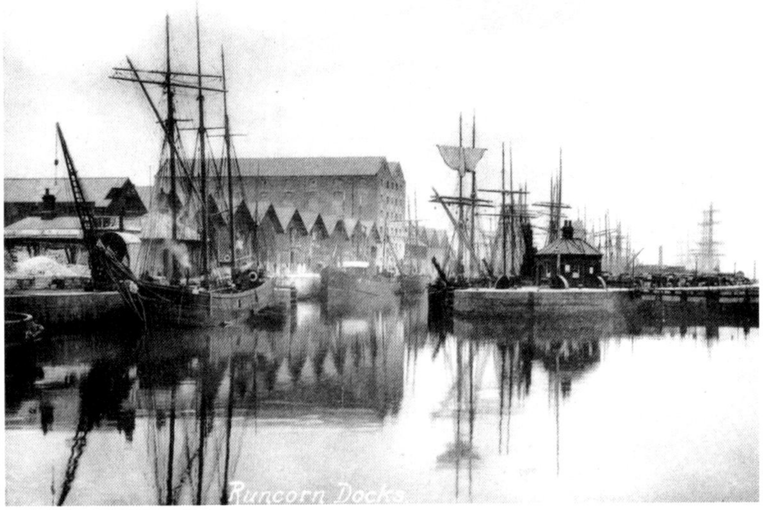

Postcard of Runcorn Docks early 20th century, showing china clay on the quay ready for transhiptment. *By courtesy of Diane Stanley*

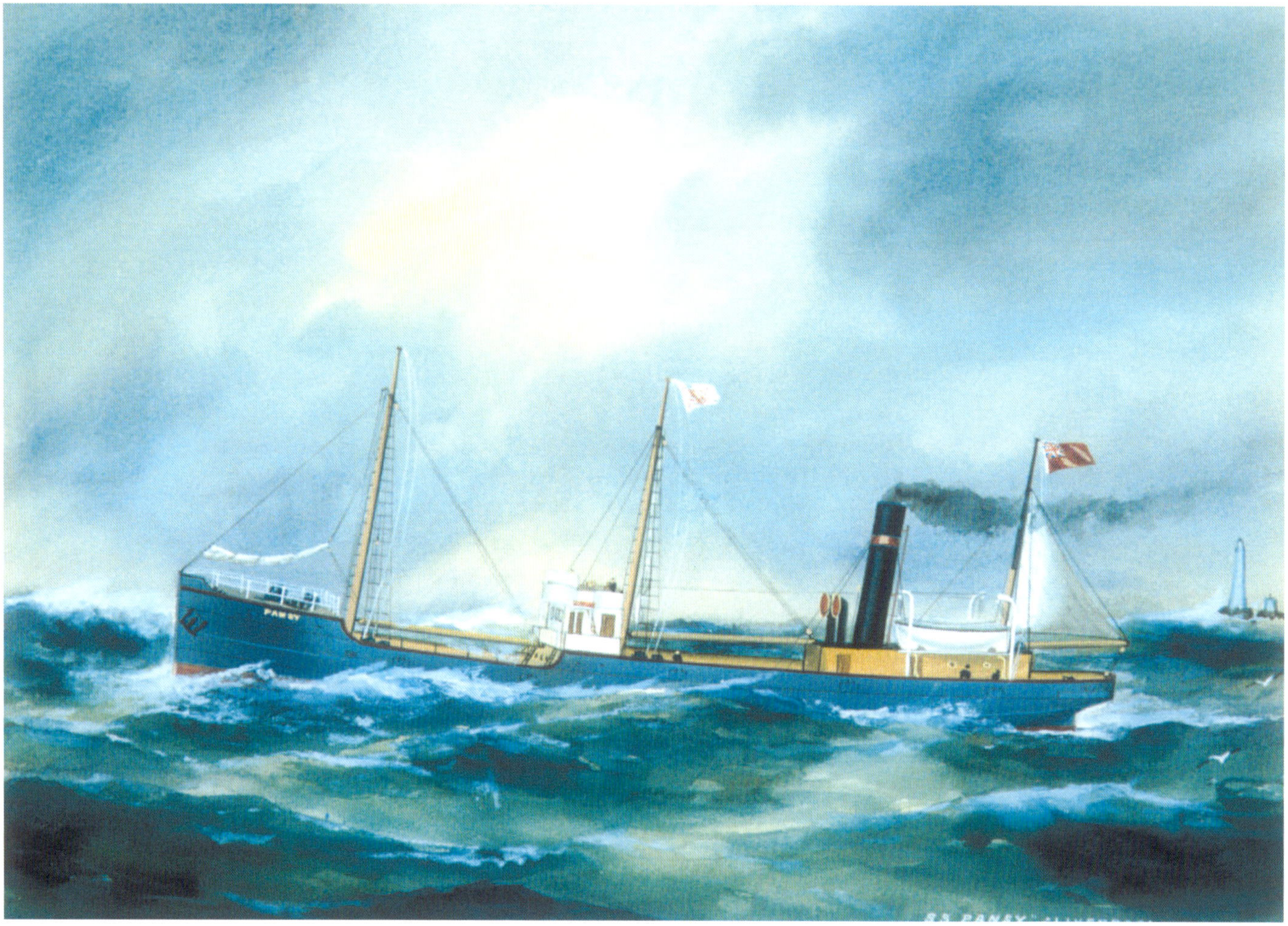

Courtesy of the British Mercantile Marine Memorial Collection.

SS Pansy

ON 109433; steel steam coaster; built 1898 by Grangemouth Dockyard; 555 gross tons; 175' x 26.3' x 11.6'; owned by Hughes & Hutson of Liverpool.

SS Pansy was built for Richard Hughes of Liverpool and she was employed carrying bulk cargoes from the large manufacturing cities of the North West. By 1918 the Hughes fleet had increased to 14 ships, their principal cargo being china clay from Fowey which was brought to Liverpool/Runcorn for transshipment by canal barge to the porcelain factories in the Potteries. Sold in March 1920 as part of Hughes's entire fleet, SS Pansy was reacquired after her purchasers became insolvent, and in March 1937 was renamed Pink Rose.

On 4th May 1941 whilst on a passage from Swansea to Dublin with a cargo of coal, Pink Rose was in collision with the Greek steamship Georgios P ten miles off the South Bishop Light, and caught fire, after which she was taken in tow but later sank.

SS Blush Rose

ON 13482; steel screw three-masted steam ship; 645 reg. tons; 178.4' x 28.1' x 11.1'; built 1918 Hardingxvld by N. V. Schpsb; 3 cylinder 83RHP engine; owners O. H. Donell & R. Leeson; reg. Liverpool.

The steam coaster Blush Rose, 645 g.r.t., was built in 1913 in Hardinxveld, Holland, for Richard Hughes & Co of Liverpool. She was sold in March 1920 when Richard Hughes disposed of the whole of his then fleet, but she was reacquired 16 months later following the failure of her purchasers. On 8th February 1942, whilst on a passage from Dublin to Swansea in ballast, she was damaged by air attack three miles south of St Ann's Head, and was beached in Dale Roads, Milford Haven. Later repaired and returned to service, she was sunk on 2nd August 1945 in collision with the SS Glaucus of the Ocean Steam Co.

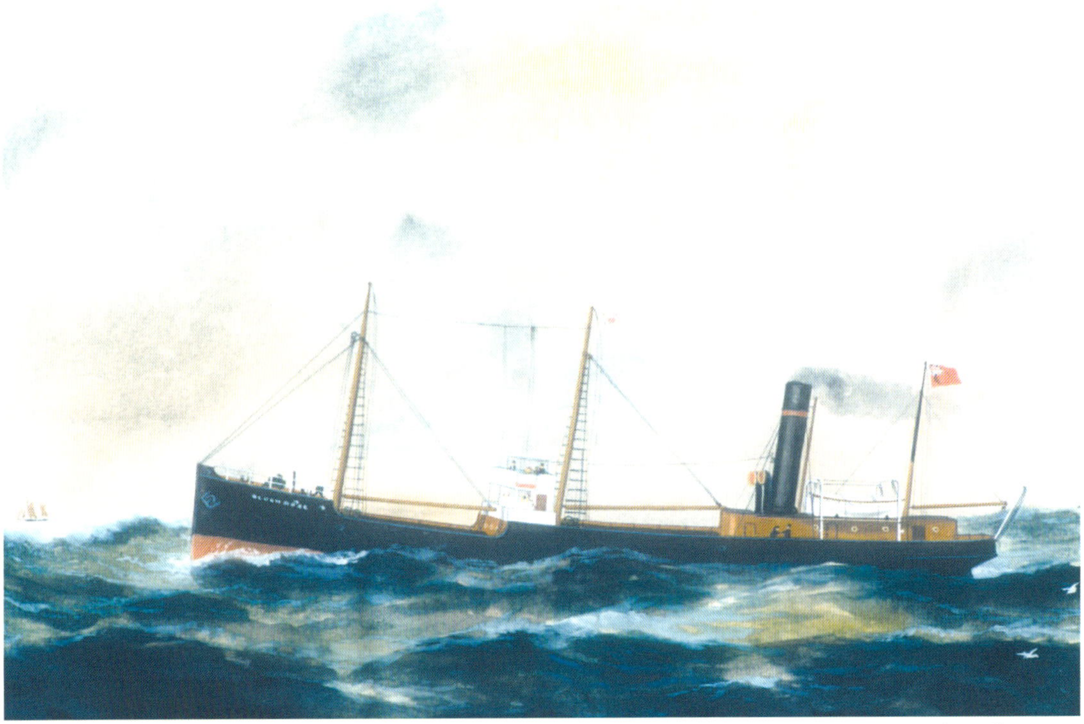

Courtesy of the British Mercantile Marine Memorial Collection.

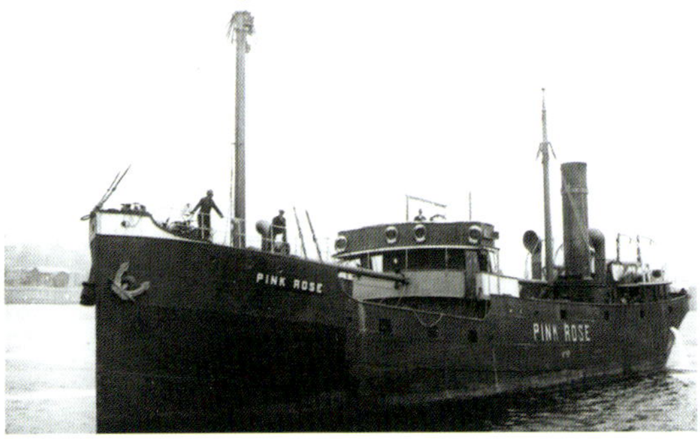

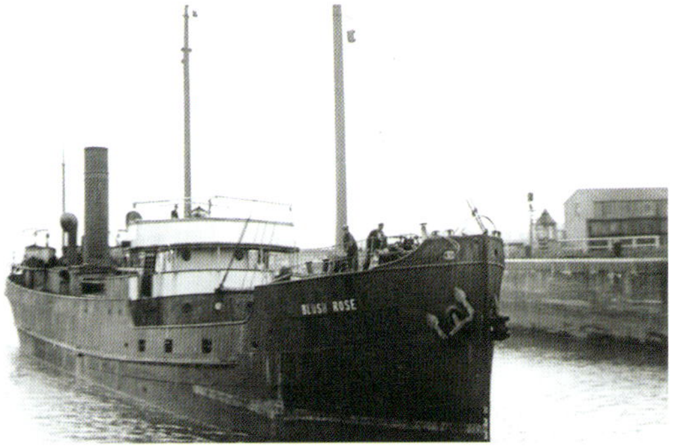

P. Dunbavand

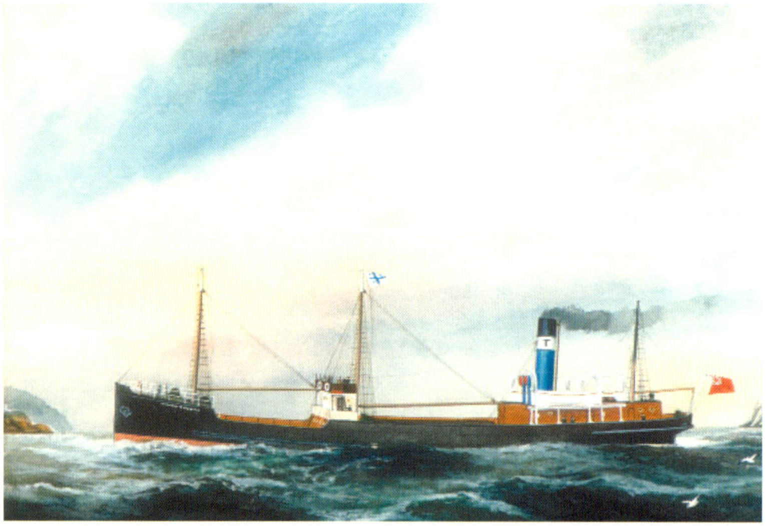

Courtesy of the British Mercantile Marine Memorial Collection.

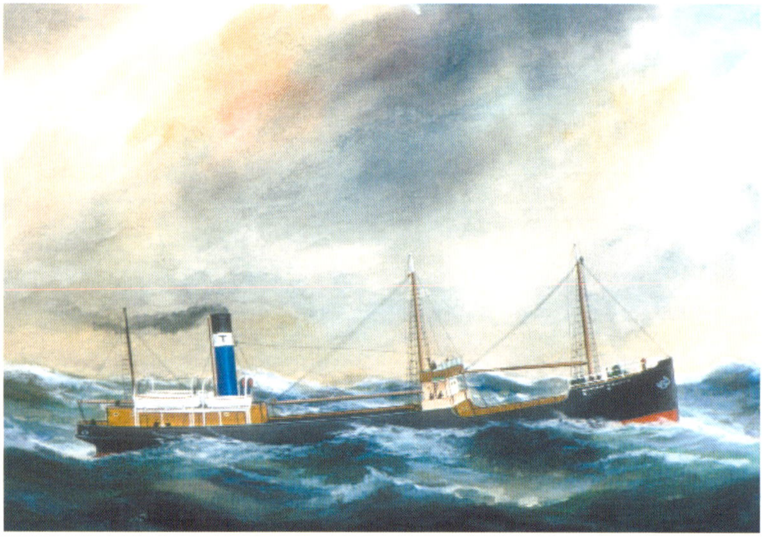

Courtesy of the British Mercantile Marine Memorial Collection.

SS Miriam Thomas

ON 143680; steel hull; built 1920 in Lowestoft by Colby Bros; 430 gross tons; 142.2' x 24.1' x 10.6'; screw propulsion; owners Thomas Bros; reg. Liverpool.

The steam coaster Miriam Thomas, 430 g.r.t., was built in 1920 by Colby Brothers Ltd of Lowestoft for Thomas Brothers Shipping Co. Ltd. of Liverpool. During the depression of the 1930s she changed hands several times between members of the Thomas family and their creditors, being acquired finally, in 1937, by the Carriers Shipping Co. Ltd. of Liverpool, managed by Owen Thomas. On 15th March 1942, whilst on passage from Weston Point to Newry, she was in collision in St George's Channel with the SS Vasna of the British India Steam Navigation Co., then serving as Naval Hospital Ship No 4, and she sank on the following day.

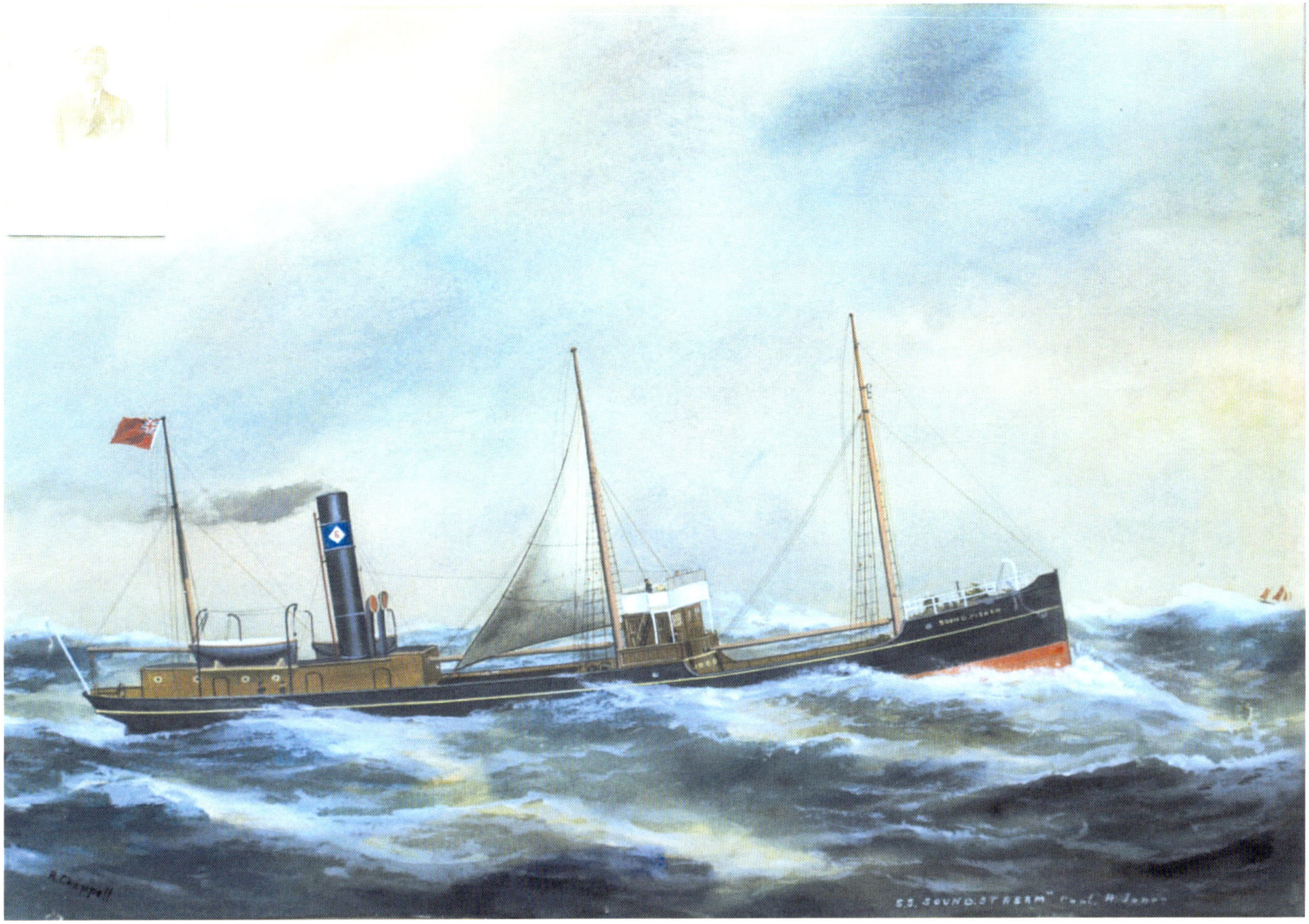

Private Collection.

SS Sound Fisher

ON 142774; built 1919 Ardrossan Dry Dock & Shipbuilding Co Ltd.; 510 gross; 142.4' x 26.1' x 10.9'.

At times Reuben Chappell would have to work into the night to complete a painting before the ship sailed, and this may account for the occasional mistake. For example, in this painting, while the name Sound Fisher is seen on the bow of the vessel, the inscription along the bottom of the painting reads 'Sound Stream' Capt R Jones. The starboard light is absent from the bridge; nevertheless this is a striking painting with an exceptionally convincing rendition of the sea. This was a quality in his work that was no doubt recognised by those who bought his paintings.

Built in 1919 and originally named 'Independence' the ship changed hands a number of times before being bought by James Fisher & Sons Ltd. of Barrow in Furness in 1929. Renamed 'Sound Fisher,' she remained in the company until 1939 when she was sold to Brazil. The vessel sank in 1949 after a collision.

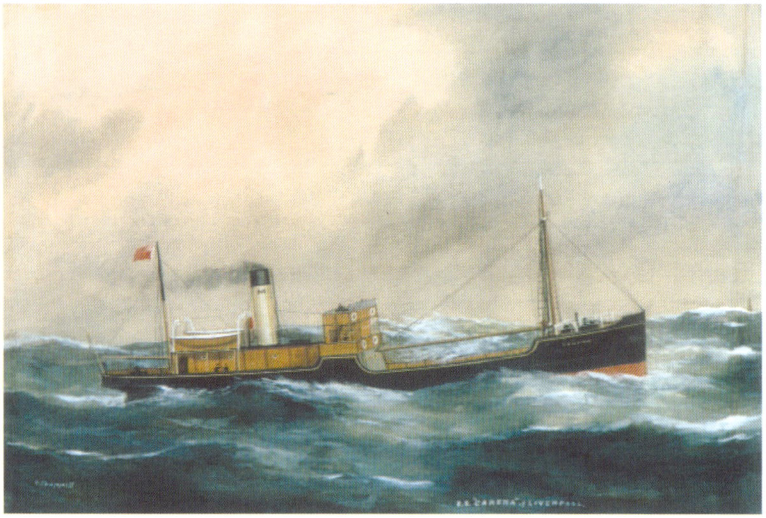

Courtesy of the British Mercantile Marine Memorial Collection

SS Carena

ON131990; steel steam coaster; built 1911 by J. P. Rennoldson of South Shields for Joseph Monks & Co. Ltd. of Warrington. 98 reg tons; reg Liverpool.

The steam coaster Carena was aquired in 1920 by the Monroe Shipping Company of Cardiff, and in this painting she is shown in their livery. On 8th January 1924 she sailed from Liverpool with a cargo of maize for Penrhun on the coast of North Wales, and was never heard of again.

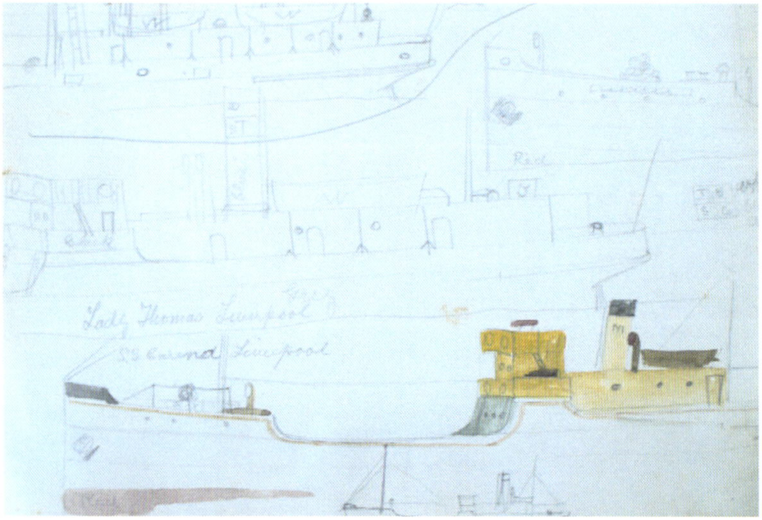

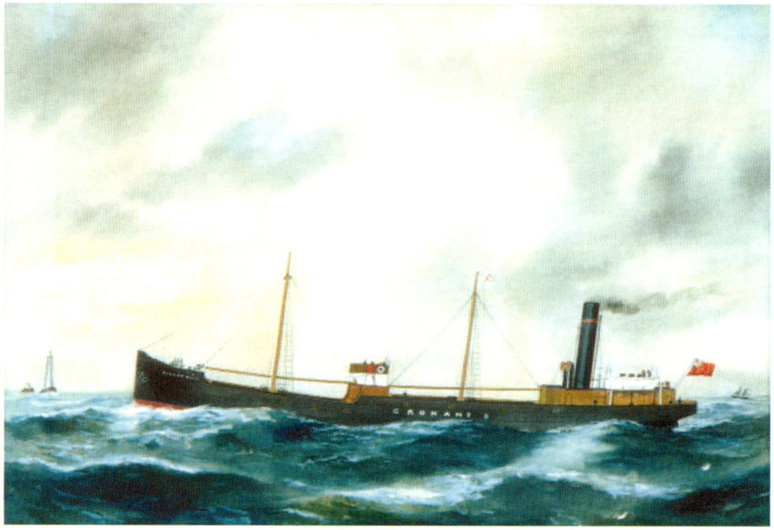

Courtesy of the British Mercantile Marine Memorial Collection

SS Gronant Rose

ON 147286; steel screw; built 1924 Paisley by J. Fullerton & Co; 1110 reg. tons; 220.5' x 34.2' x 13.2'; 169 NHP engine; owners R. Hughes & Co; Reg. Liverpool.

Part of Richard Hughes's 'Rose Fleet', SS Gronant Rose was employed in the china clay and coal trade. On 27th September 1920 whilst on passage from Cardiff to Brest with a cargo of coal she foundered off Pierres Vertes, south of Ushant.

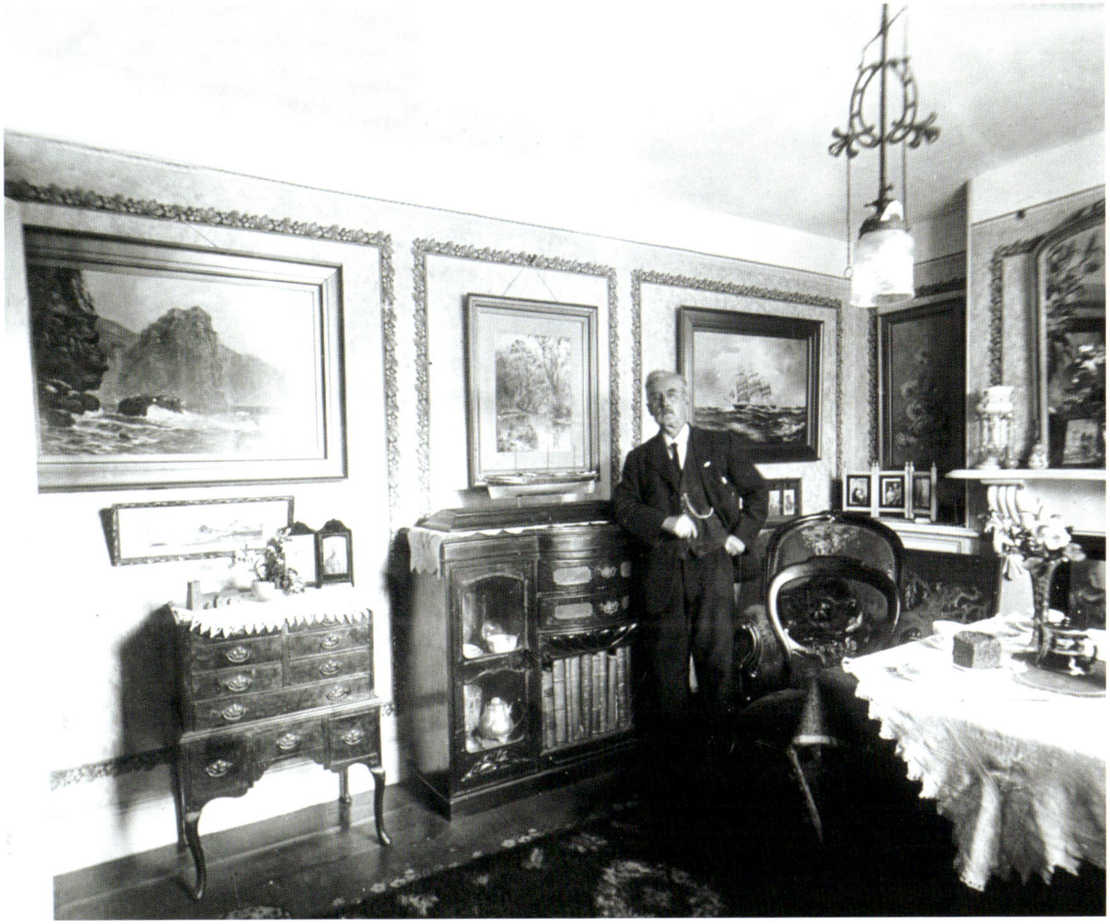

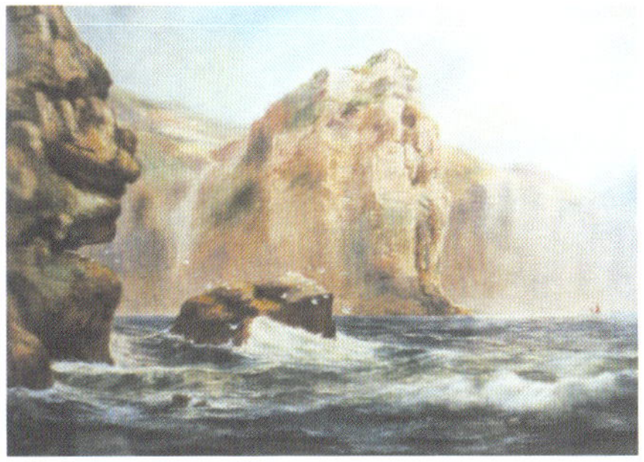

Cliffs at Tintagel

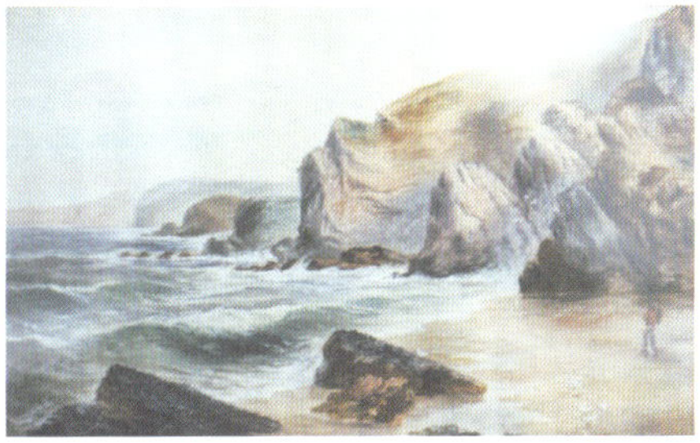

North coast cliffs

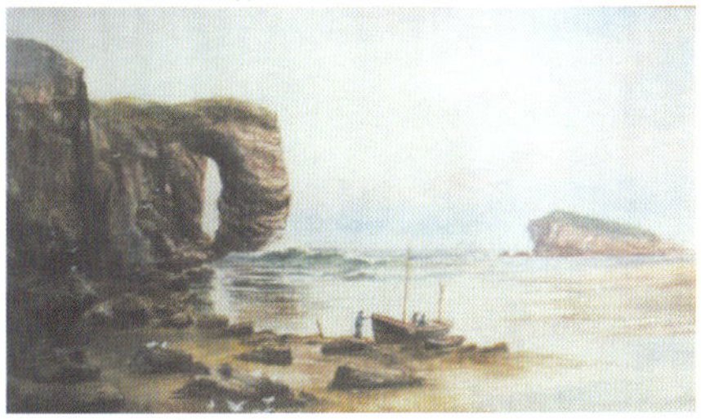

Perranporth

Chappell sometimes painted landscapes of coastal views for himself to decorate his home or as presents for friends and relatives. About 1930 he made a series of postcards of his work these were sold in local stationers and shops.

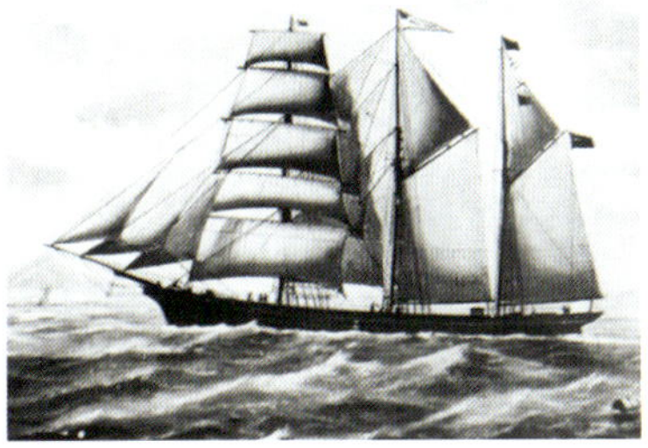

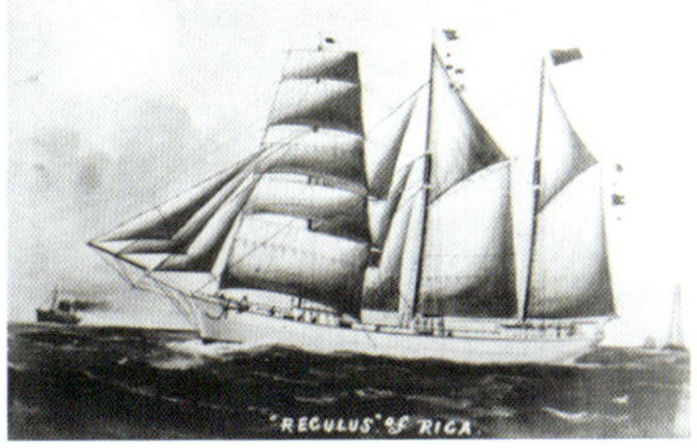

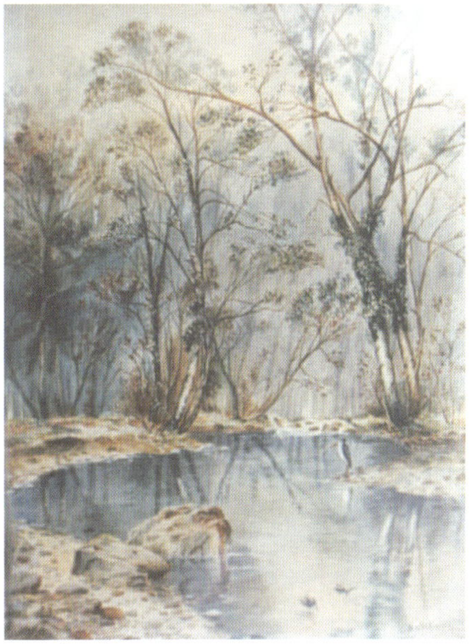

Woodland

Cutty Sark

Opium, The Tea and Wool Trades and the Cutty Sark

The opium trade was part of our nation's history. British traders, including the British East India Company, had been shipping opium from India to China since 1780. By 1840 the value of the trade in this addictive and destructive drug was enormous, far exceeding the value of the total China tea exports. The misery opium addiction caused amongst the Chinese people contrasted with the huge profits which were made by the people in the trade. This trade called for fast vessels. The opium clippers were all small vessels, mostly brigs and schooners designed for speed, partly to evade pirates in the South China Sea. Huge fortunes were being made by the companies involved, and despite requests from China, the British government did nothing to stop the trade. In 1839 a Chinese official ordered stocks of the drug destroyed, and twenty thousand casks of opium were thrown into the river at Canton. British gunboats were sent to the area and the naval skirmishes that followed showed that the Chinese junks were no match for the British forces. After British Marines killed thousands of Chinese people in Canton, the Chinese signed the Treaty of Nankin allowing the opium trade to continue, and signing Hong Kong over to the British. It also opened up other Chinese ports to British trade. What followed was the rapid expansion of trade in Chinese goods, silk, porcelain, and particularly tea. The British continued the lucrative opium trade until 1915 before their government managed to stop it.

The treaty of Nankin opened Canton, Whampoa, Macaw, Shanghai and Foochow, and these ports became centres for the export of tea. This was a seasonal trade, dependent on the tea harvest. Tea clippers would assemble at the ports towards the end of April. Tea was brought down rivers, sometimes as far as 100 miles, from the plantations by sampans, and was quickly loaded onto the ships. In Britain and America customers were willing to pay high prices for the freshest tea, and speed of delivery became a primary concern for merchants. The result of the intense competition was that extraordinary races developed between tea clippers sailing home. Their routes took them through the South China Sea, across the Indian Ocean and around the Cape of Good Hope. In the Atlantic they passed the west coast of Africa to the Azores, and on to the Bay of Biscay. After entering the Western Approaches they sailed up the English Channel where they were met by steam tugs which towed them into the Thames, thence to their docks in London where stevedores quickly unloaded the cargo.

The tea trade was not unique to London. In America there were promises of fabulous profits to the first tea-laden clippers to reach New York. The American ships were very fast and efficient vessels. In Britain the races between the Clipper ships were covered in the newspapers. The names of the ships became household names: Ariel, Taeping, Fiery Cross, Serica, Tait Sing, Chrysolyte, Stornaway etc. A great deal of money was wagered on the outcome of these races.

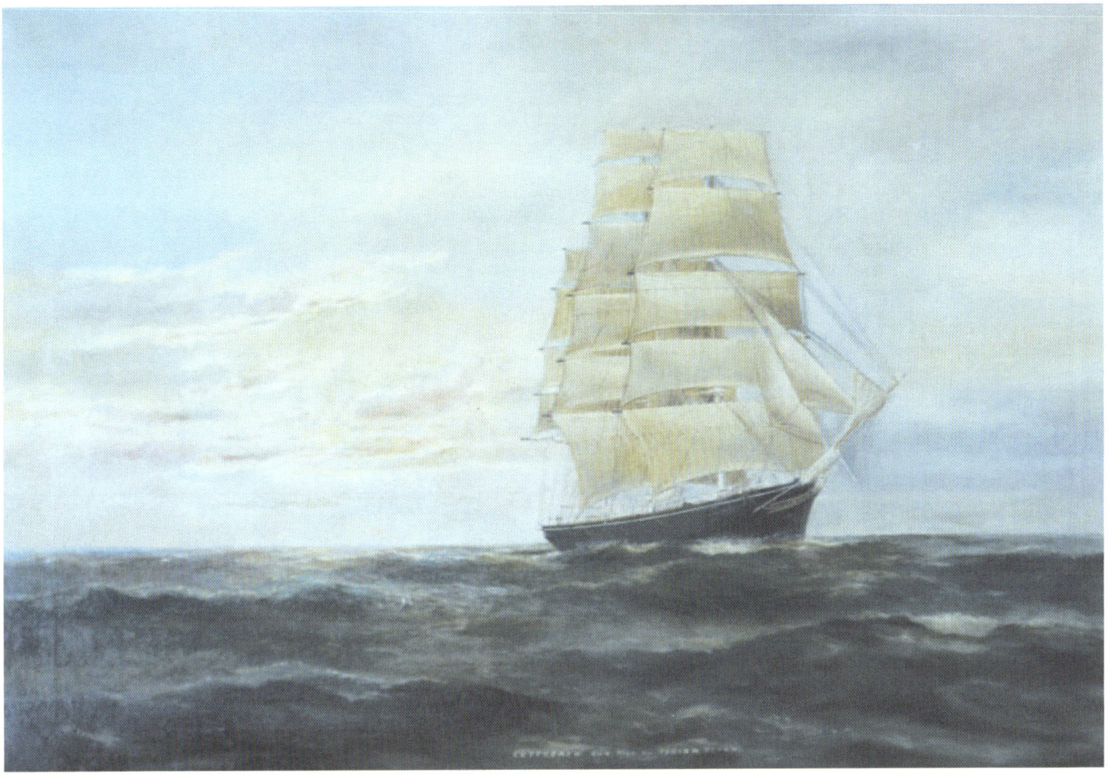

Private collection

The need for speed intensified the development of design in these ships. The intense competition of the races home added to the mystique and public interest in these vessels. They are seen as the supreme development in the design of sailing vessels. This was the zenith of the age of sail. The designers were constantly developing new rig and sail plans as well as refining the hull lines.

In 1869 the clipper Cutty Sark was built for the China trade. At this time the clippers were still viable for voyages to the the Far East, but merchants were already turning to steam ships to carry their goods. The range of the steam ships at that time was limited by the amount of coal they could carry from their home port. However the Suez Canal was opened a month before the Cutty Sark was launched. The canal was of no use to sailing ships, but to steam ships it meant that they could avoid the difficult passage around Africa and the Cape of Good Hope. For steam ships using the canal to the Orient their journey was shortened by 4,000 miles.

For some years Cutty Sark made successful voyages to the China tea ports, and became one of the fastest ships in the trade. On one occasion while racing with another famous clipper, the Thermopylae, she lost her rudder and instead of making for port for repairs, the crew fashioned a rudder from what was available aboard ship. It took four days to do this work at sea, and she then sailed on for London which she still made in remarkably quick

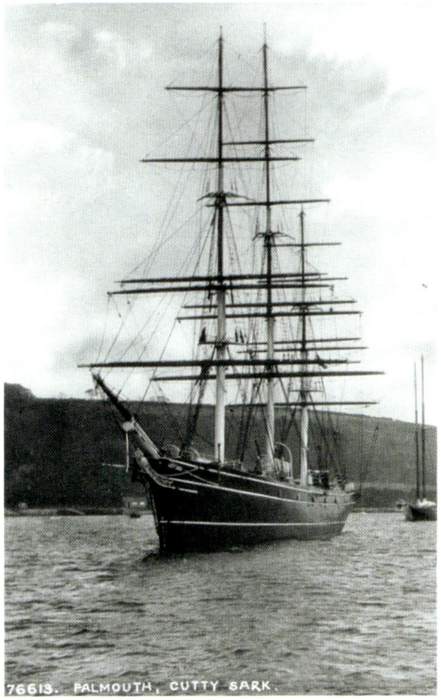

Old postcard image of the Cutty Sark

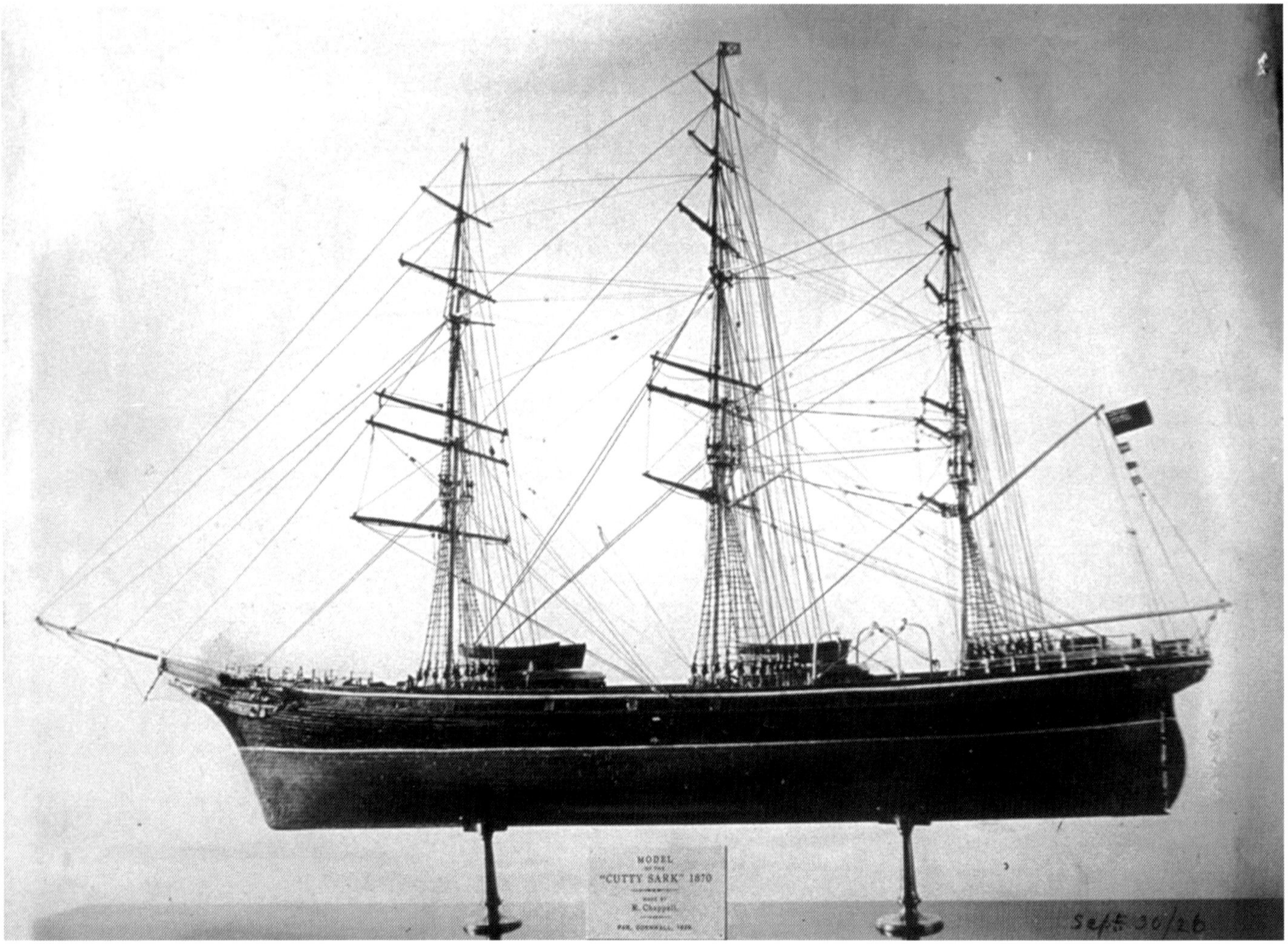

Collection of the Honourable Company of Master Mariners

time. This story caught the public's imagination, and Cutty Sark became a heroine overnight.

As the steam ships improved in design, and with the advantage of the Suez Canal, they entered the tea trade. In time they took the best of the tea and made the fastest passages home. Many of the clippers became uneconomical in that trade and had to seek work elsewhere.

For five years, Cutty Sark, like many of the other clippers, carried coal and any other cargo that was available. However by 1883 there had been a boom in Australian wool production and the clippers found new work carrying wool from Australia to Britain. For the steam ships at that time, Australia was still beyond their practical reach. So for a few years the clippers had an exclusive trade that gave them a new lease of life.

Ships in the Australian wool trade sailed east around the world going out from Britain by way of the Cape of Good Hope and returning around Cape Horn. Competition between the ships was as strong as ever and record speeds were achieved. Cutty Sark for example made London from Sydney in 73 days.

Eventually steamships took this trade as well and in 1895 Cutty Sark was sold to a Portuguese company. She carried cargo from Lisbon to such ports as Rio de Janeiro and New Orleans.

In 1922 there was a storm in the Channel and Cutty Sark came in to Falmouth for shelter. Captain Wilfred Dowman, a retired sailing master who ran a sail training ship for young seamen, saw Cutty Sark and offered to buy her from her Portuguese owners. In 1894, when he was an apprentice seaman, he had seen the Cutty Sark when it sailed past his ship, and like many others, had a deep affection for the ship. He paid £3,750 for her and spent over a year repairing and re-rigging her. She remained in Falmouth for several years and during this time Dowman asked Reuben Chappell to make a model of her. When he was building this model Reuben Chappell visited the ship many times to make drawings and watercolours, taking photographs of the ship's lines and rigging.

Of all the many clipper ships, Cutty Sark seems to have found a special place in the nation's heart. It must also have touched Reuben Chappell's, for he spent a considerable amount of time on this model and became very fond of it. The model he made was a real labour of love, and was a considerable undertaking. For a great many years it has been housed aboard the HQS Wellington moored at the Victoria Embankment, London, where it is in the collection of the Honourable Company of Master Mariners.

As well as the models, Reuben Chappell also made paintings of Cutty Sark. In 1924 he did a trio of paintings of her, one for each of his sons. The Cutty Sark stayed in Falmouth until 1938, and is now in a specially built dry dock in Greenwich.

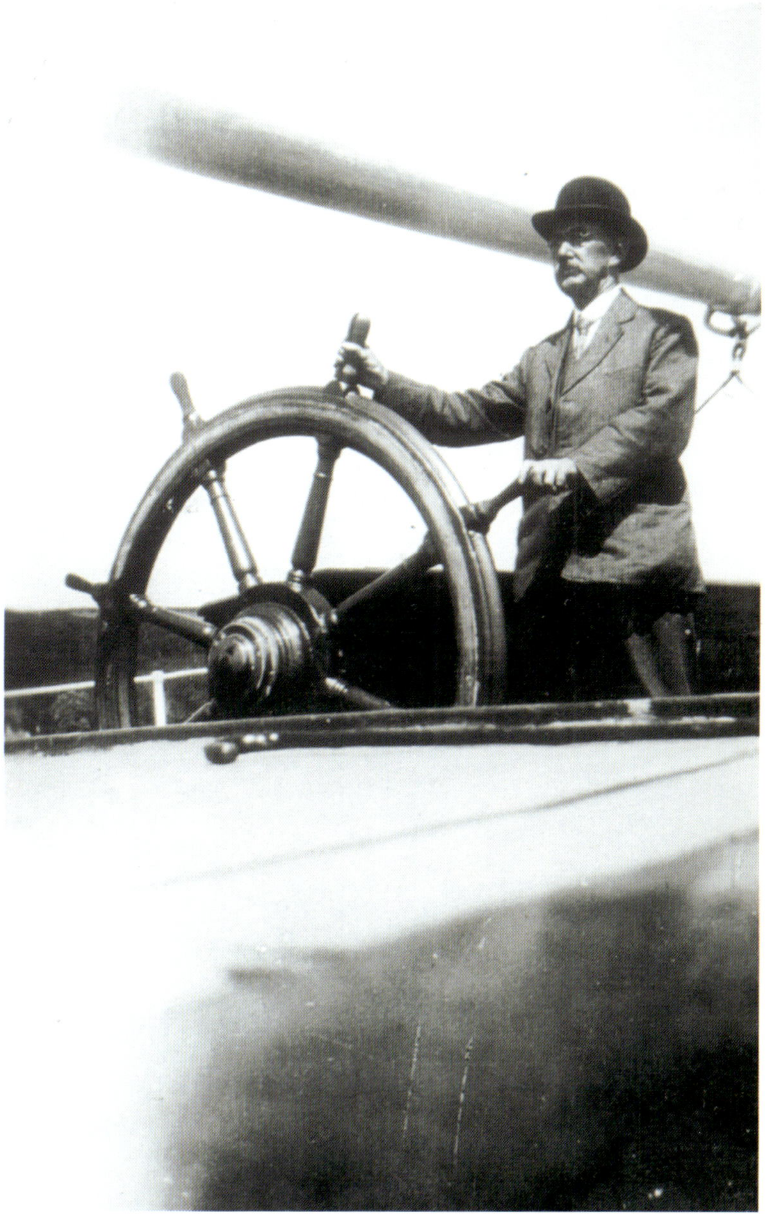

List of paintings

Most of the oils on canvas are usually no more than 21"x 35" and the sizes of the watercolour paintings indicate that Chappell worked on paper measuring approximately 15" x 22". The watercolours either include highlights of gouache, or are a mixture of watercolour and gouache.